STUDY GUIDE

to accompany

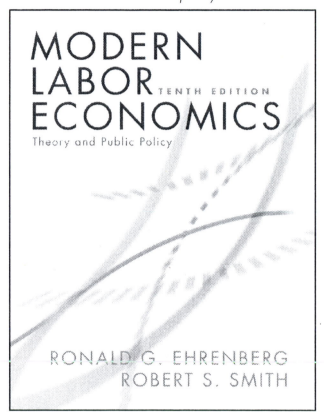

MODERN
LABOR TENTH EDITION
ECONOMICS
Theory and Public Policy

RONALD G. EHRENBERG
ROBERT S. SMITH

LÉONIE STONE

STATE UNIVERSITY OF NEW YORK AT GENESEO

PEARSON

Addison
Wesley

Boston   San Francisco   New York
London   Toronto   Sydney   Tokyo   Singapore   Madrid
Mexico City   Munich   Paris   Cape Town   Hong Kong   Montreal

Contents

Preface

■ Preface To The Tenth Edition

The tenth edition of the *Student Learning Guide*: *Labor Market Problems and Applications* continues a long-standing team effort. The seventh edition, by Professor Larry Wohl, drew heavily on the sixth edition, as prepared by Professor George Kosicki of the College of the Holy Cross, who was unavailable to work on the update. For the eighth–tenth editions, I have revised, changed, and added problems as required by changes in the text.

Previous editions included the preface to the sixth edition as prepared by Professor Kosicki, and I still think it appropriate to include it here, as it best explains the method and intent of this study guide as well as the overall format. Any remaining errors or inconsistencies are my responsibility. Please address any corrections, comments, or suggestions to Professor Léonie Stone, School of Business, SUNY Geneseo, Geneseo, NY 14454, or e-mail me at *stone@geneseo.edu*. I continually seek to improve this guide, and corrections and suggestions are equally appreciated. In any guide filled with exercises, errors inevitably creep in! Many diligent students have emailed me with corrections and clarifications, and I've included all of those in this edition . . . but if you find more, please let me know!

■ Preface To The Sixth Edition

Labor Market Problems and Applications is written for any student enrolled in a labor economics course who wishes to become a more precise and critical thinker about labor market issues. Any good principles of microeconomics text is capable of exposing a student to labor market ideas and concepts. Being a critical thinker about labor market issues, however, involves the ability to strip away the rhetoric that often surrounds labor market policies and focus on the consequences of the policy. Thinking critically involves going beyond just understanding labor market arguments to see alternative sides to these arguments. But how does one develop this ability?

The key to critical thinking is to first have information you can bring to bear on the issues. Just as you cannot write a book review if you have never before read anything related to that topic, so too you cannot critique arguments you read in newspapers or magazines, or hear about on television or in conversation, without understanding the basic principles, tendencies, and linkages that labor market variables display. What has always impressed me most about the text *Modern Labor Economics* has been not so much its interesting policy applications, but its careful and balanced presentation of the theory necessary to make sense of those policy applications.

What I have tried to do in this book is to construct a set of materials that would complement and supplement the excellent text crafted by Ron Ehrenberg and Robert Smith. Unlike some study guides that exercise great care never to present anything that cannot be found in the text, I have tried to assemble material that would add to the text, while still being consistent with the organization, general topic selection, terminology, and notation of the text. My feeling is that readers can benefit immensely from seeing similar ideas being presented in new and different ways. But what could I do that the authors have not already done? The approach I have taken in this companion volume is a very analytical one that emphasizes numerical solutions and careful graphing of labor market scenarios. In each chapter, I have tried to set up a wide variety of scenarios that can be solved for explicit numerical answers. I believe this approach enables the reader to see with great clarity and precision many of the relationships between labor market variables that follow from the models presented in the text.

While the numerical set up of many of the scenarios may at first seem intimidating to some readers, I think that the book also shows that it is possible to be precise and analytical without using complicated mathematics. Simple high school algebra and graphing skills, along with clear and careful thinking, are all that is needed to solve the problems. Knowing calculus may occasionally assist the reader in solving a problem or seeing additional connections, but calculus is never required. Knowing how to work with numbers, simple equations, and precise graphs is a valuable skill for anyone wanting to be a serious thinker about economic issues. In addition these are valuable skills for the workplace and everyday life.

Each chapter in the book begins with a detailed summary of the material in the *Modern Labor Economics* text. Unlike most study guides that provide such vague summaries that they are useless to anyone but the most experienced readers, I have tried to briefly and concisely rewrite many of the major points discussed in the text. My hope is that the summaries will be detailed enough so that anyone who chose to read just the summaries would still be able to get started answering many of the questions and problems. Each summary section also contains at least one numerical example designed to more precisely convey one of the analytical sections of the text. The example also serves as a guide in solving many of the later problems. The summary section is followed by a set of multiple choice questions designed to help the reader review the main concepts and points made in the chapter. Following the review questions is an extensive problem section designed to give the reader a chance to really work with the models and see the linkages between the variables that follow from the models. Once these problems have been mastered, students are presented with a variety of scenarios where they can apply the relationships seen in the previous problems. Complete and detailed answers to all questions, including the multiple choice questions, are provided at the end of the book. The most difficult problems are indicated by an asterisk before the question. Numerous headings and subheadings are used throughout the book to keep the material organized and accessible. My hope is that the book will serve as a valuable resource manual for both students and professors.

Chapter 1
Introduction

■ Summary

Labor market issues dominate our lives and the lives of those around us. It is almost impossible to read a newspaper or watch a television news program without encountering a story related to jobs, wages, education, discrimination, unemployment, or a similar topic. The purpose of *Modern Labor Economics* is to provide a logical framework for thinking critically about these kinds of issues.

To think critically one must have information to bring to bear on the issues. A publisher of an introductory economics text, for example, does not rely primarily on the reviews of introductory students, but rather on the reviews of experienced professors. Why? Students with no background in economics would simply be reading the text for content, to try to understand what was written. In contrast, a professor who is already familiar with the topics would be able to assess whether the text contributed anything original, or whether there were better ways to handle a particular topic. The theories and evidence presented in *Modern Labor Economics* are designed to give the reader knowledge of how labor market variables are linked together. These relationships can then be drawn upon to analyze different labor market issues, particularly the effects of various government policies on wages and employment.

Labor economics centers on the **labor market**. Labor markets are different from most other markets because labor can only be rented; workers cannot be bought and sold. There are thus many **nonpecuniary factors** relating to work environment and conditions of employment that are not relevant in other types of markets. However, labor markets are much like other markets in that the market facilitates contact between buyers and sellers, exchanges information about price and quantity of labor services, and allows contracts to be executed.

Chapter 1 of the text focuses on the methodology of modern labor economics. When the focus of the economic inquiry is identifying, understanding, and measuring labor market relationships (i.e., when the focus is trying to uncover "what is" true about the labor market), the analysis is characterized as **positive economics**. When the analysis turns to an evaluation of appropriate labor market outcomes (i.e., when the focus is trying to uncover "what should be" the labor market outcome), the analysis is characterized as **normative economics**.

The methodology of positive economics assumes that when employers and employees come together in the labor market to buy and sell labor services, they will be pursuing specific objectives in a consistent manner subject to certain constraints. Consistency in this case means simply that people's behavior can be predicted—their choices are made with a purpose in mind and are not random. It does not mean that people do the same thing all of the time. They (usually) learn from mistakes, and they respond differently to different incentives.

The underlying assumption of all economics is resource **scarcity**. Since resources are scarce, individuals and society cannot meet all their wants, and thus must make choices, each of which has a cost, since something else must be given up.

Regarding their specific objectives, it is assumed that the firms will be trying to **maximize profits** and that individual workers will be trying to **maximize their happiness** or satisfaction (called utility). The basic decision rule that leads to both profit maximization and utility maximization is that a particular course of action should be undertaken if the benefits associated with that course of action (the marginal benefits) exceed the (marginal) costs. Combining these elements—pursuing objectives and behaving consistently, yet adapting to changing incentives—constitute what is frequently referred to as a **rationality** assumption, or an assumption of "rational" behavior.

Some benefits (e.g., wages, health insurance, and pension benefits), can be measured in dollars, but others are nonpecuniary (e.g., safety, status, a feeling of fairness, and a sense of meaningful participation in the decision-making process of the firm). These nonpecuniary factors are especially prevalent in the labor market because when labor services are traded, a human being is "attached" to the transaction, and a human being's happiness can be influenced not only by the wages he receives for his services, but also by a wide range of emotions, feelings, needs, beliefs, and principles.

To help in identifying and understanding the relationships between workers and firms in the labor market, economists build models. A **model** is a deliberate simplification of reality designed to highlight certain key characteristics while pushing other less important aspects into the background. Because of the millions of interactions in markets, each involving unique preferences, information, and constraints, an accurate and "realistic" depiction of all of these interactions would be neither feasible nor useful. Instead, less important aspects can be eliminated or de-emphasized by making simplifying assumptions. For example, the model of labor supply (which will be presented in Chapter 6) assumes individuals derive happiness from just two things, their level of income and their leisure (non-work) time. One critical simplifying assumption economists frequently rely on in an attempt to highlight certain relationships is the concept of *ceteris paribus* (holding all else constant). For example, to trace out the relationship between the wage and the firm's labor demand, the price the firm charges for its product is often assumed to remain constant.

The success of a model hinges on how well it predicts behavior. It is not always necessary that any particular individual or firm actually behaves as the model assumes. The model can be considered a success if we observe people are behaving "as if" they followed the model—that is, if the model accurately predicts their behavior. What if the model fails to consistently predict how people behave? The model may still be useful in a normative sense. For example, suppose a group of individuals under observation consistently made choices seemingly contrary to a model's predicted behavior for utility maximization. Further investigation might indicate that they were doing so because of ignorance, misunderstanding, or misperception. In such a case, the model may have helped identify a market imperfection that was impeding rational choice, and might also suggest an appropriate solution to the imperfection.

Most of the normative assessments economists make about labor market outcomes are based on the concept of **Pareto (economic) efficiency**. Pareto efficiency means that an outcome has been reached where all mutually beneficial transactions have been made. These are the kinds of transactions that people enter into voluntarily. If all mutually beneficial transactions have been made, all that remains are transactions where some people gain and some people lose. This satisfies the Pareto criterion.

Rational individuals will not voluntarily enter into exchanges in which they would lose, unless they could be fully compensated by those who gain. If the relative size of the gains and losses do not permit such compensation (or if there is no method to bring about such compensation), then an assessment must be made as to whether the transaction is justified. This is a question, however, that often involves value judgments. Societies can and do make these kinds of assessments from time to time, but they require the government to mandate certain behavior, and the basis of such mandates must be ethical principles.

One such principle might be that the distribution of income should be more equal. Another might be that workers should not be allowed to place themselves at risk of significant physical or financial harm. Such principles may drive government mandates on the minimum wage, welfare programs, and health and safety regulations. Government mandates based on distributional considerations can be problematic, however, because they often require that adjustments be undertaken that move the participants away from a Pareto efficient outcome.

Example

Consider a labor market where there are 10 firms and 10 workers. Each firm can hire only one of these workers. Each firm has a maximum wage it would be willing to pay the worker. It would like to hire its worker for as far below this maximum as possible, but if no other options exist, it will hire a worker at a wage equal to the firm's maximum willingness to pay. The maximum wage each firm is willing to pay is shown in Table 1-1.

Also suppose that each worker in this market can work for only one firm. Each worker has a minimum wage that will just be acceptable. Any offer below this minimum will be rejected and the worker will not participate in the market. Each worker would like to be hired at a wage as much above their minimum acceptable wage as possible, but if no other options exists, will work at a wage just equal to this minimum. The minimum wage acceptable to each worker is also shown in Table 1-1.

Table 1-1

Firm #	Maximum Acceptable Wage ($)	Person #	Minimum Acceptable Wage ($)
1	95	1	45
2	90	2	50
3	85	3	55
4	80	4	60
5	75	5	65
6	70	6	70
7	65	7	75
8	60	8	80
9	55	9	85
10	50	10	90

What is the Pareto efficient outcome in this market? In answering this question, note that at any given wage W^*, all those firms with maximum willingness to pay values greater than or equal to W^* will be willing to hire a worker. On the other hand, all those workers with a minimum acceptable wage less than or equal to W^* will be willing to work.

For purposes of discussion, suppose that W^* is initially set at $80. Could this be a Pareto efficient outcome? At a wage of $80, only firms 1, 2, 3, and 4 will be willing to hire a worker. On the other hand, workers 1 through 8 would be willing to work. For simplicity, suppose workers 1 through 4 are actually hired. Notice that each firm and each worker benefit from this voluntary exchange of labor services. For example, if worker 1 were hired at firm 1, firm 1 gains $15, the difference between what it was willing to pay and what it actually had to pay the worker. Similarly, worker 1 gains $35 from the transaction. He would have been willing to work for $45 but actually is paid $80.

This is not a Pareto efficient outcome, however, because opportunities exist for the parties to strike additional deals that are mutually beneficial. For example, if worker 5 offered to work for $74, firm 5 would be willing to hire her (thus gaining $1), and worker 5 would gain $9 by being hired.

At what point are there no mutually beneficial deals left to be struck? This occurs when all the firms pay a wage of $70 and workers 1 through 6 have been hired by firms 1 through 6. At a wage of $70, the first 6 firms all gain by hiring, and the first 6 workers gain by being hired. The firms and workers that are left not transacting have willingness to pay or accept values that preclude them from striking mutually beneficial deals. For example, at a wage of $64, firm 7 would now clearly be interested in hiring a worker, but none of the workers that are left would be willing to work at a wage below $75.

It is important to realize, however, that this Pareto efficient outcome is not unique. To see another set of transactions that could satisfy the criterion, suppose that the maximum willingness to pay values in Table 1-1 represents values for a single firm that is the only buyer of labor. Also suppose that this firm is aware of each worker's minimum acceptable wage. In this situation, the firm could offer the first worker a wage of $45, and since the only other option would be not to work at all, the worker would accept. Similarly, the second worker could be offered a wage of $50 (the first would still earn $45) and he would accept. Such a firm is called a wage-discriminating monopsony.

How many workers would be hired under this pay scheme? Notice that when the firm reaches the sixth worker, the maximum the firm is willing to pay just equals the minimum the worker is willing to accept. If the firm tried to go beyond the sixth worker to the seventh, it would find itself in a situation where it was paying the worker $75, but the worker was only worth a maximum of $65, so a "rational" firm would not do so.

Notice that the employment level in this situation of 6 is the same as when there were many firms. An employment level of 6 where each worker is paid his minimum acceptable wage is also a Pareto efficient situation since there is no way to make any worker better off without hurting the firm. The difference between this Pareto efficient situation and the one described initially is that the firm has reaped all of the benefits of the transactions—all workers received only the minimal acceptable wage, but the firm hired all but the last worker for considerably less than they would have been willing to pay. Since many people would find such an outcome unfair, this example illustrates that Pareto efficient outcomes are not necessarily "fair" outcomes. An attempt by the government to move from this second outcome back to the first can be viewed as a choice between two Pareto efficient outcomes.

While the voluntary transactions that take place in the labor market are usually consistent with the concept of Pareto efficiency, the market does not always assure that all Pareto efficient transactions are made. In such cases, government may be able to play a role in facilitating such transactions. Why might the market fail to bring about all Pareto efficient adjustments?

Market failure can occur due to **ignorance** or lack of information about alternatives. Other times there are legal barriers or distortions in incentives created by taxes or subsidies, **transaction barriers**. The cost of completing a Pareto efficient transaction can also be an inhibiting factor, particularly where there are **price distortions** due to taxes or subsidies. **Externalities** occur when costs or benefits are imposed on people who were not a part of the original transaction, since their costs or benefits are not considered. A specific case of externalities is the **free rider problem** created by **public goods**, goods that can be consumed by many people at the same time, including those who do not pay.

What can the government do when these kinds of problems arise? The government may provide or subsidize the cost of public goods, which will otherwise be underprovided by the market. In other instances the government may be able to disseminate information that will help parties see that a mutually beneficial transaction exists. The government may also be able to step in and remove some transaction barriers, as in the case of **capital market imperfections**. The government may be in a position to provide financial support that enables parties to undertake mutually beneficial but costly transactions. The government may also act to overcome other types of transactions barriers by creating regulations that act in the place of missing markets. Often the government must simply realize that its own policies are the source of the problem and get out of the way, as is the case when price distortions are due to taxes or subsidies. In deciding whether government should get involved in such a situation, however, it is important to realize that government intervention itself is costly, and so it is important to weigh the potential gains against these costs.

Normative economics is also concerned with issues of economic efficiency versus equity or fairness. There may be any number of transactions that are equally efficient but not similarly equitable. Also, increasing equity may involve moving away from efficiency.

The appendix to Chapter 1 is an introduction to the empirical methodology of modern labor economics. To put this methodology in perspective, the authors focus on the specific problem of testing the hypothesis that, holding all else constant, a firm's quit rate is inversely related to the wage it pays. Hypothetical data on wages and quit rates for 10 firms are used to generate numeric examples. One of the first lessons of the appendix is that when there are a small amount of data and just two variables, it can be very useful to plot the data with the dependent variable (quit rates) on the vertical axis and the independent variable (wages) on the horizontal axis.

To measure the relationship that exists, on average, between the two variables, a linear relationship can be fitted to the data using **least squares regression** analysis. This is a technique where the parameters of the linear relationship (the vertical intercept and the slope) are chosen so that they minimize the squared difference between the actual and estimated values of the dependent variable. (The actual and estimated values of the dependent variable are presumably different because of the existence of random factors.) Most statistical computer programs, as well as most spreadsheet programs, contain commands that will compute **parameter estimates** using the least squares approach.

Along with the parameter estimates, most programs also generate a standard error for each estimate. The smaller the standard error, the greater the chance that the estimated parameters lie close to the true value. A useful rule of thumb is that if the ratio of the estimated parameter to its **standard error** is 2 or more, we can be statistically confident in ruling out the possibility that the true value of the parameter equals zero. This is a valuable piece of information, since if one can rule out the possibility that the slope of a linear relationship is zero, then one has established that a relationship exists between the independent and dependent variable.

Most economic relationships, however, involve more than a dependent variable and a single independent variable. For example, in the quit rate/wage relationship, it is very possible that for a given wage, older workers are less likely to quit than younger workers. The relationship between the dependent variable and two or more independent variables can be estimated using **multiple least squares regression** analysis.

Problems can occur in a regression analysis when independent variables that should be included are not, and these **omitted variables** are correlated with one or more of the independent variables that are included. In such cases, the differences between the actual and estimated values of the dependent variable will not reflect simple random errors, but will vary in a systematic pattern. Since these systematic differences are correlated with other independent variables, these differences will be attributed to the variables that are included, thus giving a misleading picture of the true relationship.

For example, in the quit rate/wage regression, a worker's age is likely to be correlated with the wage. If age is omitted from the regression, some of the negative effect on quits due to a worker's age will be attributed to the wage level instead, making it seem as if high wage rates exert stronger negative effects on quit rates than is actually the case. To avoid such biases, it is important to try to uncover through economic theory as much as possible about the nature of the relationship before making any attempt at empirical measurement.

■ Review Questions

Choose the letter that represents the **BEST** response.

Labor Economics: Some Basic Concepts

1. A unique feature of the labor market relative to standard product markets is
   a. individuals are the sellers, firms are the buyers.
   b. nonpecuniary characteristics play a larger role in labor market transactions.
   c. intense competition exists among the sellers.
   d. both **a** and **b**.

2. Feelings, emotions, personalities, and working conditions play an important role in labor market transactions because
   a. labor services cannot be separated from workers.
   b. people strive to make themselves as happy as they can.
   c. people are sometimes irrational.
   d. both **a** and **b**.

3. Which of the following is a statement associated with positive economic reasoning?
   a. Workers are entitled to a just wage.
   b. An increase in the payroll tax paid by firms will reduce wages and employment opportunities.
   c. Employers should be required to pay for health insurance for their employees.
   d. Professional athletes are overpaid.

4. Which of the following is a statement associated with normative economic reasoning?
   a. It is important that everyone who wants to attend college be able to do so.
   b. Holding all else constant, workers in more dangerous occupations earn more than those employed under safer conditions.
   c. Welfare programs can lead to reductions in work incentives.
   d. Subsidies given to firms that purchase new capital equipment will lead to an increase in employment.

5. Which of the following is a true statement about economic models?
   a. A model is deliberately abstract.
   b. A model accurately captures the all of the complexity of the real world.
   c. A model shows the thought process people go through when making decisions.
   d. A model must accurately predict behavior to be useful.

The Models and Predictions of Positive Economics

6. The goal often pursued in positive economic models of the labor market is
   a. utility maximization.
   b. profit maximization.
   c. income maximization.
   d. either **a** or **b**.

7. Positive economic models typically assume
   a. people cannot get everything they want and so must make choices.
   b. people undertake a particular course of action if the marginal benefits of that action outweigh the marginal costs.
   c. people are often inconsistent and inflexible when making their choices.
   d. both **a** and **b**.

8. Predictions of positive economic models are usually conditional on
   a. individuals caring only about themselves.
   b. the transactions being mutually beneficial.
   c. everything else being held constant.
   d. both **a** and **b**.

9. For a positive economic model to be useful, it must
   a. explain how people should behave.
   b. tend to predict how people behave on average.
   c. explain how people actually behave.
   d. apply to everyone.

Normative Economics

10. Normative economic statements
    a. must be based on the principle of mutually beneficial gain.
    b. are based on ethical principles or goals.
    c. relate to voluntary transactions only.
    d. both **b** and **c**.

11. A Pareto efficient outcome has been achieved when
    a. all mutually beneficial transactions have been made.
    b. it is impossible to make someone better off without making someone else worse off.
    c. at least one person can gain and no one else will lose.
    d. both **a** and **b**.

12. Which of the following is true about a Pareto efficient outcome?
    a. The outcome must have been purely voluntary.
    b. The outcome may not satisfy society's sense of fairness.
    c. The outcome is unique.
    d. Both **a** and **b**.

13. Policies that move two parties from one Pareto efficient outcome to another
    a. will make one of the parties worse off.
    b. are often influenced by the parties' initial endowment of resources.
    c. can be designed scientifically outside of the political system.
    d. both **a** and **b**.

14. Pareto efficient transactions may not occur because
    a.   parties may not have all the relevant information.
    b.   they may be against the law.
    c.   the cost associated with completing the transaction may deter one or more of the parties.
    d.   all of the above.

15. Government may help to bring about Pareto efficient outcomes by
    a.   producing public goods.
    b.   eliminating capital market imperfections.
    c.   providing a way to substitute for market transactions.
    d.   all of the above.

Statistical Testing of Labor Market Hypotheses (Appendix 1A)

16. Least squares regression assumes that
    a.   the relationship between the independent variables is linear.
    b.   the coefficients associated with the independent variables are greater than zero.
    c.   a random error term accounts for any differences between the actual and predicted values of the dependent variable.
    d.   all of the above.

17. One can be reasonably confident a relationship between an independent and a dependent variable has been found if
    a.   the standard error of the estimated parameter is small.
    b.   the standard error of the estimated parameter is less than half the value of the estimated parameter.
    c.   the error term of the least squares regression is random.
    d.   the t-statistic for the estimated parameter is about 0.5.

In answering Questions **18** through **20**, please refer to the following information.

Suppose that for a sample of 10,000 individuals, the relationship between annual hours supplied (H), the hourly wage rate in dollars (W), and the level of nonlabor income in dollars (V) (e.g., interest income, gifts, public assistance) was estimated by multiple regression to be

$$H_i = 1200 + 0.5W_i - 0.04V_i.$$
$$(225) \quad (0.2) \quad (0.01)$$

The subscript i refers to the ith household where $i = 1$ to 10,000. Standard errors of the estimated parameters are in parentheses.

18. The coefficient of −0.04 associated with the independent variable V means that
    a.   on average, when a person's wage and nonlabor income both increase by $1, he wishes to work 0.04 hours less.
    b.   on average, when a person's nonlabor income increases by $1, he wishes to work 0.04 hours less, holding all else constant.
    c.   the true value of the parameter associated with the V variable is equal to zero.
    d.   both **b** and **c**.

19. Comparing the size of the coefficient on the W variable and its standard error, one can conclude that
    a. the relationship between H and W has been estimated with reasonable precision.
    b. statistically, one can be confident that the true relationship between H and W is not zero.
    c. from an economic standpoint, the relationship between H and W is insensitive to changes in W.
    d. all of the above.

20. Suppose W and V are positively correlated (e.g., people with high wages save more and thus earn more interest income). What would happen if V were omitted from the multiple regression?
    a. The coefficient on W would become smaller.
    b. The coefficient on W would become larger.
    c. The standard error associated with the coefficient on W would become smaller.
    d. Both **b** and **c**.

■ Problems

Labor Economics: Some Basic Concepts

21. The concept of a model is one of the most important concepts in economics. Helping the reader to understand and apply labor market models is the primary purpose of this book. Figure 1-1 is an example of a model, but in this case, it is a model of a human being.

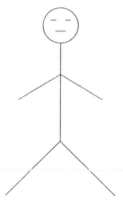

Figure 1-1

21a. What does it mean to call this drawing a model?

21b. What essential characteristics of a human being does it capture? What characteristics does it push into the background?

21c. Why do you think such a simple drawing was used to illustrate the concept of a model? Would a more realistic drawing make for a better model?

21d. Is this model a positive or normative model? Explain your reasoning.

22. Models of positive economics typically assert that people weigh costs and benefits in a consistent manner. That is, if the benefits of following a particular course of action exceed the costs, then that action will be taken, otherwise it will not.

Consider a worker who is told he can save $5 on his dental insurance premium of $50 if he goes to the company's personnel office and fills out a form. The whole process will take 30 minutes. Suppose the worker fills out the form.

A month later, the same worker is told that he can reduce his health insurance premium from $1,000 to $995 by taking 30 minutes to fill out a form in the personnel office. The worker declines the offer.

22a. Does the model of rational choice based on costs and benefits serve as a positive economic model for this person? If not, can you explain why the person might have acted as he did?

22b. When an economic model fails to predict behavior accurately, does that mean it is useless? What other purpose could the model serve?

Pareto Efficiency

23. Consider a labor market in which there are 10 firms and 10 workers. Each firm can hire only one of these workers. Each firm has a maximum it would be willing to pay the worker. It would like to hire its worker for as far below this maximum as possible, but if no other options exist, it will hire a worker at a wage equal to its maximum willingness to pay value. The maximum wage each firm is willing to pay is shown in Table 1-2.

Suppose that each worker in this market can work for only one firm. Each worker has a minimum wage that will just be acceptable. Any offer below this minimum will be rejected and the worker will not participate in the market. Each worker would like to be hired at a wage as much above the minimum acceptable wage as possible, but if no other options exists, will work at a wage just equal to this minimum. The minimum wage acceptable to each worker is also shown in Table 1-2.

Table 1-2

Firm #	Maximum Acceptable Wage ($)	Person #	Minimum Acceptable Wage ($)
1	520	1	240
2	500	2	260
3	480	3	280
4	460	4	300
5	440	5	320
6	420	6	340
7	400	7	360
8	380	8	380
9	360	9	400
10	340	10	420

23a. Suppose that the first 8 workers are hired by the first 8 firms and each worker is paid a wage of $380. Show why this is a Pareto efficient outcome.

23b. Concerned that workers will be exploited by firms, suppose that the government passes a law that prohibits deals below $480; that is, individuals and firms must contract for work at $480 or above. What will be the consequences of this law?

23c. Assuming the Pareto efficient outcome from **23a** would have emerged without government interference, which workers gain because of the law in **23b**? How much do they gain? Who loses because of the law? How much do they lose?

23d. Is it possible for the winners in **23c** to fully compensate the losers and still come out ahead? If not, how could such a law be justified?

23e. Now suppose that the maximum willingness to pay values in Table 1-2 represent values for a single firm that is the only buyer of labor. Also suppose that this firm is aware of each worker's minimum acceptable wage. In this situation, the firm could offer the first worker a wage of $240, and since the only other option would be not to work at all, the worker would accept. Similarly, the second worker could be offered a wage of $260 (the first would still earn $240) and he would accept. How many workers would be hired under this pay scheme?

23f. Is the answer to **23e** a Pareto efficient outcome? Is it an equitable outcome?

Statistical Testing of Labor Market Hypotheses (Appendix 1A)

24. Up until the 1970s economists believed there was a stable tradeoff between the unemployment rate and the rate of wage inflation. This relationship is known as the Phillips curve. To summarize briefly, the logic of the Phillips curve rests on two assertions. The first is that the general rate of change in wages is proportional to the amount by which the number of jobs exceeds the number of people looking for work on a percentage basis. For example, when the number of jobs exceeds the number of people willing to work by 10%, the wage is presumed to rise at a faster pace than when the number of jobs exceeds the number of people willing to work by only 5%.

The second assertion is that the unemployment rate is inversely related (probably in a nonlinear way) to the percentage difference between the number of jobs and the number of people willing to work. As Chapter 15 will point out, even when the number of jobs and the number of people willing to work are equal, there will still be a small positive rate of unemployment. This rate should diminish (probably at a decreasing rate) as jobs become more plentiful relative to the supply of workers. On the other hand, as the number of jobs falls below the number of workers, the unemployment rate will rise.

The result of these two assertions is that the rate of wage inflation will be inversely related (probably in a nonlinear way) to the unemployment rate. By the 1970s economists began to realize that there were also a number of other factors that could change over time and cause the terms of the entire tradeoff to either worsen or improve. In other words, a stable tradeoff exists only at a particular point in time. The difficulties a shifting tradeoff can cause for economists wishing to empirically measure the Phillips curve are explored in the problems below.

24a. Plot the 1960–69 data in Table 1-3 with the unemployment rate on the horizontal axis and wage inflation on the vertical axis.

24b. Fitting a linear equation to the data for 1960–69 using the least squares regression technique yields

$$\%\Delta W_t = 9.2 - 1.1 UR_t,$$
$$(1.21)\ (0.25)$$

where $\%\Delta W_t$ refers to the wage inflation for any year t, and UR_t refers to the unemployment rate for any year t. The standard errors of the estimated parameters (the vertical intercept and the slope) are in parentheses. Add this line to the graph produced in Question **24a**.

Table 1-3 contains the annual unemployment rate and rate of wage inflation experienced by the U.S. economy each year over the period 1960–79.

Table 1-3

Year	Unemployment Rate (%)	Rate of Wage Inflation (%)
1960	5. 4	3. 4
1961	6. 5	3. 0
1962	5. 4	3. 4
1963	5. 5	2. 8
1964	5. 0	2. 8
1965	4. 4	3. 6
1966	3. 7	4. 3
1967	3. 7	5. 0
1968	3. 5	6. 1
1969	3. 4	6. 7
1970	4. 8	6. 6
1971	5. 8	7. 2
1972	5. 5	6. 2
1973	4. 8	6. 2
1974	5. 5	8. 0
1975	8. 3	8. 4
1976	7. 6	7. 2
1977	6. 9	7. 6
1978	6. 0	8. 1
1979	5. 8	8. 0

Source: *Economic Report of the President: 1989*, Table B-39 (p. 352) and Table B-44 (p. 358).

*24c. Assess how well this line fits the data. For each of the years 1960–69, find the difference between the actual level of wage inflation and the level predicted by the regression line (these differences are called residuals). Make a plot where the unemployment rate is on the horizontal axis and the corresponding residual value is on the vertical axis.

*24d. Do the residuals plotted in **24c** seem to be the result of just random errors? Is there a curve other than a straight line that could fit this data a little better?

*24e. To capture the nonlinearities suggested by the plot of the data and the residuals from the linear regression line, the rate of wage inflation was regressed on the reciprocal of the unemployment rate (since the reciprocal function decreases at a decreasing rate). The least squares technique yielded the following relationship.

$$\%\Delta W_t = -1.43 + 24.6 \ \frac{1}{UR_t}.$$
$$(0.98) \ (4.25)$$

Add a plot of this line to the graph created in **24a** and **24b**.

*24f. Compute the residual errors using the nonlinear relationship estimated above. Plot the new residuals (using different symbols) on your previous residual plot. Where has the fit of the line improved most?

24g. Create a graph where all of the data in Table 1-3 are plotted with unemployment on the horizontal axis and wage inflation on the vertical axis. Use one symbol to denote data from the period 1960–69 and a different one to denote data from the period 1970–79.

24h. Since the data from the 1970s generally seem to follow a different pattern than the 1960s data, suppose we define a variable $D70$ such that $D70 = 1$ if the data come from the period 1970–79, otherwise it takes on a value of zero. Adding this variable to the basic linear model yielded the following least squares estimates:

$$\%\Delta W_t = 5.4 - 0.28\ UR_t + 3.7\ D70_t.$$
$$(1.17)\quad (0.24)\qquad (0.61)$$

Plot the estimated line implied by this equation for the 1960s data on the graph from **24g**. Do the same for the 1970s data.

24i. If a researcher assumed that the tradeoff between unemployment and wage inflation was the same during the 1960s and 1970s, then the variable $D70$ would be omitted and linear least squares regression yields the equation

$$\%\Delta W_t = 2.9 + 0.53\ UR_t.$$
$$(1.86)\quad (0.34)$$

Add a plot of this line to the graph from **24h**. Why does the omission of the $D70$ variable make such a difference in the estimated line? Does omitting an independent variable from a regression equation always make such a difference?

*24j. The equation estimated in Question **24h** assumed that the position of the entire curve shifted during the 1970s but that the slope remained the same. Write the equation that would be estimated if both the position and slope of the curve were allowed to change.

■ Applications

Alternatives to the Norm of Pareto Efficiency

25. On May 15, 1891, Pope Leo XIII, leader of the Roman Catholic Church, circulated a letter to church members in which he wrote

> When there is question of defending the rights of individuals, the defenseless and the poor have a claim to special consideration. The richer class has many ways of shielding itself, and stands less in need of help from the state; whereas the mass of the poor have no resources of their own to fall back on, and must chiefly depend on the assistance of the state. It is for this reason that wage-earners, since they mostly belong to the latter class, should be especially cared for and protected by the government.
>
> *Source*: Leo XIII, encyclical letter *Rerum Novarum* (May 15, 1891).

This teaching has been reaffirmed by Pope John Paul II and has generally come to be known as exercising a "preferential option for the poor."

25a. How does the notion of a "preferential option for the poor" compare with the norm of Pareto efficiency?

25b. How does the role of government envisioned by Pope Leo XIII compare with the role government would play in a society where the norm was strictly Pareto efficiency?

26. In May 1990 a telephone survey of Moscow and New York City residents was conducted to gauge popular attitudes toward free markets. One of the questions was

> Suppose the government wants to undertake a reform to improve the productivity of the economy. As a result, everyone will be better off, but the improvement in life will not affect people equally. A million people (people who respond energetically to the incentives in the plan and people with certain skills) will see their incomes triple while everyone else will see only a tiny income increase, about 1%. Would you support this plan?

The responses are presented in Table 1-4.

Table 1-4

Response	U.S.S.R.	U.S.A.
Yes	55%	38%
No	45%	64%

Source: Robert J. Shiller, et.al. "Popular Attitudes Toward Free Markets: The Soviet Union and the United States Compared." *The American Economic Review* 81 (June 1991): 385–400.

26a. If individuals cared only about their personal levels of income, the expected response to the above question would be "yes," and yet a significant portion of the respondents in both countries answered "no." What do the survey responses suggest that people care about?

26b. Are the answers to the survey question consistent with the norm of Pareto efficiency?

26c. How do you think the premise of the question would have had to be different to gain a more favorable reaction?

Estimating the Relationship between Wages and Productivity (Appendix 1A)

27. An important relationship in labor economics is the one between employee earnings (E) and the revenue (R) an employee generates for the firm. One problem in estimating this relationship, however, is that in many instances (e.g., when employees work in groups or teams) it is difficult to know or measure precisely what an employee contributes to the firm. In occupations like automobile or real estate sales, however, the amount of revenue a particular worker generates for the firm is very clear. The question then becomes, to what extent do differences in employee productivity translate into differences in pay? And to what extent do other factors, like concern about economic status and fairness, play a role? This problem explores the methodology involved in answering these questions.

Consider the equation

$$E_i = \alpha_0 + \alpha_1 R_i + e_i,$$

where e is a random error term, and the subscript i refers to one individual. The parameters to be estimated are α_0, the vertical intercept of the line, and α_1, the slope of the line.

27a. Briefly outline how one would go about estimating the parameters α_0 and α_1.

27b. How can you tell the degree to which these estimated values approach the true underlying values of the parameters? How could you test the hypothesis that the parameter α_1 was different from zero?

*27c. The standard theory of the demand for labor (to be studied in Chapter 3) says that the parameter α_1 should equal 1. That is, differences in productivity should be reflected in differences in pay on a one-to-one basis. How could you test this hypothesis?

*27d. In practice, pay schemes seem to put much less emphasis on productivity than the standard theory predicts. Most firms determine pay by looking at variables such as experience, education, and years at the firm, rather than an employee's output. In his book *Choosing the Right Pond: Human Behavior and the Quest for Status* (New York: Oxford University Press, 1985), economist Robert H. Frank argues that pay is relatively insensitive to productivity differences because people care about their relative position in the wage hierarchy of the firm. Frank's hypothesis is that high productivity workers earn less than the standard theory predicts because they must pay a price for occupying the top ranked positions in the firm. On the other hand, low productivity workers command a premium for occupying the low status positions of the firm. (See Example 8.1 in Chapter 8 of the text.) If relative standing is something workers care about, fairness dictates that pay reflect all of a worker's contributions to a firm, including any effects his position in the wage hierarchy has on the well-being of coworkers.

What does Frank's hypothesis imply about the values of the parameters α_0 and α_1 relative to the standard model?

*27e. Frank goes on to argue that the more closely workers interact in their day-to-day routines, the greater the price paid by the top ranked workers, and the larger the premium received by low ranked workers. Suppose we define the dichotomous variable D to represent the level of interaction in the workplace between coworkers. D would take on the value of 1 if employees interacted extensively, 0 if they did not. What equation would you use to test this additional hypothesis?

*27f. Discuss the consequences for the estimates of the parameters α_0 and α_1 of omitting the variable D from the analysis.

Chapter 2
Overview of the Labor Market

■ Summary

The purpose of Chapter 1 was to introduce the methodology of modern labor economics, particularly the art of model building. In Chapter 2, the discussion shifts from models in general to the demand and supply model of the labor market. This is one of the most important positive economic models of the labor market, and it forms the foundation for most of the chapters that follow.

In the demand and supply model of the labor market, firms are the buyers and individuals are the sellers of labor services. Although this represents a reversal of the roles played in traditional product markets, the labor and product market roles are linked. A firm's success in the product market will influence its decision about how much labor to demand. The prices consumers face in the product markets determine the real purchasing power of the wages they earn, and wages in turn influence labor supply behavior. Before summarizing the demand and supply model of the labor market, it may be helpful to briefly review the labor market definitions, facts, and trends also presented in Chapter 2.

Labor markets can be **national** or **local** depending on how far buyers and sellers are willing to search. Sometimes, when firms follow strict practices such as filling key positions only from within the firm (as in some unionized workplaces and in some parts of the government), the labor market is so localized that it can be characterized as being **internal** to a particular firm.

All individuals aged 16 or older who are employed, waiting to be recalled from a layoff, or actively seeking work, are classified as being in the labor force. Those in the labor force who are not employed are classified as unemployed. Labor markets are very dynamic, and individuals are constantly flowing among the categories of employment, unemployment, and out of the labor force. The four major flows between labor market states are becoming unemployed due to either voluntary quits or involuntary layoffs, becoming employed either as a new hire or being recalled from a layoff, exiting the labor force by retiring or dropping out, and entering the labor force either as a new worker or reentering after dropping out.

In general, while the unemployment rate has fluctuated considerably over the years, the percentage of the population in the labor force, known as the **labor force participation rate**, has increased steadily. This increase has come about because of large and steady increases in the labor force participation rate for women. The labor force participation rate for men has been gradually falling throughout most of the 20th century.

The **unemployment rate** is computed by dividing the number of unemployed by the number in the labor force. Unemployment rates around 5% or less (in the United States) indicate **tight** markets, in which there are many job openings relative to workers. As the rate rises, labor markets become **loose**, and it is more difficult for workers to find a job and easier for firms to hire.

The types of work people do change over time. Employment in good-producing industries has fallen, while jobs in private-sector services increased rapidly. Workers have moved from manufacturing into wholesale and retail trade, education, heath care, hospitality and leisure services, and professional and business services. Within sectors, the types of jobs have changed as well. For example, within the service sector, management, administrative, and sales jobs have increased as a percentage of total service employment.

The price per hour of the labor services that are bought and sold in the labor market is the wage rate. In thinking about wages, it is useful to distinguish between **nominal wages** (sometimes called money wages) and **real wages**. Nominal wages are what a worker earns in today's current dollars, while real wages are computed by dividing nominal wages by an index of prices, usually the Consumer Price Index (CPI). This calculation essentially holds prices constant, leaving only the real physical output per hour that the wage could purchase. Real wages are useful because they allow one to compare workers' actual ability to purchase goods and services over time. Constructing an index of real wages can further facilitate these comparisons.

Example 1

Table 2-1 presents data on average nominal wages and consumer prices for the years 1945, 1980, and 1997.

Table 2-1

Year	Average Nominal Wage	Consumer Price Index
1945	$ 1.02	100
1980	$ 7.27	458
1997	$13.38	892

The year 1945 was chosen as the base year for the price index, which means that its index number was set to 100. (The CPI is just the ratio, multiplied by 100, of the total expenditures needed to buy a certain bundle of goods in a particular year to the total expenditures needed to buy that same bundle of goods in the base year.) The index 458 for 1980 says that in general, prices were 4.58 times higher in 1980 than they were in 1945.

To construct the index of real wages (assuming 1945 is the base year), first express the nominal wages for each year as a percentage of the wage in 1945. This is done by dividing the nominal wage in each year by the wage in 1945 ($1.02) and multiplying by 100. The resulting index numbers are then divided by the CPI numbers (carried over from the previous table) and multiplied by 100 to form the index of real wages reported in Table 2-2.

Table 2-2

Year	Index of Nominal Wages	Price Index	Index of Real Wages
1945	100	100	100
1980	713	458	156
1997	1312	892	147

The index 156 for 1980 says that on average, real wages were 1.56 times higher in 1980 than they were in 1945, but only 1.47 times higher in 1997 than they were in 1945. Thus real wages fell between 1980 and 1997.

Examining the data on real wages suggests that for many workers, particularly less-skilled workers, real wages fell in the 1980s and rose in the 1990s, leading overall to a very slight increase from 1980 to 2003. However, this may not be completely accurate, in part due to problems with using the CPI as a price measure. Since the CPI measures the cost of a fixed bundle of goods, it does not allow for either the fact that consumers substitute products when relative prices change or for changes in quality of goods that consumers buy. Thus the CPI may be overstated by as much as 1%, suggesting that actual purchasing power may have risen modestly over the period.

In interpreting the real wage index numbers, it is important to keep in mind that wage earnings are only one component of the total compensation workers receive. Many employers now provide workers with a wide range of benefits such as health insurance, paid vacations, and pensions.

How are compensation and employment levels determined in labor markets? Labor market outcomes are the result of the forces of **demand and supply**. The key to properly using the demand and supply model of the labor market is to remember that it is only a model. It is made simple deliberately to highlight a few important factors. At any one time, it pushes a number of factors into the background by utilizing the assumption of *ceteris paribus*, i.e., by holding all else constant and allowing just one variable to change.

When economists talk about a firm's **demand for labor**, they are referring to a schedule of wages and employment levels that represent the quantity of labor the firm would like to hire over a particular period of time (e.g., a year) at any given wage, holding all else constant. A table of numbers or a simple algebraic expression usually represents this schedule. For example, a hypothetical demand schedule could take the form of the data in Table 2-3.

Table 2-3

Wage ($)	Desired Employment
12	0
10	5
8	10
6	15
4	20
2	25

Alternatively, that same data could be represented algebraically by the equation

$$L = 30 - 2.5W,$$

where W represents the wage and L the employment level.

In Figure 2-1, the demand schedule data are transferred to a graph, plotting the wage on the vertical axis and the employment level on the horizontal. The resulting graph (labeled D) is called a demand curve. Note that the wage is graphed on the vertical axis of the graph even though it plays the role of the independent variable in the construction of the demand schedule. To be more consistent with the graph, sometimes an algebraic demand schedule is written with the wage on the left side of the equation, which in this case would yield the equation

$$W = 12 - 0.4L.$$

In the **long-run** (defined as a period of time in which there are no fixed inputs), demand curves are thought to slope downward for two reasons. As the wage rises, for example, holding all else constant, additional units of output become more costly to the firm and the firm has a tendency to cut back on its output. (The firm's higher costs will usually translate into higher prices. As a result, consumers will want to buy less of the output, so the decision to reduce output is actually driven by end consumers.) When the firm produces less output, it uses fewer inputs. The resulting reduction in the quantity of labor demanded is called the **scale effect** of a wage increase. Also, as the wage rises, the firm will try to minimize the effect of the increase on its total costs by substituting other inputs (e.g., capital) for labor. This is called the **substitution effect** of a wage increase. In the **short-run** (defined as a situation where the firm's capital stock is fixed), the substitution effect cannot come into play, but the scale effect still operates to create a downward sloping demand curve.

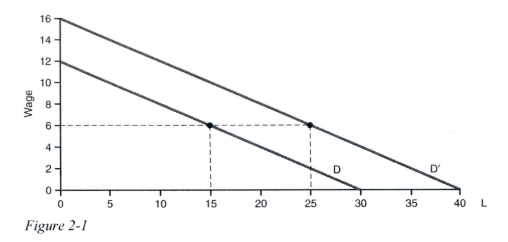

Figure 2-1

In tracing out the demand curve D in Figure 2-1, all other factors that can influence a firm's hiring decision besides the wage rate have been held constant. If one of those factors is now allowed to change, holding the wage constant at any given level, the entire curve will shift. An increase in the demand for the product the firm produces, for example, tends to create a **scale** (or **output**) effect that shifts the entire schedule to the right, say to D' in Figure 2-1, because it is now more profitable to produce goods and thus more profitable to hire workers. At any given wage (e.g., $6), the quantity demanded is now 10 units higher along curve D'.

Changes in the price of other inputs the firm uses, like capital, produce an ambiguous effect on the position of the demand curve. A reduction in the price of capital, for example, would tend to produce a positive **scale** effect since the cost to the firm of producing another unit of output would be less. On the other hand, when the price of capital falls, **substitution** of more capital for the now relatively more expensive labor will occur. If the scale effect of the capital price decrease dominates the substitution effect, then the demand for labor will shift outward to the right. However, if the substitution effect of the capital price decrease dominates the scale effect, the labor demand curve will shift inward to the left.

It is also important to note that the analysis so far has referred only to the demand for labor by a particular firm. In general, it is possible to aggregate the labor demand schedules for individual firms to produce **industry or market demand** curves for particular categories of labor. These aggregate curves combine with labor supply to determine the various labor market outcomes.

The **supply** side of the labor market is modeled in a similar fashion to the demand side. For those who have already decided to work, the attractiveness of a particular occupation will be directly related to the wage it pays, holding all else constant. Thus the market supply curve for any particular occupation is upward sloping—more people will want to work in this occupation at $9.00 per hour than at $8.00. It will tend to shift outward to the right at any given wage if working conditions improve or wages in other occupations tend to fall. Even at $8.00 per hour, for example, a job offering flexible scheduling of hours may be more attractive to some than less flexible jobs paying $9.00 per hour.

One important difference between the demand and supply side of the labor market occurs at the level of the individual firm. Once a person has decided to join a particular occupation, the choice of which firm to work for is made on the basis of the wage that is offered, assuming all the other terms of employment are the same. Knowing this, an individual firm will be constrained to offer the going wage or risk losing all its applicants to other employers of the same type of labor. The result is that the supply curve of labor facing any individual firm in a competitive environment is simply a horizontal line at the going wage rate. That is, the firm can hire as much or as little labor as it wants provided it pays the going wage. From the perspective of the supply side of the labor market, each firm is essentially a **wage taker**.

How is the going wage determined in a particular labor market? Left alone, markets tend to settle to a wage called the **market** or **equilibrium wage** (equilibrium meaning there is no tendency for change). The market wage is one that leads to the quantity of labor demanded being equal to the quantity of labor supplied. This occurs at the intersection of the demand and supply curves. The best way to see why this is the equilibrium wage is to look at other wage levels and see that a tendency for change exists at each.

Example 2

Suppose the market demand and supply curves are given by the equations

$$\text{Demand: } L_D = 60 - 5W,$$
$$\text{Supply: } L_S = 5W,$$

where the subscripts D and S are used to distinguish between the quantity of labor demanded and the quantity of labor supplied. W is the real wage. These equations are shown graphically in Figure 2-2.

To understand where the equilibrium occurs, first consider a wage of $8. Note that at this wage, the quantity of labor supplied is 40, but the quantity of labor demanded is only 20. When such a **surplus** of labor (excess supply) exists, the tendency is for firms to experience many new applicants and low quit rates. The result is that firms start to offer lower wages (perhaps by just keeping nominal wages constant while prices are rising). As the wage falls, the quantity firms wish to hire starts to increase as we move down the market demand curve, and the quantity of people wishing to work in that occupation falls as we move down the market supply curve. These two forces combine to eliminate the excess supply. Hence, a wage of $8 could not be the equilibrium wage because a tendency for change still exists at that wage. When excess supply of labor exists, workers can be thought of as **overpaid** in an economic sense.

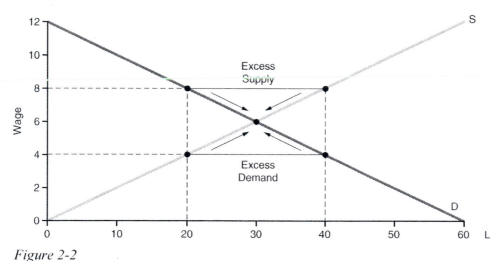

Figure 2-2

In the same way, it is clear that a wage of $4 can not be the equilibrium wage. At a wage of $4, the quantity of labor demanded is 40 but the quantity of labor supplied is only 20. When such a **shortage** of labor (excess demand) exists, quit rates are high and the firm has trouble getting enough people to serve its customers. The result is that firms tend to raise wages. As they do, a reduction in the quantity of labor demanded and an increase in the quantity of labor supplied eliminate the shortage. When excess demand for labor exists, workers can be thought of as **underpaid** in an economic sense.

The only wage where there is no tendency for change is $6. At this wage, the quantity of labor demanded and the quantity of labor supplied are equal at 30 units. This wage and employment level can be determined algebraically by solving for that wage (W^*) that equates L_D and L_S.

$$L_D = L_S \implies 60 - 5W = 5W \implies W^* = \$6.$$

An alternative way to view equilibrium is to realize that at any wage and employment level other than the equilibrium, it is possible to make someone better off without making anyone worse off. That is, the possibility for mutually beneficial exchange still exists. In the language of Chapter 1, the condition for Pareto efficiency is not satisfied at outcomes other than the equilibrium.

To see why this is true requires viewing the demand and supply curves from a slightly different perspective. Instead of thinking of the demand curve as the quantity of labor the firms wish to hire at any given wage rate, think of the curve as representing, at any given employment level, the maximum a firm would be willing to pay for a unit of labor. Similarly, the supply curve could be viewed as representing, for any given employment level, the minimum that would be necessary to induce an individual to enter that market. This minimum acceptable wage is called the **reservation wage**.

With this perspective in mind, consider a situation where the same demand and supply curves as in Figure 2-2 pertain and suppose that currently 20 units of labor are transacted at a wage of $8. At this employment level, some firm will be willing to hire an additional unit of labor at a wage of $8 or below, and some worker would be willing to accept $4 or more for supplying additional labor. These tendencies are shown graphically by the arrows in Figure 2-3. Note that the current situation leaves a window of opportunity for one of the workers currently shut out of the market to strike a mutually beneficial deal with one of the firms.

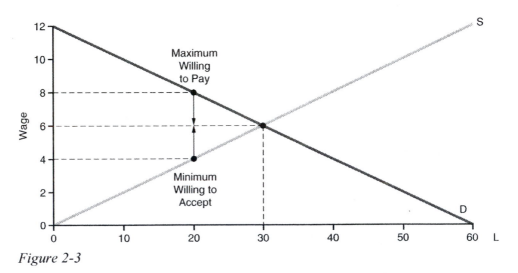

Figure 2-3

Suppose a worker willing to work for $4 offers to work for $7. Since at least one firm is willing to hire at $8, the offer of $7 will seem like a bargain to it. The firm will gain $1 by hiring an additional unit of labor, and the worker will gain $3 by being hired. (The difference between what the worker is willing to accept and the wage actually attained is called **economic rent**.) Whenever the wage is above or below equilibrium, thus creating an employment level below the equilibrium (note that employment can only occur along the heavier portions of the demand and supply curves in Figure 2-3), an opportunity exists for a mutually beneficial deal that will move employment closer to the equilibrium value.

While the demand and supply model predicts that the wages and employment levels will settle toward their equilibrium values, it is important to note that these values can change as the position of the demand and supply curves change. Changes in demand tend to push equilibrium wages and employment levels in the same direction (as demand goes up, both increase), while changes in supply tend to push wages and employment levels in opposite directions (as supply increases, the equilibrium wage falls and employment rises). When both curves shift at the same time, the effect on one of the outcomes can be ambiguous.

Sometimes wage and employment levels fail to reach their equilibrium values because of nonmarket forces such as minimum wage laws and unions. In an industry where a single union negotiates a wage above equilibrium that applies to all employees, the union effectively creates a horizontal supply curve at that wage (and makes the analysis identical to that for an effective minimum wage law). Other unions that directly limit and control the supply of labor effectively create a vertical supply curve to the left of the equilibrium employment level. While such arrangements make some people better off, they also tend to make some people worse off relative to the equilibrium outcome. Hence, the normative basis for such arrangements must rest on a principle other than that of mutually beneficial exchange. An examination of international differences in unemployment rates, particularly long-term unemployment rates, suggests that nonmarket forces are probably stronger in Europe than in the United States.

■ Review Questions

Choose the letter that represents the **BEST** response.

The Labor Market: Definitions, Facts, and Trends

1. The labor force consists of
    a. all individuals aged 16 or older who are employed or unemployed.
    b. all individuals aged 16 or older who are employed or looking for work.
    c. all individuals aged 16 or older who are employed or waiting to be recalled from layoff.
    d. all of the above.

2. The labor force participation rate is defined as
    a. the percentage of the total population aged 16 or older that is in the labor force.
    b. the percentage of the total population aged 16 or older that is employed.
    c. the percentage of the labor force that is employed.
    d. either **a** or **b**.

3. The unemployment rate is defined as
    a. the number unemployed divided by the labor force.
    b. the number unemployed divided by the sum of the employed and unemployed.
    c. the percentage of the population aged 16 or older that is not employed.
    d. either **a** or **b**.

In answering Questions **4–6**, please refer to the information in Table 2-4.

Table 2-4

Year	Average Nominal Wage	Consumer Price Index
1990	$ 9.54	100
1996	$11.18	127

4. Assuming 1990 is the base year, what would the index of nominal wages be for 1996?
   a. 85
   b. 92
   c. 117
   d. 164

5. Assuming 1990 is the base year, what would the index of real wages be for 1996?
   a. 67
   b. 92
   c. 109
   d. 117

6. What was the percentage change in real wages over the period 1990 to 1996?
   a. −10%
   b. −8%
   c. 9%
   d. 17%

7. When the real wage of a worker falls, one cannot necessarily conclude that the real income of the worker has also fallen because
   a. total earnings equal the wage rate times the number of hours worked.
   b. total compensation includes employee benefits provided by the firm.
   c. total income includes unearned income such as interest, dividends, and transfer payments.
   d. all of the above.

How the Labor Market Works

In answering Questions **8–19**, please refer to Figure 2-4. Suppose that the curves labeled *D* and *S* in Figure 2-4 represent the long-run market demand and supply curves for construction workers in Boston, Massachusetts during the summer of 2004.

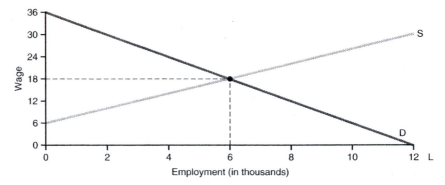

Figure 2-4

The Demand for Labor

8. The curve labeled D shows the number of workers firms wish to hire at each wage assuming
   a. the prices charged by construction firms for homes, office buildings, road construction, etc., remain constant.
   b. the price of construction equipment remains constant.
   c. the supply of construction workers remains constant.
   d. both **a** and **b**.

9. An economic reason why the curve labeled D slopes downward in the long run is that
   a. as wages increase, the firm will substitute equipment for workers.
   b. as wages increase, the optimal level of output for the firm will decrease.
   c. as wages increase, the number of workers the firm wishes to hire will decrease.
   d. both **a** and **b**.

10. An algebraic expression consistent with the demand curve in Figure 2-4 would be
    a. $L = 12 - (1/3)W$.
    b. $W = 36 - 3L$.
    c. $L = 12 - 3W$.
    d. both **a** and **b**.

11. The demand curve in Figure 2-4 would shift to the right if
    a. the market clearing wage fell.
    b. more workers are accepted into unions representing construction workers.
    c. the price of construction equipment rises and the substitution effect dominates the scale effect.
    d. all of the above.

The Supply of Labor

12. The curve labeled S in Figure 2-4 shows the number of workers willing to work in construction at each wage assuming
    a. wages in other occupations are less than in construction.
    b. working conditions are held constant.
    c. there is no union.
    d. all of the above.

13. An algebraic expression consistent with the supply curve in Figure 2-4 would be
    a. $L = 3 - 0.5W$.
    b. $W = 6 + 2L$.
    c. $L = -2 + (1/3)W$.
    d. both **a** and **b**.

14. Assuming all construction jobs offer comparable working conditions, the supply curve facing an individual construction firm will be
    a. a vertical line.
    b. a horizontal line at a wage of $18.
    c. the same as the market supply curve.
    d. flatter than the market supply curve.

Determination of the Wage and Employment Level

15. At the market clearing wage
    a.   the quantity demanded equals the quantity supplied.
    b.   no shortages or surpluses exist.
    c.   it is impossible to make someone better off without making someone else worse off.
    d.   all of the above.

16. At the market clearing wage, the total economic rent earned by all the workers employed would be
    a. $0.
    b. $36,000.
    c. $90,000.
    d. $108,000.

17. Suppose a union represents all construction workers and the union achieves a collective bargaining agreement with employers that specifies a wage of $24. If the firm still chooses what number of workers to hire given the negotiated wage, the result of the collective bargaining agreement will be
    a.   the supply curve of workers will become a vertical line located at an employment level of 4,000 workers.
    b.   there will be a surplus of 2,000 construction workers.
    c.   only 4,000 construction workers will be employed.
    d.   all of the above.

18. If demand increases while supply is constant
    a.   a shortage will exist at the original equilibrium wage.
    b.   the equilibrium wage will increase.
    c.   the wage will rise, causing labor demand to decrease to its original position.
    d.   both **a** and **b**.

19. If supply and demand both increase
    a.   the market clearing wage will rise but employment will stay the same.
    b.   employment will rise but the market wage may rise, fall, or stay the same.
    c.   both employment and the market clearing wage will rise.
    d.   there will be no change in the equilibrium.

20. If demand and supply are represented by the equations

$$\text{Demand: } L_D = 13 - \frac{1}{3}W,$$

$$\text{Supply: } L_S = \frac{1}{2}W - 2,$$

    then the equilibrium wage (W^*) and employment level (L^*) will equal
    a. $W^* = \$18$, $L^* = 6$.
    b. $W^* = \$18$, $L^* = 7$.
    c. $W^* = \$16$, $L^* = 8$.
    d. $W^* = \$12$, $L^* = 4$.

Problems

The Labor Market: Definitions, Facts, and Trends

21. Suppose that the population aged 16 or over in the United States could be categorized as follows

    Not in the labor force (N) = 75 million,

    Employed (E) = 115 million,

    Unemployed (U) = 10 million.

21a. Compute the unemployment rate for this economy.

21b. By historical standards, would your answer to 21a represent a relatively high level of unemployment?

21c. What has been the general trend in the unemployment rate since 1950?

21d. Compute the labor force participation rate for this economy.

21e. By historical standards, would your answer to **21d** represent a relatively high labor force participation rate?

21f. What has been the general trend in the labor force participation rate in the United States since 1950? Has the trend been the same for men as it has been for women?

21g. What has been the general trend since 1950 in the type of work Americans perform?

22. Consider Table 2-2 from Example 1 in the Summary section.

22a. What is the rationale behind computing an index of real wages?

22b. Redo Table 2-2 making 1980 the base year for both the price index and the index of real wages.

22c. What was the percentage change in real wages between the years 1980 and 1997?

22d. Is the change in **22c** likely to overstate or understate the change in the real compensation per worker over this period?

The Demand and Supply Model

23. Suppose labor demand and supply are represented by the equations

$$\text{Demand: } L_D = 10 - 0.5W,$$

$$\text{Supply: } L_S = 0.5W.$$

23a. Find the equilibrium wage and employment level.

23b. Graph the curves and indicate the equilibrium on the graph.

23c. Explain why $6 cannot be the market clearing wage.

*23d. Suppose 3 workers are hired at a wage of $6. Give an example of a mutually beneficial exchange that can still take place. Indicate the economic rent that is generated by your transaction.

23e. If workers earn economic rent, does that mean they are being overpaid?

*23f. Suppose all hiring in this market must be done through a union and the union has limited the supply of labor to 4 units. What wage will emerge in this market? How much economic rent have the employed members of the union gained? How much economic rent has been lost due to the limitation on union labor?

23g. Give an example of one thing that might cause labor demand to increase. Also give an example of one thing that might cause labor supply to decrease.

■ Applications

An Imperfection in the Unemployment Rate

24. The unemployment rate is defined as the percentage of the labor force that is unemployed at any particular point in time.

24a. What happens to the unemployment rate when an unemployed worker drops out of the labor force?

24b. Suppose the worker would like to work but has dropped out of the labor force because jobs are very hard to find. Has the labor market become tighter or looser because of the worker's withdrawal from the labor force?

Identifying the Demand and Supply Curves

25. Consider the following hypothetical scenario in which the president of a major labor union was presented with the data in Table 2-5. He concluded that the union was operating in a labor market where there was a rare upward sloping demand curve for union labor.

25a. Do you find his conclusion reasonable? What other conclusion could you draw?

25b. Using the demand and supply model, present an alternative explanation for the pattern shown in the data.

Table 2-5

Year	Average Wage of the Members	Member Employment (thousands)
1993	$10.00	4.0
1994	$11.25	4.5
1995	$12.50	5.0

Changes in the Demand for Labor

26. In September 1992, *The Wall Street Journal* reported that the Internal Revenue Service (IRS) was planning to cut 414 positions at the same time it was going to expand its auditing, collection, and taxpayer assistance and education programs. The increase in output was to be made possible by expanding its computer system. Based on these facts, what can you say about the size of the substitution and scale effects at the IRS? Assume that the expansion of the computer system was triggered by a reduction in the price of computers.

27. An investment tax credit is effectively a subsidy paid to a firm that spends money on a new plant and equipment. It effectively reduces the price of capital the firm faces.

27a. What effect does economic theory predict an investment tax credit will have on employment opportunities in the industries that take advantage of it?

27b. Under what circumstances will workers gain from the investment tax credit?

Disturbing the Market Equilibrium

28. Consider the following statement.

    "An increase in the supply of labor will cause the wage to fall. With a decrease in the wage, the demand for labor will increase, and an increase in the demand for labor tends to push the wage up. Therefore, an increase in labor supply will result in practically no long-run change in the wage because labor demand will increase also."

28a. Is this an accurate assessment of how the labor market operates? If not, what is wrong with the reasoning in this statement?

28b. Carefully explain how an increase in the supply of labor disturbs the equilibrium. What kinds of things cause labor supply to increase?

Chapter 3
The Demand for Labor

■ Summary

The demand and supply model of the labor market presented in Chapter 2 provides an effective framework for thinking about a wide variety of labor issues. To properly use that framework when analyzing policy issues, however, one must fully understand each component of the model. In this chapter, the focus is on the demand side of the model. The demand for labor is called a derived demand, because it comes from the demand for the products that workers produce.

The key to understanding where an individual firm's demand curve for labor comes from is to realize that every point on the demand curve is the result of an optimization decision by the firm. At a given wage rate, the quantity that is read off the demand curve represents the profit-maximizing level of employment for that wage rate.

As the firm hires more workers, total output will increase. But the marginal product of labor (MP_L), the amount of additional output associated with an additional unit of labor, is assumed to eventually decrease. Holding the stock of capital constant, hiring one more worker may initially result in an increase in the marginal, due to gains from specialization or cooperation. However, at some point, hiring one more worker will eventually result in a lower marginal product than that of the previous worker. This occurs because with a fixed stock of capital, capital will become scarce relative to the number of workers, and thus the productivity of each additional worker will be less, **diminishing marginal returns**.

In the short run, with the firm's capital stock fixed, there is one guiding principle behind the profit-maximization strategy. The firm will maximize profits when the marginal (extra) revenue associated with hiring an additional unit of labor (MR_L) just equals the marginal expense of hiring an additional unit of labor (ME_L). If this condition is not met, a window of opportunity exists for the firm to change its employment level and increase its profits. The marginal revenue associated with an additional unit of labor is called the **marginal revenue product** of labor (MRP_L) since it can be shown that it is equal to $(MR) \times (MP_L)$. MR is the marginal revenue associated with the sale of an additional unit of output, and MP_L is the marginal product (physical output) associated with an additional unit of labor ($\Delta Q/\Delta L$).

The details of the profit-maximization exercise, however, are also influenced by the firm's position in both the input and output markets. Is the firm the sole buyer of labor (a monopsony, discussed in Chapter 5) or just one small buyer among many (a competitor in the input market)? Is the firm the only seller of its product (a monopoly), or does it face such vigorous competition that is essentially a price taking firm (a competitor in the output market)? These are the key questions that must be answered before the exact nature of the short-run profit-maximization exercise can be described.

When the firm faces competition in the output market, MR will simply be the price of the product (P). Similarly, when the firm faces competition in the input market, ME_L will equal the wage rate (W). The various possibilities for expressing the short-run profit-maximization condition in a competitive labor market are summarized in Table 3-1.

Table 3-1

Output Market Structure	Maximization Condition
Competition	$P \times MP_L = W$
Monopoly	$MR \times MP_L = W$

To see how these short-run profit-maximization conditions lead to the firm's demand curve for labor, suppose the firm has a fixed capital stock of 10 units and a production function given by the equation

$$Q = KL - .0125KL^2,$$

where K stands for units of capital. Then in the short run the production function can be written as $Q = 10L - 0.125L^2$. For this production function, the marginal product of labor is always declining and given by the equation $MP_L = 10 - 0.25L$. (For the reader with calculus training, the marginal product of labor can be computed by taking the first derivative of the short-run production function.) Also assume the firm takes prices as given in both input and output markets, selling its product at a price of $2, and hiring labor at the going wage rate of $10.

Given the assumption of competition in the output market, marginal revenue equals the market price, so the marginal revenue product (MRP_L) equals $P \times MP_L = 20 - 0.5L$. Given the assumption of competition in the input market, the marginal expense of labor ME_L equals the wage of $10. Solving for L, $MRP_L = 20 - 0.5L = 10 = ME_L$, which yields $L^* = 20$. At any (*) level of employment less than 20, the MRP_L exceeds the ME_L and the firm can increase its profits by increasing the quantity of labor it uses. Alternatively, at values of L greater than 20, the MRP_L is less than the ME_L, signifying that the firm hired some workers who added less in revenue than they added in costs. By reducing employment, the firm could increase its profits. Only at $L = 20$ has the firm made all the profit-increasing hires and none that reduce profits. Therefore, the coordinates $W = \$10$, $L = 20$ denoted by point a in Figure 3-1 represent a point on the firm's short-run demand curve for labor.

(*) Readers should note that profits would not rise when increasing employment from 19 to 20 in this example, since by construction, the 20th unit of labor adds exactly as much to revenues as to costs. However, note that the 19th worker adds $.50 to profits, just as a 21st worker would reduce profits by $.50. Employing labor, or any input to the point where $MRP = ME$, or, if they cannot be precisely equated, to the point where the next unit's MRP would be less than its ME, assures that all possible profits have been extracted, although when MRP exactly equals ME, the last unit employed has no impact on profits.

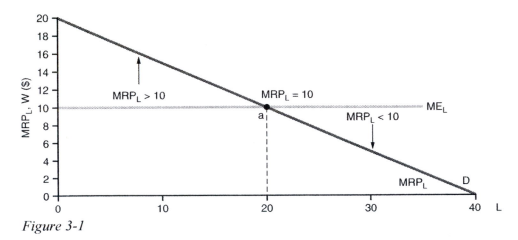

Figure 3-1

As the wage changes, the firm simply moves up or down along the MRP_L curve, tracing out the entire short-run demand curve, the curve that by definition represents what the firm wishes to hire at any given wage rate. The curve can also be depicted as the quantity of labor associated with any given value of the real wage (W/P). In this case, the marginal product schedule becomes the firm's labor demand curve. Note that changes in the original specification of the production function (i.e., the firm's technology), the level of capital, or the price of the final product (through, say, a shift in the demand for the product) would all change the position of the MRP_L curve.

Once the firm's labor demand curve is identified, the **market demand** curve can be constructed by summing horizontally all the individual firm demand curves (i.e., adding the quantities of labor demand by each firm at a given wage rate, and then repeating for all wage rates), provided the individual firm demand curves are expressed in terms of the real wage.

The long-run demand for labor is also generated through a profit maximization exercise. Assuming competitive input markets with a given wage and price of capital, the key is to find the **cost-minimizing combination** of labor and capital associated with the firm's optimal output. The cost-minimizing combination occurs when

$$\frac{W}{MP_L} = \frac{C}{MP_K},$$

where C refers to price of capital, and MP_K refers to the marginal product of capital. The ratio of an input's price to its marginal product gives the marginal cost of producing output using that input. If this equality did not hold, there would be a window of opportunity to produce the same output level at lower cost by using a different input mix.

What is the optimal output for the firm to produce? This occurs where the marginal revenue (MR) just equals the marginal cost (MC). Here the MC refers to the change in total cost (expense) associated with an additional unit of output. In the short run, as the wage changes, the firm facing competition in the input markets simply moves along its MRP_L curve. In the long run, however, a rise in the wage typically brings about a substitution of capital for labor and vice versa. In addition to this **substitution effect**, an increase (decrease) in the wage increases (decreases) the marginal cost of production, leading to a decrease (increase) in output. The change in output causes the firm to change the quantity of labor and capital it demands in the same direction. This change is called the **scale effect**.

Example

Consider a firm with a production function given by the equation

$$Q = \sqrt{L}\sqrt{K}.$$

This equation is an example of a Cobb-Douglas production function. For a firm facing competition in the input markets, it can be shown (using the cost-minimizing conditions mentioned earlier along with the production function) that for any given level of output the cost minimizing levels of L and K are given by the equations

$$L^* = \frac{\sqrt{C}}{\sqrt{W}}Q, \quad \text{and} \quad K^* = \frac{\sqrt{W}}{\sqrt{C}}Q.$$

If $W = \$4$ and $C = \$16$, for example, then $L^* = 2Q$ and $K^* = .5Q$. But what is the optimal level of Q?

Recall that the firm finds its optimal output where $MR = MC$. If the firm is a monopolist in the output market and faces a demand curve given by the equation $P = 36 - Q$, then its marginal revenue will be $MR = 36 - 2Q$. But what is its marginal cost? The firm's total cost (TC) can always be expressed as $TC = WL + CK$. Substituting the expressions for the optimal levels of L and K yields

$$TC = W \frac{\sqrt{C}}{\sqrt{W}} Q + C \frac{\sqrt{W}}{\sqrt{C}} Q,$$
$$\Rightarrow TC = 2\sqrt{W}\sqrt{C}\, Q.$$

Since every time Q changes by one, TC changes by $2\sqrt{W}\sqrt{C}$, and the expression for marginal cost must be

$$MC = 2\sqrt{W}\sqrt{C}.$$

Assuming $W = \$4$ and $C = \$16$, $MC = \$16$. Setting $MC = MR$ ($= 36 - 2Q$) implies that the optimal level of output is $Q^* = 10$. Substituting this value back into the simplified L^* and K^* expressions yields $L^* = 20$ and $K^* = 5$. The total cost associated with this input use would be $\$4(20) + \$16(5)$ for a total of $\$160$.

Now suppose the wage rises from $\$4$ to $\$9$, what would be the effect on the quantity of labor demanded in the long run? With the new wage rate, notice that the optimal expressions for L and K become $L^* = (4/3) Q$ and $K^* = (3/4)Q$. If Q were to remain at 10, then the firm would change its input mix to $L^* = 13.33$ and $K^* = 7.5$. This reduction in L from 20 to 13.33 and the increase in K from 5 to 7.5 is called the substitution effect of the wage increase. It occurs because labor is more expensive relative to capital than it was originally, so the firm economizes on labor to limit the amount of the cost increase it faces. Notice that after the firm substitutes capital for labor, costs rise from $\$160$ to $TC = \$9(13.33) + \$16(7.5) = \$240$, reducing profits to $\$20$. However, this rise is significantly less than if the firm had not changed its input mix at all. Staying with the original combination of inputs would have led to $TC = \$9(20) + \$16(5) = \$260$ and eliminated profits.

The problem is that with the increase in the wage from $\$4$ to $\$9$, the optimal output of the firm will not stay at 10 units. Why? Substituting the new input price into the marginal cost expression, notice that MC has risen from $\$14$ to $\$24$. With this rise in the MC, the optimal output falls to $36 - 2Q = 24$, and $Q^* = 6$. Substituting this new output into the new L^* and K^* expressions yields $L^* = (4/3)6 = 8$, and $K^* = (3/4)6 = 4.5$.

The net result of W increasing from $\$4$ to $\$9$ was that L^* fell from 20 to 8 (a reduction of 12 units), and K^* fell from 5 to 4.5 units (a reduction of 0.5 units). This can be explained by a substitution effect where L^* fell from 20 to 13.33 (a reduction of 6.67) and a scale effect where L^* fell from 13.33 to 8 (an additional reduction of 5.33). Similarly, the reduction in K^* can be explained by a substitution effect where K^* increased from 5 to 7.5 (a 2.5-unit increase), but also a scale effect where K^* fell from 7.5 to 4 (a 3-unit decrease). Total costs are now $\$9(8) + \$16(4.5) = 144$. With output reduced to 6, price rises to $36 - 6 = \$30$, so total revenue is $\$30(6) = 180$, and profits equal $180 - 144 = \$36$.

Notice that for labor (the input whose price changed) the substitution and scale effects reinforce one another, leading to a downward sloping demand curve. However, for capital (the other input), the substitution and scale effects counteract. In general, when the scale effect dominates the substitution effect (as it did in this example) so that L^* and K^* move together, labor and capital are called **gross complements**. On the other hand, it is possible for the substitution effect to dominate the scale effect, in which case L^* and K^* would move in opposite directions and be called **gross substitutes**. In the event that labor and capital are used in fixed proportions, there is no substitution effect and so labor and capital will be gross complements.

In actually applying this theory to the labor market, it is usually more interesting to look at what happens to labor when the price of the other input changes, but the same basic principles apply. In such situations, if labor and capital are gross complements, the firm's long-run labor demand curve shifts to the left as the price of capital increases, and shifts right if they are gross substitutes. Also, the framework can be used to think about how different types of labor interact (e.g., full-time vs. part-time, teenagers vs. adults, union vs. non-union, men vs. women) when the wage of just one group changes.

When the firm has monopoly power in the product market, the details of the analysis are different. For a firm with monopoly power in the output market, the given information must include the market demand curve for the product the firm produces. Marginal revenue for a monopolist will always be less than the price of the last unit of output, because for a monopolist, selling more requires lowering the price of all units. (If the demand curve is linear, it could be written in the form $P = a - bQ$, where a and b are constants greater than zero, and Q stands for quantity demanded. Marginal revenue is then given by the equation $MR = a - 2bQ$. To find the marginal revenue product (MRP_L) expression, one substitutes the short-run production function for the variable Q in the marginal revenue expression and then multiplies the resulting expression by the marginal product.) Thus the MRP_L curve for a monopolist will lie below the MRP_L curve for an otherwise identical competitive firm. If it is assumed that both firms hire at a competitive wage rate, monopolists will hire fewer workers than equivalent competitive firms.

The rest of the chapter uses the concept of market demand to look at the question of who bears the burden of payroll taxes and whether differences in payroll tax rates across countries can explain differences in unemployment rates. The flip side of payroll taxes—wage subsidies—are also examined for their effectiveness in expanding employment and raising the incomes of low-wage workers. The analysis shows that a significant portion of payroll taxes can fall on workers, and this burden increases when the supply of labor is not particularly responsive to changes in the wage. Additionally, wage subsidies have not been found in practice to be very effective at raising the employment or wages of low-wage workers. A lack of employer awareness of the availability of subsidies and eligibility requirements for prospective employees both appear to diminish the potential effectiveness of wage subsidies.

The appendix to this chapter develops aspects of short-run and long-run demand graphically, using the tools of **isoquants** and **isoexpenditure lines**. Isoquants represent all the different combinations of labor and capital that can produce the same output level. The slope of the isoquant expressed positively is called the **marginal rate of technical substitution (MRTS)**. Its magnitude can be found by taking the ratio of the marginal product of labor to the marginal product of capital at any combination of L and K along the isoquant. Isoquant maps reflect the assumption that short-run production functions will exhibit diminishing marginal productivity.

Isoexpenditure lines show all the combinations of L and K that cost the same. The magnitude of the slope of the isoexpenditure line is given by the ratio of the price of labor to the price of capital. The appendix clearly shows that cost minimization in the long run occurs when the firm reaches the lowest isoexpenditure line associated with a given isoquant. This typically occurs when the firm chooses values of L and K associated with a tangency between the two curves. Since tangency points equate slopes, this implies that the ratio of marginal products equals the ratio of input prices, which was earlier demonstrated to be a cost-minimizing condition. Finally, substitution and scale effects for an increase in the wage are shown graphically.

■ Review Questions

Choose the letter that represents the **BEST** response.

Assumptions of the Labor Demand Model

1. When a firm faces competition in the labor market
   a. the wage the firm pays can be treated as constant.
   b. the firm can buy as much or as little labor as it wants at a going wage rate.
   c. the firm's marginal expense of labor equals the wage rate.
   d. all of the above.

2. When a firm faces competition in the product market
   a. the product price the firm receives can be treated as a given.
   b. the firm can sell as much or as little of its product as it wants at a going price.
   c. the firm's marginal revenue equals the product price.
   d. all of the above.

3. As the firm increases its employment, it is typically assumed that the marginal product of labor will eventually decline. An economic reason for why this occurs is that
   a. the law of diminishing returns applies.
   b. an increase in employment causes the wage to fall and this, in turn, causes workers to exert less effort.
   c. at some point, additional units of labor bring about a smaller change in total output than previous units did.
   d. Each additional worker has a smaller share of capital with which to work.

Short-Run Demand for Labor

4. A firm will maximize its profits in the short run when
   a. the difference between MR_L and ME_L is as large as possible.
   b. MR_L equals ME_L, or the difference between them is as small as possible.
   c. the money wage workers receive (W) equals the marginal product.
   d. the marginal revenue product (MRP_L) equals the marginal cost (MC).

5. The marginal revenue product curve is the firm's short-run demand curve for labor provided
   a. the firm faces competition in the labor market.
   b. the firm faces competition in the output market.
   c. $MRP_L = MR \times MP_L$.
   d. both **a** and **b**.

6. For a firm to survive in a competitive environment
   a.   it must follow the $MRP_L = ME_L$ rule.
   b.   it must act as if it is following the $MRP_L = ME_L$ rule.
   c.   it must be able to verbalize the conditions for profit maximization.
   d.   it must be able to accurately measure the marginal revenue product of its workers.

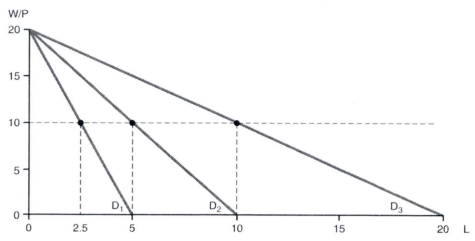

Figure 3-2

7. Figure 3-2 shows the short-run labor demand curves (expressed as a function of the real wage) for the three individual firms that hire this type of labor. At a real wage of 10, the quantity associated with the market demand curve would be
   a.   15 units of labor.
   b.   17.5 units of labor.
   c.   20 units of labor.
   d.   35 units of labor.

Long-Run Demand for Labor

8. Assume the price of labor (W) equals $10 and the price of capital (C) equals $36. Also suppose that at the current mix of labor and capital, $MP_L = 5$ and $MP_K = 12$. Using the rule for cost minimization, which of the following correctly describes what the firm should do to its labor and capital mix?
   a.   Increase L and decrease K.
   b.   Decrease L and increase K.
   c.   Increase both L and K.
   d. L and K should not change.

9. Suppose the price of capital falls. If the scale effect associated with the price change dominates the substitution effect,
   a.   the quantity of labor demanded will increase.
   b.   the quantity of labor demanded will decrease.
   c.   labor and capital can be called gross substitutes.
   d.   both **b** and **c**.

10. Suppose the price of capital falls. If capital and labor are used in fixed proportions in the production process,
    a. the substitution effect is zero.
    b. the scale effect will dominate the substitution effect.
    c. labor and capital will be gross complements.
    d. all of the above.

11. If the price of capital rises and the long-run demand for labor curve shifts right, one can infer that
    a. the scale effect dominated the substitution effect.
    b. the substitution effect dominated the scale effect.
    c. labor and capital are gross substitutes.
    d. both **b** and **c**.

Who Bears the Burden of the Payroll Tax?

In answering Questions **15–18**, refer to Figure 3-3. The curve labeled D_0 represents the short-run market demand before the payroll tax is imposed, while D_1 represents the curve after a tax (in real terms) of X per employee has been imposed on the firm. The curve labeled S is the market supply curve for labor. The wage on the vertical axis represents the real wage (W/P) employees actually receive.

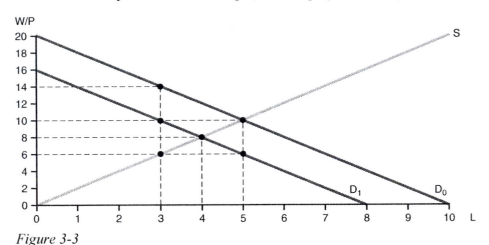

Figure 3-3

12. What is the amount of the tax?
    a. $X = 0.5$
    b. $X = 1$
    c. $X = 2$
    d. $X = 4$

13. The percentage of the tax the workers bear in the form of lower wages is
    a. 10%.
    b. 25%.
    c. 50%.
    d. 100%.

14. What has been the effect of the payroll tax on the employment level?
    a. Employment has fallen by 1.
    b. Employment has fallen by 2.
    c. Employment has risen by 1.
    d. There has been no change in employment.

15. What percentage of the tax would the worker bear in the form of lower wages if the supply curve (*S*) were perfectly vertical (i.e., quantity supplied was extremely insensitive to changes in the wage)?
    a. 0%
    b. 25%
    c. 50%
    d. 100%

A Graphical Approach to Labor Demand (Appendix 3A)

In answering Questions **19–21**, refer to Figure 3-4, which shows the cost-minimizing combination of *L* and *K* for producing 100 units of output when *W* = $16 and *C* = $25.

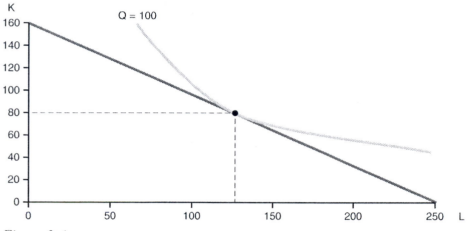

Figure 3-4

16. At the cost-minimizing combination of *L* and *K*, the ratio of *MPL* to *MPK*, the marginal rate of technical substitution (*MRTS*), equals
    a. 0.64.
    b. 1.5625.
    c. 2.
    d. 2.25.

17. The total cost level associated with the optimal combination of *L* and *K* is
    a. $4,000.
    b. $4,100.
    c. $4,405.
    d. $4,750.

18. If the price of capital were to rise to $40, which of the following statements would be true?
    a.   If the firm wanted to stay at the same cost level, the output of the firm would have to fall.
    b.   If the firm wanted to stay at the same output level, the total cost would have to rise.
    c.   If the firm stayed at the same output level, it would adjust its input mix to use less capital and more labor.
    d.   All of the above.

■ Problems

The Short-Run Demand for Labor

19. Recall that the marginal revenue product of labor (MRP_L) is defined as $MR \times MP_L$.

19a. Using the definitions of marginal revenue and marginal product of labor, prove that $MR \times MP_L$ equals the marginal revenue associated with an additional unit of labor (MR_L).

19b. Explain why the MRP_L curve slopes downward.

20. The demand for labor is called a derived demand since without the demand for the final product, there would be no demand for labor. Using the data associated with Figure 3-1 in the **Summary** section, show what would happen to the demand for labor when each of the following changes takes place.

20a. Suppose the demand for the product increased in such a way that the product price rose to $4. Find the equation for the firm's new demand curve for labor. What would be the new optimal level of labor assuming W stays at $10?

20b. In the short run, by definition, the capital stock is fixed. Show what would happen to the demand for labor if the capital stock were fixed at 20 units instead. Find the equation for the firm's new demand curve for labor. What would be the new optimal level of labor, assuming W stays at $10?

20c. Finally, show what would happen to the firm's demand for labor if labor became more productive so that the production function could now be represented by the formula

$$Q = 2KL - 0.025KL^2,$$

which would make the marginal product expression at $K = 10$

$$MP_L = 20 - 0.5L.$$

Find the equation for the firm's new demand curve for labor. What would be the new optimal level of labor assuming W stays at $10?

21. The demand for labor can be expressed in terms of real or nominal (money) wages. Figure 3-1 in the **Summary** section is expressed in terms of the nominal wage.

21a. Redraw Figure 3-1 expressing the demand for labor in terms of the real wage.

21b. What curve plays the role of the firm's demand curve for labor when the real wage is plotted on the vertical axis?

22. Suppose the following equations represent the demand for two firms demanding a particular type of labor. The curves are expressed as functions of the real wage.

$$Firm\ 1:\ L_1 = 50 - (W/P).$$

$$Firm\ 2:\ L_2 = 25 - 0.5(W/P).$$

22a. Plot the two curves on the same axes and then construct the market demand.

22b. Find the equation for the market demand curve.

The Long-Run Demand for Labor

23. Suppose the firm currently employs 500 workers and 100 units of capital and that the following relationship holds.

$$\frac{W}{MP_L} = \frac{16}{4} = 4 < \frac{C}{MP_K} = \frac{50}{10} = 5.$$

Prove that the firm is not at an equilibrium mix of labor and capital by showing there is a window of opportunity for it to reduce its total cost.

*24. Use the data in the **Summary** section **Example** problem to answer the following questions.

*24a. Find the substitution and scale effects associated with an increase in the wage from $4 to $9 assuming the firm faces a market demand given by the equation $P = 56 - 2Q$.

24b. Are labor and capital gross substitutes or gross complements? Will the demand for capital shift right or left as the wage increases?

*25. Use the data in the **Summary** section **Example** problem to answer the following questions.

*25a. Find the substitution and scale effects associated with an increase in the price of capital from $16 to $36. Assume the wage rate is constant at $4.

25b. Are labor and capital gross substitutes or gross complements? Will the labor demand curve shift left or right as the price of capital increases?

A Graphical Approach to Labor Demand (Appendix 3A)

26. Consider the isoquants shown in Figure 3-5. Assume the level of capital is fixed at 4 units in the short run.

26a. Find the marginal product of labor associated with a movement from point a to point b. Do the same for a movement from point b to point c.

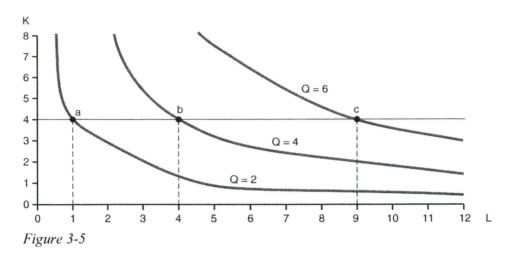

Figure 3-5

26b. Is the diagram consistent with the notion of a diminishing marginal product of labor? If so, does it help to explain why the marginal product declines?

27. Figure 3-6 depicts a situation where the firm must use capital and labor in a fixed one-to-one proportion. For example, if the firm uses 70 units of capital and 70 units of labor, it will be able to produce 70 units of output. However, if it adds another unit of capital without adding another unit of labor, output would remain at 70 units. Suppose that originally the price of labor is $5, the price of capital is $10, and the optimal level of output is 70.

The cost-minimizing point is where the firm uses 70 units of labor and 70 units of capital (point *a*). Now suppose the price of capital rises to $20 and the firm responds by moving to point *b*.

27a. Find the substitution effect on labor and capital of the capital price change.

27b. Find the scale effect on labor and capital of the capital price change.

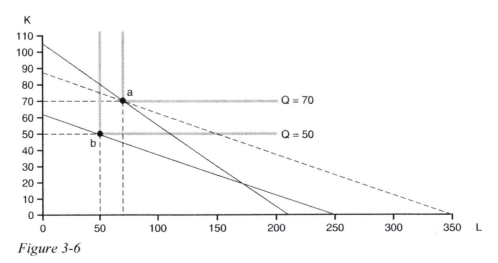

Figure 3-6

27c. Are labor and capital gross substitutes or gross complements?

27d. Has the firm's total cost level increased or decreased after the change in the price of capital?

■ Applications

Who Bears the Burden of the Payroll Tax?

28. Consider a labor market where the labor demand and supply curves are given by the equations

$$\text{Demand: } W_D = 30 - 0.04L.$$
$$\text{Supply: } W_S = 0.05L - 15.$$

28a. Calculate the equilibrium wage and employment level.

28b. Suppose the government imposes a payroll tax of $9 per labor unit on the employer. Calculate the new equilibrium wage and employment level. What is the new per-unit cost of labor to the firm?

28c. What percentage of the tax is ultimately paid by the workers? What percentage is paid by the firm?

28d. What similarity do you see between the analysis of payroll tax burdens and proposals that employers be required to provide certain benefits (like health insurance or parental leave) to their employees? What are the likely effects of such mandates?

Effects of Deregulation on the Demand for Labor

*29. The theory behind deregulating various product markets like air travel, trucking, and so on was to break down monopoly power, do away with regulation that was generally ineffective, and make the markets more competitive. Holding all else constant, when monopoly power is broken down, an industry should be able to produce more output at a lower price.

Consider a firm with a production function given by the equation

$$Q = \sqrt{L}\sqrt{K}.$$

In the short run suppose the level of capital is fixed at 16 units. The marginal product of labor in the short run is given by the equation

$$MP_L = \frac{2}{\sqrt{L}}.$$

Suppose initially that a firm has been granted monopoly power by the government and faces a demand curve given by $P = 20 - 0.5Q$. The firm faces competition in the labor market where the going price of labor is $10. Suppose that regulation is ineffective and the firm acts as a normal profit-maximizing monopolist.

*29a. Find the equation for the firm's labor demand curve. Find the optimal level of labor for the firm to demand.

29b. Given your answer to **33a**, how much output will the firm produce and what price will it charge?

*29c. Now suppose the market in which the firm sells its product is deregulated and new competitors enter the market. Suppose the price of the product falls to $15. Find the equation for the firm's demand curve for labor under competition. Using the new demand curve expression, find the optimal level of labor for the firm to demand. How much output will the firm produce now?

*29d. On the same graph, plot the demand curves and the quantity of labor demanded before and after deregulation.

29e. In general (without computing specific numbers), what effect do you think deregulation would have on a firm's long-run demand for labor? Explain your reasoning.

29f. If regulators are actually effective in keeping a firm from exploiting its monopoly status, some economists suspect that such firms may actually pay a wage that is higher than the going rate. Explain the reasoning behind this argument.

Wage Subsidies

*30. Consider a firm that hires low-skilled workers. The firm's demand for this labor is given by the equation

$$W = 16 - 0.1L,$$

or equivalently,

$$L = 160 - 10W.$$

To stimulate the employment of low-skilled workers, suppose the government institutes a wage subsidy program. The program is a "targeted" subsidy in that the firm will receive a subsidy only if it hires people previously on welfare. The program is also a "marginal" or "incremental" subsidy in that the subsidy applies only to new hires made from the targeted groups. The firm will not receive subsidies for existing workers. Finally, the subsidy will be structured so that the firm receives 50% of the difference between the wage they pay and the program's "target wage" of $8. (If the firm pays the workers $8 or more they receive no subsidy.) Suppose the firm currently pays the going wage for unskilled labor of $4.

30a. Before the subsidy was enacted, what was the quantity of labor demanded? Graph the demand curve before the subsidy and indicate the firm's wage and employment level.

*30b. Under the program, assuming the wage actually paid is $4, what subsidy does the firm receive for each new hire? What is the effective cost to the firm of each new hire?

*30c. What is the quantity of labor the firm will demand at a wage of $4 under the subsidy program? On the same graph as in **34a**, draw the demand for labor under the subsidy program.

*30d. At a wage of $4, is the demand for labor flatter or steeper under the subsidy program? Would the slope increase or decrease if the subsidy were 75% of the difference between the target wage and the actual wage?

*30e. Given the original information, what is the total payment the government must make to the firm? What would the cost to the government be if the subsidy applied to all workers, not just new hires?

*30f. If the original demand for labor were steeper, would the employment effects of the subsidy be larger or smaller? Explain your reasoning.

*30g. Why do subsidy programs targeted to specific groups not always have the type of effect this example predicts?

Chapter 4
Labor Demand Elasticities

■ Summary

Chapter 3 presented a framework for thinking about the demand side of the labor market. The framework explained why the quantity of labor demanded is inversely related to the wage both in the short run and the long run. It also explained what causes labor demand to increase or decrease when the prices of other inputs change. Knowing why these things happen provides a foundation for correctly analyzing the effects of different policies (e.g., payroll taxes) on the direction of employment and wages. Chapter 4 extends the labor demand framework to look at the issue of how responsive the quantity of labor demanded is to changes in the wage or the price of other inputs. Does the quantity firms demand change by a little or a lot when the wage changes? Under what circumstances is the substitution effect accompanying a change in the price of capital likely to be large and the scale effect small? These are the types of questions taken up in Chapter 4.

The main measure of how responsive employment is to changes in the wage or the price of other inputs is the **elasticity of demand**, which is denoted by the Greek letter eta (η). An elasticity is simply the ratio of two percentage changes. If the focus is how responsive the quantity of labor demanded is to a change in the wage rate, the elasticity is called the own-wage elasticity of demand. Letting E stand for employment, W the wage, the subscript i a particular category of labor, and $\%\Delta$ a percentage change, the own-wage elasticity is defined as

$$\eta_{ii} = \frac{\%\Delta E_i}{\%\Delta W_i} = \frac{\frac{\Delta E_i}{Ei}}{\frac{\Delta W_i}{W_i}} = \frac{\Delta E_i}{\Delta W_i} \frac{W_i}{E_i}.$$

The elasticity can be interpreted as the percentage change in employment induced by a one percentage point change in the wage. Since the own-wage elasticity will always have a negative sign (since demand curves slope downward), usually reference is made to just the magnitude (the absolute value) of the elasticity. When the magnitude of η is less than one, demand is said to be **inelastic**, meaning employment is relatively unresponsive to changes in the wage. A magnitude greater than one is called **elastic** and means that employment is relatively responsive to changes in the wage.

What factors lead the own-wage elasticity to be elastic or inelastic? In the case of a straight line demand curve, whether the own-wage elasticity is elastic or inelastic depends in part on the current position along the curve. Straight line demand curves exhibit the same *unit* changes throughout the entire curve. For example, a demand curve with a slope of −1 will show an increase of employment by one unit for every one-unit fall in the wage. The same curve, however, will have changing elasticities as wages change. In particular, demand will be more elastic toward the top and get less elastic as wages fall. The logic behind this is simple: When wages are high and employment low (at the top of the curve), any given wage change will be small in percentage terms while a given change in employment will be large in percentage terms. The reverse is true when wages are low and employment high (at the bottom of the curve). So although slope alone is not a good universal indicator of elasticity, when comparing two demand curves, it is still usually possible to generalize whether one tends to be more elastic than another. For example, in Figure 4-1, for any small change at a given wage rate, say from $25 to $26, curve D_1 will always be more elastic ($\eta_{11} = -1.67$ at $25) than curve D_2 ($\eta_{22} = -1$ at $25), even though each will eventually exhibit an inelastic range if the wage goes low enough.

Secondly, the size of the own-wage elasticity can be explained by the size of the substitution and scale effects resulting from a change in the wage. The size of the substitution and scale effects, in turn, are influenced primarily by four factors. These factors have come to be known as the **Hicks-Marshall laws** of derived demand. These laws state that the elasticity of demand for labor will be greater (more elastic):

1. the greater the elasticity of demand for output,

2. the easier it is to substitute other factors of production for labor,

3. the more elastic is the supply of other factors, and

4. the greater is labor's share in the total costs of the firm.

To understand the Hicks-Marshall laws, consider a situation where the wage increases, holding all else constant. What kinds of things would tend to *diminish* the substitution and scale effects, and hence result in a very unresponsive (inelastic) labor demand curve?

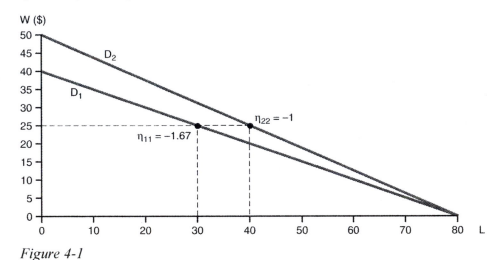

Figure 4-1

Considering the substitution effect first, the substitution effect will be small if circumstances exist that make it difficult to substitute capital for labor. For example, in a production process where labor and capital are used in fixed proportions, there can be no substitution effect. Alternatively, union rules may limit firms from undertaking certain tasks with less than some minimum number of workers. Supposing that the firm can and does try to substitute capital for labor, are there any factors that could limit this substitution? Usually we think of the firm being able to buy as much or as little capital as it wants at the going price. This would be the case if the supply of capital is perfectly elastic (horizontal). But suppose instead that the supply of capital is actually upward sloping and relatively inelastic. As the firm tries to substitute capital for labor, the demand for capital will be shifting outward along a relatively inelastic supply curve. This bids up the price of capital significantly and limits the firm's incentive to continue substituting additional units of capital for labor. So substitution can be limited or perhaps even unfeasible due to either technical or economic factors.

What would lead to a small scale effect? The best way to answer this is to think of the linkages through which the scale effect occurs. When the wage increases, the marginal cost of production (MC) rises, and a rise in the MC destroys the equality between marginal revenue (MR) and MC. That forces the firm to adjust its output downward to restore the $MR = MC$ condition for profit maximization. As the optimal output (Q^*) is adjusted downward, the firm's use of labor (L) and capital inputs (K) are reduced. This chain of reasoning is summarized schematically below.

$$W \uparrow \Rightarrow MC \uparrow \Rightarrow Q^* \downarrow \Rightarrow K^* \downarrow \quad \text{and} \quad L^* \downarrow.$$

The important thing to realize is that if the first two links in the chain are weak, the last cannot help but be weak. But what would cause the MC of production not to rise much as the wage increases? The answer is if the cost of employing labor is a small share of total cost. As an extreme example of this, suppose a firm did not use any labor to begin with (so that labor's share of total cost was 0%). In such a case, an increase in the wage would have no effect on the MC. (See the discussion accompanying footnote 5 in the text for a situation where a category of labor could still be highly elastic even when it accounts for a very small share of total costs.) What about the second link? What would make the level of output not fall very much for a given increase in MC? The answer here is an inelastic demand for the final product the firm sells. The more unresponsive quantity demanded is to changes in price, the more the MC increase can be passed along in the form of higher prices, and the less output has to adjust downward.

If the focus is how responsive the quantity demand of labor input i is to a change in the price of another input j, the elasticity is called the **cross-price elasticity of demand** (cross-wage elasticity of demand when the other input is a different category of labor) and is defined as

$$\eta_{ij} = \frac{\%\Delta E_i}{\%\Delta Wj} = \frac{\dfrac{\Delta E_i}{Ei}}{\dfrac{\Delta W_j}{Wj}} = \frac{\Delta E_i}{\Delta Wj}\frac{W_j}{E_i}.$$

Similarly, one could define a cross-price elasticity η_{ji} (though readers should note that the two elasticities will **not** have the same value). Unlike the own-wage elasticity where the sign is typically ignored, both the sign and magnitude of the cross-price elasticities are important. If the sign is positive, the employment of input i moves together with the price of input j (and hence presumably opposite to that of the quantity of input j) indicating that i and j are **gross substitutes**. If the sign is negative, inputs i and j are **gross complements**.

What factors lead two inputs to be gross substitutes or gross complements? When focusing on the long-run demand for labor, the size of the substitution and scale effects are again the determining factors in whether demand will be relatively elastic or inelastic, and whether any two inputs will be gross substitutes or gross complements. (In the short run only the scale effect is relevant to the choice between capital and labor since there can be no substitution effect. However, if the focus is on two types of labor, there often can be substitution between the two types even in the short run.)

Focusing on these four factors (the ease of substitutability between labor and other inputs, the supply elasticity of the other inputs, the share of total costs that are labor costs, and the product demand elasticity) provides a good place to start in assessing the likely consequences for employment of different changes that may take place in the labor market. By assembling evidence on each of these factors, one would be in a strong position to gauge the magnitude of the employment change due to a change in the wage. Also these four factors can provide focus when assessing the employment effects of changes in the price of other inputs. In the problems and applications that follow, these four factors will be employed in a number of different contexts to assess and explain a variety of labor market phenomena. Proper use of the Hicks-Marshall laws is one of the most important and versatile tools for anyone interested in being a serious thinker about labor market issues.

The next section of the chapter uses the concept of elasticity to consider the effects of **minimum wage** legislation. The basic model of labor demand under competitive labor market conditions predicts that the minimum wage will produce both winners and losers. The winners are those who retain their jobs at the higher wage. The losers include those covered by the law who lose their jobs, and those not covered by the law who experience lower wages because of the rightward supply shift that accompanies the migration of these unemployed workers to the uncovered sector. The key issue is the degree of the employment loss among low-wage workers and the resulting impact on poverty levels, and ultimately this is a question of labor demand elasticity. Factors that can complicate the empirical estimation of the employment effects of the minimum wage are reviewed and an overview of recent empirical results is presented. Empirical findings have been sensitive to the design of the study, and overall it is difficult to reach a definite conclusion as to the effects of the minimum wage on employment, although certainly there are many reasons to doubt its effectiveness as a tool to fight poverty.

The chapter also applies the labor demand framework to the issue of how **technological change** affects employment. Technological change can affect the demand for labor in two ways. Technological change involving the introduction of new or improved products causes demand shifts in the product markets—an outward shift for the newly created product, an inward shift for the product that is superseded—which in turn translates into shifts in labor demand. Labor demand will increase in the sectors producing the new product, and decrease in the sectors producing the outdated product. New and improved products also tend to increase competition in the product markets as consumers have more substitution possibilities. Increased competition means each firm faces a more elastic product demand. A more elastic product demand, according to the Hicks-Marshall laws, results in a more elastic labor demand curve for the firm. An elastic labor demand greatly diminishes the ability of unions to bargain for wage increases since employment losses are greater for a given wage increase when labor demand is elastic.

Technological change can also affect employment by reducing the price of capital directly, or making available a new type of capital that can serve as a substitute for labor. The latter occurrence can be treated as a reduction in the price of capital since when something is unavailable it essentially has an infinite price. When the capital does become available through technological change, it is as if its price has fallen to a point where at least some firms can afford to buy it. Direct or indirect price changes like these induce the firm to substitute capital for labor, but also create a scale effect that causes the firm to use more capital and more labor. By examining the factors listed in the Hicks-Marshall laws, the likely size of the substitution and scale effects can be determined, thereby providing a solid foundation for assessing the likely employment effects of the technological change on particular industries. Even when employment falls in a particular industry, however, it is important to keep in mind that these labor resources are now free to flow to those industries that will be expanding because of the technological change.

However, while it is fairly simple to demonstrate that technological change involves a net benefit to society (since more goods and services can be obtained from limited resources), it is more difficult to prove whether technological change results in benefits to society as a whole. The answer to this question depends largely on how the gains (and losses) from change are distributed, and whether any losers are compensated. This in turn suggests that for society as a whole to gain from these changes requires attention to minimizing the costs to the losers, perhaps through unemployment insurance, job banks, and retraining programs that facilitate the move from declining to expanding sectors.

■ Review Questions

Choose the letter that represents the **BEST** response.

The Own-Wage Elasticity of Labor Demand

1. If the wage paid to automobile workers goes up by 3.5% and the quantity of workers demanded goes down by 5.25%, the own-wage elasticity of demand for these workers is
   a. −0.67.
   b. −1.5.
   c. −1.75.
   d. −5.25.

2. If the wage paid to automobile workers goes up by 3.5% and the own-wage elasticity of demand for automobile workers is −0.5, the percentage change in the quantity of workers demanded must be
   a. −1.5%.
   b. −1.75%.
   c. −3%.
   d. −7%.

   In answering Questions **3–4**, please refer to Figure 4-3.

3. The own-wage elasticity of labor demand associated with a wage increase from $7 to $8 would be
   a. −0.5.
   b. −0.71.
   c. −1.4.
   d. −2.

4. The firm's total expenditures on labor (the total income received by labor) equals the wage multiplied by the number of workers employed. What is the change in the firm's total expenditures on labor as *W* rises from $7 to $8?
   a. +$5
   b. −$15
   c. +$15
   d. −$22.5

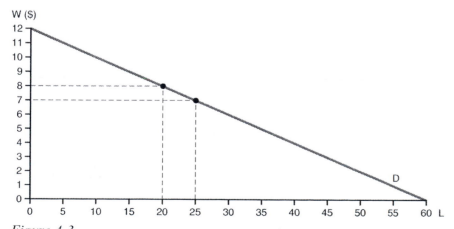

Figure 4-3

Hicks-Marshall Laws of Derived Demand

5. A firm's demand curve for labor is thought to be more elastic in the long run than in the short run because
   a. the firm can not substitute capital for labor in the short run.
   b. consumers may not be able to easily find substitutes for the firm's product in the short run.
   c. the producers of capital equipment might face skilled-labor and capacity constraints in the short run.
   d. all of the above.

6. The own-wage elasticity of demand is thought to be higher at the firm level than at the industry level because
   a. labor's share of total cost will be higher at the industry level than at the firm level.
   b. the supply of capital is more inelastic at the industry level.
   c. all the firms acting together have monopoly power.
   d. the demand curve facing an individual firm under competition is highly elastic.

7. A union bargaining for wage increases will be in a stronger position if the demand for labor is inelastic, since increases in the wage will not bring about significant reductions in employment and the total income received by members will rise. According to the Hicks-Marshall laws, which factor will be a contributor to union success?
   a. Elastic product demand.
   b. The production process is very labor intensive.
   c. Supply of capital is very elastic.
   d. Labor and capital are used in fixed proportions.

The Cross-Wage Elasticity of Demand

8. If the wage of teenagers falls 5% and the employment of adults rises by 1%, the cross-wage elasticity between adults and teenagers is
   a. −0.2.
   b. +0.2.
   c. −4.
   d. −5.

9. If the cross-wage elasticity between adult and teenage labor is negative,
   a. adults and teens are gross complements.
   b. adults and teens are gross substitutes.
   c. the substitution effect associated with a rise in the price of teenage labor will dominate the scale effect.
   d. both **b** and **c**.

10. As the price of teenage labor rises, adults and teens are more likely to be gross complements if
    a. it is easy to substitute adults for teens.
    b. the supply of adult labor is elastic.
    c. teen labor accounts for a large share of total costs.
    d. the demand for the product workers are producing is inelastic.

Employment Effects of the Minimum Wage

11. In a competitive labor market where everyone is covered by the minimum wage, if employment increases when the minimum wage increases, one can conclude
    a. all other factors affecting employment were not held constant.
    b. employment would have been even higher in the absence of the minimum wage increase.
    c. labor and capital are gross complements.
    d. both **a** and **b**.

12. The possibility that an increase in the minimum wage could create an intersectoral shift in product demand implies that the employment effects of the minimum wage are best measured
    a. by looking at the employment changes of individual firms.
    b. by looking at the employment changes of large groupings of firms from many different industries.
    c. by looking at only those firms that comply with the minimum wage law.
    d. by using the monopsony model of the labor market.

Employment Effects of Technological Change

13. Technological change that results in the introduction of new and improved products typically results in
    a. labor demand becoming more elastic.
    b. job losses for those producing outdated products.
    c. increases in employment in those sectors producing the new products.
    d. all of the above.

14. Technological change that results in a reduction in the price of capital (or equivalently, the availability of a new type of capital) is more likely to stimulate demand for a particular type of labor if
    a. capital costs accounts for a small share of total costs.
    b. the demand for the final product is elastic.
    c. the supply of labor is inelastic.
    d. all of the above.

15. Technological progress of all kinds tends to lead over time to
    a. declining real wages.
    b. persistent unemployment.
    c. scale effects that enlarge and change the mix of output and employment.
    d. all of the above.

■ PROBLEMS

The Own-Wage Elasticity of Labor Demand

16. Suppose labor demand is given by the equation

$$L = 50 - 2W,$$

where L is the number of workers and W is the wage rate.

16a. The slope of the demand curve can be viewed as the amount by which L changes for every 1 unit change in W. This can be expressed formally as

$$\text{Slope} = \frac{\Delta L}{\Delta W},$$

where Δ refers to a small change in the value of L or W. Using this definition, find the slope associated with a wage change from $5 to $6. Would your answer be different if the wage rose from $20 to $21?

16b. Calculate the own-wage elasticity of labor demand as the wage changes from $5 to $6. How would your answer be different if the wage rose from $20 to $21?

16c. How does the slope change as one moves up this labor demand curve? How does the elasticity change as one moves up this labor demand curve? Graph this labor demand curve.

16d. The firm's total expenditures on labor (the total income received by labor) equals the wage multiplied by the number of workers employed. Calculate the change in the firm's total expenditures on labor when the wage changes from $5 to $6. Do the same for a change from $20 to $21.

16e. Considering your answer to **16b** and **16d**, what relationship can you find between the own-wage elasticity of labor demand and the change in a firm's total expenditures on labor (the total income received by labor)?

16f. Suppose each worker at this firm always works 40 hours a week. If L were expressed in terms of labor hours instead of the number of workers, the labor demand curve would be represented by the equation

$$L = 2000 - 80W.$$

Find the slope of the curve and the elasticity as the wage rises from $5 to $6. Does the change in the units in which L is measured make any difference to your answers (when compared to the answers in **16a** and **16b**)?

16g. Why do you think the economists prefer the elasticity when compared to the slope as a measure of labor's responsiveness to wage changes?

*17. Consider the labor demand curve given by the equation

$$L = \frac{100}{W}.$$

For small changes in the wage around any given point on the curve, the slope of the curve (the change in L divided by the change in W) is given by the formula

$$\text{Slope} = -\frac{100}{W^2}.$$

(For the reader with calculus training, the slope can be computed by taking the first derivative of L with respect to W.)

*17a. Find the slope of the curve for a small change in the wage around $W = \$5$. Do the same for a small change in the wage around \$10. How does the slope change as one moves up this demand curve?

*17b. Find the own-wage elasticity of labor demand for a small change in the wage around \$5. Do the same for a small change in the wage around \$10. How does the elasticity change as one moves up this labor demand curve?

*17c. Graph this labor demand curve.

Hicks-Marshall Laws of Derived Demand

18. Consider two possible demand curves for a firm with monopoly power in the output market

$$\text{Demand 1: } P = 36 - Q.$$

$$\text{Demand 2: } P = 56 - 2Q.$$

Recall that the marginal revenue (MR) for a firm with a demand curve $P = a - bQ$ is given by the equation $MR = a - 2bQ$. Also, recall that a firm's optimal output occurs where marginal revenue equals marginal cost.

18a. The price elasticity of demand is given by the equation

$$\eta_{QP} = \frac{\%\Delta Q}{\%\Delta P} = \frac{\dfrac{\Delta Q}{Q}}{\dfrac{\Delta P}{P}} = \frac{\Delta Q}{\Delta P}\frac{P}{Q}.$$

At any given price (e.g., $P = \$20$), which of the market demand curves would be the more elastic?

18b. For each demand curve, how would the optimal output of the firm change if marginal costs increased from \$16 to \$24 because of a change in the price of labor?

18c. Would the scale effect associated with a wage change be larger if demand 1 or demand 2 applied? Would the long-run demand be more elastic if demand 1 or demand 2 applied?

Cross-Wage Elasticity of Demand

19. An empirical study by Daniel Hamermesh (*Economic Inquiry*, July 1982, pp. 365–380) found that for every 100 teenagers who might be employed as a result of a youth subminimum wage, between 11 and 33 adult workers would be displaced.

19a. According to this finding, are teenagers and adults gross complements or gross substitutes? Would the cross-wage elasticity between teenagers and adults have a positive or negative sign?

19b. Would the substitution effect associated with a decrease in the teen wage dominate the scale effect or would the scale effect dominate the substitution effect?

19c. How would the demand curve for adult workers change if the wage paid to teenagers falls?

■ Applications

The Own-Wage Elasticity of Labor Demand and Minimum Wage Increases

20. The empirical evidence summarized in the text suggests that the overall elasticity of demand for labor in the long run is close to unitary in magnitude. For particular categories of labor, however, the results can be different. Demand for unskilled workers tends to be more elastic than demand for educated or highly skilled workers. Consequently, the magnitude of the own-wage elasticity of demand for teenage workers, for example, may be significantly greater than one in the long run. If the demand for unskilled labor is elastic at the current value of the minimum wage, will raising the minimum wage, holding all else constant, increase or decrease the total income flowing to those workers receiving the minimum wage? Explain your reasoning.

Union Bargaining Strength and the Hicks-Marshall Laws

21. A union's ability to bargain for higher wages is thought to be constrained by the degree to which such wage increases cause significant reductions in employment for its members. When wage increases cause large reductions in union employment, unions are thought to have little power when bargaining over wages.

21a. Before the airline industry was deregulated (i.e., before competition increased), the union representing pilots flying for commercial airlines was generally regarded as one of the most successful unions in raising the wages of its members. On the other hand, the union representing garment workers had only very limited success in raising the wages of its members. Using the Hicks-Marshall laws of derived demand, rationalize why these unions might have had such different experiences.

21b. Trace through the effect increased airline competition should have had on the bargaining strength of the pilots' union. Similarly, trace through the effect that increased emphasis on free trade (i.e., the elimination of tariffs and quotas) would have on the power of the garment workers' union.

Health Care Reform and the Hicks-Marshall Laws

22. One approach to health care reform is the so called "play or pay" approach. Under this approach, employers are required to either provide health insurance to their employees or contribute to a fund which the government would use to provide insurance for all those lacking coverage. Consider three competing proposals for how these contributions could be determined.

    Plan A: Contributions would be required for every hour an employee works (e.g., 10 cents per hour).

    Plan B: Contributions would be some percentage of the value of the firm's buildings, land, and machinery (e.g., 2% of the total property value).

    Plan C: Contributions would be required for every unit of output a firm produces (e.g., 50 cents per unit of output).

22a. While all the plans have the potential to reduce employment opportunities, which plan would probably have the least impact on employment? Explain your reasoning.

22b. For each plan, list the conditions that would lead to the largest reduction in employment.

Employment Effects of the Minimum Wage

23. Suppose market demand is given by the equation

$$W = 25 - 0.5L.$$

The current wage is $4. An above equilibrium minimum wage of $6 is imposed at the same time labor demand shifts out to

$$W = 25 - (1/3)L.$$

23a. What was the original employment level? What is the new employment level?

23b. Has the minimum wage reduced employment opportunities? If so, by how much?

Technological Change and Job Losses

24. In an article in *Forbes*, June 29, 1987 (pp. 68–70), economist Richard B. McKenzie criticized the obsession many policymakers have with preserving jobs. McKenzie asks:

"[I]s job creation, apart from any corresponding increase in output, the proper measure of economic success? If so, then forget all those costly and complex programs to make America competitive. I have a simple one-line statute that will create 60 million jobs overnight: Outlaw farm machinery."

24a. What is a better measure of economic success than the number of jobs created?

24b. How can one argue that technological advances (like the invention of new and better farm equipment) improves the well-being of society when it clearly results in lost jobs?

24c. Do you see any similarities between laws designed to make plant closings more difficult and McKenzie's tongue-in-cheek suggestion to ban farm machinery?

Chapter 5
Frictions in the Labor Market

■ Summary

In previous chapters, it has been assumed that firms were always wage takers; in other words, a firm would have to hire at the market wage or all employees would leave. Similarly, all labor costs have been considered to be variable, directly proportionate to the amount of time that an employee works. Thus we are implicitly assuming that it is easy for workers to change firms and easy for firms to hire and fire workers. However, there are usually frictions in the labor market, which implies that it is costly for one or both groups to make such changes.

The chapter first considers costs to workers of changing jobs, and thus how hiring decisions are different when there are mobility costs. If mobility is costless, then workers who have identical skills and who are performing the same job must receive equal wages. However, real-world data does not generally support this prediction; there are significant differences in wages for similar jobs in different geographic markets and for jobs requiring similar skills within the same geographic markets. This implies that there must be a cost to mobility, or low-wage workers would simply move to higher paying jobs. Some mobility costs are monetary (printing résumés and moving, for example), but there are also nonmonetary costs such as time, stress, and possible nonwage benefits of the current job. These nonmonetary costs are likely to vary significantly between workers.

If there are positive mobility costs, then the supply of labor to the firm is now upward-sloping rather than horizontal. As the firm raises wages, it will attract some workers from other firms (presumably those with relatively lower mobility costs), and likewise, if the firm lowers wages, it will lose some but not all workers. Mobility costs also influence the elasticity of labor supply; relatively low mobility costs imply a more elastic supply of labor. Upward-sloping labor supply curves facing *individual firms* are called monopsonistic conditions.

A labor-market **monopsonist** has traditionally been defined as the sole employer of labor in a given market, and thus the firm faces the *market* supply of labor. However, while cases of pure monopsony power in labor markets are considered very rare at best, degrees of monopsony power exist in a wide variety of labor markets. To determine optimal employment levels in the case of a firm having monopsony power, the given information must include specification of the labor supply curve. For a monopsonist, labor supply is upward sloping (because it is the sole employer of labor or because there are mobility costs). Thus the marginal expense of hiring one more worker is not constant, because to attract one more worker, the firm must raise the wage. Raising the wage for one worker is assumed to require raising the wages of all workers, and thus the marginal expense for the last worker is greater than the wage rate. (Assuming that the labor supply curve is linear, it could be written in the form $W = a + bL$, where a and b are typically assumed to be positive constants. Assuming that the firm is free to set any wage and that it pays the same wage to all its workers, the marginal expense of labor is given by the expression $ME_L = a + 2bL$. This expression is then set equal to the marginal revenue product expression to find the optimal employment level of the firm. The wage the workers receive is found by taking the optimal employment level and substituting back into the market supply equation.) Thus the monopsonist will hire fewer workers than an equivalent competitive firm and will use its market power to pay them lower wages.

Within the same labor market, firms may have different marginal revenue product curves (due to differences in plant and equipment and other factors influencing productivity) and different labor supply curves (due to differences in the nonwage benefits of different employers and other mobility cost factors that may vary between firms), and thus workers with similar skills performing similar jobs may well earn very different wages.

Shifts in the supply of labor change the marginal expense of labor and thus change the monopsonist's desired level of employment and wage. For example, a decrease in the supply of labor increases the marginal expense of labor and thus reduces desired employment and increases the wage. In the long run, this may also lead the firm to substitute capital for labor, and employment will decrease further.

Sometimes a monopsonist is bound by a government-enforced minimum wage law or has negotiated a union scale wage, above the market equilibrium in either case. In these situations, the stipulated wage functions as a portion of the firm's ME_L curve and again the ME_L is equated to the MRP_L. Depending on the exact level at which the minimum or union wage is set, it is possible for the firm's optimal employment level to increase relative to the level that is optimal when there is no market interference. Why? Mandated wages increase the average cost of hiring, at least initially, but they can reduce the marginal cost, since hiring one more worker no longer implies raising the wages of all workers. With a lower marginal expense of labor, the firm is likely to wish to hire more workers. In such cases, minimum wages can increase *both* the wage and the level of employment (in contrast to the competitive model discussed in Chapter 4).

Since there are positive mobility costs, workers must decide whether it is worth incurring the costs of a job search or whether it is better to stay with the existing job. While there are many reasons (some of which are discussed later in the text) why wages differ, one reason may simply be luck. Some workers may initially be hired by high-wage firms and stay there, while those who are initially matched with a low-wage employer may wish to search more. More searching may result in a better match but also involves costs; depending on the level of costs and the expected increase in the wage, it may not be worth searching for a better match.

Costs of job search provide one explanation for why we observe that wages tend to increase with overall labor-market experience and with time on the job. One reason why job search is costly is because it takes time and effort, and job openings may appear randomly. Thus workers who have been in the labor market longer will have had more chances to acquire better offers and improve their matches (and thus earn higher wages). Likewise, workers who have chosen to stay with an employer are probably those who found a good match to begin with, and thus are observed to have higher wages. High search costs may also be correlated with longer unemployment spells and higher unemployment rates, as workers are more likely to turn down an offer if it is more costly to search again once employed.

We now turn to issues relating to labor demand. The major friction on the demand side of the labor market is the existence of **quasi-fixed labor costs**, costs that vary with the number of workers hired, but not with the number of hours existing employees work. For example, when an additional worker is hired to regularly work forty hours per week, the firm will almost certainly incur hiring and training costs, contribute to the provision of employee benefits (e.g., medical insurance), and be required by the government to make payments on the worker's behalf (e.g., contributions to the unemployment insurance fund). These quasi-fixed costs fall into two categories: *investments* in the workforce (such as hiring costs and training), and *employee benefits*.

Hiring costs involve such factors as advertising positions and screening applicants, as well as the record-keeping costs of having another employee. Training costs are of three types: the explicit cost of materials and trainers used in the training process; the implicit cost of using existing employees and capital equipment to train the new employee; and the implicit (opportunity) cost of the new employee's time. Finally, there may be a cost of terminating the worker, if necessary. Hiring and training costs are considered to be investments because the costs occur in the present and have benefits in the future and, like most investments, are inherently risky.

Employee benefits include both legally mandated expenses, such as contributions to unemployment insurance Social Security programs, and privately-provided benefits such as medical insurance and vacation pay. These costs all vary with number of workers rather than number of hours and thus are categorized as quasi-fixed costs. Treating the average workweek of existing workers (H), and the number of workers (M), as two distinct inputs, the cost-minimization rules developed in Chapter 3 require that

$$\frac{ME_M}{MP_M} = \frac{ME_H}{MP_H},$$

where ME refers to the marginal expense of an additional unit of the input M or H, and MP refers to the marginal product of an additional unit of the input M or H. The ratio of ME to MP gives the marginal cost of producing an additional unit of output using either more workers or longer hours. The growth of quasi-fixed costs increases ME_M, destroying the equality and raising the marginal cost of producing output using workers. This creates a window of opportunity for the firm to produce the same output in a less costly manner by substituting longer hours for some of its existing workers.

Some have proposed increasing ME_H by increasing the overtime pay premium, with a goal of expanding employment by making additional hours per worker more costly and hence less attractive to employers. Such an increase in ME_H, however, may not translate into significant employment gains for a number of reasons. The optimal output of the firm is likely to be reduced because of higher costs (a scale effect). Also, the firm may shift to more capital-intensive production processes (a substitution effect). In addition, the unemployed available for hire may not be good substitutes for those currently working overtime, and the straight-time wage rate may be adjusted downward so as to keep total compensation the same.

The cost-minimization framework can also be adapted to look at the effect quasi-fixed costs, such as those associated with the mandated provision of health insurance, have on the choice between different categories of labor. For example, the choice between full-time and part-time workers, or skilled and unskilled workers can be affected by the growth of quasi-fixed costs in the same manner the employment/hours choice is affected.

Training costs create a different type of friction because they are often paid in part by the workers themselves. For training to be desirable, it must be true that the training increases the marginal productivity of the employee by more than it increases the wage (so that the employer receives some return on the training investment), and secondly, the worker must stay with the firm for long enough for the employer to receive this return.

In the case where the training expenditures are **general** (i.e., they make the employees more productive in the eyes of all employers), all training expenses must be recovered during the current or training period. This means that, in equilibrium, the wage must equal marginal productivity less the training cost, meaning the employee is "paying" for the training. In all future periods, we should expect the worker to be paid the value of his productivity. If it were not so, workers, now more productive due to the training received in the first period, could be bid away by competing firms. Firms will only pay for general training if mobility costs are so high that trained workers will not seek a different job (and thus the firm can recoup its training cost).

However, in the case where the training expenditures are **specific** (i.e., they make the employees more productive *only* in the eyes of the current employer), employers will pay for at least some of the training costs with a training wage that exceeds marginal productivity less the training cost. It is expected the firm will recover this training investment gradually over time by setting the wage in future periods to be less than the corresponding marginal product, provided the present value of the entire compensation package remains at least competitive with what employees can attain elsewhere. The firm is willing to incur some of the initial training cost because it can recoup these costs by underpaying the worker (relative to productivity) in later periods; the worker is willing to stay even though paid less than the value of marginal productivity in the future because with specific training, the value of the worker's skills is higher at this firm than it would be to other firms. In other words, where training is specific, the worker is overpaid relative to productivity during training and underpaid relative to productivity in later periods. Both workers and employers have invested in training, and thus both have an incentive to make the employment relationship work and share in the rewards. The share of the training cost borne by the employer will reflect the size of mobility costs as well; if mobility costs are high, then the firm will be willing to pay more of the training cost as it will not need to increase the post-training wage much in order to retain workers.

The gap that exists in equilibrium between the MP and the post-training wage gives the worker some protection from temporary layoffs caused by declining demand. It will not be in the firm's interest to lay off workers as long as it is still recovering some of its training investment. The gap between MP^* and the post-training wage suggests that the firm will not have to worry about the worker quitting since the wage it is paying is higher than what the worker could earn elsewhere. Thus the existence of quasi-fixed costs like hiring and training costs can foster a more stable employment relationship. It can also explain why average productivity tends to fall at the beginning of a recession. Firms may "hoard" skilled labor, as they are unwilling to lay off trained employees. This surplus of labor relative to utilized capital causes average productivity to appear to fall during a recession, but it also means that firms can easily expand output without incurring new hiring and training costs when the economy picks up.

An alternative strategy for responding to quasi-fixed hiring costs may be to attempt to reduce them as much as possible. One method some firms use is to rely on credentials or screening devices instead of closely investigating each individual applicant. This can lead to **statistical discrimination** in the hiring process. For example, a firm may prefer hiring men, not out of prejudice against women, but because data suggested that on average, men had longer expected job tenures, which in turn would make the recovery of hiring and training costs more likely. In situations where upper-level positions require extensive firm specific knowledge, firms may rely on an **internal labor market** policy of filling most positions from the ranks of current employees, thus learning about future applicants gradually over time and eliminating the need for extensive screening.

■ Review Questions

Choose the letter that represents the **BEST** response.

Definitions

1. The best definition of quasi-fixed costs is
    a. nonwage labor costs.
    b. hiring and training costs.
    c. costs that vary with the number of workers employed.
    d. costs that vary with the number of workers employed, but not with the number of hours worked by existing employees.

2. Which of the following is not a quasi-fixed cost?
   a. The hourly wage the firm pays.
   b. Costs associated with a defined benefit pension.
   c. Costs associated with a defined contribution pension.
   d. Employer contributions to Social Security.

*3. Consider a law that would require employers to provide the same package of nonwage benefits that is offered to full-time employees to part-time employees on a prorated basis. (For employees working 25% of the normal workweek, employers would pay for 25% of the benefit package offered to full-time employees, and so on.) Assuming most part-time workers do not currently receive any benefits, such a law would
   a. increase quasi-fixed costs.
   b. increase labor costs that vary with hours worked.
   c. have no effect on quasi-fixed costs.
   d. both **b** and **c**.

4. Suppose that during the training period, a firm spends in real terms 3,000 per trainee on labor and materials for its training program. Trainees in the program each produce 2,000 in output during the period, but could produce 3,500 if not occupied with training activities. What is the total cost of training per worker to the firm?
   a. 1,000.
   b. 1,500.
   c. 4,500.
   d. 6,500.

Use the following information in answering Questions **5–8**.

Suppose the firm has 500 employees each working a standard workweek of 40 hours. The typical worker earns a real wage of 10 per hour and receives another 200 in weekly benefits and training, 150 of which are quasi-fixed costs to the firm.

5. The marginal expense an employer faces when increasing its average workweek by an hour (ME_H) is approximately the sum of wage and variable benefit costs (on a per-hour basis) multiplied by he number of employees. Assuming no overtime wage premium, an approximate value for ME_H would be
   a. 11.25.
   b. 60.
   c. 5,625.
   d. 30,000.

6. Recomputing ME_H assuming an overtime wage premium of 50%, an approximate value would be
   a. 16.875.
   b. 8,125.
   c. 8,437.5.
   d. 11,250.

7. The marginal cost an employer faces when employing an additional worker (ME_M) for a typical workweek is approximately total weekly wages plus the employee benefits that are variable costs plus the quasi-fixed costs. An approximate value for ME_M would be
   a. 15.
   b. 550.
   c. 600.
   d. 7,500.

The Employment/Hours Trade-Off

8. Suppose the marginal product of an additional worker is 50 and the marginal product associated with expanding the workweek by 1 hour is 625. Using the ME_H and ME_M values computed in Questions **6** and **7**, employ the rule for cost minimization to find the firm's optimal adjustment of its employment/hours mix.
   a. Increase M and decrease H.
   b. Increase H and decrease M.
   c. Increase both H and M.
   d. M and H should not change.

9. Increasing the overtime pay premium to double time may not result in overtime hours being converted to additional employment because
   a. firms may shift to more capital-intensive production methods.
   b. the optimal output of many firms is likely to be less.
   c. the unemployed may not be substitutes in production for those currently working overtime.
   d. all of the above.

In Questions **10** and **11**, consider again the law that would require employers to provide the same pack age of nonwage benefits offered to full-time employees to part-time employees on a prorated basis. (For employees working 25% of the normal workweek, employers would pay for 25% of the benefit package offered to full time employees, and so on.) Also, assume most part-time workers do not currently receive benefits.

*10. Holding output and capital constant, how would firms adjust the employment/hours mix of part-time workers?
   a. H would increase and M would decrease.
   b. M would increase and H would decrease.
   c. No change in M or H.
   d. Can not be determined without more information on the ME and MP values.

*11. Holding output and capital constant, what effect would there be on the firm's mix of part-time and full-time workers?
   a. Full-time workers would increase and part-time workers would decrease since the marginal cost of part-time workers is now higher.
   b. Full-time workers would decrease and part-time workers would decrease since the marginal cost of part-time workers is now higher.
   c. There would be no change in the mix of part-time and full-time workers since part-time workers are still cheaper than full-time workers.
   d. Part-time employment would actually increase since more people would now want to work part-time.

In Questions **12** and **13**, consider a law that would mandate full health insurance coverage for all employees. Assume that currently most, but not all, full-time employees have health insurance coverage, but that few part-time employees are covered.

12. Holding output and capital constant, how would firms adjust the employment/hours mix of part-time workers?
    a. H would increase and M would decrease.
    b. M would increase and H would decrease.
    c. M and H would both decrease.
    d.   There would be no change in M or H.

13. Holding output and capital constant, what effect would there be on the firm's mix of part-time and full-time workers?
    a.   Full-time workers would increase and part-time workers would decrease since the marginal cost of part-time workers is now higher.
    b.   Full-time workers would decrease and part-time workers would decrease since the marginal cost of part-time workers is now higher.
    c.   There would be no change in the mix of part-time and full-time workers since part-time workers are still cheaper than full-time workers.
    d.   Part-time employment would actually increase since more people would now want to work part-time.

Firms' Hiring and Training Investments

14. A basketball team promises to pay its top draft choice in real terms a 1 million bonus for signing with the team. The player receives 250,000 now and 250,000 each year for the next three years. Assuming an interest rate of 6%, the present value of this payment stream is
    a.   918,253.
    b.   925,251.
    c.   943,396.
    d.   1,093,654.

15. When a firm provides specific training, what happens to the gap between the post-training wage and the marginal product as the market interest rate decreases?
    a.   It increases.
    b.   It decreases.
    c.   It stays the same.
    d.   It persists for a longer period of time.

16. Workers want the firm to pay some of the initial cost of specific training because
    a.   this will create a gap between the marginal product and the post-training wage.
    b.   workers will have some protection from layoffs due to declining demand.
    c.   the present value of the total compensation package will be higher.
    d.   both **a** and **b**.

17. Firms want the workers to pay some of the initial cost of specific training because
    a.   the firm will recover more of its investment in the workers.
    b.   the post-training wage will be farther above the workers' marginal product in other firms.
    c.   workers will be less likely to quit the firm.
    d.   both **b** and **c**.

18. Specifically trained workers will be predisposed to quit the firm when
    a. the post-training wage is less than their marginal product at the firm.
    b. the firm employs statistical discrimination.
    c. the present value of the entire compensation scheme is not equivalent to what can be earned elsewhere.
    d. the firm utilizes an internal labor market strategy.

19. Firms faced with high hiring and training costs may
    a. pay workers substantially less than their marginal product while they are in training.
    b. use statistical discrimination in hiring.
    c. use internal labor markets.
    d. all of the above.

20. If firms rely on old data that suggest women have shorter job tenures than men, firms may
    a. pay women less.
    b. offer fewer training opportunities to women.
    c. employ fewer women.
    d. all of the above.

Mobility Costs and Monopsony

21. In a labor market that is monopsonistic
    a. firms pay a competitive wage.
    b. firms face an upward-sloping supply of labor curve.
    c. are monopolists in output markets.
    d. all of the above.

22. When mobility costs are high
    a. the supply of labor is more elastic.
    b. the supply of labor is less elastic.
    c. the supply of labor is perfectly elastic.
    d. the elasticity of supply of labor can no longer be determined.

*23. Assuming the market supply curve of labor is linear, the marginal expense of labor curve for a monopsonist that pays all workers the same wage will
    a. have a lower vertical intercept and the same slope when compared to the supply curve.
    b. have a lower vertical intercept and a steeper slope when compared to the supply curve.
    c. have a higher vertical intercept and the same slope when compared to the supply curve.
    d. have the same vertical intercept and a steeper slope when compared to the supply curve.

24. In a monopsonistic labor market where everyone is covered by the minimum wage, it is possible for the minimum wage to lead to
    a. higher employment.
    b. lower employment.
    c. no change in employment.
    d. all of the above.

■ Problems

The Definition of Quasi-Fixed Costs

25. Consider a firm where workers are typically employed for 40 hours a week and 50 weeks a year. Workers at this firm earn a real wage of $12.50 per hour. Suppose the firm is liable for a contribution on behalf of each worker to a fund that will help finance a program of national health insurance. This contribution is 5% of the first $50,000 the worker earns. ($50,000 is called the wage base.)

25a. How much would the firm typically have to contribute for each worker? Prove that this contribution is not a quasi-fixed cost.

25b. Holding the typical hours and the wage base constant, at what wage level would this contribution become a quasi-fixed cost? On the other hand, holding typical hours and the wage constant, what wage base would transform this contribution into a quasi-fixed cost?

The Employment/Hours Trade-Off

26. Immigration laws now require employers to determine whether newly hired workers are legally residing in the country.

26a. Assuming for simplicity that output and capital are constant, what effect does this law have on the employment/hours mix used by firms?

26b. How would the analysis be different if output were not constant?

27. Suppose the firm currently employs 500 workers at 40 hours per worker per week and that the following relationship holds.

$$\frac{ME_M}{MP_M} = \frac{800}{400} = 2 > \frac{ME_H}{MP_H} = \frac{9,000}{6,000} = 1.5.$$

Prove that the firm is not at an equilibrium mix of workers and hours by showing there is a window of opportunity for it to reduce its total cost.

Firms' Hiring and Training Investments

28. Consider a multiperiod labor demand scenario where for simplicity the interest rate is assumed to be zero. Assume the firm makes real specific training expenditures of 200 per worker, and the expected length of employment (after training) is 15 months. In equilibrium, the workers' inherent marginal productivity is 225. During training the workers have a marginal product of 200 and are paid a real wage of 150. After training the marginal product is expected to rise to 250. Also, assume an equal wage in the post-training periods.

28a. Find the maximum monthly wage the workers could be offered in the post-training periods if the firm wants to recover fully its training costs by the time the workers are expected to leave. Will the training program be attractive to the workers?

28b. In this scenario, workers and the firm share in the cost of training during the initial period since workers are contributing a marginal product of 200 but are only being paid 150. What would happen to the post-training wage if the firm bore the full cost of training? Why does the firm want the workers to initially bear some of the cost of training?

28c. What would happen to the post-training wage if the worker initially bore the entire cost of training? Why does the worker want the firm initially to bear some of the cost of training?

28d. Suppose the expected length of employment after training is only 10 months. What does this do to the gap between the marginal product and the wage the workers receive?

28e. Assuming a monthly minimum wage of 225, could the firm recover its training costs in only 5 months after training? What is the shortest time over which the firm could recover its training costs?

28f. Given the initial information in the problem, what is the highest the inherent marginal product of the workers could be and still make the recovery of training costs possible?

29. Consider a firm that incurs real expenditures for specific training in the current period equal to 150 per worker. During the training period, the workers have a marginal product of 400 and are paid a real wage of 375. Next year, after the training is over, marginal productivity is expected to rise to 535.

29a. If the firm wanted to recover all its training costs in the initial year after training, what would be the maximum wage it could offer the workers, assuming the interest rate is 6%?

29b. Are workers likely to find this training program attractive?

30. A firm expects to hire workers for three years. The interest rate is constant at 6%. In the current period the firm incurs real training costs of 500 per worker. Suppose the workers' marginal product during training is 1,800 and then rises to 2,500 in the second year and 2,800 in the third.

30a. If the firm pays the workers a real wage of 1,600 during the training year, 2,200 during the second year, and 2,600 during the third year, will the firm recover its training costs on a present value basis?

30b. Do you think such a pay schedule could persist over time?

31. A firm expects to hire workers for three years. The interest rate is constant at 6%. In the current period the firm incurs real general training expenditures of 3 per worker. A typical worker's marginal product during training is 5.50. In the second and third years, the worker's marginal product is expected to increase to 9.

31a. To fully recover its training costs, what real wage will the firm offer to pay the worker in each year?

31b. Why could the firm not pay the worker a post-training wage of 7.5?

31c. Suppose there is a minimum wage of 4 in this economy. How would this change your analysis?

*32. Suppose a firm has a marginal product schedule given by the equation

$$MP_L = 50 - 2L,$$

where L is the number of workers. Suppose the money wage is $40 and the product price is $2.

*32a. Find the optimal employment level assuming no training investment.

*32b. If the price of the product the firm sells falls to $1, find the new employment level.

*32c. Suppose that at the employment level found in **28a**, the firm only paid the workers a money wage of $20 because it was recovering an earlier investment in specific training. Find the new employment level when the product price falls to $1.

■ Applications

Effects of Equal Pay Laws

33. Consider a firm that incurs expenditures for specific training in the current period equal to 3,000 per worker in real terms. During the training period, workers and the firm share the cost of training. The firm pays its workers a real wage of 10,500 and their marginal product is 11,000. Next year, after the training is over, the marginal product is expected to rise to 16,000, and then to 17,000 the year after that. The interest rate is 6%.

33a. Robin, a college senior, applies for the job and promises to stay two years after the training program is complete. Robin has other offers to work at 11,500, but they do not offer any training. If the firm wanted to recover all its training costs by the time Robin leaves, what would be the maximum wage it could offer in the post-training years? Assume an equal wage in the years following training.

33b. Would the firm be likely to attract Robin with this offer?

33c. A short time later, Ann also applies to this firm. She is a comparable applicant in all ways except that she plans to stay only one year after training is complete. What would be the maximum wage the firm could offer Ann in the post-training year if they want to recover their training investment?

33d. Assuming she has had offers similar to those made to Robin, would the firm be likely to attract Ann with its offer?

33e. Suppose the firm is required by law to pay workers who do comparable jobs the same wage. Discuss the likely effects on Ann.

Effects of Minimum Wage Laws

34. In April 1990, a lower minimum wage was instituted for teenagers. It applied to 16- to 19-year-olds for the first six months of their first job.

34a. How would you predict such a youth subminimum wage would affect the likelihood of teens receiving on-the-job training? Would general or specific training opportunities be most affected?

34b. Construct a simple numerical example to illustrate your reasoning.

Effects of Subsidized Training

35. Under the Job Training Partnership Act, the government substantially subsidized employer costs incurred in training certain disadvantaged groups in the population. Refugees from the Vietnam War, for example, were a group targeted by the program, although other groups also qualified.

35a. How would this program affect a firm's employment/hours choice?

35b. How would this program affect the job stability of the targeted groups?

Monopsony

*36. Consider a monopsonist with a production function given by the equation

$$Q = LK.$$

The firm's marginal product is given by the equation

$$MP_L = K.$$

The labor supply curve for this market is given by the equation

$$W = 3L.$$

Suppose the firm has monopoly power in the output market and faces a demand curve for its product given by the equation

$$P = 64 - Q.$$

The level of capital is held constant at 3 units in the short run. The price of capital is $5 per unit.

*36a. Find the equation for the marginal revenue product of labor (MRP_L).

*36b. What simplifying assumption about the firm's production process was made in this problem that is not typically made when examining the firm's short-run demand for labor? Why do you suppose it was made in this problem?

*36c. Find the equation for the marginal expense of labor (ME_L).

36d. Calculate the optimal level of labor for this firm.

36e. Calculate the wage paid to the typical worker and the resulting output, price, and profits for the firm.

36f. Suppose a minimum wage of $30 is mandated in this market. Find the optimal employment level for the monopsonist. Compare your result with the answer to **36d**. Finally, suppose the minimum wage was set at $66. Find the optimal employment level.

Chapter 6
Supply of Labor to the Economy:
The Decision to Work

■ Summary

The number of hours an individual actually works is something jointly determined by employers and employees. Chapter 5 discussed factors affecting the number of hours a firm requires its employees to work. This chapter looks at factors affecting the number of hours employees wish to work. While one may not usually think of hours of work as something individuals control, choices can be made which influence the total number of hours worked, particularly over longer time periods. The decision to participate in the labor market, the decision to seek part-time or full-time work, and the number of jobs a person works are important ways in which individuals affect the supply of labor. The choice of occupation will also affect an individual's total hours, as will vacations, leaves, and absenteeism.

Two notable trends in labor force participation in the U.S. and other developed countries are the increase in the participation of women, particularly married women, and the decrease in the length of working life for men. Other trends include the decrease in the length of the work week and changes in the flexibility of work hours.

Given that individuals have some discretion over the supply of labor, what kinds of factors affect the choices they make? In answering this question the approach that is taken in this chapter is to view the individual's supply of labor hours as the total time available less the individual's **demand for leisure time**. Here, leisure time refers simply to any time not spent working for pay, i.e., it does not necessarily have to be time spent in a relaxing or enjoyable manner. By thinking about labor supply in this way, it is possible to analyze the demand for leisure hours—and inversely, the supply of labor—much like one would analyze the demand for food, clothing, or any other good that households regularly consume.

The standard approach to modeling consumer demand is to assume that an individual chooses between two goods so as to maximize happiness, or utility, subject to a budget constraint. Any particular level of utility can be represented graphically by an **indifference curve**, a curve that represents all different combinations of the two goods that yield equal satisfaction. The maximization process can be represented graphically as an individual trying to attain the highest possible indifference curve subject to a **budget constraint**. The result of this maximization process yields the demand function for each good, where this function relates the desired quantity of the good to the opportunity cost of the good, the level of household wealth, and the particular preferences of the person. In the labor supply model, the two goods are assumed to be leisure and income (which represents the consumption of all other goods at fixed prices). The demand for leisure can eventually be expressed in terms of the wage rate, the amount of nonlabor income the individual receives, and certain parameters representing the individual's willingness to trade off leisure and income.

In constructing the individual's labor supply curve, we ask: what happens to the number of hours the individual wishes to supply when the wage rate changes, holding all else constant? In the case of a wage increase, the opportunity cost of leisure time increases, so the number of leisure hours demanded decreases, increasing hours of labor supplied. This is called the **substitution effect** of a wage increase. However, as the wage rate increases, the individual is also wealthier for any given number of hours of work beyond zero. An increase in wealth allows an individual to consume more of all normal goods, including leisure, decreasing the number of hours of labor supplied. This effect of a wage increase is called the **income effect**.

In general, the substitution effect refers to the individual's response to a change in the opportunity cost of the good, holding all else constant, while the income effect refers to the individual's response to a change in wealth, holding the opportunity cost of the good constant. Since for leisure the substitution and income effects of a wage change typically oppose one another, whether the labor supply schedule is upward or downward sloping depends on the relative magnitude of the two effects. What drives the size of the income and substitution effects? Because normal preferences, with convex indifference curves, exhibit a changing marginal rate of substitution between income and leisure, the number of hours a person already works is important. Generally, the more a person is already working, the more valuable a marginal hour of leisure will be and hence the larger the income effect. The substitution effect grows larger when leisure and work hours are viewed as being highly substitutable. This could happen when the individual's leisure time consists largely of work around the home.

Example 1

Suppose an individual ranks combinations of leisure (L) and income (Y) according to the formula

$$U = L^{\alpha} Y^{\beta}.$$

U denotes the utility level, or happiness ranking (higher levels of U are better), the individual places on the particular combination of leisure and income. The symbols α and β are constants greater than zero and represent the relative importance the individual places on leisure and income. Such a formula is called a **Cobb-Douglas utility function**. Letting W stand for the wage rate, H the number of work hours, T the total time available, and V nonlabor income, the budget constraint an individual faces can be written as

$$Y = WH + V \Rightarrow Y = W(T - L) + V.$$

Maximizing U subject to the budget constraint yields the following expression for the **optimal value of L**

$$L^{*} = \frac{\alpha}{\alpha + \beta} \frac{WT + V}{W}.$$

(For the reader with calculus training, this expression can be derived using the method of Lagrangian Multipliers; or by substituting the budget constraint into the utility function and then maximizing the resulting function.) Note that this expression applies only for the Cobb-Douglas utility function used in this example. If one changes the formula depicting preferences, the expression for the optimal value of L also changes.

Suppose the individual gives equal weight to units of leisure and income and that α and β are both equal to one. Assuming the analysis pertains to one month and that $T = 400$ hours, $W = 4$, and $V = 400$, then the optimal value for L is

$$L^{*} = \frac{1}{1 + 1} \frac{(4)(400) + 400}{4} = 250.$$

This, in turn, implies that the number of hours supplied to the market (H^*) is 150, and the total income of the consumer is $1,000 [(4 × 150) + 400]. This optimal combination of L and Y which yields utility level U_1 is denoted by point a in Figure 6-1. The highest level of utility in this case is achieved where the indifference curve representing utility level U_1 is just tangent to the budget constraint. Note that the constraint starts at $400 when H is zero, reflecting the nonlabor income of the individual. Its highest value of $2,000 (called the individual's full income) is determined by summing the nonlabor income of the individual and his total earnings when working the maximum time of 400 hours at a wage rate of $4. The wage rate is reflected in the slope of the constraint.

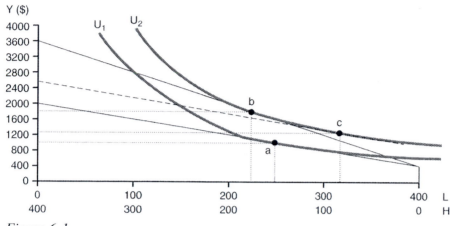

Figure 6-1

What happens if the wage rate rises to $8? The slope of the budget constraint increases in magnitude showing the higher opportunity cost of leisure. The constraint also lies further to the right (except at its starting point) since the higher wage rate will imply a higher income (and wealth) at any given level of work hours. Given the preferences in this example, the individual responds by reducing leisure to 225 and increasing work hours to 175 (point b). The move from point a to b is a result of both the opportunity cost change and the income level change.

How much of the move is due to each factor? Holding the opportunity cost constant, suppose the consumer attained the higher level of utility U_2 through an increase in nonlabor income. In this case, the budget constraint would be the dotted line parallel to the original budget constraint (having the same wage and slope), and the optimal choice would have been point c. The movement from point a to point c is the income effect of the wage increase. Holding the level of utility constant at U_2 and allowing the slope of the constraint to increase, reflecting the rise in the wage, moves the individual from point c to point b. This movement represents the substitution effect of the wage increase. Here the income and substitution effects oppose one another, but because the substitution effect is larger, the net effect of the wage increase is for leisure hours to fall and work hours to increase. The reader should note that this need not be the case, since the location of point b is determined by the preferences of the individual represented by the indifference curves. Point b must be to the left of point c, reflecting the positive substitution effect. But depending on the preferences (and the shape of the corresponding indifference curves), point b could, theoretically, end up left, right, or directly above point a.

Allowing the wage rate to vary over the entire range between $0 and $10 yields the individual labor supply schedule shown in Figure 6-2. Note that for any labor hours to be supplied the wage must be greater than one.

The lowest wage that will induce a person to participate in the labor market is called the **reservation wage**. When there are significant unpaid time obligations (e.g., commuting time) that accompany a job, the reservation wage will be associated with a certain minimum number of work hours.

Also note that for the preferences represented here, the substitution effect always dominates the income effect and so the curve is always upward sloping. (For differing preferences, represented by a differently shaped indifference curve mapping, the results might differ.) The wage and work hour combinations associated with the optimal points depicted in Figure 6-1 are shown again in Figure 6-2 to emphasize the close connection between the two graphs.

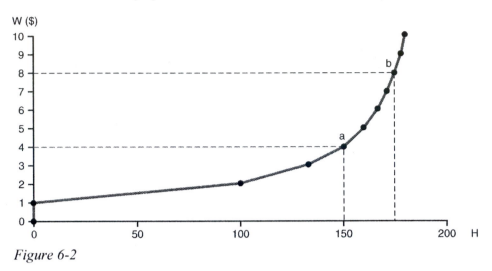

Figure 6-2

The main application of labor supply theory is to the analysis of **income replacement** and **income maintenance** programs like workers' compensation, unemployment insurance, and welfare. By analyzing how these programs change the budget constraints, the work incentive effects of these programs can be analyzed for any given set of preferences.

For example, in some income maintenance programs, the person who does not work at all receives a subsidy S from the government, perhaps as compensation while injured or as payment of unemployment benefits. This causes a "spike" in the budget constraint, because the person receives income even when supplying zero hours of work. This program clearly has serious work disincentives; when the worker goes from zero hours to some positive number of hours, income initially drops. Also, it allows the worker to consume a bundle that contains the same amount of income but more leisure than at least one point on the original budget constraint, and that may well be preferred to other possibilities. Thus these programs stop or slow the return to work by injured or unemployed workers.

Programs such as welfare are needs-based; they pay the recipient the difference between what he earns and some standard. Thus the more income the worker earns, the lower the amount of benefits received. Benefits are scaled back by some fraction for every dollar individuals earn on their own. Letting this fraction, called the **implicit tax rate**, be denoted by t, where $0 \leq t \leq 1$, then the basic budget constraint can be written as

$$Y = S + WH - tWH + V$$
$$\Rightarrow Y = S + (1 - t)\, WH + V$$
$$\Rightarrow Y = (1 - t)\, W(T - L) + S + V.$$

Notice that the effective wage rate (the slope of the budget constraint) becomes $(1 - t)\, W$ and the total level of nonlabor income (the initial height of the budget constraint) is $S + V$. The lower the level of t, the higher the opportunity cost of leisure, and in most instances, the stronger the incentive to work. However, the lower the level of t, the longer people remain eligible for the program, thus increasing the number of people receiving payments and thereby increasing the cost of the program. This tradeoff between work incentives and program costs is a fundamental tension running through all income replacement and income maintenance programs.

The point on the budget constraint separating those who receive benefits from those who do not is called the **breakeven point**. Given the type of program structure mentioned above, the level of income associated with the breakeven point could be computed by finding earnings such that

$$S - tWH = 0 \Rightarrow WH = \frac{S}{t}.$$

The actual level of income at the breakeven point, of course, would be $(S/t) + V$.

Example 2

Consider an individual with preferences given by the formula

$$U = L^{3/4} Y^{1/4}.$$

Assume the going wage rate is $4 per hour and that the maximum time available per month is 400 hours. Also assume initially that the person has no nonlabor income. Now suppose a welfare program provides low income individual's with a benefit of $200 if they do not work at all. As the person earns income, however, benefits are scaled back 20 cents for every dollar earned. What would be the breakeven point of the program and what effect would such a program have on the work incentives of this individual?

The breakeven level of income would occur when the person earned enough to have the initial $200 subsidy "taken away," that is, the total subsidy received should be zero. Algebraically, this occurs when

$$200 - 0.2(WH) = 0 \Rightarrow WH = \$1,000.$$

This would occur when the person worked 250 hours and leisure was 150 hours.

Substituting the appropriate values into the expression for the optimal level of L yields a choice of $L^{*} = 300$ before the welfare program. This implies 100 work hours and a total income of $400. After the adoption of the welfare program, however, the person's nonlabor income effectively becomes $S + V = \$200$, and the effective wage rate becomes $(1 - t)W = \$3.20$. Substituting these values into the demand function for L yields $L^{*} = 346.875$ which implies work hours of 53.125. This yields total earnings of $212.50, plus a subsidy of $157.50, for a total income of $370.

An indifference curve/budget constraint graph showing these results is plotted in Figure 6-3. The budget constraint before the welfare program is denoted by the line *ab*. After the welfare program is established the constraint becomes the line *acdb*. Note that the breakeven point of the program occurs at point *d*. The individual's optimal combination of L and Y before the program was at point *e*, leading to a utility level at U_1. After the program is enacted, the individual's optimum is at point *f* and involves more leisure and less work (and just slightly less total income). The large gain in leisure at the cost of little income leads to the higher level of utility U_2. This tendency to consume more leisure makes sense since the program creates income and substitution effects that in this case both work in the same direction to reduce work hours. Notice how the program shifts the constraint out, thus making individuals eligible for the program richer. When people are richer they typically consume more of all goods, including leisure. Notice also that the constraint is flatter, representing a lower effective wage rate, and hence a lower opportunity cost to leisure time. When the opportunity cost of a good is lower, people typically respond by substituting more of that good for the other, in this case, more leisure for less income.

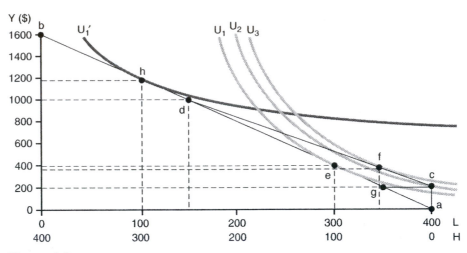

Figure 6-3

While this program does reduce work incentives, it is also important to note that it does not eliminate them. This would occur, however, if the program were set up with an implicit tax rate of $t = 1$. The constraint then would be *acgb* and the person would maximize utility at point *c* by dropping out of the labor force entirely. As the effective wage rate goes to zero, notice the L^* expression gets extremely large, but since L has a maximum of 400, that is where the optimum occurs. This is an example where the optimum does not occur at a tangency between the indifference curve and the budget constraint. Graphically, while a tangency has not been attained, the person still has reached the highest possible indifference curve consistent with the budget constraint. Notice that by dropping out of the labor force the individual would actually increase utility from U_1 to U_2. In general, when analyzing the work incentive effects of income maintenance programs, be sure to watch for the tendency of individuals to cluster around sharp **corners** on the constraint like point *c*. Also, note that such corner points do not necessarily occur at the end of the constraint, and sometimes the corners lack the accompanying horizontal segment between points *c* and *g*. When there is no such horizontal segment (i.e., the program pays out a subsidy only at one specific leisure value) the point is characterized in the text as a budget constraint **spike**.

While for many individuals the program in this example will reduce work incentives, it does not follow that all individuals will respond in this way. For example, if someone inherently placed more value on units of income such that his preferences could be depicted by the equation

$$U = L^{1/4}Y^{3/4},$$

then the original optimum would occur at $L = 100$ and $Y = \$1,200$ (point *h*), and the program would have no effect on his behavior. The program does not enable the individual to attain a higher level of utility than the original U_1'. (Note how the shape of the U_1' reflects the new preferences relative to the original set of indifference curves—its flatness shows the stronger emphasis on income over leisure.) This is not to say that a person above the breakeven point could never be affected by an income maintenance program, however. If the initial optimum is close enough to the breakeven point, the individual can be pulled into the program. This possibility, and many others, will be explored in the problems and applications that follow.

Another possibility is to create work incentives. An illustration of this type of program is the Earned Income Tax Credit (EITC). Under this program, a tax credit of $1 reduces the workers tax liability by $1, and for workers with sufficiently low incomes, this can result in an actual increase in earnings (if the tax credit exceeds the tax liability, the government pays the worker the difference). The actual amount of the tax credit depends on both earnings and number of dependent children and are phased out as income rises. Thus there are a variety of effects, depending on the worker's original income. For workers who work few or zero hours, the tax credit is the greatest, making the after-tax wage greater than the market wage. Thus while there are both income and substitution effects, it is likely that income effects will dominate and thus that some workers will enter the labor force or work more hours. For the middle income range, the net wage is equal to the market wage, so there is an income effect but not a substitution effect. Thus workers may actually work less. In the upper income range, the net wage is less than the market wage, as the credit is phased out. Thus the implicit reduction in the wage will create income and substitution effects, both of which will cause workers to supply less labor (because the opportunity cost of leisure has fallen while income has increased), and thus it is likely that workers at that income range will choose to work less.

■ Review Questions

Choose the letter that represents the **<u>BEST</u>** response.

The Labor/Leisure Choice: The Fundamentals

1. Although firms have an important say in how many hours an employee works, workers can adjust their hours through
   a. choice of occupation.
   b. choice of full-time or part-time work.
   c. absenteeism.
   d. all of the above.

2. Indifference curves representing preferences for leisure and income should be drawn in such a way that they do not cross. If they do, it can be inferred that
   a. the steeper curve represents an individual who places a low value on an extra hour of leisure.
   b. the individual is inconsistent in his ranking of different income and leisure combinations.
   c. the indifference curves that cross pertain to different individuals.
   d. either **b** or **c**.

In answering Questions **3** and **4**, please refer to Figure 6-4. The budget constraint is represented by line *abc*.

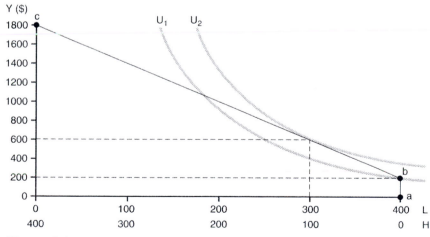

Figure 6-4

3. Which of the following is true in Figure 6-4?
   a. The wage rate is $4.
   b. Nonlabor income is $400.
   c. The optimal number of hours to supply is zero.
   d. All of the above.

4. The convex shape of the indifference curves in Figure 6-4 means that
   a.   when leisure is low and income is high, additional units of leisure are very valuable.
   b.   when leisure is high and income low, additional units of leisure are not very valuable.
   c.   people generally prefer having some leisure and some income to having much income and little leisure, or much leisure and little income.
   d.   all of the above.

5. The optimal level of leisure occurs where
   a.   the level of leisure is maximized subject to the budget constraint.
   b.   the level of income is maximized subject to the budget constraint.
   c.   the highest attainable indifference curve is tangent to the budget constraint.
   d.   both **a** and **b**.

6. An individual with standard downward-sloping indifference curves will participate in the labor market provided
   a.   the indifference curves between leisure and income are steep.
   b.   a tangency between the budget constraint and the indifference curve is reached.
   c.   at the point where leisure is at its maximum, the indifference curve is steeper than the budget constraint.
   d.   at the point where leisure is at its maximum, the indifference curve is flatter than the budget constraint.

In answering Questions **7** and **8**, please refer to Figure 6-5. The budget constraint is given by line *abcd.*

7. The shape of the indifference curves in Figure 6-5 means that
   a.   after a certain number of leisure hours is reached, additional leisure hours become very valuable.
   b.   after a certain number of leisure hours are reached, additional leisure hours have no value.
   c.   after a certain number of leisure hours are reached, work hours are actually viewed as a good thing.
   d.   as leisure hours increase, additional hours of leisure fall in value, but after some point, start to increase again.

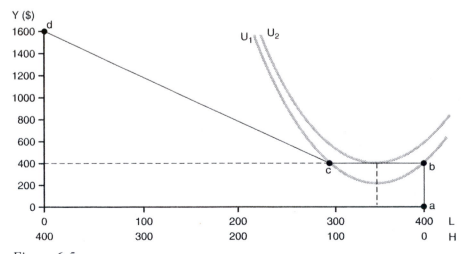

Figure 6-5

8. Which of the following statements is consistent with Figure 6-5?
   a. The market wage rate is $6.
   b. Low-income individuals receive a subsidy of $400 and face an implicit tax rate of zero.
   c. The optimal number of hours to supply is 50.
   d. The optimal number of hours to supply is zero.

Income and Substitution Effects

9. If a person has preferences that lead to a choice of zero work hours, an increase in the wage rate will result in
   a. an income effect only.
   b. a substitution effect only.
   c. counteracting income and substitution effects.
   d. a dominant substitution effect.

10. Suppose leisure is an inferior good (a good whose consumption goes down as income goes up). As the wage rate goes up
   a. hours supplied should go up.
   b. hours supplied should go down.
   c. hours supplied go up provided the substitution effect dominates the income effect.
   d. hours supplied go up provided the income effect dominates the substitution effect.

11. A backward-bending labor supply curve occurs when
   a. leisure is a normal good and the substitution effect dominates at low wage levels.
   b. leisure is a normal good and the income effect dominates at high wage levels.
   c. at low wages level, leisure is a normal goods, but then is an inferior good at high wage levels.
   d. both **a** and **b**.

12. What should be the effect on labor supply of reducing marginal income tax rates while keeping the total taxes paid by a worker constant?
   a. Hours supplied should go up.
   b. Hours supplied will go down.
   c. Hours supplied stay the same.
   d. Hours supplied should go up if the substitution effect dominates the income effect.

Basic Income Replacement and Income Maintenance Programs

13. Suppose the government promises to pay workers who lose their sight in a workplace accident $100,000 regardless of their earnings before the accident. This payment would create
   a. a pure income effect.
   b. a pure substitution effect.
   c. reinforcing income and substitution effects.
   d. counteracting income and substitution effects.

14. An income replacement program based on scheduled benefits generally preserves work incentives better than one that guarantees replacement of the actual income loss because the scheduled benefits approach

a.   creates a pure substitution effect.

b.   does not alter the price of leisure.

c.   leads to a higher level of utility.

d.   overcompensates workers for their injuries.

In answering Questions **15–18**, please refer to Figure 6-6. The original constraint is line *ab*. The constraint associated with the income maintenance program is line *acdb*.

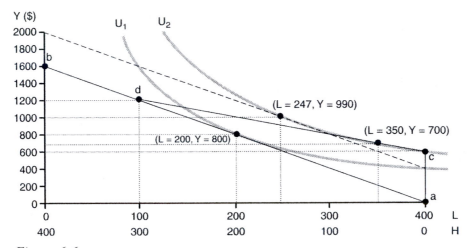

Figure 6-6

15. The implicit tax rate (*t*) used in this income maintenance program is

a.   1.

b.   0.

c.   .4.

d.   .5.

16. The actual subsidy paid to the individual will be

a. $100.

b. $500.

c. $600.

d. $1,200.

17. The substitution effect associated with this income maintenance program is

a.   an increase of 47 leisure hours.

b.   an increase of 103 leisure hours.

c.   a decrease of 103 leisure hours.

d.   an increase of 150 leisure hours.

18. The income effect associated with this income maintenance program is

a.   a decrease of $100.

b.   an increase of 47 leisure hours.

c.   an increase of 103 leisure hours.

d.   an increase of leisure hours.

19. In the typical income maintenance program, the higher the implicit tax rate
    a.   the higher the breakeven point.
    b.   the lower the work incentive.
    c.   the higher the cost of the program.
    d.   all of the above.

20. The problem with reducing the implicit tax rate pertaining to the welfare program is that
    a.   individuals well above the poverty level may receive benefits.
    b.   the cost of the program increases.
    c.   people will have less incentive to work.
    d.   both **a** and **b**.

21. Under the Earned Income Tax Credit program, the theoretical effects on labor supply are _____
    for the lowest income recipients, and _____ for the highest income recipients.
    a.   an increase; a decrease
    b.   a decrease; an increase
    c.   ambiguous; a decrease
    d.   an increase; ambiguous

22. The Earned Income Tax Credit is now viewed by many as being the most effective way of raising
    the incomes of the working poor because
    a.   it is much more closely targeted on the working poor than the minimum wage.
    b.   the estimated impact on hours worked by the working poor is positive.
    c.   since the subsidy comes through the tax system rather than through employers, there is no
         negative stigmatizing effect on recipients.
    d.   all of the above.

■ Problems

The Labor/Leisure Choice: The Fundamentals

23. Suppose an individual's preferences for leisure and income can be represented by a Cobb-Douglas
    utility function of the form

$$U = L^{\alpha}Y^{\beta}.$$

Assume the analysis pertains to one day and the maximum time available is 16 hours.

23a. Plot the $U = 1,000$ indifference curve assuming $\alpha = 1$ and $\beta = 1$.

23b. Plot the $U = 8,000$ indifference curve assuming $\alpha = 2$ and $\beta = 1$.

23c. What effect does an increased appreciation for leisure time have on the slope of a typical
     indifference curve?

24. Suppose the analysis pertains to one month and the maximum time available is 400 hours.

24a. Plot the budget constraint facing an individual receiving $400 in nonlabor income and a wage of $5 per hour.

24b. On the same graph, plot the budget constraint facing an individual receiving $200 in nonlabor income and a wage of $7 per hour.

Income and Substitution Effects

25. Consider Figure 6-7, which depicts a wage decrease. The original constraint is line *abc*. The new constraint is line *abd*.

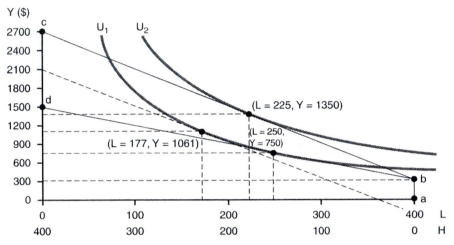

Figure 6-7

25a. By how much has the wage decreased?

25b. What is the income effect of the wage decrease? What is the substitution effect of the wage decrease?

25c. Find the coordinates of two points on this individual's labor supply curve. Is the labor supply curve upward or downward sloping over the range of the wage change?

Basic Income Replacement and Income Maintenance Programs

26. Consider an individual with preferences given by the formula $U = LY$. Suppose the total time available per day is 16 hours, the wage rate is $5, and nonlabor income is zero.

26a. Calculate the optimal level of leisure and labor hours, and the resulting earnings and utility level.

26b. Suppose the person is injured on the job in such a way that he cannot work at all. Prove that a policy that compensates the worker for his lost income will increase his utility.

26c. Find the minimum percentage of income that could be replaced and just keep the worker at the same level of utility as before his injury. Do you see any problems with this analysis?

27. Consider an individual with preferences given by the formula $U = LY$. Assume the going wage rate is $4 per hour and that the maximum time available per month is 400 hours. Also assume initially that the person has no nonlabor income. Now suppose that a welfare program is developed that provides low-income individuals with a benefit of $500 if they do not work at all. As the person earns income on his own, benefits are scaled back by the fraction t for every dollar earned.

27a. Find the change in hours supplied for each of the following implicit tax rates: $t = 1$, $t = 0.5$, $t = 0$.

27b. Which rate provides the least work disincentive? Explain why this happens.

28. Figure 6-8 shows two income maintenance programs that provide a maximum subsidy of $350 to anyone who does not work at all. One program is represented by the constraint $acdb$, while the other is represented by the constraint $aceb$.

28a. What are the implicit tax rates associated with each program?

28b. Given the preferences depicted on the graph, which program provides the strongest work incentives? Explain the intuition behind your finding.

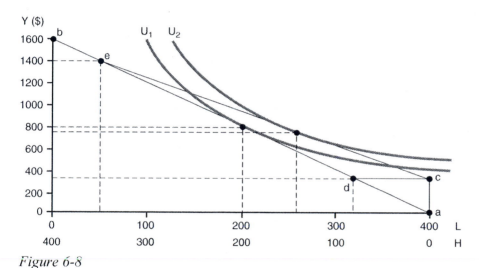

Figure 6-8

A Variation on the Basic Income Maintenance Program

29. Consider an individual with preferences for leisure and income given by the Cobb-Douglas utility function $U = LY$. Suppose an income maintenance program is created where individuals who do not work receive $2,000. Those who do work also receive the full subsidy provided they earn $4,000 or less. Those earning above $4,000 have their subsidy reduced by a dollar for every additional dollar earned beyond $4,000. The maximum time available is 2,800 hours per year, and the going wage is $5. The person initially has no nonlabor income.

29a. Graph the budget constraint facing a typical individual before the program is enacted. Then draw the constraint after the program is enacted. What is the breakeven point?

29b. Find the optimal number of hours before the adoption of the program. Calculate the level of utility the individual achieves.

29c. Using the graph as a guide, find the optimal number of hours after the program is enacted. Calculate the new level of utility. Would your answer have been different if all benefits were simply cut off once a person earned $4,000?

■ Applications

Reforming Income Maintenance and Income Replacement Programs

30. A common theme in welfare reform proposals is the notion of mutual obligation. That is, society has an obligation to help the poor, but the poor also have a responsibility to strive to become self-sufficient. A concrete way in which this notion is implemented is to make the receipt of benefits conditional on the recipient first performing some task, e.g., enroll in job training or accept part-time government employment, etc.

   Suppose an individual's preferences for leisure and income can be represented by a Cobb-Douglas utility function of the form

   $$U = L^{\alpha}Y^{\beta}.$$

   Assume the going wage rate is $4 per hour and that the maximum time available per month is 400 hours. Also assume initially that the person has no nonlabor income. Concerned about the work disincentives that can accompany income maintenance programs, suppose Congress legislates that to qualify for the maximum benefit of $200 you must work 100 hours per month. Those working in excess of 100 hours will see the maximum benefit scaled back by 40 cents for each additional dollar they earn once they have qualified for the program.

30a. Draw the budget constraint facing an individual in the absence of the welfare program. Then draw the constraint with the welfare system in place. What is the breakeven point under this program?

30b. Using the graph as a guide, find the effects of the welfare program on hours worked for each of the following preference parameter combinations.
   1. $\alpha = 0.65,\quad \beta = 0.35$.
   2. $\alpha = 0.75,\quad \beta = 0.25$.
   3. $\alpha = 0.85,\quad \beta = 0.15$.

30c. Assess the usefulness of threshold provisions such as this in reforming welfare programs.

The Earned Income Tax Credit

31. Suppose that the Earned Income Tax Credit (EITC) program is set up so that a maximum payment of $2,700 can be earned when a qualified worker earns $9,000. This represents a payment of 30 cents for each additional dollar earned. Suppose also that workers earning between $9,000 and $12,000 are eligible for the maximum payment, but that once earnings exceed $12,000, additional earnings cause the payment to be reduced by 45 cents for each additional dollar earned.

   Assume the maximum number of hours a person can work in a year is 3,000, and that the going wage rate is $6 per hour. Recall that individuals who do not work receive no benefits under this program.

31a. Graph the budget constraint facing a typical individual before the program is enacted. Then graph the budget constraint after the program in enacted. Be sure to find the coordinates of the point where a person is no longer eligible for the program.

31b. What is the slope of the constraint for anyone earning less than $9,000? What is the slope of the constraint for anyone earning more than $12,000?

31c. Consider a worker with preferences such that before the tax credit program she would have worked 500 hours. Is this individual likely to work more or less because of the tax credit program? How can you tell?

31d. Discuss the work incentives for someone with preferences such that before the program he worked more than 1,500 hours.

Effects of Progressive Taxes on Labor Supply

*32. Suppose an individual's preferences for leisure and income can be represented by a Cobb-Douglas utility function of the form

$$U = L^\alpha Y^\beta.$$

Assume the going wage rate is $4 per hour and that the maximum time available per month is 400 hours. Also assume that the person has nonlabor income of $200. Suppose that the government raises revenue through a tax on total income. As an example, suppose that when total monthly income is $1,000 or less, income is taxed at the rate of 20%. Anyone with income above $1,000 must pay 20% on the first $1,000 they received, but also 40% on every dollar over $1,000. Such a system is called a progressive tax, and the two rates are called marginal tax rates. For simplicity, ignore the issue of how the tax revenues would be used.

*32a. Draw the before-tax budget constraint facing an individual. Then draw the constraint with the income tax system in place.

*32b. At what point on the leisure (hours worked) axis does the 40% marginal tax rate begin to apply? Find the slope of the constraint to the left and to the right of this point.

*32c. Assuming $a = b = 1$, find the optimal hours supplied by this individual before and after the tax. What is the average tax rate the individual faces?

*32d. If one follows the budget line associated with the 40% marginal tax rate to the point where leisure is at its minimum (the full income level), it will be as if the level of nonlabor income has increased above $200. Use the value of income at this point, and the formula for full income $(WT + V)$ to find the height of the constraint (the implicit value of V) at this point.

*32e. Assume $\alpha = 1$ and $\beta = 3$. Using your answer to **32d**, find the optimal hours supplied by this individual before and after tax. What is the average tax rate this individual faces?

*32f. Assess the consequences for labor supply of tax proposals that call for the wealthy to face significantly higher marginal tax rates.

Reducing the Costs of Working Through Telecommuting

33. Consider an individual with preferences given by the formula $U = LY$. Assume the going wage rate is $4 per hour and that the maximum time available per month is 400 hours. Also assume initially that the person has nonlabor income of $200. Suppose the individual incurs a fixed monetary cost of $100 per month associated with working and a fixed time cost of 30 hours per month.

33a. Find the optimal amount of leisure and work that can be attained and the level of utility achieved. Verify that the level of utility is greater than that attained by not working at all.

33b. Suppose both the monetary and time costs of working are eliminated by telecommuting; that is, the person now works at home and sends her work to the office via a home computer equipped with a modem. Find the optimal number of leisure and work hours and the level of utility achieved.

Chapter 7
Labor Supply: Household Production, the Family, and the Life Cycle

■ Summary

The labor supply model presented in Chapter 6 assumed that individuals derive utility from consumption and leisure time. At any given point in time, the model postulates that individuals try to maximize their utility subject to the constraint that they cannot consume more than their income. Their income in turn is a function of the wage rate, the level of nonlabor income, and the number of hours they work (which equals the total time available less what they demand in leisure). This approach provides a valuable framework for thinking about labor supply issues, particularly the effects of government social welfare policies on work incentives.

The purpose of this chapter is to discuss three modifications to the labor supply model presented in Chapter 6. These modifications reflect more recent developments in labor supply theory. First, the assumption that individuals divide their time only between leisure and market work is relaxed. Instead, it is assumed that individuals divide their time between market work, **work at home**, and leisure time, and a model of the choice between market work and work at home is developed. Second, the assumption that decisions about the allocation of time are made independently by individuals is relaxed. Instead, decisions are looked at as part of a **joint husband-wife decision**. Third, the assumption that labor supply decisions are essentially the same at any point in time is abandoned. Instead, it is recognized that important differences in wages, market and household productivity, and preferences for leisure exist over an individual's **life cycle** and that these differences affect decisions about labor supply. A life-cycle perspective is then used to model the choice of retirement age.

The model of the choice between market work and work at home is a recasting of the labor supply model from Chapter 6. The model assumes that an individual or family derives utility from consuming market goods, household goods (such as meals and laundry), and leisure. These goods are, to some extent, substitutes for each other, and thus, as in Chapter 6, we can graph indifference curves showing the tradeoff between market goods and household time (a combination of time spent producing and consuming household goods and consuming leisure). The budget constraint is again a function of any nonlabor income, the wage rate, and available hours. From this model, we can derive the same implications about labor supply as in the previous chapter. Increases in nonlabor income will increase consumption of household time and reduce hours spent on paid work, while increases in the wage rate have both income and substitution effects, and thus the effect on hours of work is undetermined. The size of these effects will depend on preferences and the ease with which market and household goods can be substituted. For example, a particularly good cook may have a harder time substituting restaurant meals for home production of food. And preferences may change over the life cycle of the family; as children get older, mothers may be more likely to enter the labor force.

The chapter also explores the **interdependency** between the labor supply decisions of husband and wife. One possibility is that there will be complete specialization: one partner will work full time in the market while the other will stay at home. Historically, men's wages have been higher than those of women, while there are indications that women have been more productive at child-rearing, and thus this decision may be the result of optimizing behavior.

Another possibility is that both partners will work for pay. In general, each person should work additional hours in the market provided an extra hour of work makes up for the household production lost because of the time spent at work. This weighing of costs and benefits, however, is complicated by the interdependency between a spouse's productivity at home and the other spouse's labor supply. In most instances, spouse A's productivity at home rises when spouse B increases his or her market work (implying that they are *substitutes* in household production), increasing the incentive for A to work at home instead of in the market. However, the utility A derives from a certain amount of household production is likely to be inversely related to the time B works, dampening A's incentive to work at home (and implying that they are *complements* in production).

Cross effects are also common when one member of the household loses a job due to a recession. When this results in the spouse decreasing time spent in household production to enter the labor market, the increase in the labor force is called the **added worker effect**. This effect tends to raise the observed unemployment rate. At the same time this is happening, however, the person who has been laid off may actually withdraw from the labor force because of the substitution effects associated with a lower expected wage. This counteracting effect on the labor force is part of the **discouraged worker effect**, and it tends to lower the observed unemployment rate. Overall, however, discouraged worker effects appear to dominate, because the labor force tends to shrink during recessions and grow during recovery.

Market and household productivity can also vary for an individual because of differences that occur over the **life cycle**, or **intertemporal** aspects of the labor supply. Over the life cycle, workers will tend to work most when their earning capacity is high (relative to home production). As reflected by the wage, market productivity starts lowwhen the worker is young, rises quickly with age, and then levels off or even falls. Workers familiar with this traditional path of wages may be able to generate an estimate of expected lifetime wealth. Then, as these *expected* wage changes occur over time, they produce a substitution effect but no income effect (since they do not change expected lifetime wealth). In a life-cycle context, only unexpected wage changes can produce both income and substitution effects.

An intertemporal perspective can also be used to model a worker's **choice of retirement age**. In general, delaying retirement means a higher yearly Social Security benefit, and it also allows the additional accumulation of market earnings. The additions to remaining lifetime income that come from delaying retirement an additional year can be thought of as the effective wage associated with delaying retirement. It is this wage, together with overall level of benefits, that must be combined with a worker's preferences for leisure and income to arrive at the optimal retirement age.

Example

Consider a worker who is currently 65 years old and expects to live until age 80. His or her current and expected future wage is $20,000 per year. After retirement, the person will not work and will receive only Social Security payments for income. Table 7-1 shows the hypothetical yearly Social Security payments (in thousands of dollars) the worker is eligible for at retirement ages between 65 and 70.

Table 7-1 also shows the lifetime Social Security payments that will accrue (yearly Social Security payments multiplied by the number of years left to live), additional lifetime earnings (yearly wage multiplied by number of years to retirement), and the total lifetime income remaining at different retirement ages (all dollar values in thousands). For simplicity, assume the market interest rate is zero so that future dollars do not have to be discounted.

Table 7-1

Retirement age	Yearly social security	Lifetime social security	Lifetime earnings	Total lifetime income
65	8.0	120	0	120
66	8.5	119	20	139
67	8.9	115.7	40	155.7
68	9.2	110.4	60	170.4
69	9.4	103.4	80	183.4
70	9.5	95	100	195

If the worker ranks combinations of leisure and income according to a Cobb-Douglas utility function given by the formula

$$U = L^{\alpha}Y^{\beta},$$

where U is the index of satisfaction (higher values are better), L is the number of years to be spent at home in retirement, and Y is remaining lifetime income, what is the optimal retirement age for this worker? Assuming for simplicity that L and Y are each given equal weight in the worker's preferences, the constants α and β can both be set equal to 1. Having computed the remaining lifetime income associated with each retirement age, Table 7-2 shows the ranking of various leisure/income combinations. Under this ranking the optimal retirement age is 68.

Table 7-2

Retirement age	Leisure years (L)	Lifetime income (Y)	Utility ranking ($U = LY$)
65	15	120	1,800
66	14	139	1,946
67	13	155.7	2,024.1
68	12	170.4	2,044.8
69	11	183.4	2,017.4
70	10	195	1,950

The lifetime income/retirement age constraint is shown graphically by points a through f in Figure 7-1. The slope between any two points can be thought of as the effective wage rate associated with working an additional year, while the height of the constraint in the earliest year can be thought of as the level of nonlabor income associated with the model. As Figure 7-1 makes clear, the effective wage rate varies from year to year.

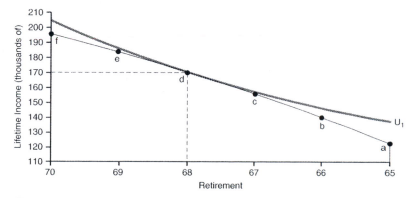

Figure 7-1

The preferences of the worker are represented by the indifference curve U_1. The optimum retirement age occurs at point *d* where the highest indifference curve consistent with the constraint is attained.

The chapter concludes by returning to the basic model of the choice between household and market work, where household work includes time spent in child rearing. The model is used to analyze a proposal for a child support assurance program. Under this proposal, a single parent eligible for child support would receive the child support payments from the government in the event that the absent parent does not make the payment. The proposal is evaluated within the context of a welfare system that provides a certain guaranteed income level if the person does not work at all, and then reduces welfare benefits dollar for dollar with income earned. In contrast, the guaranteed level of child support is available regardless of how much the parent earns in the labor market, but if the parent chooses not to work, the child support payment is subtracted from the maximum welfare subsidy.

Child care subsidies that reduce the fixed cost of child care encourage work among those who would otherwise be out of the labor force but create an income effect that may reduce hours for those already working. Subsidies that reduce the hourly cost of child care are more likely to create work incentives for all workers, because substitution effects dominate in participation decisions and, generally, at low levels of income.

■ Review Questions

Choose the letter that represents the **BEST** response.

The Theory of Household Production

1. The theory of household production assumes that the family derives utility (satisfaction) from
   a. income.
   b. time spent in home production.
   c. the wage rate.
   d. leisure, commodities (e.g., meals, a clean home, the growth of children) produced by the family, and goods purchased with family income.

2. In a graphical representation of the household production theory, an indifference curve represents
   a. all the combinations of household production time and market purchased goods and services that can produce a certain level of utility.
   b. all the combinations of household production time and market purchased goods and services that can produce a certain level of output.
   c. all the combinations of leisure time and work that can produce a certain level of utility.
   d. both **a** and **b**.

3. Which of the following is a true statement about the budget constraint in a household production model?
   a. For any given level of household production time, it shows the maximum amount of goods and services that the family can purchase in the market.
   b. The magnitude of its slope equals the level of nonlabor income.
   c. The height of the constraint equals the wage rate.
   d. All of the above.

4. Consider a household production model where only one member of the family works for pay and there is zero nonlabor income. Which of the following statements are true if the working member receives a wage increase?

   a. The working member will experience an income effect that will drive him or her to spend less time in home production activities.

   b. The working member will experience a substitution effect that will drive him or her to spend more time in home production activities.

   c. The overall effect of a wage increase on labor supplied to the market cannot be determined from theory alone.

   d. All of the above.

5. The household production model reminds us that individuals really have three ways to allocate time: market work, household production, and leisure time. In such a context, an increase in the wage leads to

   a. a substitution effect where household work is cut back.

   b. a substitution effect where leisure time is cut back.

   c. income effects that lead to more household work and more leisure time.

   d. all of the above.

6. Data from time-use diaries show that for men, household production time increased, market work decreased, and leisure time increased between the years 1965 and 1981. Assuming the real wages of men were rising over this time, one can infer that

   a. the substitution effect between household and market work dominated the income effect.

   b. the substitution effect between leisure and market work dominated the income effect.

   c. the income effect dominated the substitution effects occurring between household and market work and leisure and market work.

   d. both **a** and **b**.

7. Data from time-use diaries show that for women, household production time decreased, market work increased, and leisure time decreased between the years 1965 and 1981. Assuming the real wages of women were rising over this time, one can infer that

   a. the substitution effect between household and market work dominated the income effect.

   b. the substitution effect dominated the income effect between leisure and market work.

   c. the substitution effect between household and market work was so strong that it counteracted the substitution effect between leisure and market work.

   d   both **a** and **b**.

8. The substitution effect of a wage change tends to be larger in the household production model than in the labor/leisure choice model because

   a. some types of purchased goods and services can easily make up for lost household production time.

   b. purchased goods and leisure time are likely to be used in a complementary fashion.

   c. household production time and market work can be thought of as perfect substitutes for some workers, particularly women.

   d. both **a** and **b**.

Joint Husband-Wife Labor Supply Decisions

9. According to the household production model, if a married couple decides to have one spouse stay at home, it should be
   a. the spouse who earns less in the labor market.
   b. the spouse who is more productive at home.
   c. the spouse for whom the difference between the wage and the household marginal productivity is lowest.
   d. both **a** and **b**.

10. According to the household production model, when a household decides that both spouses can work for pay, a wife should continue to supply extra hours to the market provided
    a. the husband is a substitute in household production.
    b. the husband and wife are complementary in the consumption of household commodities.
    c. the wage rate of the wife is higher than that of the husband.
    d. the extra hours spent working allow the wife to purchase goods and services that can at least make up for the time lost in household production.

11. In a household production model where both spouses work, if the wife increases her work hours, the husband will tend to work less if
    a. he and his wife are complements in household production.
    b. he and his wife are complementary in the consumption of household commodities.
    c. his marginal productivity in household production increases.
    d. both **b** and **c**.

12. When a husband's time in the labor market becomes less valuable because of a health problem, the wife is more likely to increase her time in the labor market if
    a. his health problems do not impact his marginal productivity in household production.
    b. the husband and wife are substitutes in household production.
    c. the husband and wife are complementary in the consumption of household commodities.
    d. both **a** and **b**.

13. The "discouraged worker" effect occurs when an unemployed household member drops out of the labor force during a recession. This occurs because
    a. other members of the household may be joining the labor force due to the "added worker effect."
    b. the expected wage of unemployed workers tends to fall during a recession.
    c. changes in the expected wage create a substitution effect by lowering the opportunity cost of time at home.
    d. both **b** and **c**.

14. Consider a household where currently only the husband works for pay. If the family becomes eligible for an income maintenance program that increases family income and reduces the effective wage, the household production model predicts that
    a. the husband will supply less labor to the market.
    b. the wife may begin to work for pay.
    c. more total hours will be supplied to household production.
    d. all of the above.

Life-Cycle Aspects of Labor Supply

15. A recent empirical study found that the labor force participation rates of married women tend to rise over time, with the largest increases being after age thirty. One explanation for this is that
    a. wages tend to rise as a person ages.
    b. marginal household productivity tends to fall as children get older.
    c. men have increasingly been spending more time in household production and less time working for pay.
    d. the invention of new time-saving devices (e.g., microwave ovens) makes work at home less necessary.

16. If workers are aware of the general path that their wage will take over their lifetime, what will happen when an anticipated increase in the wage occurs?
    a. there will be no change in the quantity of labor supplied.
    b. the quantity of labor supplied will decrease.
    c. there will be a substitution effect but no income effect.
    d. both **b** and **c**.

17. Under the Social Security program, yearly pension benefits rise as the retirement age is delayed. However, at some point the increase is not enough to offset the reduced number of years the benefits will be received. The result is that lifetime benefits eventually fall as the retirement age is delayed. Suppose this payment structure were replaced by one where lifetime benefits remained constant as the retirement age increased. How would this affect the decision about retirement age?
    a. the retirement age would tend to increase.
    b. the retirement age would tend to decrease.
    c. the retirement age would increase only if the income effect of the change dominated the substitution effect.
    d. the retirement age would decrease only if the income effect of the change dominated the substitution effect.

■ Problems

The Theory of Household Production

18. Consider two families that derive satisfaction (utility) from the consumption of market goods and household goods (including leisure). Of course, there is no requirement that all families see the tradeoff between goods and household time the same way. In Figure 7-2, suppose that curve U_1 represents the combinations of goods and time that yield a certain level of utility for family 1, while curve U_2 represents the combinations of goods and time that yield the <u>same</u> level of utility for family 2.

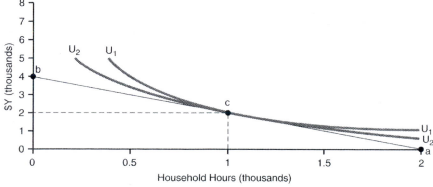

Figure 7-2

18a. Describe the differences in how each family views the tradeoff between goods and household production time.

18b. Suppose that each family has no nonlabor income and that only one member works for pay at an initial wage of $2. This leads to the initial budget line *ab*. Given the tradeoffs perceived by each family, the initial point chosen by each is point *c*. Now suppose the market wage facing the working member of each family increases to $4. Will the substitution effect of the wage increase be greater for family 1 or family 2? Show the substitution effects for each family graphically.

Joint Husband-Wife Labor Supply Decisions

19. According to the text, "The basic premise of the household production model is that people are productive in two places: in the home and in a 'market' job. Their decisions about whether to seek market work and for how many hours are a function of their *relative* productivities in both places. As long as an extra hour of market work allows the person to buy more goods than are required to make up for the hour of lost production time at home, the person will work for pay that extra hour."

Consider a family that ranks combinations of household production time (N) and purchased goods and services (Y) according to the formula

$$U = NY,$$

where U represents the level of utility (associated with the production of some household commodity). Suppose the maximum time available in a day is 16 hours and currently a spouse devotes 4 hours to market work (H) at a wage of $10 per hour.

19a. What is the level of utility associated with the spouse's current choice?

19b. How much additional purchasing power would the spouse contribute if the number of hours worked in the market rose to 8?

19c. How much of an increase in purchased goods and services would be necessary to compensate for the additional 4 hours of lost household production?

19d. Is the additional 4 hours of market work a good deal for this family?

19e. If this couple is raising a child, suppose that combinations of household production and purchased goods are now ranked according to the formula

$$U = N^2Y.$$

Would the additional 4 hours of market work be a good move for the family in this situation?

19f. Returning to the situation where the family ranks combinations of household production time and purchased goods according to the formula $U = NY$, suppose the spouse has already made the move to working 8 hours per day. Would one additional hour of market work make the family better off or worse off?

19g. Technological advancements like microwave ovens, disposable diapers, and video cassette players have transformed the tradeoff between household production time and purchased goods. For a small increase in purchased goods, households can now obtain a large decrease in household production time without reducing the quantity of the final commodities that are produced. The change in the tradeoff can be represented by giving purchased goods more weight in the household's ranking formula.

Suppose that technological advancements result in the ranking formula becoming

$$U = NY^2.$$

Under these conditions, would a family where the spouse already works 8 hours per day benefit from having him or her work an additional hour?

20. Consider a household where the husband can earn a market wage of $15 per hour and has a marginal productivity in the household that is the equivalent of $12. The wife can earn a market wage of $20 and has a marginal productivity in the household that is the equivalent of $15. Suppose initially that their marginal household productivities do not depend on the time that the other spouse spends at home.

20a. If the couple decides to have only one of them work for pay outside the home, who should it be?

20b. Would it make sense for both the husband and wife to work for pay outside of the home?

20c. Assuming both members of the couple are working, how would an increase in the wife's wage affect her work hours? Would an increase in the wife's wage cause the husband to increase or decrease his work hours?

20d. How would your answer to **20c** be different if you knew that the couple were substitutes in household production?

20e. How would your answer to **20c** be different if you knew that the couple were complementary in household consumption?

The Discouraged Worker Effect

*21. Consider a family that ranks the combination of household production time (N) and purchased goods (Y) according to the formula

$$U = NY,$$

where U represents the level of utility (associated with the production of some household commodity). Suppose the maximum time available in a day is 16 hours and currently a spouse devotes 7 hours to market work (H) at a wage of $5 per hour. Suppose the family also receives $10 per day in nonlabor income (e.g., food stamps).

21a. What is the level of utility associated with the current mix of market work and household production?

21b. Assume that a recession occurs and the worker is laid off from his or her job. What is the level of utility at the new mix of market work and household production?

*21c. Suppose the probability of finding a comparable job during this recession is π. What is the return to taking an hour away from household production activities to look for a job?

*21d. Assuming $\pi = 0.5$, would an hour spent in the labor force searching for a job make this person better off or worse off? Would the worker continue to be a member of the labor force under these conditions? If not, how would he or she be categorized?

*21e. Assuming $\pi = 0.1$, would an hour spent in the labor force searching for a job make this person better off or worse off? Would the worker continue to be a member of the labor force under these conditions? If not, how would he or she be categorized?

*21f. Suppose that if the worker were willing to accept a job paying only $2 per hour, the probability of finding a job would rise to $\pi = 1/3$. Would the worker continue to be a member of the labor force under these conditions?

■ Applications

Changes in the Allocation of Time by Men and Women

22. Data from time-use diaries suggest that as wages have risen, leisure consumption has increased for both men and women. At the same time, however, women have devoted more hours to market work and less to household production, while men have devoted less time to market work and slightly more time to household production. One key to explaining these differences is to realize that the substitution effect between market work and leisure is likely to be much smaller than the substitution effect between market work and household production.

Figure 7-3 represents a model of an individual's choice between market work and leisure, while Figure 7-4 shows the choice between market work and household production. In each figure, the person has no nonlabor income and an initial wage of $3, leading to the initial budget line *ab*. Preferences between purchased goods or income (*Y*) and non-market time are indicated by the curves labeled U_1. The initial point chosen is point *c* in Figure 7-3, and point *a* in Figure 7-4.

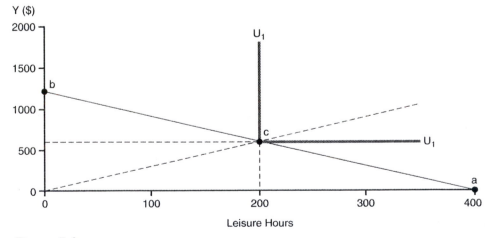

Figure 7-3

22a. For Figure 7-3, compute the substitution effect associated with an increase in the wage from $3 to $5.

22b. For Figure 7-4, compute the substitution effect associated with an increase in the wage from $3 to $5.

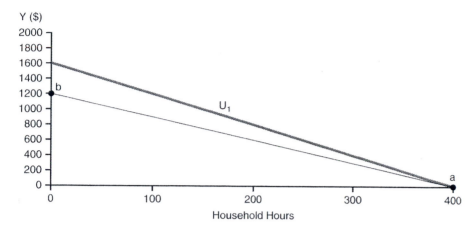

Figure 7-4

22c. Although Figures 7-3 and 7-4 represent extreme situations, why is Figure 7-3 a better model of the choice between market work and leisure?

22d. Similarly, why is Figure 7-4 a better model of the choice between market work and household production?

22e. Explain how these different substitution effects could help to explain the different changes in the allocation of time made by the men and women completing the time-use diaries.

Effects of Social Security on the Choice of Retirement Age

23. Consider again the situation presented in the Example problem in the Summary section of this chapter.

23a. Why is the constraint shown in Figure 7-1 a concave curve rather than a straight line? What would it take to make it a straight line?

23b. Analyze the work incentives associated with changing the constraint to a straight line. Given the formula for ranking combinations of leisure time and income used in the Example, how would the optimal retirement age be affected?

Changes in the Social Security Retirement Test

24. Prior to 1990, Social Security recipients whose earnings after retirement exceeded some threshold level saw their benefits reduced by 50 cents for each additional dollar earned in excess of the threshold amount. Effective in 1990, the reduction in benefits was lowered to 33 cents for each additional dollar earned in excess of $10,200.

Consider a 65-year-old Social Security recipient who is eligible for a maximum yearly benefit of $11,000. If the person chooses to work, suppose that he or she can earn a wage of $20 per hour. Also suppose that the maximum number of hours that can be worked in a year is 3,000.

24a. Draw the budget constraint facing this recipient assuming the reduction in benefits is 50 cents for every dollar earned in excess of $10,200. How many hours would the person have to work before they no longer qualified for Social Security benefits? How much would the person be earning at this point?

24b. On the same graph as in 24a, draw the budget constraint facing this recipient assuming the reduction in benefits is 33 cents for every dollar earned in excess of $10,200. How many hours would the person have to work before they no longer qualified for Social Security benefits? How much would the person be earning at this point?

24c. Analyze the change in work incentives associated with reducing the rate at which benefits are scaled back. What would be the effect of the change on someone who was previously working 1,000 hours? What would be the effect of the change on someone who was previously working 1,800 hours?

24d. For the worker previously working 1,000 hours, how would this change in the Social Security program be likely to affect his or her labor supply over the entire life cycle?

Chapter 8
Compensating Wage Differentials
and Labor Markets

■ Summary

The focus of the previous two chapters was on the question: Will an individual work for pay, and if so, how much? But assuming the person does decide to look for work, what type of work will it be? What benefits will accompany the job? These are the kinds of questions taken up in Chapter 8. The purpose of the chapter is to provide a framework for thinking about the role that recurring job characteristics play in an individual's labor supply decision and the repercussions such characteristics have on labor market outcomes such as the level of wages. The framework is then used to analyze the effects that regulations governing workplace safety and the provision of employee benefits can have on worker well-being.

One of the unique features of the labor market emphasized in Chapter 1 was that participants are much more sensitive to the nonpecuniary aspects of a transaction than in other markets. Labor services cannot be separated from the person rendering them. Therefore, given two offers of employment that are identical in all respects except working conditions, individuals trying to maximize their utility (satisfaction) will choose to supply their labor under the more desirable conditions. Hence, firms wishing to attract workers are faced with a dilemma. If they wish to attract more workers, they must either incur the costs necessary to make working conditions better, or they must pay higher wages. If the firm chooses to pay higher wages, the extra wage it pays relative to the firm with the more desirable working conditions is called a compensating wage differential. The compensating differential can be viewed as a reward to those workers accepting undesirable conditions, or alternatively, as the amount workers must pay to receive desirable conditions.

Of course, there are many things other than working conditions that influence a worker's wage. Training, skill, experience, age, race, gender, union status, and location may all exert an influence on the wage received. It is important to realize that the theory of compensating differentials does not imply that workers experiencing bad conditions will earn more than those experiencing good. After all, the chief executive at General Motors earns more and works under better conditions than the typical worker on the assembly line. What the theory does imply is that, **holding all else constant**, comparable workers will receive higher wages when they work under unpleasant conditions. The theory is also based on the assumptions that workers seek to **maximize utility** rather than income, have **complete information** about the characteristics associated with a particular job, and that they have enough **mobility** so that they can potentially accumulate a number of different job offers.

Empirical studies that attempt to measure the size of compensating differentials are inherently difficult, since not everyone will agree on whether certain job characteristics (e.g., outdoor work) are desirable or undesirable. Also, it is essential to control for all the other factors that influence wages. Still, studies that have focused on the risk of fatal injury in manufacturing industries have found that wages are 1% higher when workers face twice the average risk of a job-related fatality. Compensating differentials have also been associated with such characteristics as night shifts, longer work hours, inflexible schedules, lower job security, and dangerous, expensive, or distant work locations.

But what is the process through which compensating differentials emerge? What roles do employers and employees play in the process? The answers to these questions can be found in a framework known as the **hedonic theory of wages**. This theory is illustrated in Figure 8-1, where the undesirable characteristic is assumed to be **risk of fatal injury**.

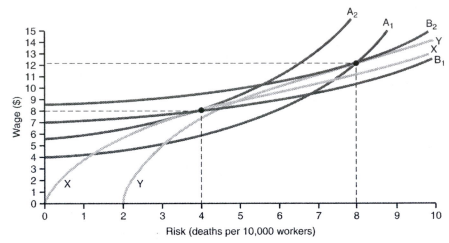

Figure 8-1

The preferences of two workers are summarized by the series of **indifference curves** labeled *A* and *B*. Any given curve shows all the combinations of risk and wages that will yield a certain level of utility. Higher curves (i.e., movements to the northwest) yield higher levels of utility and are denoted by higher subscript numbers. The curves are upward sloping since as the level of risk increases, the only way to keep the worker at the same level of utility would be to raise the wage. The convexity of the curves suggests that when the workplace is very risky, workers are willing to forgo a large amount in wages in return for a given reduction in risk. However, as the workplace grows safer, workers are less willing to give up wages for that same reduction in risk. The steeper slope to person A's indifference curves suggests that preferences about risk and wages are not the same for all individuals. Person A is more concerned about safety (more averse to risk) and so is willing to forgo more in wages than person B is for a given reduction in the level of risk.

The constraints facing two employers are summarized by the **isoprofit curves** labeled *X* and *Y*. Any given curve shows all the combinations of risk and wages that will yield a certain level of profit. Higher curves (i.e., movements to the northwest) would yield lower profits. The curves shown are assumed to be wage/risk combinations associated with zero economic profits, or just a normal rate of return. Zero economic profits are consistent with the notion that firms face perfect competition in the input and output markets. The curves are upward sloping since reducing the level of risk is costly, and so reductions in risk must be accompanied by wage reductions if the firm is to remain at a certain profit level. The convexity of the curves suggests when the level of risk is high, risk reductions are relatively easy to find and a given reduction in risk can be found at a relatively low cost. However, once the workplace has been made safer, additional risk reductions are likely to be difficult and that same reduction in risk will be more costly. The steeper slope to firm Y's isoprofit curve suggests that at any given level of risk, firm Y finds a given reduction in risk more costly than firm X.

Note that at low levels of risk, firm X will be able to offer higher wages than firm Y and still stay on the zero-profit isoprofit curve. At high levels of risk the opposite will be true. This suggests that the final outcome is constrained to lie along the portions of the zero-profit isoprofit curves that lie furthest to the northwest. The set of potentially acceptable offers is called the **offer curve**.

Given that the employees will be trying to maximize their utility given the offers made by the firms, person A will choose to work for employer X at a risk level of 4 and a wage of $8, while worker B will choose to work for employer Y with a risk of 8, but will receive a wage slightly over $12 for accepting this higher level of risk. Such a matching allows each firm to obtain the workers they need and at the same time allows the workers to obtain the highest feasible level of utility. Note that if *A* accepted the offer *B* did, *A* would be on a much lower indifference curve. The same would be true if *B* accepted the offer *A* did. Note that the process results in the worker least sensitive to risk (person B) being matched with the firm that finds risk reductions most costly (firm Y). Similarly, the worker most averse to risk (person A) is matched with the firm that finds risk reductions least costly (firm X).

Note that if Figure 8-1 is an accurate depiction of the matching process through which compensating differentials are generated, mandatory safety standards may make at least some workers worse off. For example, if all firms were forced to reduce the risk level to 4, workers like *B* would be forced onto a lower indifference curve. Mandatory reductions in risk below 4 would make both workers worse off. Additionally, while businesses may initially bear the costs of additional safety, they may eventually try to cut costs elsewhere. This may result in permanent layoffs (or reduced hiring of new workers), and workers will have to find other jobs (presumably less desirable jobs, since they could have chosen them before and did not).

Recall, however, that Figure 8-1 was based on the assumption that workers had complete information about the actual risk associated with different employment offers. If this is not true, a window of opportunity may be created for mandatory risk reductions to make at least some workers better off. Even in these situations, however, it is important that the standards not be set too strict. In setting standards for workplace safety, it is important that a **benefit/cost study** be done to see whether the value that workers place on risk reductions is at least as great as the costs borne by firms, which invariably will be paid by the workers in one form or another. In such a study, the benefits can often be estimated by using the compensating differentials that are generated in markets where there is complete information.

For example, some empirical studies of compensating differentials have suggested that manufacturing workers may be willing to give up as much as $700 for a 1 in 10,000 reduction in the risk of a fatal injury. Using this information, it would be possible to extrapolate what a worker might be willing to give up, say, for a 4 in 10,000 reduction in risk. The regulation would thus seem to be worth up to (4)($700) or $2,800 per worker. This benefit level could then be compared with the estimated cost per worker of implementing the regulation.

Benefits computed in this manner, however, are often criticized for not taking into account the benefits from increased safety that would accrue to people not directly affected by the regulation. Also, the extrapolation takes worker willingness to pay for increased safety as a given. This ignores the convexity of indifference curves as well as changes in preferences and attitudes such regulations can bring about over time.

Another recurring job characteristic that can be analyzed using the hedonic wage theory is the level of employee benefits that workers receive. Employee benefits include **payments in kind** (e.g., medical insurance or paid vacations) or **deferred compensation** (e.g., pension fund contributions). Figure 8-2 shows how the model is adapted when the recurring characteristic is something of benefit to the workers.

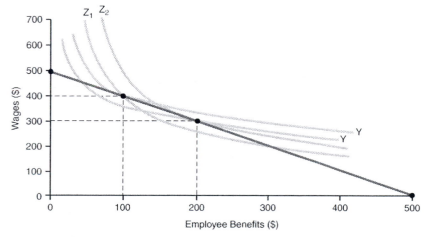

Figure 8-2

The preferences of two employees are summarized by the series of indifference curves labeled Y and Z. Any given curve shows all the combinations of employee benefits and wages that will yield a certain level of utility. Higher curves (i.e., movements to the northeast) yield higher levels of utility and are denoted by higher subscript numbers. The curves are downward sloping since as the level of benefits increases, the only way to keep the worker at the same level of utility would be to lower the wage. The convexity of the curves suggests that when the workers do not receive many benefits, they are willing to give up a significant amount in wages for a given increase in benefits. This occurs because in-kind benefits are not subject to income taxes, and deferred benefits will generally be taxed at a lower rate than current income. However, as the level of benefits rises, workers are less willing to give up wages for that same increase in benefits. This occurs because receiving compensation in the form of benefits does reduce the discretion workers have in how they allocate their income. The steeper slope to person Z's indifference curves suggests that person Z finds additional benefits more valuable than person Y, and so is willing to give up more in wages than person Y for a given increase in benefits.

As income tax rates change over time, the benefits associated with taking compensation in the form of fringe benefits also changes. Holding all else constant, indifference curves between wages and benefits should become steeper as tax rates increase. Of course, preferences for wages and benefits will be heavily influenced by exactly what benefits are being modeled and the characteristics of the individual worker. For example, if the benefits on the horizontal axis consist primarily of child-care benefits, and the worker is without children, the benefits will be of little use and so we would expect the indifference curve for this individual to be much flatter than that for someone with small children.

The constraint facing employers is summarized by the **isoprofit curve** labeled X. (Since all firms are assumed to have the same isoprofit curves in this analysis, the line labeled X can also be thought of as the offer curve facing workers.) The curve shows all the combinations of fringe benefits and wages that will yield the same total cost of compensation to the firm. With the total cost of compensation constant along the curve, it can be inferred that profits will also be constant along the curve. Higher curves (i.e., movements to the northeast) represent higher total compensation levels and so would yield lower profits. The curve shown is assumed to be that level of compensation associated with zero economic profits.

In Figure 8-2, the compensation level associated with zero economic profits is assumed to be $500. Since the isoprofit curve is drawn with horizontal and vertical intercepts at $500 (resulting in a slope of -1), it is also assumed that the firms can trade off between benefits and wages on a one-to-one basis and still keep total compensation costs the same. From the firm's perspective, then, paying employees a dollar of fringe benefits is the same as paying a dollar in wages.

Although a one-to-one tradeoff is a useful starting point in the analysis, it is important to realize that the tradeoff is likely to be different. Business taxes like Social Security and workers' compensation are computed as a percentage of a firm's payroll, and so compensating workers in the form of wages can lead to additional costs that would not be incurred if the compensation was made in the form of benefits. So, for example, the firm may find that it can offer only $400 in wages in place of $500 in benefits (or $1 in benefits for every 80 cent reduction in wages).

Other reasons that benefits can be offered on more than a one-to-one basis include the reduced turnover costs that come when benefits tie people to firms, as well as possible volume discounts that firms may be able to obtain when buying things like medical insurance for their workers. There are also factors, however, that can counteract this tendency. For example, some benefits may result in more absenteeism, raising the cost of providing benefits relative to the cost of wages.

Combining the indifference curves for each individual with the employers' isoprofit curves yields the equilibrium combinations of wages and benefits shown in Figure 8-2. If allowed to choose the mix of wages and benefits, worker Y would choose $400 in wages and $100 in benefits, while worker Z would choose only $300 in wages but $200 in benefits. Although some firms do give employees some flexibility as to the form of their compensation, most firms will choose a particular point along the isoprofit curve to offer to prospective employees. The result, of course, is that firms will tend to attract different types of workers. A firm offering only $300 in wages but $200 in benefits would have no trouble attracting a worker like Z, but such a package would put Y on a lower indifference curve and create an incentive for Y to seek employment at a firm with a compensation package more suited to his or her preferences. Similarly, a firm offering more in wages but less in benefits would have trouble attracting workers like Z since such a package would put Z on a lower indifference curve.

Knowing that different types of compensation packages will appeal to different kinds of workers, firms will structure their compensation strategically to attract the types of workers they want. For example, what kinds of workers are likely to have preferences like person Z in Figure 8-2? Since the indifference curves are relatively steep, this means that additional benefits are highly valued. If the benefits are traditional things like pensions and health insurance, this is likely to be an older worker. Alternatively, if the benefits are maternity leave and child care, the person could be a young woman. By appropriately setting the type of benefits and their levels, the firm would be sure to attract workers like Z while discouraging applicants like Y.

Regardless of the compensation mix offered by the firms, note that Figure 8-2 clearly shows that workers pay for additional benefits in the form of lower wages. Holding all else constant, firms that offer comparable workers more generous benefits must pay lower wages to remain competitive. Figure 8-2 also provides a framework for rationalizing the growth of fringe benefits documented in Chapter 5. Higher income tax rates tend to steepen the indifference curves at the same time higher payroll taxes tend to flatten the isoprofit curves. As the indifference curves steepen and the isoprofit curves flatten, the optimal combination of wages and benefits moves in a southeast direction.

Example

Consider a worker who ranks combinations of employee benefits (E) and wages (W) according to the utility function

$$U = E^\alpha W^\beta,$$

where α and β are positive constants and U is the index of satisfaction. Suppose α and β are both equal to one and that firms are able to remain competitive (i.e., keep profits at zero) if they offer $400 in wages and no employee benefits. If they offer benefits, wages must be reduced by 80 cents for every dollar of benefits offered. Suppose that currently, the firm is offering a compensation package of $250 in benefits and $200 in wages. Would the worker be made better off or worse off by a regulation that forced this firm to increase the value of its benefit package to $300?

The original wage/benefit package yielded an index of satisfaction equal to

$$U = (250)(200) = 50,000.$$

If the level of benefits is increased to 300, the workers would stay at the same level of utility if wages fell to

$$W = \frac{50,000}{300} = \$166.67.$$

In other words, the worker would be willing to give up $33.33 for the additional $50 in benefits.

However, to provide the additional $50 in benefits and still keep profits at zero, by how much will the firm have to reduce wages? Since every dollar of fringe benefits requires the firm to reduce wages by 80 cents, an additional $50 in benefits would require the firm to reduce wages by (0.8)($50) or $40. Since the cost of providing the additional benefits exceeds what the worker is willing to pay, the regulation will make the worker worse off. Note also that the level of utility associated with the new compensation package of $E = 300$ and $W = 160$ falls to $U = (300)(160) = 48,000$.

The appendix to Chapter 8 provides a framework for thinking about the size of the compensating differential that must arise when workers are constrained by employers in their choice of work hours. For example, employees may be forced through excessive layoffs to consume more leisure than they consider optimal. Using the labor supply framework from Chapter 6, the appendix illustrates how to determine the income necessary to keep workers at their original utility when the level of leisure is forced away from its optimum. Once the level of income is found that will keep the worker's utility constant, the wage that the firm must pay can be found by dividing the income level by the constrained number of work hours.

The appendix also provides a framework for thinking about why compensating differentials will be necessary when workers are subjected to uncertain layoffs. In such a situation, compensating differentials will arise if workers are **risk averse**, that is, if they have preferences such that they place a larger value on negative changes from a given income level than they do on positive changes of the same magnitude. In such a situation, the average level of utility associated with a job that always involves, say, 200 hours will be greater than the average utility that results from a job that averages 200 hours, but where hours range from 300 hours 50% of the time to 100 hours the other 50% of the time. Since the more variable schedule results in a lower average level of utility, a compensating differential will be necessary to attract risk-averse workers to this type of workplace.

■ Review Questions

Choose the letter that represents the **BEST** response.

A Verbal Analysis of Occupational Choice

1. If all jobs were exactly alike and located in the same place, an individual would tend to seek work at employers that
    a. paid the highest wages.
    b. had the most applicants.
    c. had the fewest applicants.
    d. had the most job openings.

2. In practice, jobs are not exactly alike and can be located in very different places. When this happens, a compensating wage differential can be expected to arise to attract workers to the jobs with less desirable characteristics. Such a differential is in equilibrium when
    a. all the workers are employed for the higher wage firm.
    b. all the workers who are indifferent about the adverse conditions are employed at the firm offering the most adverse conditions.
    c. each firm can obtain the quality and quantity of workers that it wants.
    d. the wage rises enough so that the firm with the worst working conditions has an incentive to improve its conditions.

3. Workers performing dangerous jobs in the economy are typically people that
    a. cannot find work offering better conditions.
    b. see the jobs as paying well compared to alternative employment.
    c. are poorly paid.
    d. enjoy danger.

4. Suppose that the compensating differential associated with working in a noisy workplace is $500 per year. This $500 payment can be interpreted as
   a.   the amount sufficient to attract any worker to the noisy environment.
   b.   the amount that the marginal worker is willing to pay for a quiet environment.
   c.   the minimum amount necessary to attract a worker to the noisy environment.
   d.   the most that any worker would pay for a quiet work environment.

5. The theory of compensating differentials predicts that
   a.   workers with poor conditions will earn more than those with good conditions.
   b.   holding worker characteristics constant, workers experiencing poor conditions will earn more than those experiencing good conditions.
   c.   holding wages constant, highly skilled workers will work under better conditions than less skilled workers.
   d.   both **b** and **c**.

6. Which of the following is not an assumption on which the theory of compensating differentials is based?
   a.   Workers always try to choose the highest paying job available to them.
   b.   Given a certain wage, workers will always choose the job with more pleasant conditions.
   c.   Workers know about the job characteristics associated with different employment opportunities.
   d.   Workers have a variety of employment opportunities from which to choose.

A Hedonic Theory of Wages: The Risk of Injury

In answering Questions **7–13** please refer to Figure 8-3. The curves labeled A_2 and B_2 refer to indifference curves between the wage and risk of injury for two individuals, while the curves X and Y refer to zero-profit isoprofit curves for two firms.

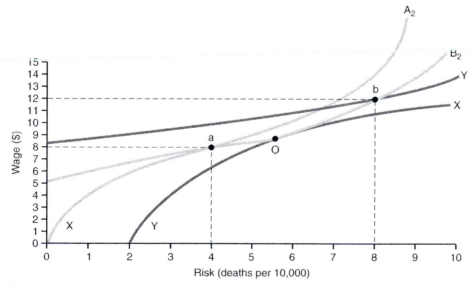

Figure 8-3

7. In Figure 8-3 the indifference curves between the wage and risk of injury are drawn upward sloping. This is consistent with the statement that
   a. workers enjoying safe workplaces also typically earn higher wages.
   b. firms with safer conditions must pay less because risk reduction is costly.
   c. safer workplaces increase worker utility, so the only way to keep utility constant as risk is reduced is to lower the wage workers receive.
   d. both **b** and **c**.

8. In Figure 8-3 the indifference curves between the wage and risk of injury are drawn with a convex shape (when viewed from below). This is consistent with the statement that
   a. when a person feels relatively safe, he or she is not willing to give up much in wages for a given reduction in risk.
   b. when a person is in imminent danger of injury, he or she is willing to give up a large amount in wages for a given reduction in risk.
   c. the flatter the slope of the indifference curve, the more risk averse the person is.
   d. both **a** and **b**.

9. In Figure 8-3 the isoprofit curves between the wage and risk of injury are drawn upward sloping because
   a. reducing risk is costly, and so to stay at the same profit level, the firm must lower the wage.
   b. profits fall as the firm offers safer conditions.
   c. the firm must pay workers higher wages to accept higher levels of risk.
   d. increased risk of injury means that the firm must pay more in insurance and medical costs.

10. In Figure 8-3 the isoprofit curves between the wage and risk of injury are drawn with a concave shape (when viewed from below). This is consistent with the statement that
   a. When the workplace is relatively unsafe, a given reduction in risk can be attained cheaply.
   b. When the workplace is relatively safe, a given reduction in risk can only be achieved at a high cost.
   c. The steeper the isoprofit curve, the less costly are risk reductions to the firm.
   d. Both **a** and **b**.

11. In Figure 8-3 the offer curve for wage and risk is formed by the darkened portions of the isoprofit curves (including points *a*, *b*, and OC). Which of the following statements is **not** true about the offer curve?
   a. The offer curve represents the wage/risk combinations that firms can afford to make and workers are willing to accept.
   b. Every point on the offer curve is a point of positive economic profit for some firm.
   c. Every point on the offer curve is potentially an optimal combination of wage and risk for some worker.
   d. Constructing an offer curve could help to simplify the hedonic wage theory graph in the case when there are more than two firms.

12. In Figure 8-3 the matching process between firms and workers results in the wage/risk combinations indicated by points *a* and *b*. This diagram predicts that
   a. holding all else constant, wages rise with risk.
   b. workers most averse to risk will be matched with employers that find risk reductions least costly.
   c. workers with undesirable conditions are being exploited by their employers.
   d. both **a** and **b**.

13. If the workers in Figure 8-3 are mobile and perfectly informed about the degree of risk associated with a particular occupation, a mandatory risk reduction to 4 deaths per 10,000 workers would

   a.   make both workers worse off.

   b.   make person B worse off.

   c.   force person B to change employers.

   d.   both **b** and **c**.

14. In general, if a worker is imperfectly informed about the degree of risk associated with a particular occupation, a mandatory risk reduction

   a.   will always make the worker worse off.

   b.   will always make the worker better off.

   c.   will make the worker better off provided the worker's willingness to pay for the risk reduction exceeds the cost to the firms of providing it.

   d.   will result in the optimal level of risk being attained.

15. Benefit/cost analyses of occupational safety and health standards may understate the benefits associated with such standards because

   a.   benefits of safety and health standards can extend beyond just those workers protected by the standards.

   b.   workers may not always know what is best for themselves.

   c.   if workers experience safer standards, their attitudes may change and they may be willing to pay more for increased safety.

   d.   all of the above.

Hedonic Wage Theory and Employee Benefits

16. As income tax rates increase, the advantage of receiving compensation in the form of employee benefits (payments in kind or deferred payments) increases. Assuming employee benefits are graphed on the horizontal axis and wage earnings on the vertical axis, what effect would income tax rate increases have on the indifference curves between benefits and wages?

   a.   They would become steeper.

   b.   They would become flatter.

   c.   They would become more convex.

   d.   The would eventually become upward sloping.

17. Firms may be able to offer employees an extra dollar in employee benefits and reduce wage earning by less than a dollar if

   a.   the tax and insurance payments made by firms are based on a percentage of their total compensation.

   b.   a more attractive tradeoff between wages and benefits attracts workers that are more stable and hence involve lower hiring, screening, and training costs.

   c.   employees prefer having the discretion over spending that comes with receiving compensation in the form of wages.

   d.   all of the above.

18. The hedonic wage theory of employee benefits typically assumes that
   a.   firms are well informed about the compensation packages offered by their rivals.
   b.   workers have a number of employment opportunities from which to choose.
   c.   workers are offered a certain level of compensation and then are free to decide how it is split between wage and employee benefits.
   d.   all of the above.

19. Employers that tailor their compensation packages to include a relatively large proportion of employee benefits will tend to attract workers that
   a.   have steeper indifference curves (assuming benefits are plotted on the horizontal axis and wage earnings on the vertical axis).
   b.   tend to be older and have higher family incomes.
   c.   tend to be more present oriented.
   d.   both **a** and **b**.

20. If workers are mobile and well informed about the compensation packages available at different firms, the mandated provision of employee benefits (e.g., health insurance) will tend to
   a.   make all workers better off.
   b.   make all workers worse off.
   c.   make all firms worse off.
   d.   make workers worse off if the reduction in wages that is necessary for firms to provide the benefits exceeds what workers are willing to pay for the benefits.

Compensating Wage Differentials and Layoffs (Appendix 8A)

In answering Questions **21–23**, please refer to Figure 8-4. Point *a* shows the unconstrained labor/leisure choice for an individual with no nonlabor income that faces a market wage of $4 per hour. The maximum time available is 400 hours. Leisure time is denoted by *L*, work hours by *H*, income by *Y*, and utility by *U*.

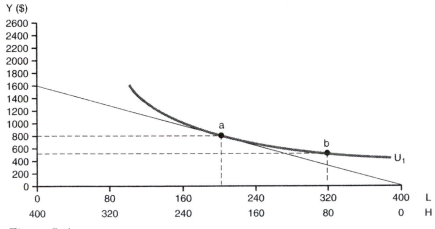

Figure 8-4

21. In Figure 8-4 the optimal number of work hours for this individual is 200 hours. Which of the following statements is true about this point?
   a.   The choice may involve the person being laid off for part of the period.
   b.   The choice may involve the person being laid off for part of the period provided the wage adjusts to reflect a compensating differential.
   c.   The choice reflects a desire for part-time work.
   d.   The choice reflects a desire for full-time work.

22. Suppose that the individual is offered a job that involves only 80 work hours per period because of a predictable temporary layoff. What is the compensating wage differential required to keep the worker at the level of utility consistent with the unconstrained choice? In other words, what compensating differential would allow the person to attain point b? (Note that point b has the coordinates $H = 80$, $Y = \$500$.)

    a. $2.25
    b. $6.25
    c. $180
    d. $300

23. If one were to draw the budget constraint consistent with compensating differential required when work hours are constrained to 80, the vertical intercept of that budget constraint would be

    a. $1,780.
    b. $1,900.
    c. $2,100.
    d. $2,500.

    In answering Questions **24–25**, please refer to Figure 8-5 which shows an individual's relationship between income (Y) and utility. The wage rate is constant at $20. Work hours are denoted by H. Suppose the individual is offered a job that involves uncertain layoffs. In this job the person will work 50 hours half of the time and 450 hours the other half of the time.

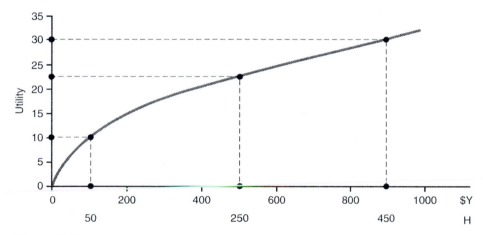

Figure 8-5

24. The average level of utility experienced by this person would be

    a.   20.
    b.   22.5.
    c.   250.
    d.   500.

25. If instead of the job with uncertain layoffs, the person was offered a job that involved 250 hours of work with certainty, the average level of utility would

    a.   decrease since the person is risk averse.
    b.   increase since the person is risk averse.
    c.   increase unless a compensating differential developed to make the two jobs yield the same average level of utility.
    d.   both **b** and **c**.

■ Problems

The Hedonic Theory of Wages and the Assumption of Perfect Mobility

26. Figure 8-6 represents the matching process between employers and employees that occurs when working conditions differ across jobs. The curves labeled A_1 and B_2 refer to indifference curves between the wage and risk for two individuals, while the curves X and Y refer to isoprofit curves for two firms. Suppose that both workers are well informed about the wage/risk combinations offered at different workplaces.

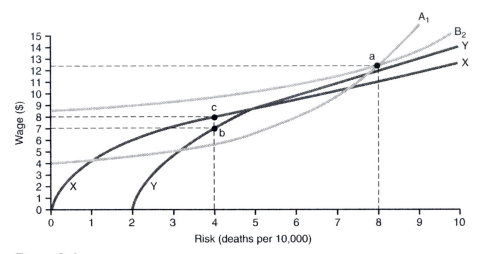

Figure 8-6

26a. Suppose that person B is mobile, but person A is constrained to work only for firm Y. If firm Y offers the wage and risk combination indicated by point a (Risk = 8, Wage = $12.25) to all workers, what effect does the lack of alternative offers have on person A's level of utility (relative to what could be attained if person A was mobile)?

26b. Given the situation in Question **26a**, what effect would a regulation that reduced risk to 4 deaths per 10,000 workers have on worker A's level of utility?

26c. What effect would a regulation that reduced risk to 4 deaths per 10,000 workers have on person B's level of utility? Would the effect of the regulation be better or worse if B was constrained to work for employer Y?

The Hedonic Theory of Wages and the Assumption of Perfect Information

27. Figure 8-7 represents the matching process between employers and employees that occurs when working conditions differ across jobs. The curves labeled A_1, A_2, and A_3 refer to indifference curves between the wage and risk of injury for one individual. The curve OC refers to the offer curve formed by the isoprofit curves of many different employers. The matching process shown in Figure 8-7 assumes that the worker is perfectly mobile but imperfectly informed about the degree of risk associated with a particular job. In particular, suppose that the worker receives a wage of approximately $10.60 and thinks that he or she is being exposed to a risk level of 3 deaths per 10,000 workers (point a) when in fact the actual level of risk is 7 deaths per 10,000 workers (point b). Also assume that the firms know the degree of risk actually associated with a particular job, but are not aware of the worker's misconception.

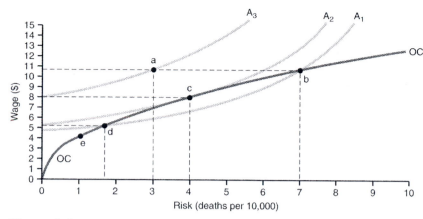

Figure 8-7

27a. Suppose that the government does a study, learns about the worker's misconception, and decides to regulate a reduction in risk. What would be the optimal level of risk exposure to allow? What wage would person A receive when exposed to the optimal level of risk?

27b. What would be the lowest level of risk exposure the government could set without actually making the worker worse off?

27c. Assuming the results of the government study are not made public, would person A be in favor of a regulation limiting risk exposure to 1 death per 10,000 workers per year?

27d. Now suppose the worker is perfectly informed and mobile. What wage/risk combination would he or she choose?

27e. Would a perfectly informed and mobile worker support a regulation limiting risk exposure to 1 death per 10,000 workers per year?

The Benefits and Costs of Reduced Risk

28. Figure 8-8 represents the matching process between employers and employees that occurs when working conditions differ across jobs. The curve labeled A_2 refers to the indifference curve between the wage and risk of injury for one individual while the curve OC refers to the offer curve formed by the isoprofit curves of many different employers. The matching process shown in Figure 8-7 assumes that the worker is perfectly informed and perfectly mobile. The utility maximizing choice for person A is a job with a wage of $8 and a risk level of 4 (point *a*). Now consider a regulation that would mandate a decrease in risk exposure to 1 death per 10,000 workers.

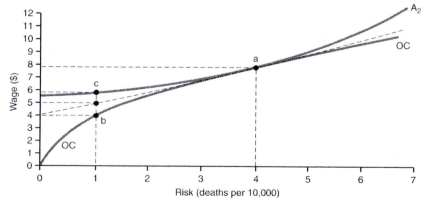

Figure 8-8

28a. Approximately how much per hour would person A be willing to pay for such a risk reduction?

28b. How much per hour would it cost firms to comply with the regulation?

28c. Would such a regulation pass a benefit/cost test?

28d. Empirical studies of compensating differentials attempt to measure the tradeoff between wage and risk (holding all else constant) based on people's actual choices. In Figure 8-8, at person A's actual choice, the rate at which person A (and A's employer) are willing to trade off wages and risk is given by the slope of the dashed line. What is the slope of this line?

28e. In actually carrying out benefit/cost studies of various safety regulations, the observed tradeoffs between wages and risk are extrapolated to measure the benefits associated with the regulation. If the tradeoff between wages and risk implicit at point *a* is assumed to be constant for any change in risk, how much would one predict person A would be willing to pay for a risk reduction to 1 death per 10,000 workers?

28f. Does the extrapolation in **28e** overstate or understate person A's actual willingness to pay for such a risk reduction? Why does the difference occur? What are the implications for benefit/cost studies of safety regulations?

Hedonic Wage Theory and Employee Benefits

29. Consider a worker that ranks combinations of employee benefits (*E*) and wages (*W*) according to the utility function

$$U = E^{\alpha}W^{\beta},$$

where α and β are positive constants and *U* is the index of satisfaction. Suppose that firms are able to remain competitive (i.e., keep profits at zero) if they offer $90 in wages and no employee benefits. If they offer benefits, wages must be reduced by 75 cents for every dollar of benefits offered. Suppose that currently, the firm is offering a compensation package of $40 in benefits and $60 in wages.

29a. Suppose an individual's preferences are such that $\alpha = 1$ and $\beta = 2$ (i.e., they give more weight to wages than to benefits in the ranking process). Why might such a weighting occur?

29b. What is the utility level associated with the initial compensation package?

29c. How much would this individual be willing to give up for a $20 increase in benefits? What would such an increase in benefits cost the firm? Would the worker be made better off by such an increase in benefits?

29d. Suppose that workers are now given more freedom over the choice of benefits so that α and β are both given an equal weight of one. Given the original compensation package, how much would the individual be willing to give up for a $20 increase in benefits? What would such an increase in benefits cost the firm? Would the worker be made better off by such an increase in benefits?

Compensating Wage Differentials and Layoffs (Appendix 8A)

30. Consider a worker who ranks combinations of leisure hours (L) and income (Y) according to the utility function

$$U = L^{\alpha}Y^{\beta},$$

where α and β are positive constants and U is the index of satisfaction. Suppose $\alpha = 2$ and $\beta = 1$, the total time available (T) is 300 hours, the wage rate (W) is \$4, and the level of nonlabor income (V) is \$0. In such a situation, the optimal number of leisure hours is 200, and the optimal number of work hours (H) is 100. When the person works 100 hours, the resulting level of income is \$400.

30a. What is the level of utility associated with the unconstrained choice of leisure hours?

30b. Now suppose that this individual is forced through additional layoffs to consume 250 leisure hours. What must the level of income be for this individual to stay at the level of utility that was attainable before the additional layoffs?

30c. What wage rate would make it possible for the individual to attain the level of income found in **30b**? What is the compensating differential associated with the firm's higher layoff policy?

*30d. Redo Questions **30b** and **30c** assuming the person derives utility from consuming leisure and income in fixed proportions, where the proportion is \$2 of income for every one hour of leisure. Note that if utility is generated in this way, once the person is at the designated proportion, increases in leisure that are not accompanied by increases in income will not increase utility. Similarly, increases in income that are not accompanied by increases in leisure will not increase utility. Such a situation means that leisure and income are viewed as perfect complements.

*30e. How did the change in preferences affect the size of the compensating differential associated with constrained work hours? Explain the intuition behind your findings.

*31. Consider a worker with a utility function given by the equation

$$U = \sqrt{Y},$$

where Y is total income and U is the level of utility. Assume the individual receives no nonlabor income.

*31a. Suppose that Job A pays \$5 per hour and involves working 5 hours per day every day during the year. What is the level of utility the person will attain on a daily basis? What will be the average level of utility attained (per day) during the year?

*31b. Suppose that Job B also pays \$5 per hour but involves working 2 hours per day 50% of the year, and 8 hours per day the other 50% of the year. How many work hours will the person average (per day) during the year?

*31c. What level of utility will be attained during the 2-hour days? What level of utility will be attained during the 8-hour days? What will be the average level of utility attained (per day) during the year?

*31d. Will the typical worker prefer Job A or Job B?

*31e. What wage must the firm with the less desirable schedule pay to just make their job comparable to the job with the more desirable schedule? What would the compensating differential be for accepting the less desirable schedule?

■ Applications

The Effects of Mandating Higher Wages

32. It has been well documented that a wage differential exists between union and non-union workers with the same personal skills (see Chapter 13). In the June 1980 issue of the *American Economic Review*, economists Greg Duncan and James Stafford argued that a significant portion of the differential reflected not the bargaining power of unions, but rather a compensating wage differential. Duncan and Stafford reasoned that the differential arose because workers in unionized industries typically had to work under more structured conditions (e.g., had fewer opportunities to take unscheduled breaks) and at a faster pace than their non-union counterparts. The primary reason for this is that a large proportion of unionized employees work on an assembly line. For the sake of argument, suppose Duncan and Stafford are correct. Shown below in Figure 8-9 are zero-profit isoprofit curves for two firms hiring comparable workers. The isoprofit curve for the union firm is labeled *U*, the isoprofit curve for the non-union firm is labeled *NU*. Also shown in Figure 8-9 are indifference curves for two sets of workers (call these workers A and B). These indifference curves were drawn in such a way that a compensating differential arises between union and non-union work.

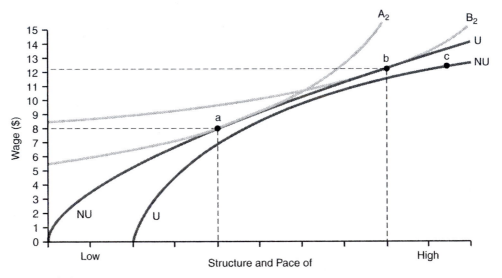

Figure 8-9

32a. Assuming workers are tied to their current employers, analyze the effects of a law requiring non-union firms to pay the union wage rate.

32b. What would be the effect of such a law if workers were perfectly mobile?

32c. Assuming again workers are perfectly mobile, will the law prevent a compensating differential from arising?

32d. Some economists argue that the minimum wage law does not significantly reduce the quantity of labor demanded since firms just adjust working conditions to neutralize the impact on costs of the higher mandated wages. Do you see any similarity between this argument and the effects seen in this problem? When such a legal minimum wage is imposed, what are the effects on the least skilled workers in the labor market?

Health and Safety Regulation When Relative Income Matters

*33. In his book *Microeconomics and Behavior* (New York: McGraw-Hill, 1994, p. 599), economist Robert H. Frank explores the impact that health and safety regulation has in a world where workers care strongly about their levels of income relative to one another. To illustrate the point, Frank proposes a utility function of the form

$$U = Y + S + R(Y),$$

where Y is income, S is a measure of the utility connected with working under safe conditions, and $R(Y)$ is a measure of the utility gained through rank in the income distribution. Suppose that Y equals \$200 if the person works under safe conditions, but rises to \$300 if the person works under unsafe conditions. Suppose S takes on the value of 200 if conditions are safe, and zero if conditions are unsafe. If person A and person B have the same income, $R(Y)$ equals zero for both. However, if person A's income exceeds B's, $R(Y)$ will equal 200 for A but –250 for B. Similarly, if person B's income exceeds A's, $R(Y)$ will equal 200 for person B but –250 for person A.

*33a. Make a table with two rows and two columns that shows the levels of utility available to persons A and B. The rows should show the options (work under safe or unsafe conditions) for person A, while the columns should show the options (work under safe or unsafe conditions) for person B. Within each cell of the table compute the utility that would be derived by each person.

*33b. Assuming each worker is trying to maximize utility, what condition will person A choose? What condition will person B choose?

*33c. Would the workers be better or worse off if the government were to regulate working conditions so that both jobs could be considered safe?

*33d. Discuss the reasonableness of the assumption that a significant determinant of a person's utility is his or her *relative* income.

The Benefits and Cost of Occupational Safety and Health Regulation

34. On March 20, 1992 (p. A3), *The Wall Street Journal* reported on an attempt by the Bush administration to change the way benefit/cost analyses of regulations are performed. Specifically, when computing the cost of a regulation, the administration wanted agencies to take into account the reduction in income that the regulation brings about. The theory behind this suggested change, according to W. Kip Viscusi, an economist not affiliated with the plan, was that "Regulations cost people money . . . and the poorer people become, the more likely they are to get ill or die early." One study cited by the Labor Department estimated "that each \$7.5 million of regulatory expenses could result in one additional death from lowered incomes." In a letter to President Bush 12 Democratic senators called the plan "cruelly insensitive" and said that the plan was based on "a dangerous notion: that America's working men and women have to make a choice between their jobs and their health."

34a. Was the premise of the proposed change sound? Was it insensitive?

34b. While the proposed change would affect calculations of the cost of regulations, the benefit calculations would basically be unchanged. Are there any factors that are typically left out of benefit calculations that perhaps should not be?

Issues Related to the Provision of Employee Benefits

35. According to data presented in Chapter 5, deferred benefits such as pensions make up about 4% of total compensation. Such plans, however, can be very costly to administer, particularly if they are defined benefit pension plans. As discussed in Chapter 5, a pension can be either a defined plan benefit or a defined contribution plan. Under a defined benefit plan employers guarantee the employee a certain monthly payment upon retirement, and then it is up to the firm to make sure the money is put aside to make such payments in future years. However, under a defined contribution plan, employers simply put aside a certain amount of money each pay period for the employee who then invests this money subject to certain rules. Defined contribution plans are typically much easier to administer. Defined benefit plans, on the other hand, typically involve complying with a wide array of government regulations, and so the paperwork associated with such a plan can be very costly.

35a. How would an increase in the paperwork cost of providing a pension plan be modeled using the hedonic wage theory of employee benefits?

35b. Assuming workers have perfect information and are mobile, how would an increase in the cost of administering employee benefits affect the optimal mix of wages and employee benefits in the model?

36. One of the key issues in the debate over health care reform is the tax treatment of employee health benefits. Traditionally, such benefits have not been counted as part of an employee's taxable income. Also, since these benefits are a business expense, they tend to reduce the firm's corporate tax liability. Opponents of the status quo argue that if employees had to pay taxes on the benefits, and if firms could not automatically deduct the cost of benefits from their income, both employees and employers might shop more carefully for health coverage. If employers and employees pay greater attention to the cost of different plans, providers of both health insurance and health services would face greater incentives to keep costs down.

36a. How would the hedonic wage model of employee benefits change if employees had to pay taxes on health care benefits?

36b. How would the hedonic wage model of employee benefits change if employers could count only part of their health care expenses as a business expense?

36c. How would the changes in **36a** and **36b** affect the optimal combination of wage and employee benefits?

37. Throughout the 1990s, it was reported that various forms of family assistance grew even as companies struggled to contain overall benefit costs. Benefits such as paternity leave or work-at-home policies, virtually unheard of in the 1980s, became quite common in the late 1990s.

37a. Discuss why firms would make such changes in their compensation packages.

37b. Although the provision of family benefits has been growing, such benefits do not extend to all working families. Discuss whether such benefits should be mandated for all employees.

The Effect of Unemployment Insurance on Compensating Differentials for Layoffs

38. Consider the scenario discussed in problem **30** where the unconstrained choice of leisure hours was 200. Also suppose that the worker is constrained to consume 250 leisure hours and that these extra 50 leisure hours come about through anticipated layoffs.

38a. If the worker receives a payment of $56 through the unemployment insurance program for the extra time spent on layoff, find the size of the compensating differential that the firm would have to pay for subjecting the worker to these excessive layoffs.

38b. Suppose the firm pays only $30 per worker into the fund used to make the unemployment insurance payment. What would be the consequences for the use of temporary layoffs in the economy?

Chapter 9
Investments in Human Capital: Education and Training

■ Summary

The purpose of Chapter 8 was to provide a framework for thinking about the role that working conditions and employee benefits play in an individual's choice of occupation and employer. But supplying labor involves more than just showing up at a particular employer. What quality of labor will an individual supply? What level of education and training will an individual bring to the labor market? These are the kinds of questions taken up in Chapter 9.

Activities designed to enhance the value of the labor supplied by an individual are considered **investments in human capital**. Specific examples discussed in *Modern Labor Economics* include education and training, migration to locations where labor market opportunities are better, and job search. Each of these activities can be classified as an investment because they involve initial costs that the individual then hopes to more than recover over time. The term *human capital* is used to emphasize the similarity between these activities and a firm's investment in new plant and equipment (physical capital). Individual education and training investments are discussed in this chapter, while migration and job search decisions are analyzed in Chapter 10. Job search issues are also taken up within the context of the unemployment discussion in Chapter 14.

Investments in physical or human capital will add to an individual's wealth provided the present value of the benefits exceeds the present value of the costs. These investments should continue as long as the marginal benefit of an additional unit of capital exceeds the marginal cost. In the case of education and training investments, the costs include **direct expenses for tuition and books**, **forgone earnings** during the time devoted to education, and **psychic losses** due to the difficulty, stress, and anxiety of schooling. The prospective benefits include higher future earnings, access to more interesting, challenging, or pleasant jobs, the satisfaction that comes with being a more educated person, and the psychic benefits that come from some of the more pleasant aspects of student life.

The benefits and costs of investment in human capital will not occur at the same time, and thus any benefits occurring in the future must be converted to a present value basis before a comparison can be made. After all, a dollar of benefits received today is worth more than a dollar received next year, since dollars received today can be invested. Also, benefits received in the future may not be as valuable as benefits today because there is no guarantee the person will live long enough to enjoy the future benefits.

Letting r be the rate at which the yearly benefits of education (B_1, B_2, . . .) are discounted, and assuming the costs of education (C) all occur in the initial year (year 0), the **present value method** suggests that an educational investment should be undertaken provided

$$\frac{B_1}{1+r} + \frac{B_2}{(1+r)^2} + \cdots + \frac{B_T}{(1+r)^T} > C.$$

The subscripts refer to different years along an interval 1 to T with 1 being the first year after the initial year and T the last. When the benefit values and the discount rate are constant, the entire present value of the benefit stream (PVB) can be found using the formula

$$PVB = B \frac{1 - \dfrac{1}{(1+r)^T}}{r}.$$

This formula is called the **annuity formula** and applies for any value of T. Note that if T is very large, the formula reduces to $PVB = B/r$.

An alternative, but equivalent, approach to evaluating educational investments is the **internal rate of return method**. Under this method, one solves for the discount rate that will just set the present value of the benefits equal to the present value of the costs. If this rate exceeds the discount rate required by the individual (usually the going interest rate on alternative investments), then the investment is considered to be worthwhile.

Both the present value and internal rate of return methods predict that educational investments (e.g., a college education) are more likely (holding all else constant) the lower the values of r and C, and the higher the values of B and T. A lower value of r is a way of saying the person is less present-oriented and more future-oriented, while higher values of T are associated with younger persons. Changes in the value of B and C can typically explain a large part of the change in college enrollments over time. In general, this model predicts that present-oriented people are less likely to go to college than future-oriented people, that most college students will be young (because they receive the benefits from a college education for more years), that college attendance will fall as costs rise, and that college attendance will increase if the gap between earnings of college graduates and high school graduates increases. An additional aspect of cost is the cost of credit, which may vary widely for different potential students; programs that make borrowing easier or cheaper are also likely to increase college enrollments.

Although higher levels of benefits create a greater incentive to make educational investments, the level of B is largely determined by the extent to which educational investments enable a person to earn higher wages. The level of wages associated with any educational investment, however, is determined in part by how many people make the investment—in other words, the supply of educated workers. It is the supply of educated workers, together with the demand for such workers, that determines the wage workers receive, and ultimately the benefits associated with making the investment. When more people attend college, the supply of college-educated workers eventually rises, which (all other things equal) causes the wage to decline, and thus the benefits received may be lower than expected.

After using the basic human capital investment model to discuss investment in a college education, the discussion in the text turns to the relationship between education, earnings, and on-the-job training. The focal point of the discussion is the **age-earnings profiles** of men and women as of 1997. These profiles, presented in graphical form, show the relationship that exists on average between age and earnings for workers with various levels of education.

The age-earnings profiles constructed for men and women display four tendencies. The first tendency is for the average earnings of full-time workers to rise with the level of education. The second tendency is for earnings to rise rapidly with age, then flatten out, and eventually fall. Graphically, this leads to age-earnings profiles that are concave. The third tendency is for higher levels of education to be associated with steeper age-earnings profiles. This steepening leads to the education-related differences in earnings becoming more pronounced as a person ages. Graphically, this shows up as a *fanning out* of the age-earnings profiles. While, the previous three tendencies related to the age-earnings profiles of both men and women, the fourth tendency relates to a comparison of the profiles between men and women. Such a comparison reveals that the profiles for women display less concavity and are less steep than the profiles for men.

How does the human capital investment framework account for these four tendencies? The first tendency, the positive relationship between earnings and education, must occur because without it, there would be little incentive to invest in education.

The second tendency, the concavity of the age-earnings profiles, is attributed to formal or informal on-the-job training. General on-the-job training can be viewed much like any other educational investment. Workers typically pay for such training in the form of lower wages. In return, the workers receive training that they hope will pay off in the form of higher wages and better jobs in the future. This combination of lower wages early on, and higher wages later, forms the initial steep segment of the concave age-earnings profile. However, like any other investment, the chance of fully recovering educational costs decreases as a person ages, holding all else constant. Thus, job training (whether sought by the worker or initiated by the firm) can be expected to decline as the worker ages, with older workers receiving so little training that their skills begin to deteriorate. The leveling off of training opportunities and the resulting deterioration of older worker skills is thought to explain the leveling off, and eventual decline, of the age-earnings profile.

The third tendency, the tendency for more educated workers to display a steeper age-earnings profile, is also thought to be related to on-the-job training. The basic principle is that investments such as job training are more likely the lower the expected costs. Holding all else constant, workers who have completed higher levels of education typically have displayed the ability to learn more quickly. This in turn shortens the training period and lowers the psychic costs of the investment, and so lowers the total cost of the investment. Thus, the higher the level of formal education, the more likely it is that workers will seek out or be offered job training. The tendency of better educated workers to invest more in job training means that their age-earnings profiles will rise more quickly than for less educated workers, thus leading to a fanning out of the age-earnings profiles.

When comparing the age-earnings profiles of men and women, it is clear that the fourth tendency is for women's profiles to be less concave and to fan out less as education rises. This tendency is again thought to be connected to job training opportunities. Because of the role women have traditionally played in child rearing and household production, historically it has been expected that, on average, women will work fewer years for pay. Also, within a given occupation, women have averaged fewer hours of work per week than men. Because of the shorter expected work life of women, the human capital investment model predicts that the benefits to the average women of investing in on-the-job training will be less. Thus, historically women have had less of an incentive to seek out, and firms have had less incentive to offer them job training opportunities at the level received by males. To the extent that job training accounts for the concavity and fanning out of the age-earnings profiles, the model predicts that these effects should be less pronounced for women. However, as the traditional role of women has changed, and their work lives have become less interrupted, the model also predicts that the profiles should start to more closely resemble the patterns displayed by men. This prediction is supported by a comparison of the age-earnings profiles for women in 1999 with those from 1977.

According to the human capital investment framework, longer expected careers for women should also lead to an increased incentive to undertake formal educational investments. Comparisons of college and university graduates by field of study verify a dramatic increase in the percentage of women receiving bachelor's and master's degrees. Also, women have dramatically increased their representation in highly technical fields where it is widely perceived that continuous experience is important.

The presentation of the age-earnings profiles for men and women clearly revealed that higher levels of education tend to be associated with higher earnings. But what is the rate of return on educational investments? Is additional education a good investment? Studies of the monetary costs and benefits of educational investments have typically revealed a real internal rate of return in the range of 5% to 15%, suggesting that education is at least as good an investment over time as stocks, bonds, or real estate. Internal rate of return studies of education are difficult to interpret, however, because of several conflicting biases which affect the data. Most of these biases are connected to the problem of omitted variables (see Appendix 1A).

However, estimates of the rate of return to schooling may be biased in three ways. First, they may be overestimated, because it is not possible to separate the contribution of ability to earnings. This "ability bias" suggests that more-able workers are likely to obtain more schooling (because both the direct and implicit costs of schooling may be less), but these more-able workers would be likely to receive a higher-than-average wage even if they did not obtain more schooling.

Secondly, the rate of return to education may be underestimated for a number of reasons. Some benefits of education are not reflected in productivity but rather in such things as a greater appreciation of life and thus cannot be measured. Typical studies also tend to measure money earnings rather than total compensation, and benefits tend to rise as a percentage of total compensation as earnings rise. Finally, some of the benefits of education are nonmonetary, such as having a more interesting or pleasant job, another return that cannot be quantified.

Thirdly, a subtle and sometimes important source of bias in labor economics is **selection bias** (also known as the selectivity problem). Selection bias occurs when the samples being compared differ in some systematic, but typically unobservable way. For example, someone who ends up as a college graduate is in that group because they chose (selected) to be there. They did this presumably because they did not find the alternatives available to them without a college degree very appealing, perhaps because they had little aptitude for jobs not requiring a degree. Hence, measuring the returns to education by comparing the actual average earnings of different groups will tend to understate the return to those who made the investment (and overstate the return possible for those that did not) due to this "ability bias."

Despite the difficulty in interpreting estimates of the rate of return on educational investments, empirical studies are basically supportive of the notion that additional education is a reasonable investment from an **individual** perspective. Similarly, empirical studies of the labor market experiences of adult women indicate that government training programs generate enough of an earnings increase for the participants to justify government expenditures. But just because additional education may be a reasonable investment from an individual perspective, it does not follow that additional education is a reasonable investment from the perspective of **society** as a whole. This uncertainty is associated with the view that education serves primarily as a **signaling device** in the labor market. For example, if education does nothing to enhance individual skills, but rather simply helps firms to identify which individuals have the highest skills to begin with, then fostering higher levels of education may be unnecessary from a social standpoint.

Example

Consider Figure 9-1 which shows the present value of lifetime earnings (PVE) that firms are willing to offer to workers who have attained different levels of education (E). Those workers who have completed 16 years or more of education (4 or more years after high school) will be offered a wage leading to a present value of lifetime income of $1,600,000 (PVE$_2$), while those completing less than 16 years of education will be offered a wage leading to a present value of lifetime income equal to $800,000 (PVE$_1$).

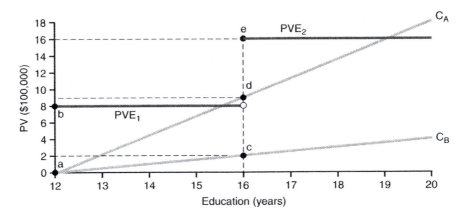

Figure 9-1

Suppose that the total cost of various levels of education is given by the equations

$$C_A = 225,000(E - 12) \quad \text{and} \quad C_B = 50,000(E - 12),$$

where the subscripts A and B refer to two types of workers. Type A workers are low productivity workers while type B workers are high productivity workers. These total cost schedules are shown as lines C_A and C_B in Figure 9-1.

Note that at 12 years of education the net benefit (i.e., the difference between the present value of lifetime earnings and the total cost of additional education) for type A workers is $800,000 (the difference between points a and b), whereas at 16 years of education the net benefit falls to $700,000 (the difference between points d and e). Consequently, the best choice for type A workers is 12 years of education. In contrast, the net benefit for type B workers is $800,000 at 12 years of education and $1,400,000 at 16 years of education (the difference between points c and e). Clearly, type B workers do better by attaining 16 years of education. Given the position of the cost curves in Figure 9-1, type A workers voluntarily choose not to attain a college degree, while type B workers do attain the degree. As a result, even if additional education does nothing to enhance worker productivity, a college degree serves a useful purpose in that it enables employers to accurately distinguish low-productivity workers from high-productivity workers.

Note that in order for a college degree to play an effective signaling role, the cost to the workers of acquiring the signal must be strongly and inversely related to the worker's inherent ability. This is plausible if the psychic costs of education are included as part of the total cost of additional years of education. Individuals with low ability are likely to find additional years of education more challenging, stressful, and unpleasant than those with high ability.

Finally, note that from the perspective of society as a whole, raising the level of education that is necessary to obtain the higher income stream would result in increased costs for some workers but no increase in benefits for society. For example, if the threshold for the higher income stream were made 18 years of education instead of 16, high-productivity workers would attain the threshold amount while low-productivity workers would not. Type B workers would gain $1,200,000 by investing in 18 years of schooling versus a maximum of $800,000 if they did not. In contrast, type A workers would gain $800,000 at 12 years of schooling but only $250,000 at 18 years of schooling. Consequently, the higher educational threshold would impose additional costs on type B workers without changing the effectiveness of education as a signal.

Although evidence on whether schooling serves primarily as a signaling device or whether it actually enhances worker productivity is not conclusive at this point, it is important to note that from an individual perspective, the distinction is unimportant since in either case employers will be willing to offer higher earnings to those who complete higher levels of education. From society's point of view, however, the signaling hypothesis is important because it suggests that devoting more resources to education is not necessarily a good investment. Still, the fact that employers are willing to pay more for educated workers suggests that even if education is just a signal, it is an effective signal and one that is less costly to use than any other signal that is available to firms.

The appendices to Chapter 9 relate to the relationship between education and earnings. Appendix 9A builds on the notion that the level of wages associated with any educational investment is determined by the forces of supply and demand. When the investment in education involves a time commitment of several years, however, it is important to note that the forces of demand and supply may not work to determine the market clearing wage as smoothly or as rapidly as the demand and supply model presented in Chapter 2 suggested. The extensive time needed to train new workers for some occupations means that the quantity of labor supplied cannot adjust quickly to changes in the wage. These lags in the supply response in turn can lead to **boom-and-bust cycles** in which wages and employment opportunities fluctuate over a rather wide range when compared to other occupations that require less-extensive training.

These cycles can be depicted through an extension of the demand and supply model known as the **cobweb model**. Failure to realize that such cycles may be a normal part of the adjustment process in some labor markets may lead the government to try to smooth out the cycles through subsidizing the supply of workers at certain times. The cobweb model, however, suggests that such attempts may only make the cycles more pronounced.

Example (Appendix 9A)

Consider a labor market where the demand and supply curves for highly trained workers are given by the equations

$$L_D = 90 - 3W,$$
$$L_S = 2W,$$

where L represents the number of workers, W is the wage, and the subscripts D and S are used to distinguish between the quantity of labor demanded and the quantity of labor supplied. These curves appear as lines D_1 and S in Figure 9-2.

If the market is initially in equilibrium, the market-clearing wage occurs where the quantity of labor demanded equals the quantity of labor supplied.

$$L_D = L_S \implies 90 - 3W = 2W \implies W^* = \$18 \implies L^* = 36.$$

The market-clearing wage (W^*) and employment level (L^*) associated with the initial demand and supply curves are indicated by point a in Figure 9-2.

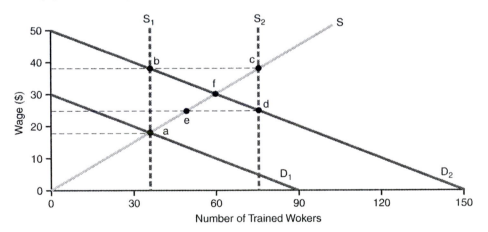

Figure 9-2

Now suppose that the demand for labor in this particular occupation increases to

$$L_D = 150 - 3W.$$

The new demand schedule results in a parallel shift of the demand curve to line D_2 in Figure 9-1. Given this new demand curve, the market-clearing wage should rise to \$30 and the new equilibrium employment level should be 60 (point f) since

$$150 - 3W = 2W \implies W^* = \$30 \implies L^* = 60.$$

However, if no new quantity of labor could be immediately supplied because of lags in the training of new workers, the wage would rise to \$38 (point b) since

$$150 - 3W = 36 \implies W^* = \$38.$$

With the number of trained workers fixed at 36 for the time being, it is as if the supply curve temporarily becomes line S_1. If workers shortsightedly based their training plans on this new wage, the quantity of workers that will be supplied when training is complete will equal 76 (point c) since

$$L_S = 2W = 2(38) \Rightarrow L_S = 76.$$

Once training is complete and 76 trained workers exist, it will be as if the supply curve is now temporarily given by the line S_2, since once workers are trained they may be reluctant to leave that occupation. With the supply of workers fixed for the time being at 76, the market clearing wage now falls to $24.67 (point d) since

$$150 - 3W = 76 \Rightarrow W^* = \$24.67.$$

If workers again shortsightedly base their training plans on this new wage, the quantity of workers that will be supplied when training is complete will equal 49.33 (point e) since

$$L_S = 2W = 2(24.67) \Rightarrow L_S = 49.33.$$

Note that instead of following a smooth path from the original wage and employment level of $18 and 36 (point a) to the new market-clearing wage and employment level of $30 and 60 (point f), the wage has cycled from $18 to $38 to $24.67, and the employment level has cycled from 36 to 76 to 49.33. Note that this spiraling effect that is occurring around the new market-clearing values (hence the name cobweb model) is bringing the market closer to a true equilibrium (where there is no tendency for change). The cycle gradually dampens out any time the magnitude of the slope of the demand curve (as it appears on the graph) is less than the slope of the supply curve. Note that in Figure 9-1, the demand curve slope has a magnitude of one-third while the supply curve has a slope of one-half. On the other hand, if the slope magnitudes were reversed so that demand was steeper than supply, the alternating shortages and surpluses would worsen over time and the market would cycle away from the new equilibrium value.

Can the government help to dampen the boom-and-bust cycles? In most cases, the answer is no. For example, suppose that when the first shortage of workers appeared in response to the demand shift and the wage was bid up to $38, the government intervened and subsidized the training of workers in this occupation. The result would have been a shift in the supply curve S to the right of its initial position. Consequently, more than 76 workers eventually would have been trained, and the market then would have overshot the new equilibrium employment level by an even wider margin, making the next downturn in the cycle even worse.

Note that in the above example, it was not only the lags in the supply of new workers that caused the boom-and-bust cycles, but also the myopic or shortsighted behavior of workers who based their decision to train for a certain occupation on the basis of the current wage, ignoring the effect their decisions may have on the future behavior of the wage. An alternative assumption is that people base their decision to train for a certain occupation on the basis of current wages and the past movement of wages. Such an extension would be called an **adaptive expectations** model and in general would lead to smaller cycles. On the other hand, if workers eventually understood exactly how the model worked and based their supply decisions on a perfect prediction of what the future wage would be, there would be no cycles, rather just an immediate movement to the new market-clearing wage. A model in which workers know the model and so can make perfect predictions about the future wage is called a **rational expectations** model. One constructive role government can play in labor markets where training takes time is to provide information to workers suggesting that the current wage is not a good indicator of the future wage. In so doing, this may help to foster rational expectations among workers in that market and speed the adjustment to the true market clearing values.

Appendix 9B adapts the **hedonic theory of wages** framework presented in Chapter 8 to explain the connection between higher levels of education and higher wage earnings. While it was emphasized in Chapter 9 that higher wages must accompany educational investments to induce workers to make the investments, this framework is valuable in emphasizing the role that employers play in actually creating such incentives. The matching of employers and employees in this model is identical to that presented in

Chapter 8 when workers had to contend with jobs offering different risks of fatal injury. The similarity in analyses suggests that the higher wages associated with education can also be viewed as a **compensating differential** workers receive for undertaking the costs of education.

■ Review Questions

Choose the letter that represents the **BEST** response.

The Benefits and Costs of an Educational Investment

1. Which of the following benefits is typically considered to be part of an individual's return on his or her educational investment?
    a. higher wages
    b. increased likelihood of on-the-job training
    c. increased satisfaction from participation in nonmarket activities
    d. all of the above

2. Which of the following costs is typically considered to be associated with an individual's educational investment?
    a. expenditures for tuition and books
    b. earnings forgone while in school
    c. the effort expended attending class and studying
    d. all of the above

3. Benefits that are received in the future must be discounted (put on a present value basis) before they can be compared with benefits that accrue today because
    a. inflation erodes the purchasing power of dollars received in the future.
    b. dollars received today can be invested.
    c. the future is uncertain, people prefer to consume benefits earlier.
    d. both **b** and **c**.

4. Assuming the discount rate is 6%, what is the present value of $1,000 received 10 years from now?
    a. $558.39
    b. $564.47
    c. $625
    d. $943.40

5. Suppose that a college education will raise the average earnings of a typical individual by $10,000, relative to those of a high school graduate, over each of the next 40 years. If the interest rate is 6%, what is the present value of the monetary benefits to a college education?
    a. $150,462.97
    b. $166,666.67
    c. $377,358.49
    d. $424,000

6. Consider a training program that will result in a worker receiving a one-time bonus of $2,500 two years from now. The cost of the training program is $2,000. What is the internal rate of return on this investment?
   a.   4.9%
   b.   11.8%
   c.   21.4%
   d.   25%

7. Holding all else constant, which of the following factors would tend to make educational investments more attractive?
   a.   An increase in the discount rate (r)
   b.   An increase in the wage earned by high school graduates
   c.   An increase in the age at which people retire
   d.   A decrease in the scores earned by high school students on tests like the Scholastic Aptitude Test (SAT)

8. According to data presented in the text, college enrollment rates for women rose during the 1970s even though the average earnings of college graduates fell relative to high school graduates during this period. These facts do not contradict the human capital theory of investment because
   a.   the discount rate used by women was rising.
   b.   as women have worked more outside the home, the time period over which the investment can be recovered has lengthened.
   c.   the cost of college was falling.
   d.   all of the above.

Signaling in the Labor Market

In answering Questions **9–12** please refer to Figure 9-3, which shows the present value of lifetime earnings (PVE) firms are willing to offer to workers who have attained different levels of education. Those workers who have completed 16 years or more of education (4 or more years after high school) will be offered a wage leading to a present value of lifetime income of $2,000,000 (PVE$_2$), while those completing less than 16 years of education will be offered a wage leading to a present value of lifetime income equal to $1,000,000 (PVE$_1$). Lines C_A and C_B show the total cost of different levels of education for two types of workers. Type A workers are low-productivity workers while type B workers are high-productivity workers.

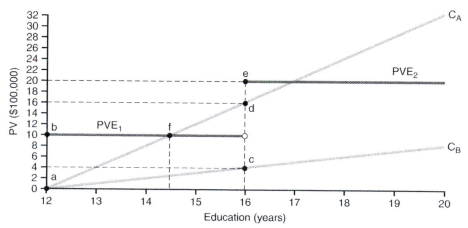

Figure 9-3

9. The optimal level of education for a type A worker is
   a. 12 years.
   b. 14.5 years.
   c. 16 years.
   d. 20 years.

10. The optimal level of education for a type B worker is
    a. 12 years.
    b. 14.5 years.
    c. 16 years.
    d. 20 years.

11. Based on the levels of education chosen by each group of workers, one can conclude that
    a. 16 years of education is not an effective signal since no worker has an incentive to attain that level of education.
    b. 16 years of education is not an effective signal since all workers have an incentive to attain that level of education.
    c. making 16 years of education the qualification for the higher paying job will effectively distinguish high-productivity workers from low-productivity workers.
    d. there is no way that educational attainment can effectively distinguish high-productivity workers from low-productivity workers.

12. From society's point of view, the optimal level of education to distinguish high-productivity workers from low-productivity workers would be
    a. slightly more than 12 years.
    b. slightly more than 14.5 years.
    c. 16 years.
    d. when education only has signaling value, there is no optimal level from society's point of view.

Education, Earnings, and Post-Schooling Investments

13. Age-earnings profiles, especially those for men, tend to be very steep early on and then flatten out. According to the human capital investment framework, this occurs because
    a. on-the-job training investments have a higher payoff for younger workers.
    b. on-the-job training investments that lead to the acquisition of general skill will be paid for by workers in the form of lower wages.
    c. on-the-job training investments lead to new skills and subsequently higher wages.
    d. all of the above.

14. Age-earnings profiles for college-educated individuals, especially men, tend to be steeper than the age-earnings profiles for individuals that only complete high school. According to the human capital investment framework, this difference occurs because
    a. the steepening is necessary as an incentive for individuals to invest in a college education.
    b. college graduates have shown that they can learn more easily than high school graduates, and so are more likely to also seek out (or be offered) on-the-job training.
    c. college graduates acquire more general skills that tend not to diminish over time.
    d. both **a** and **b**.

15. Age-earnings profiles computed for women as of 1999, while lower and less steep than the comparable profiles for men, are clearly steeper than those computed for women as of 1977. According to the human capital investment framework, this change is attributable to

   a.   changes in women's labor force participation that have led to longer worklives for women.

   b.   increased acquisition by women of on-the-job training.

   c.   increased willingness of women to pursue post-graduate education.

   d.   both **a** and **b**.

Is Education a Good Investment?

16. Education is a good investment for an individual if

   a.   workers with higher levels of education tend to earn higher wages.

   b.   given the individual's discount rate, the present value of the benefits of the investment are greater than or equal to the present value of the costs of the investment.

   c.   the internal rate of return associated with the investment is positive.

   d.   all of the above.

17. Rate of return estimates for educational investments will be biased upward if

   a.   the psychic benefits associated with educational investments are included in the measure of benefits.

   b.   the sample contains people with different inherent abilities.

   c.   differences in ability are not accounted for.

   d.   firms use educational investments as a way to screen for high-productivity applicants.

18. Failure to account for the comparative advantage people have in different occupations (the selectivity problem) when estimating the rate of return on educational investments will result in

   a.   a small upward bias in the rate of return.

   b.   a downward bias in the rate of return attained by those who actually made the investment.

   c.   an upward bias in the rate of return that is possible for those who did not make the investment.

   d.   both **b** and **c**.

19. From society's point of view, encouraging investments in the expansion or upgrading of education may waste scarce resources if

   a.   educational activities do not enhance productivity, rather they only serve to signal those individuals who are inherently more productive.

   b.   education enhances productivity, but the marginal rate of return to society on educational investments is no greater than the marginal rate of return on other forms of investment (such as investment in physical capital).

   c.   the internal rate of return on educational investments just equals the market interest rate.

   d.   all of the above.

A Cobweb Model of Labor Market Adjustment (Appendix 9A)

In answering Questions **20–24**, please refer to Figure 9-4, which depicts the demand (*D*) and supply (*S*) curves for highly trained workers in a particular occupation. Assume the demand curve has shifted out from D_1 to D_2 and that there is a significant lag in the quantity of labor that can be supplied because of the time needed to train new workers. Also suppose individuals myopically base their decision to train for this occupation on the current wage.

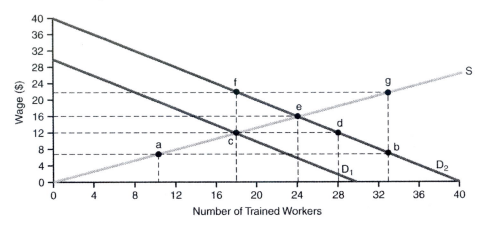

Figure 9-4

20. Assuming the market was initially in equilibrium, what is the size of the shortage created by the shift in demand from D_1 to D_2?
    a. The distance from point *a* to point *b* (22.5 workers)
    b. The distance from point *c* to point *d* (10 workers)
    c. The distance from point *c* to point *e* (6 workers)
    d. The distance from point *f* to point *g* (15 workers)

21. If there can be no immediate change in the quantity of labor supplied because of a lag in the training of new workers, what effect will the demand shift have on the market-clearing wage?
    a. The wage will rise from point *c* to point *e* ($4 increase).
    b. The wage will rise from point *c* to point *f* ($10 increase).
    c. The wage will remain unchanged.
    d. The wage will fall from point *c* to point *b* ($5 decrease).

22. If workers myopically base their training plans on the current wage, the demand shift will eventually result in a surplus of workers equal to
    a. the distance between point *a* and point *b* (22.5 workers).
    b. the distance between point *c* and point *d* (10 workers).
    c. the distance between point *b* and point *e* (9 workers).
    d. the distance between point *f* and point *g* (15 workers).

23. Assuming trained workers choose to stay in their chosen occupation, the surplus of workers that results from the myopic response to the initial wage change will cause
    a. the wage to fall from point *g* to point *b* ($15 decrease).
    b. the wage to fall from point *g* to point *e* ($6 decrease).
    c. the wage to fall from point *e* to point *b* ($9 decrease).
    d. the wage to increase from point *e* to point *g* ($6 increase).

24. In this example, the market moves farther and farther from the true equilibrium wage and employment level as the process continues. This result occurs because

   a.   the magnitude of the slope of the demand curve is greater than the slope of the supply curve.

   b.   workers are assumed not to have rational expectations.

   c.   workers are adapting their expectations to the boom and bust cycles.

   d.   both **a** and **b**.

A Hedonic Model of Earnings and Educational Level (Appendix 9B)

In answering Questions **25–27,** please refer to Figure 9-5. The curves A_2 and B_2 refer to indifference curves between the wage and the level of non-compulsory schooling for two individuals, while the curves Y and Z refer to zero-profit isoprofit curves for two firms.

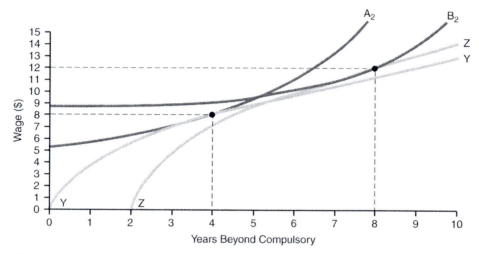

Figure 9-5

25. In Figure 9-5 the indifference curves between the wage and the level of education are drawn upward sloping. This is consistent with the statement that

   a.   individuals prefer more education and more wages.

   b.   more education is costly, and so the only way to keep worker utility constant is for the wage to rise.

   c.   more educated workers are more productive, and so they can demand higher wages.

   d.   more education signals higher productivity workers, who in turn must be paid more.

26. In Figure 9-5, the isoprofit curves between the wage and education are drawn upward sloping because

   a.   more education may signal higher-productivity workers, and higher-productivity workers must be paid more.

   b.   education causes workers to be more productive, and more-productive workers must be paid more.

   c.   highly educated workers demand more in wages so that they can recover their educational costs.

   d.   either **a** or **b**.

27. Figure 9-5 shows that those workers obtaining 4 additional years of education will be paid $8, while those obtaining 8 additional years of education will be paid approximately $12.25. This outcome is the result of a matching process where

   a.   those workers finding additional years of education most difficult are matched with those firms willing to pay the most for additional years of education.

   b.   those workers who are less averse to additional years of education are matched with firms where education adds greatly to productivity.

   c.   workers are mobile enough to have various employment opportunities.

   d.   both **b** and **c**.

■ Problems

The Benefits and Costs of Educational Investments:
The Present Value Method

28. Consider an individual who currently earns $20,000 as an unskilled laborer. Suppose that by taking courses full time at a community college for one year, the person can qualify for a more skilled job paying $23,000 that is guaranteed to last for 10 years (after which the person would retire). Assume the cost of tuition and books at the community college for one year is $2,000 and that the current interest rate is 6%. Is this a good investment?

The Benefits and Costs of an Educational Investment:
The Internal Rate of Return Method

29. Consider a worker who is offered a salary bonus of $2,000 for each of the next two years if he or she enrolls in a job training program this year. The total cost to the worker, including any forgone earnings, is $3,500.

*29a.   What is the internal rate of return on this investment?

29b.   Would this be a good investment for someone with a discount rate of 6%?

29c.   What is the highest discount rate a person could have and still find this investment attractive? Is it possible for a person to have a higher discount rate than the market interest rate?

29d.   Why are older workers less likely to seek out, or be offered, on-the-job training opportunities? How does this affect the shape of the typical age-earnings profile?

The Relationship Between Expected Inflation and the Discounting of
Future Benefits from Education

30. In evaluating educational investments in which costs are incurred in the current year (year 0), but benefits accrue over future years (years 1 through *T*) it important that the future benefits be discounted. Dollars accessible today are more valuable since they can be consumed today with certainty or invested at some rate of interest. Therefore, dollars received in the future must first be discounted if they are to be fairly compared with current dollars. However, dollars received in the future may also be less valuable than dollars today if inflation occurs, raising the general level of prices and reducing the purchasing power of future dollars.

In Chapter 2, adjustments for inflation were discussed in the context of converting nominal wages to real wages. To adjust nominal values to real values, one simply divides the nominal dollar values by the price index and then multiplies the result by 100. The result is a measure that can be compared to dollar values in the base year of the price index.

When inflation is anticipated, it is also important to note that anyone loaning (investing) money will typically require that a premium for expected inflation be built into the interest rate payable on the investment so as to assure a certain real rate of return after accounting for inflation. The nominal (market) interest rate is converted to the real interest rate by the formula

$$i = \frac{r - p}{1 + p},$$

where i is the real interest rate, r is the market interest rate (expressed as a fraction) and p is the expected rate of inflation (also expressed as a fraction). When expected inflation is small, the above formula is often approximated by the simple formula $i = r - p$.

Table 9-1 lists the costs and benefits associated with an educational investment. The price indices presented in the table reflect the expectation that in each of the two years after the investment is made, inflation will be 4%. The market interest rate throughout the period is assumed to be constant at 6% per year.

Table 9-1

Year	Price Index	Costs	Benefits
Year 0	100	$10,000	$ 0
Year 1	104	$ 0	$6,000
Year 2	108.16	$ 0	$6,000

30a. Using the market interest rate as the discount rate, convert the nominal values of the costs and benefits to present values. Does the present value of the benefits exceed the present value of the costs? If so, by how much?

30b. Compute the real rate of interest expected in each year to five decimal places.

30c. Using the expected price indices, convert the nominal values of the costs and benefits to real values.

30d Using the real interest rate as the discount rate, convert the real values of the costs and benefits to present values. Does the present value of the benefits exceed the present value of the costs? If so, by how much?

30e. Compare your answers to **30a** and **30d**. Is it necessary to convert all nominal values to real values in order to accurately assess the costs and benefits of educational investments?

Measuring the Rate of Return to Educational Investments

31. According to studies cited in the text, estimates of the individual rate of return on educational investments range (in real terms) from 5% to 15%.

31a. If you knew that these studies suffered from selection bias, would you be more inclined to believe the upper or lower range of these estimates?

31b. What similarities do you see between the notions of selection bias and ability bias?

Signaling and the Labor Market

32. Consider Figure 9-6 which shows the present value of lifetime earnings (PVE) firms are willing to offer to workers who have attained different levels of education. Those workers who have completed 16 years or more of education (4 or more years after high school) will be offered a wage leading to a present value of lifetime income of $2,000,000 (PVE$_2$), while those completing less than 16 years of education will be offered a wage leading to a present value of lifetime income equal to $1,000,000 (PVE$_1$). Lines C_A and C_B show the total cost of different levels of education for two types of workers. Type A workers are low-productivity workers while type B workers are high-productivity workers.

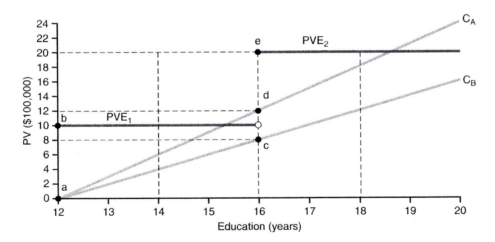

Figure 9-6

32a. What is the net benefit (i.e., the difference between the PVE and the cost of education) a type A person would derive from attaining 16 years of education? What would be the net benefit for A from 12 years of education? What is the optimal level of education for a type A person?

32b. What is the net benefit a type B person would derive from attaining 16 years of education? What would be the net benefit for B from 12 years of education? What is the optimal level of education for a type B person?

32c. Is 16 years of education an effective way to distinguish low-productivity workers from high-productivity workers?

32d. Suppose firms lowered the cutoff for the higher wage job to 14 years of education. What level of education would type A workers attain? What level of education would type B workers attain? Would the level of education be an effective signal of worker productivity?

32e. Suppose firms raised the cutoff for the higher wage job to 18 years of education. What level of education would type A workers attain? What level of education would type B workers attain? Would the level of education be an effective signal of worker productivity?

The Cobweb Model (Appendix 9A)

33. Consider a labor market where the demand and supply curves for highly trained workers are given by the equations

$$L_D = 10 - 0.5W,$$
$$L_S = 0.5W,$$

where L represents the number of workers, W is the wage, and the subscripts D and S are used to distinguish between the quantity of labor demanded and the quantity of labor supplied.

33a. Find the initial market-clearing wage and employment level.

33b. Now suppose that the demand for labor in this particular occupation increases to

$$L_D = 12 - 0.5W.$$

Find the new market-clearing wage and employment level.

33c. Suppose that because of lags in the training of new workers, no new quantity of labor could be immediately supplied in response to the demand shift. With the number of trained workers fixed for the time being at the original employment level, calculate what would initially happen to the wage.

33d. If workers shortsightedly based their training plans on the new wage (computed in Question **33c**), find the quantity of workers that will be supplied when training is complete.

33e. Once training is complete and the newly trained workers are in the labor market, calculate what will happen to the equilibrium wage. Assume that once workers are trained, they will be extremely reluctant to leave that occupation.

33f. If workers again shortsightedly base their training plans on this new wage, find the quantity of workers that will be supplied when training is complete.

33g. Is this market moving closer to the market clearing values associated with the new demand curve?

33h. Will this market eventually converge on the wage and employment values associated with the new demand curve? How can you tell?

A Hedonic Model of Earnings and Educational Level (Appendix 9B)

34. In Figure 9-7, the curves labeled *A* and *B* refer to indifference curves between the wage and the level of non-compulsory schooling attained for two individuals, while the curves *Y* and *Z* refer to zero profit isoprofit curves for two firms. Suppose that initially persons A and B have both attained 4 years of additional schooling beyond the compulsory level (point *a*).

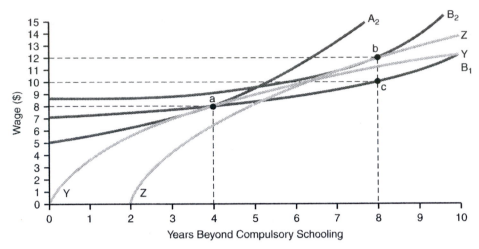

Figure 9-7

34a. What would be the monetary benefit to person B of investing in an additional 4 years of education?

34b. What is the minimum wage increase person B would accept in return for undertaking the additional years of education?

34c. Would the additional years of education be a good investment for person B? What about for person A?

■ Applications

Increases in the Cost of Education

35. According to data presented in Table 9.1 of *Modern Labor Economics*, the college enrollment rates of high school graduates rose most rapidly during the period 1980 to 1985. During that period, enrollment rates for men rose 11.9% while the rates for women rose 5.1%. On the other hand, according to data published in *The Wall Street Journal* (August 17, 1988, p. 31), the average annual cost of tuition and fees at public four-year colleges and universities rose from $706 to $1,242, a 76% increase. For four-year private colleges and universities, average tuition and fees rose 65% from $3,279 to $5,418. These increases far exceeded the 31% increase in the Consumer Price Index that took place over this time. How is it possible that college enrollment rates could be rising at the same time college costs were rising so substantially in real terms?

Changing Patterns in Graduate Business School Enrollments

36. According to data presented in Table 9.3 of the text, the percentage of women among those graduating with master's degrees in business rose dramatically from 3.9% in 1971 to 37% in 1995. In the fall of 1992, however, *The Wall Street Journal* reported on what appeared to be a change in that trend. According to an article in the September 25, 1992 issue (p. B1), women as a percentage of entering Master of Business Administration (M.B.A.) classes had fallen substantially at many top schools after peaking in the 1980s.

A career counselor interviewed in the article said the changes occurred because "a lot of women who were the pioneers in M.B.A. programs and big companies rushed blindly into what were formerly forbidden areas. . . . Now, a lot of these women have come back and told their younger sisters, 'It's not that great out there'."

Using the human capital investment framework, assess the reasonableness of this explanation.

Estimating the Relationship Between Education and Earnings

*37. The age-earnings profiles presented in Chapter 9 of the text clearly show that at any given age, workers with more education tend to earn higher wages, holding all else constant. In a 1974 book entitled *Schooling, Experience, and Earnings*, economist Jacob Mincer presented a framework for specifying what that relationship might look like. Mincer started by defining the rate of return (r) to one additional year of education, say, beyond the high school level as

$$r_1 = \frac{Y_1 - Y_0}{Y_0},$$

where Y_0 is the income level a person with a high school education could expect, while Y_1 is the income level a person could expect after receiving one year of additional education. Similarly, the rate of return to a second year of education (r_2) could be defined as

$$r_2 = \frac{Y_2 - Y_1}{Y_1}.$$

Taken together, the two equations imply that the income derived from two years of education could be expressed as

$$Y_2 = Y_0(1 + r_1)(1 + r_2).$$

If r is assumed to be constant over time, after S years of education, income could be expressed as

$$Y_S = Y_0(1 + r)^S.$$

Taking the natural logarithm (ln) of both sides of the equation yields

$$\ln Y_S = \ln Y_0 + S \ln (1 + r).$$

Mincer then noted for small values of r, $\ln(1 + r)$ could be approximated by r [e.g., $\ln (1 + 0.1) = 0.095 \cong 0.1$]. This means that the relationship between earnings and education can be simplified to

$$\ln Y_S = \ln Y_0 + rS.$$

Such an equation is often called a **human capital earnings function**.

*37a. Given the techniques discussed in the Appendix to Chapter 1, explain how one could estimate the parameter r in the above model.

*37b. Are there any variables that have been omitted from the above model that you think should be included? Would the omission of these variables bias the estimate of r at which you arrived? What would be the direction of the bias?

*37c. Would the estimate of r be likely to suffer from selection bias? If so, what would be the direction of the bias?

*37d. Given this model, the rate of return on education can be expressed as

$$r = \frac{\ln Y_S - \ln Y_0}{S}.$$

Suppose that after graduating from high school the typical student can earn $25,000. After graduating from college 4 years later, suppose the same individual can earn $35,000. What is the rate of return on the college investment?

*37e. Given the information in **37d**, would college be considered a good investment for the individual?

Lowering the Cost of Obtaining Educational Signals

38. In 1993 the Clinton administration proposed and successfully passed a program where students receive subsidies to attend college in return for agreeing to perform a national service job after graduation.

To see the effects of lowering educational costs in the context of the signaling model of education, consider Figure 9-8 which shows the present value of lifetime earnings (PVE) firms are willing to offer to workers who have attained different levels of education.

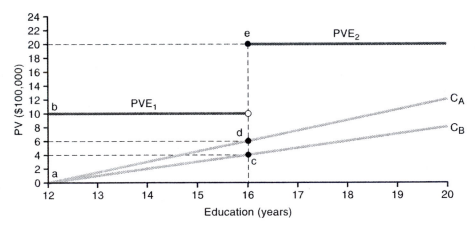

Figure 9-8

Those workers who have completed 16 years or more of education (4 or more years after high school) will be offered a wage leading to a present value of lifetime income of $2,000,000 (PVE$_2$), while those completing less than 16 years of education will be offered a wage leading to a present value of lifetime income equal to $1,000,000 (PVE$_1$). Lines C_A and C_B show the total cost of different levels of education for two types of workers. Type A workers are low-productivity workers while type B workers are high-productivity workers. The cost levels shown in Figure 9-8 are 50% of the costs assumed in Figure 9-6 from Problem 32.

38a. What is the net benefit (i.e., the difference between the PVE and the cost of education) a type A person would derive from attaining 16 years of education? What would be the net benefit from 12 years of education? What is the optimal level of education for a type A person?

38b. What is the net benefit a type B person would derive from attaining 16 years of education? What would be the net benefit from 12 years of education? What is the optimal level of education for a type B person?

38c. Is 16 years of education an effective way to distinguish low-productivity workers from high-productivity workers? Has lowering the cost of education increased or decreased the social benefits derived from education?

38d. A major concern in higher education today is grade inflation, the tendency of professors to give A_S and B_S to students who in the past would have earned C_S or D_S. What effect does grade inflation have on the ability of education to function as an effective signal of the most productive individuals?

Mandatory Increases in the Level of Education (Appendix 9B)

39. In Figure 9-9, the curves labeled A_2 and B_2 refer to indifference curves between the wage and the level of non-compulsory schooling attained for two individuals, while the curves Y and Z refer to zero-profit isoprofit curves for two firms. Suppose that initially persons A and B are perfectly informed about the wage and education combinations available in the market and mobile enough to choose the combinations that best suit their preferences. The result is that person A chooses point a and person B chooses point b.

Now suppose that the state in which A and B work passes an occupational licensing law that requires workers in this profession to attain a certain minimum level of education at accredited schools. Assume that the law requires at least 8 additional years of formal education.

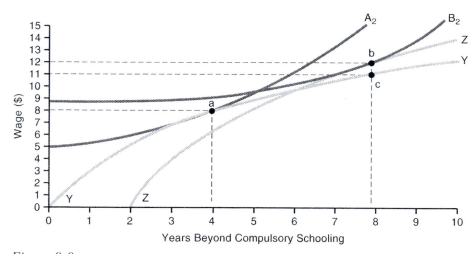

Figure 9-9

39a. Assuming A and B are not tied to any particular employer, what would be the effect of this licensing law?

39b. What would be the effect of the law assuming A and B are tied to their current employers?

Chapter 10
Worker Mobility: Migration, Immigration, and Turnover

■ **Summary**

Chapter 9 introduced the human capital investment framework and applied it to a wide variety of issues related to education and training. In this chapter the framework is used as a starting point for a more complete analysis of worker mobility, an issue closely intertwined with just about every major topic encountered so far in the text.

The ability of the labor market to bring about Pareto efficient outcomes (Chapter 1) and quickly resolve labor shortages and surpluses (Chapter 2) depends on there being a reasonable degree of labor mobility. Conclusions regarding the applicability of the monopsony model (Chapter 3), the effects of the minimum wage law (Chapters 3 and 4), and the effects of technological change and international trade (Chapter 4) also depend on the degree of worker mobility. The amount of firm-specific training offered to workers (Chapter 5) depends in part on the willingness of workers *not* to leave the firm. In turn, the amount of firm-specific training a worker receives will affect the likelihood of the worker quitting.

Assumptions regarding worker mobility also played a central role in the discussions pertaining to compensating differentials and the hedonic wage models presented in Chapter 8 and Appendix 9B. While the issue of worker mobility did not directly influence the conclusions drawn in Chapters 6, 7, or 9, the issue of mobility is closely connected to the labor supply discussions undertaken in those chapters. After all, the issue of *where* labor is supplied is a natural extension of the issues concerning the quantity and quality of labor supplied taken up in those chapters.

Worker mobility occurs when an individual makes a decision to voluntarily change either jobs and/or geographic locations. Such decisions are costly, but are made in the hopes of receiving greater benefits in the future. In that sense, these decisions are every bit as much investments in human capital as are the education and training decisions discussed in Chapter 9. Such investments will add to an individual's wealth provided the present value of the benefits exceeds the present value of the costs.

In the case of mobility decisions, the costs of the investment include direct expenses for moving if a change of residence is involved, and psychic losses due to the difficulty, stress, and anxiety of leaving friends, family, and familiar surroundings. The benefits of the investment include higher future earnings, access to more interesting, challenging, or pleasant jobs, and the psychic benefits that come from leaving problems behind and starting over in a new environment.

Letting r be the rate at which the yearly net benefits of mobility (B) are discounted, and assuming the direct costs of mobility (C) all occur in the initial year (year 0), the **present value method** suggests that employer and/or geographic changes should be undertaken provided

$$\frac{B_1}{1+r} + \frac{B_2}{(1+r)^2} + \cdots + \frac{B_T}{(1+r)^T} \geq C.$$

The subscripts refer to different years along an interval 1 to T with 1 being the first year after the initial year and T the last. Each value of B represents, for a particular year, the difference between the total compensation associated with the new position and the total compensation associated with the old position (where total compensation refers to both pecuniary and nonpecuniary compensation). It is also possible to evaluate mobility investments using the internal rate of return method discussed in Chapter 9. The annuity formula, also presented in Chapter 9, can be helpful in calculating the present value of the benefit stream when the yearly benefits are constant.

The present value method predicts that mobility investments are more likely (holding all else constant) the lower the values of r and C, and the higher the values of B and T. Evidence on **geographic mobility** within the United States has been consistent with the human capital investment framework since most studies have indicated that people are attracted to areas where the real earnings of full-time workers are highest (and are "pulled" toward higher earnings rather than "pushed" out of low-earnings areas). Areas with higher real earnings translate into higher levels of B for prospective migrants. Most moves also involve a relatively short distance, a finding consistent with prediction that higher levels of C discourage migration. But workers who live in the lowest-earning areas, who might be expected to have the greatest incentives to move, tend to also be the least willing or able to move, often because they have lower levels of wealth, education, and skills.

Evidence on the personal characteristics of migrants also supports the model, with the most important predictor of migration being age. The tendency for migrants to be young is consistent with the model, since higher values of T increase the present value of the stream of benefits. Also, since younger people are less likely to have strong community ties, the costs of migration for them should be lower.

Another important factor in the migration decision, particularly migration involving long distances, is the level of education. Occupations involving higher levels of education are more likely to have national, rather than localized, labor markets. In national labor markets information about employment opportunities is much easier to obtain. Therefore, this finding is also consistent with the prediction that lower levels of C make migration more likely.

In addition to the above predictions, the human capital model also suggests that when analyzing international migration, the distribution of earnings in the sending country, relative to that in the receiving country, will play an important role. In countries where the distribution of earnings is more equal than in the United States, skilled workers will gain the most by migrating since human capital investments have little payoff in their home countries. Immigrants from these countries are likely to be more skilled than the average worker remaining in that country. In countries with a less equal distribution of earnings, immigrants may be unable to make human capital investments in their own countries, and thus migration becomes a form of human capital investment. Immigrants from such countries will tend to be largely unskilled.

What is the rate of return on domestic migration? Studies of migration within the United States have generally confirmed that there is a substantial increase in family income that comes with migration, although the increase may take time. Workers who migrate for **economic reasons** tend to earn more, but some workers migrate for **family reasons**. The increase in family income may also occur despite a decrease in one of the spouse's income if the migration decision was based primarily on earnings prospects of the other spouse. Evidence of such gains, however, does not guarantee that migration will be beneficial. The fact that 20% of all moves occur to areas where people had previously lived suggests that comparisons of benefits and costs are often overly optimistic. Such **return migration** serves as an important reminder that mobility decisions are made based on individual expectations of benefits and costs formed in environments of uncertainty and incomplete information.

What is the rate of return on international migration decisions? Because it is often very difficult to assemble data on what migrants would have earned in the sending country, most studies have focused on how immigrant earnings compare to the earnings of U.S. natives. Such studies typically show that the age-earnings profiles of immigrants are initially lower, but then rise more steeply than those of comparable native-born workers. That is, earnings of immigrants are typically lower than natives initially, even controlling for age and education. However, earnings rise quickly (even faster than native workers) as immigrants learn English and invest in human capital. This is less true where immigrants live in "enclaves" in which business is conducted in their native tongue (or when immigrants expect to return to their native land) and thus there is less investment in learning English. Additionally, over time, each cohort of immigrants has tended to do less well upon entry than previous immigrants.

How much faster international immigrant earnings rise is a difficult question to answer since inferences drawn from cross-section data can be misleading if changes occur in the skills, work habits, and learning abilities of immigrants over time. Even with the faster earnings growth, however, the present value of lifetime earnings for immigrants is typically less than that of native-born workers. Still, the differences are relatively modest, so that given the low living standards many immigrants leave behind, the migration decision seems to have a large payoff for most immigrants. It is, however, a risky choice, and about 20% of all immigrants (presumably those who receive lower-than-expected payoffs) return to their place of origin.

While the human capital model suggests that mobility decisions can be analyzed and explained within the context of a very analytical and dispassionate framework, one mobility issue guaranteed to stir up passions is **immigration** policy. What fears do people have about immigration? Are these fears well founded? What are the consequences of immigration? These are the kinds of questions taken up in the latter part of Chapter 10.

Immigration into the United States was largely unrestricted until the 1920s when the first laws limiting the number of immigrants were passed. Since 1965, there has been an annual ceiling on the total number of immigrants and on the number that can come from any one country. Preference is given to those with family already residing in the United States, and to those who have particular skills that may be valuable in filling labor shortages. Immigrants who are spouses, children, or parents of U.S. citizens are exempt from the ceilings. Many who are shut out by this system, however, find ways to enter illegally. To discourage the flow of illegal immigrants, in 1986 Congress made it illegal for firms to hire illegal immigrants, and set up a system of fines for those that do. Due to proximity and differences in standards of living, illegal immigration from Mexico to the United States is particularly large. Although Mexican workers are, on average, less educated than American workers, most recent illegal immigrants are more likely to be from the middle of Mexico's educational distribution, as the costs of attempting to cross the border are likely to be prohibitive for the least-educated workers.

Restrictions on immigration often arise out of the fear that immigrants will harm the labor market prospects of American citizens and cost the government more than the economic benefits that they may generate. Careful analysis of the issue, however, reveals that while some workers may be hurt initially, the overall gains to society are likely to outweigh the losses.

Example

Consider a labor market where the demand curve for unskilled workers is given by the equation

$$L_D = 18 - W.$$

Suppose that the supply curve of unskilled workers who are also native-born citizens is given by

$$L_N = W - 2,$$

while the supply curve of unskilled immigrants (including unskilled illegal immigrants) is given by

$$L_I = 2W - 4,$$

where L represents the number of workers, W is the wage expressed in real terms, and the subscripts D, N, and I are used to distinguish between the quantity of unskilled labor demanded and the quantity of unskilled labor supplied by native-born and immigrant workers. These curves appear as lines D, S_N, and S_I in Figure 10-1. (The focus on unskilled labor in this problem is not meant to imply that all immigrant labor is unskilled.)

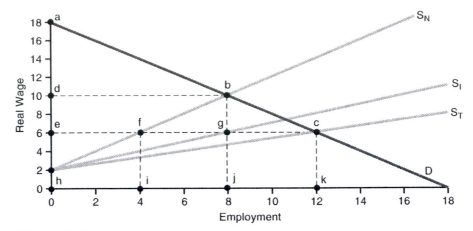

Figure 10-1

If immigration were totally prohibited, the market-clearing wage and employment level would occur where

$$L_D = L_N$$
$$\Rightarrow 18 - W = W - 2$$
$$\Rightarrow W^* = 10 \Rightarrow L^* = 8.$$

The market-clearing wage (W^*) and employment level (L^*) associated with the native supply curve are indicated by point b in Figure 10-1. The total income flowing to native workers is 80 and can be represented by the area of rectangle $dbj0$.

Allowing immigrants to enter this labor market would create a **total supply curve** given by the equation

$$L_T = L_N + L_I$$
$$\Rightarrow L_T = W - 2 + 2W - 4$$
$$\Rightarrow L_T = 3W - 6,$$

where the subscript T stands for the total quantity of workers supplied. This curve appears as line S_T in Figure 10-1. Given the two groups of workers, the market-clearing wage occurs where

$$L_D = L_T$$
$$\Rightarrow 18 - W = 3W - 6$$
$$\Rightarrow W^* = 6 \Rightarrow L^* = 12.$$

These values are denoted by point c.

Note that at the new market-clearing wage of 6, the total employment of native-born workers will be

$$L_N = 6 - 2 = 4,$$

(indicated by point f) while the employment of immigrants will be

$$L_I = 2(6) - 4 = 8,$$

(indicated by point g or the difference between points c and f). Immigration leads to lower wages and employment levels for unskilled native workers, with the total income flowing to this group decreasing from 80 to 24 (the area of rectangle efi0). Note, however, that the decrease in native employment does not consist of the 8 jobs now held by immigrants; rather, the decrease is only 4. Immigration does not reduce jobs for native-born workers on a one-to-one basis (unless there was a binding minimum wage set above point b in Figure 10-1).

If the above example is a reasonable depiction of the consequences of immigration for a particular category of labor, where do the gains from immigration come from? Would it not be better for native workers to restrict immigration? The reason the native population can gain from immigration is that **total output** also increases as a result of the immigration.

When labor demand is presented as a function of the real wage, the demand curve represents the horizontal summation of the individual firm's marginal product of labor curves, and so the area under the demand curve yields the total output associated with any particular employment level. In the above example, immigration increases output from 112 (the area of trapezoid abj0) to 144 (the area of trapezoid ack0). This increase in output makes sense because the United States now has more labor resources.

How is the distribution of output (real income) changed because of immigration? Before immigration, 80 of the 112 units flowed to native workers as real income, while the remaining 32 units accrued to the owners of the firms (area of triangle abd). This area, if one ignores the fixed costs of capital, equals the total profits of the firms. After immigration, 72 of the 144 units flow to workers (area of rectangle eck0) with 24 flowing to native workers and 48 flowing to immigrants (area of rectangle egj0 or rectangle fcki). After immigration, the remaining 72 of the 144 units flow to the owners of the firms.

While the distribution of output has been altered substantially, note that the increase in output is large enough to create a window of opportunity to keep native workers as well off as before without hurting anyone else. For example, since the supply curve represents the minimum workers are willing to accept for supplying an additional unit of labor, immigrants should be willing to give up the area represented by the difference between the wage they receive and their supply curve. This area, represented by triangle egh, was defined as **economic rent** in Chapter 2. It has an area of 16. If this amount, along with the 40 in increased profits of the firms (recall that the area accruing to the firms went from 32 to 72) were transferred to native workers, it would give native workers the same income they had before immigration (24 + 16 + 40 = 80). Firms would also have the same profits as before, and immigrants would gain the balance, just enough to make their migration investment worthwhile. When a potential exists for some workers to gain and no one else is hurt, the original situation *cannot* be considered to be Pareto efficient (see Chapter 1), and so the change to the new equilibrium may make sense from a normative perspective.

The above analysis also ignores potential shifts in the demand for products (and ultimately in the demand for labor) that the new income of immigrants is sure to bring about. Such shifts would bring about increases in the employment and wages of any workers who were **gross complements** with unskilled labor. The lower wages received by unskilled workers would also help to put downward pressure on the prices paid by consumers.

One important complication in the above analysis, of course, is the extent to which the transfers needed to keep native workers from being hurt actually take place, and whether these transfer programs also subsidize immigrants. There is little debate over the question of whether low-income native workers receive income transfers, since programs such as food stamps, welfare, unemployment insurance, public housing, and job retraining are fairly accessible and automatic. The key question remains the extent to which immigrants also receive **net subsidies** (subsidies greater than the amount they contribute in taxes) through these programs. Attempts to deny such subsidies to immigrants, particularly illegal immigrants, make sense in the context of this model, although such exclusions raise certain ethical dilemmas that cannot be resolved through economic analysis. Additionally, empirical analysis of the wage effects on natives have led to unclear results, although they do suggest that effects on native wages have been small.

Another type of employee mobility, **turnover or separations**, can take place without geographic mobility, but evidence related to **voluntary turnover** (quits) also supports the predictions of the human capital investment framework. The evidence clearly shows that workers in low-wage industries have higher quit rates than those in high-wage industries. This is consistent with the prediction of the human capital model since, holding all else constant, the lower the wage paid by the current employer, the greater the benefit associated with changing jobs.

Quit rates also tend to decline as firm size increases. Larger firms tend to pay higher wages and may offer more opportunities for transfers and promotions. It may also be more beneficial for large firms to attempt to reduce quit rates because they may have mechanized production processes that rely on team efforts, and thus quits may be more costly.

Other support for the human capital model comes from the observation that quit rates vary inversely over time with the unemployment rate and the layoff rate. This suggests that workers are more likely to quit when employment opportunities are better, suggesting that the decision to change jobs is directly related to the expected benefits.

Costs of job changing may also vary internationally. American workers tend to be more mobile than workers in Japan and Europe. This may be due to difference in housing policies that make costs of moving higher in those areas or to cultural differences.

Finally, is job mobility socially desirable? It may promote economic efficiency by leading to better job matches. In Chapter 8, it was shown that the possibility of job mobility was necessary to create compensating wage differentials.

■ Review Questions

Choose the letter that represents the **BEST** response.

The Determinants of Worker Mobility

1. Voluntary mobility is predicted when
   a.   the monetary benefits of mobility exceed the monetary costs.
   b.   a new job is available that pays more than the old one.
   c.   the present value of the benefits from mobility is at least as large as the present value of the costs.
   d.   all of the above.

2. Suppose that a baseball player eligible for free agent status signs a contract with a new team that promises to pay him $100,000 more than his current team for each of the next three years. Assuming the discount rate is 6%, what is the maximum the current costs of moving could be and still have this investment be worthwhile?
   a. $251,886
   b. $267,301
   c. $283,019
   d. $283,339

Geographic Mobility

3. Holding all else constant, higher rates of geographic mobility are exhibited by
   a. older workers.
   b. married couples.
   c. highly educated workers.
   d. both **a** and **b**.

4. Age is an important factor in determining whether a person migrates because
   a. age affects the length of the benefit stream associated with migration.
   b. age affects the psychic costs of migration.
   c. age determines whether a person participates in a local or national labor market.
   d. both **a** and **b**.

5. Lack of education appears to be a bigger deterrent to long-distance migration than age. This evidence supports the hypothesis that the primary deterrent to long-distance migration is
   a. the psychic cost of moving.
   b. the lack of information about employment prospects elsewhere.
   c. the monetary cost of the move.
   d. the difficulty of return migration.

6. Immigrants from other countries are more likely to be positively selected with respect to skills if
   a. the immigrants practice chain migration, i.e., the tendency to follow previous immigrants to particular geographic locations.
   b. the earnings distribution in the sending country is more equal than in the United States.
   c. the earnings distribution in the sending country is similar to that in the United States.
   d. both **a** and **b**.

7. Evidence suggests that the earnings of immigrants start at a lower level than the earnings of native-born workers, but then grow faster over time, and eventually meet or exceed the earnings of comparable native-born workers. This evidence demonstrates that
   a. the rate of return on an immigrant's mobility investment is likely to be high.
   b. immigrants are more productive than the average native-born worker.
   c. the present value of an immigrant's lifetime earnings is likely to exceed that of a comparable native-born worker.
   d. many immigrants set aggressive financial goals for themselves so that they can return to their homeland when the goal is met.

8. Data showing that 20% of all geographic moves are to an area in which the household had previously lived (return migration) supports the hypothesis that
   a. individual expectations about the costs and benefits of mobility are often wrong.
   b. on average, migration does not appear to be a good investment.
   c. while individuals may gain from migration, family income (the earnings of the husband and wife) tends to fall.
   d. all of the above.

Voluntary Turnover

9. Holding all else constant, workers in industries that pay higher wages have lower quit rates. This finding is consistent with the view that
    a. quits are a form of worker-initiated mobility.
    b. workers make mobility decisions based on costs and benefits.
    c. a low quit rate is a reliable sign of an above-equilibrium wage.
    d. all of the above.

10. Quit rates tend to vary over the business cycle as general labor market conditions change. Holding all else constant, the quit rate tends to decrease when
    a. labor market conditions are considered to be tight (jobs are more plentiful relative to job seekers).
    b. the unemployment rate rises.
    c. the layoff rate decreases.
    d. both **b** and **c**.

11. Based on the human capital investment framework, quit rates should be expected to fall with age because
    a. older workers are more mature and face lower psychic costs when changing jobs.
    b. older workers have longer job tenures.
    c. older workers have a shorter time over which to recover the costs associated with quitting.
    d. all of the above.

12. Holding all else constant, voluntary turnover is lower in rural areas because
    a. the costs associated with quitting tend to be higher in rural areas.
    b. rural residents tend to be less present-oriented and so have lower discount rates.
    c. wages tend to be higher in rural areas.
    d. all of the above.

The Consequences of Immigration

In answering Questions **13–19**, please refer to Figure 10-2 which depicts the demand and supply curves for a particular category of labor. D refers to the market demand, S_N to the supply of native-born workers, S_I to the supply of immigrant workers, and S_T to the total supply.

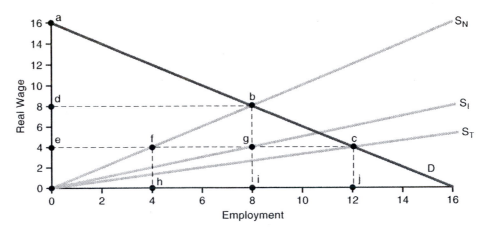

Figure 10-2

13. How many jobs for native-born workers are lost because of immigration?

    a. Native employment would not be reduced since Americans are unwilling to perform the kind of work that immigrants do.

    b. 4

    c. 8

    d. 12

14. How much is the total real income of native-born workers reduced because of immigration?

    a. 16

    b. 32

    c. 48

    d. 64

15. Ignoring the cost of capital, how much of an increase in total profit (in real terms) is generated because of immigration?

    a. 8

    b. 16

    c. 32

    d. 40

16. How much total output does society gain because of immigration?

    a. 8

    b. 16

    c. 24

    d. 32

*17. How much would immigrants be willing to pay in real terms for the right to work in this country (i.e., how much do immigrants earn in economic rent)?

    a. 4

    b. 16

    c. 32

    d. 48

18. If immigration leads to a large enough increase in output, it is possible that native workers can be kept at least as well off as before immigration without hurting immigrants or the firms. For such an outcome to occur, it is necessary that

    a. programs exist to transfer income to native workers.

    b. immigrants not receive more in government subsidies than they pay in taxes.

    c. all illegal immigrants be denied any form of government assistance.

    d. both **a** and **b**.

19. An important consequence of immigration not shown in Figure 10-2 is

    a. the downward pressure on consumer prices that results from the lower wages associated with immigration.

    b. the employment and wage gains by those categories of labor that are gross complements with the labor in this market.

    c. the migration of natives away from areas experiencing an influx of immigrants.

    d. all of the above.

■ Problems

The Determinants of Worker Mobility

20. Consider a family where both the husband and wife work, and assume each spouse has three more years to work (after the current year) before retirement. Table 10-1 indicates the projected combined salary over the remaining work years if they each stay with their current employers. It also shows the combined salary they can expect if they relocate and change employers.

Table 10-1

Year	Combined Salary at Current Jobs	Combined Salary at New Jobs
1	$80,000	$83,000
2	$82,000	$87,000
3	$85,000	$92,000

Suppose the total cost of moving, including direct expenses, forgone earnings, and psychic costs total $10,000. Assume all costs are incurred during the current year (year 0).

20a. If the discount rate is equal to the market interest rate of 6%, is this investment in mobility worthwhile?

20b. What is the maximum mobility costs could be and still make this investment worthwhile?

20c. How reasonable is it to assume that the psychic costs of mobility all occur in the current year (year 0)?

20d. Is it reasonable to expect that there will also be psychic benefits associated with moving? If so, give some examples of such benefits.

*20e. When a person moves without a new job already in hand, evidence indicates that the mobility may initially lead to lower earnings than in the current job. This reduction is then more than overcome in future periods by faster earnings growth in the new location. Holding all else constant, what is the lowest the new combined salary could be in year 1 and still have this be a worthwhile investment?

20f. Is it reasonable to expect that both spouses will gain equally because of the move?

The Gain to Society from Mobility

21. Mobility investments may lead not only to individual gains, but also to gains for society as a whole. To see why this is true, consider the information in Table 10-2. It shows the relationship between employment and output in two different labor markets.

Table 10-2

Labor Market A		Labor Market B	
Labor	Output	Labor	Output
1	12	1	17
2	20	2	30
3	25	3	40
4	28	4	48
5	30	5	55

21a. Compute the marginal product of labor for each unit of labor in market A.

21b. Graph the marginal product of labor schedule for market A.

21c. For an employment level of 5, show that the area under the marginal product schedule equals the total output associated with that output level.

21d. Compute the marginal product of labor for each unit of labor in market B.

21e. Suppose that there are 6 workers in this economy and that currently 3 work in market A and 3 work in market B. If each worker is paid in real terms the marginal product associated with the last worker hired, what will the wage rates be in each market? How much combined total output will be produced by the two markets?

21f. Assuming all other job characteristics are the same in both markets, where will workers tend to migrate? What happens to total output if one worker migrates from market A to market B? What would happen to total output if more than one worker migrated from A to B? Would there be an incentive for more than one worker to migrate?

The Consequences of Immigration

22. Consider a labor market where the demand for a particular category of labor is given by the equation

$$L_D = 20 - 2W.$$

Suppose that the supply curve of workers in this market who are also native-born citizens is given by

$$L_N = 2W,$$

while the supply curve of immigrants in this market is given by

$$L_I = W,$$

where L represents the number of workers, W is the wage expressed in real terms, and the subscripts D, N, and I are used to distinguish between the quantity of labor demanded and the quantity of labor supplied by native-born and immigrant workers.

22a. Find the market-clearing wage and employment level assuming immigration is not allowed. Then find the market-clearing wage and employment level after allowing for immigration. How many native jobs are lost to immigrants?

22b. Compute the real income of native-born workers in this market before and after immigration. How much is the income flow reduced?

22c. Ignoring the cost of capital, compute the total profits of the firms before and after immigration. What is the change in total profits?

22d. Compute the total output of this market before and after immigration. How much total output does society gain because of immigration?

*22e. Taken as a whole, how much would immigrants be willing to pay in real terms for the right to work in this country (i.e., how much do immigrants earn in economic rent)?

*22f. If immigration leads to a large enough increase in output, it is possible that native workers can be kept at least as well off as before immigration without hurting immigrants or the firms. Give an example of a transfer payment scheme that would accomplish this.

22g. What other effects do immigrants have on labor markets that are not captured in this model?

■ Applications

Migration After a Job Loss

23. Consider a worker currently making $60,000 in a defense industry plant in the New England area. Suppose the plant is closed because of government spending cutbacks and the worker loses his job. After a prolonged search, the worker decides to change occupations and move to North Carolina. His new job only pays $50,000. Has not migration made this worker worse off? Do such examples contradict the prediction of the human capital investment model that says people invest in mobility only when the present value of the benefits is at least as large as the present value of the costs?

The Causes of Higher Quit Rates for Women

*24. According to the text "It is well established that female workers have had higher propensities toward quitting than male workers." Empirical evidence also exists which shows that the job tenure of women tends to be significantly lower than that of men, a finding consistent with the view that women have had higher quit rates. The higher quit rates and shorter tenure, in turn, are attributed to the lower levels of firm-specific training obtained by women, a subject discussed in Chapter 5.

*24a. Using the lessons of Chapter 5, review why women are less likely to be offered firm-specific training.

*24b. Review why higher quit rates are expected when a worker does not receive firm-specific training. Would eliminating general training also lead to higher quit rates?

The Effects of Reducing Immigration When a Minimum Wage Applies

25. Consider a labor market where the demand for a particular category of labor is given by the equation

$$L_D = 20 - 2W.$$

Suppose that the supply curve of workers in this market who are also native-born citizens is given by

$$L_N = 2W,$$

while the supply curve of immigrants (including illegal immigrants) in this market is given by

$$L_I = W.$$

(This is the same information given in Problem **22** earlier in the chapter.) Suppose the government imposes a minimum wage (in real terms) of 6 that applies to all workers.

25a. Is the minimum wage binding? What would the market-clearing wage be in the absence of the minimum wage (assuming there are no restrictions on immigration)?

25b. What is the quantity of workers demanded at the minimum wage?

25c. What is the total quantity of workers supplied at the minimum wage? How many are native-born workers? How many are immigrants?

25d. How many native workers will actually be employed? How many immigrants will be employed?

25e. The 1986 Immigration Reform and Control Act (sometimes called the Simpson-Rodino Act) made it illegal for firms to hire illegal immigrants. Employers are required to verify if new employees are legal residents, and any firms consistently caught hiring illegal residents could face fines of up to $10,000. Suppose the law, by reducing the expected benefits of migration, has the desired effect of reducing the number of illegal immigrants in this market. In the context of this example, how many native workers will be hired for every immigrant that is not? Would your answer be the same if the minimum wage were not binding? (Based on the discussion in Chapter 5, how would the firm's cost of complying with the immigration law be classified?)

25f. Another provision of the 1986 Immigration and Control Act was that illegal immigrants who had lived continuously in the United States since 1982 could apply for amnesty and legal resident status. After 5 additional years of continuous residence, these immigrants could then apply to be U.S. citizens. Based on the human capital investment framework, what effect would such a program have on the flow of illegal immigrants?

25g. According to *The Wall Street Journal* (September 1, 1992, p. A1), in California alone, approximately 1.5 million illegal immigrants took advantage of the amnesty program, and the first wave of applicants were eligible for citizenship on November 6, 1993. Citizenship also makes the former immigrants eligible for welfare assistance. What effect does the expansion of welfare eligibility have on the likelihood that the aggregate income (the sum of earnings, profits, and net government subsidies) of the native-born population will fall?

Estimating the Earnings Growth of Immigrants

*26. Suppose that the earnings growth for an individual immigrant over time can be represented by the equation

$$\ln Y_E = \ln Y_0 + rE,$$

where ln is the natural logarithm function, Y_0 is the earnings level an immigrant can expect upon arrival, and Y_E represents the immigrant's earnings after spending E years in the new country. The variable E is best thought of as the immigrant's current age minus the age of arrival (e.g., 20 years). The rate of growth of an immigrant's earnings (r) is assumed to be constant over time. (See Question **37** in Chapter 9 for a derivation of this equation in the context of educational investments.)

Consider a situation where there have been three waves of immigrants over time. Suppose that individuals in group A arrived at age 20 in 1950, while group B arrived at age 20 in 1970, and group C arrived at age 20 in 1990. The earnings growth for each group, as well as for native-born workers (group N), can be represented by the equations

Group N: $\ln Y_E = 14 + 0.1E,$

Group A: $\ln Y_E = 12 + 0.1E,$

Group B: $\ln Y_E = 11 + 0.1E,$

Group C: $\ln Y_E = 10 + 0.1E.$

Each group's earnings are expected to grow at the same rate ($r = 0.1$) over time. However, holding all else constant, the later groups are assumed to have lower earnings prospects because of lower levels of productivity. Immigrants are also assumed to always earn less than native-born workers. These earnings schedules are show in Figure 10-3.

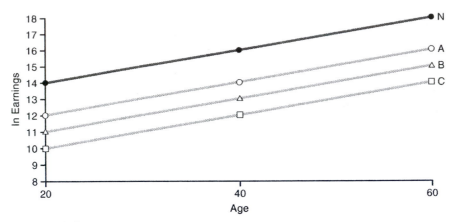

Figure 10-3

*26a. Suppose that in 1990 a cross-section sample of immigrants is selected that contains one person who is 20 years old, one person who is 40, and one person who is 60. What growth rate of immigrant earnings will be inferred from this data?

*26b. Will the growth rate give an accurate impression of the growth rate of immigrant earnings relative to that of native-born workers? Based on this estimate, what conclusion are people likely to draw?

*27. As in the previous problem, consider a situation where there have been three waves of immigrants over time. Suppose that individuals in group A arrived at age 20 in 1950, while group B arrived at age 20 in 1970, and group C arrived at age 20 in 1990. Also suppose the earnings growth for each group can be represented by the equations

Group A: $\ln Y_E = 10 + 0.1E,$

Group B: $\ln Y_E = 12 + 0.1E,$

Group C: $\ln Y_E = 14 + 0.1E.$

Each group's earnings are expected to grow at the same rate ($r = 0.1$) over time. However, holding all else constant, the latter groups are assumed to have *higher* earnings prospects because of higher levels of productivity. These earnings schedules are shown in Figure 10-4.

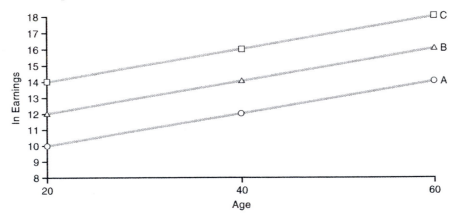

Figure 10-4

*27a. Suppose that in 1990 a cross-section sample of immigrants is selected that contains one person who is 20 years old, one person who is 40, and one person who is 60. What growth rate of immigrant earnings will be inferred from this data?

*27b. What changes in methodology could be made to eliminate the bias that occurs in these situations?

*27c. In what sense does the bias illustrated in this problem relate to the problems of ability bias and selection bias discussed in Chapter 9?

Chapter 11
Pay and Productivity:
Wage Determination within the Firm

■ Summary

Beginning with the overview of the labor market presented in Chapter 2, the organizing theme of *Modern Labor Economics* has been the demand and supply model of the labor market. Chapters 3 to 5 focused primarily on modeling demand decisions, while Chapters 6 to 10 emphasized supply. Understanding demand and supply decisions is essential for anyone wishing to think seriously and critically about labor issues. The remaining chapters in the text take up a series of special topics that build on the foundation provided by the modeling of demand and supply decisions to form a more complete framework for thinking about labor issues.

The first special topic taken up in *Modern Labor Economics* is the complex relationship between compensation and productivity. Although the early models of the firm's labor demand decision assumed that the firm simply took the market wage as a given when deciding on employment, later chapters suggested that the firm's compensation decision may be more involved than that. In Chapter 5, for example, the firm had to decide on a wage that would allow it to recover its specific training costs and at the same time keep the worker from quitting. In Chapter 8, the firm had to decide on the mix of wages and employee benefits that would allow it to attract the workers needed to stay competitive. In this chapter, additional decisions relating to the basis, level, and timing of compensation are explored. These decisions, along with the ones discussed in earlier chapters, come together to form the firm's **compensation policy**.

Managers must take into account that there are many factors that influence worker productivity, other than the human capital and physical capital issues discussed previously. Workers differ from each other in work habits, which cannot generally be observed prior to hiring. A given worker's productivity, all other things equal, may vary over time, in different environments, or according to the worker's motivation. A worker's productivity is a function of innate ability, level of effort, and factors relating to the worker's environment; being very productive is sometimes or usually related to taking initiative rather than simply following orders. Thus compensation should be designed to attract the right type of employees and give them the right incentives to be as productive as possible.

Decisions about compensation, however, are only part of a larger **employment contract** or relationship. Such a contract involves an agreement by an employee to perform certain tasks in return for current and future pay from the employer. Contracts are often analyzed in economics using the terms **principal** and **agent**. Principals are parties that hire others to help them achieve certain objectives, while agents are those hired to advance the interests of others. In the case of the labor market, the firm can be referred to as the principal and the worker as an agent.

What form do employment contracts take? Such contracts are different from the formal contracts individuals sign (e.g., when taking out an auto loan) in that they are typically **incomplete** and **implicit**. Employment contracts are incomplete because they do not specify all the actions that may be required of an individual. This gives the firm some flexibility in responding to changing business conditions. Employment contracts are also implicit because they include a number of informal understandings that can be difficult to legally enforce, and each side typically has the flexibility to end the relationship at any time. Given this structure, employment contracts have to be **self-enforcing** to be effective; i.e., each side must perceive it to be in their own interest to live up to the contract. A self-enforcing contract can be particularly hard to achieve when information in the market is **asymmetric**. This occurs when one party knows more about its intentions or performance under the contract than the other. Such asymmetries increase the likelihood of cheating on the employment contract, so many firms try to structure the terms of the employment contract in such a way that workers will **signal** their true abilities and intentions.

However, even when employers are successful in choosing workers with the right characteristics, there are incentives for **opportunistic behavior** on both sides of the employment relationship. Thus it is necessary to structure employment contracts such that both sides are induced to keep their promises about behavior, or in other words, so that it is in both parties' best interests to continue the employment relationship. These incentives are strongest when the employment relationship creates a surplus (the gap between the employee's marginal revenue product and his alternative wage) that is shared between the worker and the employer, and thus both sides benefit from the relationship. Surpluses generally arise from investment by the firm in training or through the firm's reputation as a reliable employer (which can then attract higher-quality workers).

What specific employment practices constitute the substance of an employment contract? Most of the key components of the employment contract are designed around the goal of motivating workers to exert their best efforts. Decisions related to hiring standards, supervision, compensation, and fair treatment of workers all play an important role in maximizing worker productivity.

An obvious way to motivate workers is to pay based on performance. Pay schemes based on **individual** output include **piece-rate** and **commission** pay. But whether this is effective depends first on whether the worker sees his performance as directly linked to his own effort. If performance relies in part on other workers, machines, or other factors, the worker may not be induced to optimal effort. Secondly, the output measure must bequantifiable and relate to the employer's objectives, and that may be difficult, particularly in service-related industries.

The most common method is to pay employees for their **time**. Such plans, however, may not lead workers to exert their best efforts without close supervision, unless workers are motivated by group loyalty or future considerations. Guaranteeing workers a stable wage is thought to decrease work incentives in the same way that insuring individuals against unfavorable outcomes reduces their willingness to take steps to avoid losses. This type of behavior is called the **moral hazard** problem. Essentially, since the worker is being paid for time rather than effort, why put in effort?

The role of the individual worker as part of a group is also an important issue in motivation. Workers who feel that they are not treated fairly relative to others may quit or reduce effort. Workers who feel loyal to their group may expend additional effort. Compensation methods such as **gainsharing**, **profit sharing**, and **bonus** plans tie at least part of an employee's pay to **group** achievements.

Given the variations in earnings that are sure to result from output-based pay, employees tend to prefer time-based compensation. Variations in earnings lead to lower levels of average utility if the individual is **risk averse** (see Appendix 8A). Holding all else constant, a compensating differential is expected to accompany output-based pay. However, it is possible that piece-rate pay schemes are likely to attract more productive workers, since those who gain the most from these plans are those who are more productive. Thus, workers paid under these plans are likely to earn more than time-rate workers, both because they are more productive and due to the compensating differential.

From the employer's perspective, it is the time-based compensation that leads to the more variable profit stream as well as increased screening and supervising costs. While these considerations suggest that the firm would prefer output-based pay, such schemes are not without their problems. Individually based incentive pay encourages the employee to work hard with little supervision, but such schemes may cause workers to focus so much on the quantity of output that quality suffers, equipment is damaged or misused, and group loyalty is diminished. Setting the rate for piece-rate work can also be difficult if it involves direct observation of workers. Some jobs are also not conducive to individually based incentive pay since the individual's output may be difficult to measure objectively. Even when there are clear measures of performance, tying pay to these measures may cause workers to ignore other aspects of the job.

It is the problem of measuring individual output that ultimately gives rise to pay based on group incentives. Group incentive-pay plans can take many forms. Some tie the pay of the group to gains in productivity, product quality or cost reductions achieved by the group. These are commonly called gainsharing plans. Profit sharing and bonus plans link pay or bonus payments to the firm's overall profit level. In some cases workers may even own the firm and so split the profits among themselves. The success of group incentive schemes depends on the ability of the group to control **shirking**. Particularly in large groups, the success of the group does not usually hinge on the performance of any one individual. Knowing that, some individuals may realize that they can reap the same financial rewards while doing less. This is an example of a **free-rider** problem. Of course, if everyone behaves in this way, shirking (free riding) ultimately undermines the success of the group.

One way to control shirking may be to try to hire only those workers who signal a predisposition toward cooperation and group loyalty. Alternatively, a firm may take steps to build group loyalty among existing workers. When feasible, it may help to keep the group size small so that shirking can be more easily detected and more quickly punished. However, this can conflict with the need for large team production processes.

Profit-based bonuses are most frequently used in the compensation of top executives. Such performance attainment plans usually tie the executive's bonus to the profit performance over a 3- to 5-year period. Basing the award on performance over a shorter period might create incentives to advance the short-run success of the firm at the expense of long-run profits. Longer periods are thought to involve such a long wait for compensation that the executive's performance incentives are reduced.

In an effort to keep executives focused on long-term consequences, firms increasingly tie compensation to the value of the company's stock. In general, it is more difficult to fool the stock market into thinking the earnings prospects of the firm have really been increased through strategies that only serve to increase short-run profits. The evidence suggests that such compensation plans do help to improve the performance and stock market value of the firms that adopt them. Attempts to tie the yearly pay of executives to changes in the stock market value of the firm are typically constrained by the risk aversion of the executives. Given the volatility stock prices can display in the short run for reasons beyond an executive's control, firms that use such schemes may have trouble attracting new executives without a compensating differential. Additionally, some recent evidence suggests that close relationships between CEOs and their boards of directors can lead to negotiation of excessive compensation packages, and thus that "outside" directors or other well-informed agents are necessary to align incentives efficiently.

While incentive pay has the potential for increasing productivity, the litany of problems associated with such compensation policies has led most firms to continue to rely on time-based pay for much of their work force. To improve the incentives associated with time-based pay, some firms have instituted systems involving **merit pay**. These plans attempt to award higher pay raises each year to those workers judged to be more productive.

Merit-pay plans actually share most of the same problems as output-based pay. For example, how will performance be measured? Assuming it can be measured, what about factors that are beyond the workers control? To get around this latter problem, many merit-pay systems rely on the relative ranking of workers by supervisors. Such a ranking however, can create incentives for workers to be uncooperative or disruptive towards coworkers, or divert effort into attempts to win favor with supervisors. Because such plans rely on the subjectivity of managers, they are often distrusted by workers, particularly when evidence surfaces that managers are being inconsistent in their rankings. To avoid controversy, managers may rely too heavily on the middle categories of the system, thus mitigating the increase in work incentives that the plan is designed to foster.

Given the difficulties inherent in whatever method is used as a basis for pay, it is clear that there is no system that will work for all firms. Rather, each firm must determine the appropriate basis after weighing all the costs and benefits. But the basis of pay is not the only decision needed to form a compensation policy. The **level** of pay is also an important element of the policy, and it too can have an important effect on worker productivity.

The level of pay is often a question of how to divide the surplus created when a worker and firm agree to enter an employment contract. An example of this occurred in Chapter 5 in the context of firm-specific training investments. The surplus consisted of the difference between the worker's marginal product at the current employer and the real wage a worker could expect elsewhere. The task of the firm was to set the wage so that it could recover the training investment given the expected job tenure of the worker while still keeping the wage above the worker's alternative offers. But what if the size of the surplus is a function of the wage that is set? That is, what if the worker's marginal product increases with the wage paid to the worker?

There are good reasons for suspecting that such a relationship between the wage and the marginal product exists. Higher wages expand the pool of applicants and allow the firm to be more selective in hiring. A larger gap between the wage and the worker's alternative offers should also help to reduce shirking and quits. A reduced quit rate, in turn, tends to lead to more firm-specific training opportunities. To the extent that higher wages are perceived as fair treatment, they may help to build commitment and group loyalty.

Exactly how much the wage should be raised above the market wage in these instances ultimately depends on the marginal costs and benefits of the change. The level that just equates the marginal benefit of continued increases with the marginal cost is called the **efficiency wage**. It is important to note that an efficiency wage strategy makes sense only when the firm expects a long-term employment relationship with the workers. For this reason, efficiency wage strategies are thought to be more likely in situations where firms utilize an internal labor market strategy (see Chapter 5).

Firms that foster long-term employment relationships through internal labor markets also have some discretion over the sequencing of compensation. Can this discretion be used to increase worker productivity? One productivity-enhancing technique may be to pay workers less (in real terms) than their marginal product early in their careers with the firm, and more later. Such a **deferred payment** scheme should increase work incentives early on since workers will not want to risk getting fired before they become eligible for the overpayment. Such a scheme would also be most attractive to those workers who are inherently very diligent workers and feel that the risk of being fired is very low.

This scheme will be acceptable to workers and the firm provided the present value of the real earnings stream is equal to the present value of the workers' marginal product over time. This condition, in turn, requires that for any firm using a deferred payment scheme, the present value of the overpayment must equal the present value of the underpayment. It must also be true that the present value of the earnings stream is greater than or equal to the present value of alternative streams that workers could have in other jobs (or they will leave), and that the firm must earn a normal profit. For profits less than zero, the firm will eventually exit, while supernormal profits attract entry, and thus neither state can be an equilibrium.

Example

Consider a firm where the marginal product of the typical worker varies over time according to the schedule in Table 11-1 where year 0 represents the current year. In order to motivate its workers to exert their best efforts, suppose this firm plans to sequence the pay in such a way that workers receive less than their marginal product early in their career, and then more than their marginal product toward the end of their career. If the firm has decided to pay workers the real wage values shown in Table 11-1 for years 0, 1, and 2, what is the minimum the firm could pay workers in period 3 and still have the plan be acceptable to the workers? Assume the real interest rate is 6%.

Table 11-1

Year	Marginal Product	Real Wage
0	10	6
1	15	12
2	18	18
3	20	?

Setting the present value of the underpayment equal to the present value of the overpayment yields

$$4 + \frac{3}{1+0.06} = \frac{W_3 - 20}{(1+0.06)^3} \Rightarrow \frac{W_3 - 20}{(1+0.06)^3} = 6.83$$

$$\Rightarrow W_3 = (6.83)(1.06)^3 + 20 \Rightarrow W_3 = 28.13.$$

The schedule of wage and marginal product values over time is shown in Figure 11-1. These schedules each yield identical present values of 56.96 even though the marginal product values only sum to 63, while the wage values sum to 64.13. The actual amount of the underpayment (7; area A + area B) must be less than the actual amount of the overpayment (8.13; area C) to reflect the time value of money.

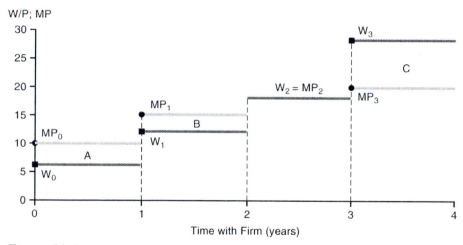

W/P; MP

Figure 11-1

What would happen, however, if the worker were laid off before reaching period 3? The result would be that the worker would never recover the earlier underpayment, and so the present value of the marginal product stream (what the worker could get elsewhere) would exceed the present value of the compensation received. One way this can be avoided is for the employment contract to guarantee that those with the shortest job tenures will be the first to be laid off if the firm cuts back its employment. Providing some of the overpayment in the form of vested pension benefits also could help to guarantee that workers receive what is coming to them.

Alternatively, what would happen if the worker wanted to stay with the firm after period 3 and the firm could not refuse or lower the wage? In this case, the present value of the overpayment would exceed the present value of the underpayment and the firm would not be able to earn even a normal profit. Given that mandatory retirement for most workers is currently illegal under the Age Discrimination in Employment Act, firms have little recourse when older workers want to stay with the firm. Most firms respond to this problem by providing financial incentives for earlier retirement or structuring defined-benefit pensions so that the present value of lifetime pension benefits declines as retirement is postponed past a certain age.

If successful, a deferred payment scheme should eventually lead to a higher present value of compensation than can be attained elsewhere. The workers' marginal product values at the firm should be shifting up over time if the workers are motivated to exert extra effort by the timing of compensation.

Firms can also affect the timing of compensation through the use of **promotion tournaments**. In such a tournament, employees compete against one another over a number of years for a prized position involving high salary and prestige. There can be only one winner. Such a scheme is similar to a deferred payment in that employees are induced to work hard now by the expectation of a large bonus later. The difference is that not everyone will actually receive the bonus. Therefore, such a scheme will be acceptable to workers only if the losers are also treated relatively well, i.e., their wage is allowed to exceed their marginal product. This helps to explain why some firms continue to employ a few workers that are easily identifiable as relatively unprofitable employees.

Tournaments create incentives for effort depending on the marginal benefits that workers expect to receive from additional effort. Marginal benefits depend on the size of the prize and the increase in the probability of winning that comes from more effort. Thus where additional effort is very costly or where extra effort is perceived to have little effect on winning the prize, prizes must be very large to create incentives. Like piece rates, tournaments may have value to the firm because they can cause more productive or more motivated workers to sort themselves into such jobs.

However, tournaments can also result in efforts to sabotage others rather than to improve one's own chances, and thus may not be appropriate where team effort is important. Also, after the tournament is over, workers may have no further incentive for effort.

The willingness of employees to work very hard early in their career is enhanced when workers view themselves more as a member of a profession or field as opposed to a member of a particular firm. In such situations, hard work may not only impress the current employer but may also improve employment prospects at other employers. When workers are highly motivated by such **career concerns**, firms may not need to employ incentive pay or pay sequencing efforts to enhance productivity.

The last part of Chapter 11 tackles two empirical puzzles using the theories of pay and productivity discussed earlier in the chapter, along with theories from previous chapters. The first puzzle is: Why do earnings increase with a worker's job tenure? Earlier chapters suggest that longer tenure and higher wages both reflect more productive matches between worker and employer. A second reason involves firm-specific investments, jointly undertaken by both workers and employers. The discussion of pay sequencing in this chapter suggests that another explanation is that higher wages earned by those with longer job tenures serve as a reward for enduring underpayment earlier in their careers.

The second empirical puzzle is: Why do large firms pay higher wages? The explanation contributed by Chapter 11 is that the complicated and interdependent production processes at most large firms require the payment of efficiency wages to reduce shirking. Also, large firms are better positioned to use internal labor markets given the wide variety of positions available in a large firm. Internal labor markets, in turn, increase the likelihood of efficiency wage and pay sequencing strategies. These strategies raise the marginal productivity of workers above what it would be in other firms, thus increasing the overall level of pay. Such productivity enhancing strategies should appeal to large firms in that it is costly to supervise a large workforce.

■ Review Questions

Choose the letter that represents the **BEST** response.

The Employment Contract

1. Employment contracts for the majority of American workers take the form of
   a. formal documents precisely specifying in advance the obligations of each party.
   b. oral agreements that can be legally enforced when necessary.
   c. a broad set of informal understandings between each party.
   d. collective bargaining agreements made between an employer and a union.

2. An employment contract is considered to be self-enforcing if
   a. it is in each party's self-interest to see to it that the contract is not broken.
   b. it is implicit.
   c. it is incomplete.
   d. it is not legally enforceable by a third party.

3. A self-enforcing employment contract may be difficult to achieve because
   a. information in the labor market may be asymmetric.
   b. employment contracts are implicit.
   c. the terms of the employment contract are typically incomplete.
   d. all of the above.

4. The likelihood of one party cheating on an employment contract can be reduced by
   a. formal sanctions for breaking certain provisions of the contract.
   b. inducing the parties to signal their true characteristics and intentions before the contract is formed.
   c. more extensive and careful interviewing.
   d. both **a** and **b**.

5. A necessary condition for the design of a self-enforcing employment contract is that
   a. a surplus of workers exists.
   b. workers' marginal revenue product at the firm must exceed their alternative offers.
   c. the surplus generated by the employment relationship be divided evenly.
   d. workers receive firm-specific training.

6. An employment practice designed to motivate workers to exert their best efforts is
   a. close supervision of workers.
   b. linking pay to an individual's output.
   c. maintaining the perception that workers are being treated fairly.
   d. all of the above.

7. The tendency of workers to identify with their employing organization means that employment practices designed to foster group loyalty are likely to
   a. create a free-rider problem.
   b. intensify workers' concern about their relative position in the firm.
   c. increase worker motivation.
   d. both **a** and **b**.

Productivity and the Basis of Pay

8. Employees typically prefer being paid on a time basis because
   a. the output a worker produces can vary for reasons beyond the worker's control.
   b. workers prefer earnings certainty (i.e., they are risk averse).
   c. over 80% of U.S. workers are paid on a time basis.
   d. both **a** and **b**.

9. Empirical evidence suggests that workers receiving output-based pay earn more than workers in comparable jobs who are paid on the basis of time. This differential in pay occurs because
   a. workers attracted to firms using output-based pay are likely to have above-average motivation and ability.
   b. time-based pay creates a moral hazard problem.
   c. workers tend to be anxious about periods of lower-than-usual pay and so require a compensating differential to work under such conditions.
   d. all of the above.

10. Which of the following is *not* a problem usually associated with individual incentive-pay schemes?
   a. Wide variations in the firm's profits
   b. Erosion of group loyalty
   c. Overemphasis on the measurable aspects of job performance
   d. Misuse of the equipment

11. Incentive pay based on the success of the group is more likely when
   a. workers are risk averse.
   b. output is produced by employees working interdependently in teams.
   c. the group is prone to the free-rider problem.
   d. all of the above.

12. A problem associated with basing the compensation of top managers partly on the value of the company's shares of stock is that
   a. it creates an incentive for the managers to emphasize short-run successes.
   b. it may be difficult to attract top managers due to the variability in earnings associated with the plan.
   c. empirical studies suggest that such plans do not help the firm's stock market performance.
   d. all of the above.

13. Merit-pay plans are more likely to be successful when
   a. workers are rated relative to one another.
   b. supervisors tend to rely on the middle rating categories and avoid the extremes.
   c. individual output is highly correlated with an individual's effort.
   d. all of the above.

Productivity and the Level of Pay

14. Suppose the employment relationship results in a gap between the workers' marginal product at the firm and their alternative wage offers (in real terms). When dividing that surplus, firms should keep in mind that
    a. the more of the surplus kept by the firm, the more likely it is that workers will quit.
    b. higher wages may actually increase the size of the surplus.
    c. the surplus should be divided evenly.
    d. both **a** and **b**.

15. Which of the following is *not* a reason why higher wages are thought to increase worker productivity?
    a. Higher wages mean that workers will be less concerned about undercutting rivals and impressing supervisors.
    b. Higher wages enlarge a firm's applicant pool.
    c. Higher wages increase the penalty associated with shirking.
    d. Higher wages tend to alleviate worker concerns about fair treatment.

16. A firm can be said to pay workers an efficiency wage when
    a. the wage is above what workers can attain elsewhere.
    b. the wage has been raised above the market level to the point where further increases are unprofitable.
    c. there is no surplus associated with the employment relationship.
    d. the surplus from the employment relationship is divided in a way that favors the workers.

17. The likelihood of a firm using an efficiency wage strategy increases if
    a. the firm utilizes an internal labor market strategy for filling upper-level positions in the firm.
    b. supervision is very costly.
    c. individual output is easily measurable.
    d. both **a** and **b**.

Productivity and the Sequencing of Pay

In answering Questions **18** and **19**, suppose that the marginal product of a typical worker varies over time according to the schedule in Table 11-2 where year 0 represents the current year. In order to motivate its workers to exert their best efforts, suppose the firm plans to sequence the pay in such a way that workers receive less than their marginal product early in their career, and then more than their marginal product toward the end of their career.

18. If the firm has decided to pay workers the real wage values shown in Table 11-2 for years 0, 1, and 3, what is the minimum the firm could pay workers in period 2 and still have the plan be acceptable to the workers? (Assume the real interest rate is 6%.)
    a. 17.8
    b. 20
    c. 21.48
    d. 22.47

Table 11-2

Year	Marginal Product	Real Wage
0	10	5
1	15	10
2	20	?
3	25	35

19. The pay scheme described in Table 11-2 is risky from the point of view of the firm because
    a. it is uncertain whether the productivity of workers will actually increase.
    b. workers may quit before the plan is completed.
    c. if the wages of older workers cannot be reduced, workers may try to stay with the firm past year 3.
    d. both **a** and **b**.

20. Suppose that a number of candidates are considered for a top position in the firm over a number of years. One is eventually selected and paid three times what the remaining candidates receive. Such a promotion tournament strategy can be undermined if
    a. the firm develops a reputation for treating the losers poorly.
    b. workers focus their efforts on undercutting one another.
    c. the firm is willing to tolerate employees widely perceived to be unprofitable.
    d. both **a** and **b**.

■ Problems

The Employment Contract

21. A firm can be thought of as a joint venture between owners and workers. Suppose that these two groups face a work environment with the incentives depicted in Table 11-3. Each entry in the table shows the level of utility attained by group members from following particular courses of action.

Table 11-3

Owners/Workers	Cooperate	Shirk
Cooperate	$U_W = 4$ $U_O = 4$	$U_W = 2$ $U_O = 5$
Shirk	$U_W = 5$ $U_O = 2$	$U_W = 3$ $U_O = 3$

21a. Assuming the workers do not know the strategy employed by the owners, what is the optimal strategy for the workers?

21b. Assuming the owners do not know the strategy employed by the workers, what is the optimal strategy for the owners?

21c. Is the employment contract between owners and workers self-enforcing?

21d. The information available to each party in this case is asymmetric, since each knows the strategy it intends to follow, but is not sure what the other will do. If each party could be sure of what the other was planning to do, would that change the outcome of the employment contract?

21e. Now suppose that the work environment changes and the two groups face the incentives depicted in Table 11-4. Carefully compare the entries in the two tables. What has happened to the payoffs associated with cooperation and shirking for each group? What could be the cause of this change?

Table 11-4

Owners/Workers	Cooperate	Shirk
Cooperate	$U_W = 6$ $U_O = 6$	$U_W = 3$ $U_O = 4$
Shirk	$U_W = 4$ $U_O = 3$	$U_W = 1$ $U_O = 1$

21f. Given the information in Table 11-4, is the employment contract self-enforcing?

The Basis of Pay

*22. Consider a firm that combines labor (L) and capital (K) to produce output (Q) according to the formula

$$Q = \sqrt{L}\sqrt{K}.$$

The firm has monopoly power in the output market and faces a demand curve given by the equation

$$P = 58 - Q,$$

where P is the price of output. The firm faces perfect competition in the input market where the going price of labor (W) is \$9 and the going price of capital (C) is \$9. The profit-maximizing combination of labor and capital in the long run is

$$L^* = 20, \; K^* = 20 \Rightarrow Q^* = 20, \; P^* = 38.$$

In order to increase work incentives, suppose the firm institutes a profit-sharing pay plan under which the workers would receive a guaranteed wage (W_g) plus some fraction (s) of a measure of firm profits. The measure used by this firm is the "profit pool" (π) divided by the number of workers, where the profit pool is defined as

$$\pi = PQ - W_g L - CK.$$

This means that the compensation per worker (Y) under profit sharing will be given by the equation

$$Y = W_g + s\frac{PQ - W_g L - CK}{L}.$$

*22a. If the firm sets $W_g = \$7$, prove that the firm must set the profit-sharing parameter (s) equal to one-eleventh in order to make monetary compensation in the long run equivalent to what workers can earn elsewhere.

*22b. Even if the monetary compensation under profit sharing is the same as what workers can attain elsewhere, will most workers perceive profit sharing to be equivalent to a standard time-based wage? If not, what adjustment will the firm be forced to make?

*22c. The total expense for labor (E_L) incurred by this firm under profit sharing is given by the equation

$$E_L = (Y)(L) = W_g L + s(PQ - W_g L - CK).$$

The marginal expense of labor (ME_L) is

$$ME_L = W_g + s(\text{MRP} - W_g),$$

where MRP_L is the marginal revenue product of labor. Recall from Chapter 3 that

$$\text{MRP}_L = (MR)(MP_L),$$

where, in this example,

$$MR = 58 - 2Q \quad \text{and} \quad MP_L = \frac{1}{2}\sqrt{\frac{K}{L}}.$$

(For the reader with calculus training, the ME_L is the first derivative of the E_L expression.) Assuming the firm is at its long-run equilibrium values, find the marginal expense of labor facing the firm if $W_g = 7$ and $s = 1/11$.

*22d. Assuming the firm is at its long-run equilibrium values, compare the MRP_L and ME_L expressions. Does the firm have any incentive to increase its employment level?

*22e. Suppose the firm expands its employment from 20 to 21. Find the new output and price for this firm.

*22f. What is the size of the profit pool assuming the firm expands employment to 21?

*22g. Find the compensation per worker under profit sharing if the firm expands employment to 21. Would the firm be able to retain 21 workers?

*22h. Evaluate the effects of profit sharing on the stability of the employment relationship. Is the firm more likely to lay off workers? Are workers more likely to quit the firm?

The Level of Pay

23. Consider a firm where the optimal output is 36 units per day. If the firm pays its workers a wage of $50 per day, each worker produces an output of 4 units. If it pays its workers a wage of $100 per day, each worker produces an output of 9.

23a. What is the profit-maximizing strategy for producing 36 units of output?

23b. Assuming the going wage rate for comparable workers is $50, can the firm be described as paying an efficiency wage?

The Sequencing of Pay

24. Consider a firm where the marginal product of the typical worker varies over time according to the schedule in Table 11-5 where year 0 represents the current year. In order to motivate its workers to exert their best efforts, suppose this firm plans to sequence the pay in such a way that workers receive less than their marginal product early in their career, and then more than their marginal product toward the end of their career.

Table 11-5

Year	Marginal Product	Real Wage
0	6	3
1	10	8
2	13	12
3	15	15
4	16	?

24a. If the firm has decided to pay workers the real wage values shown in Table 11-5 for years 0, 1, 2, and 3, what is the minimum the firm could pay workers in period 4 and still have the plan be acceptable to the workers? Assume the real interest rate is 6%.

24b. Why is such a pay scheme more likely to be found in firms using an internal labor market strategy?

24c. Explain how such a pay scheme is thought to bring about increases in worker productivity?

24d. Why is the prohibition of mandatory retirement policies thought to decrease the likelihood firms will employ such schemes?

■ Applications

The Basis of Pay

25. In a health maintenance organization (HMO), subscribers pay a fixed annual fee to the organization. In return, the member is entitled to comprehensive care through the organization's network of physicians. Some HMOs contract with physicians who also have private practices (i.e., serve non-HMO patients as well). In such instances, patients go to the physician's private office for care. Other HMOs maintain their own staff of physicians who are located at a few central locations. According to an article in *The Wall Street Journal*, January 25, 1993 (p. B1, B4), doctors employed by HMOs typically receive a flat fee (e.g., $10) for every HMO member they see. Such fees are easier to administer than other systems where doctors are compensated on the basis of the services actually performed. In order to improve the quality of care patients receive, some HMOs have been experimenting with individual incentive-pay plans.

25a. Why might the quality of care be a concern under a system where doctors are paid a flat fee for each patient served?

25b. Besides being easier to administer, why do you suppose organizations might use such a flat fee system instead of paying for each service rendered?

25c. What determines how low the fee can go? What role do doctor's preferences toward risk play in the setting of the rate?

25d. One individual incentive-pay plan gives doctors bonuses of between 5% and 15% of their base pay depending on how they score on patient satisfaction questionnaires and a review of office records. What are the advantages of such a pay plan? What are the disadvantages? What kinds of questions should be asked in the questionnaires?

25e. Are such incentive pay plans likely to work better with staff doctors who are private practitioners or with the doctors who work exclusively for the HMO at a central location?

25f. Other organizations have moved away from the flat fee method to a merit-pay system. Under these plans, doctors receive bonuses if they are rated as "exemplary" or "commendable" by their section chiefs. What problems might occur in such a system?

25g. Would it make sense to tie the doctors' pay to the overall success of the HMO? If so, what would be an appropriate measure of group success? What problems might you expect from such a group incentive-pay plan?

25h. Given all the problems associated with performance-based pay, why do HMOs not just compensate doctors for their time?

The Level of Pay

26. An article on the career paths of top executives contained the following quote.

"Forget about the straight climb to the top of the company you started with. Increasingly, the fast track up will be a zigzag through different companies. Whoever wants to run General Motors in the future should leave it now." [*The Wall Street Journal*, March 15, 1993 (p. B1)]

26a. Assuming this statement is true, what are its implications for the use of efficiency wage strategies?

26b. One explanation for why large firms pay more is that large firms are more likely to utilize an efficiency wage strategy. What is the reasoning behind this assertion? Is the reasoning consistent with the above quote?

The Sequencing of Pay

27. Faced with pressures to employ a diverse workforce, some firms have abandoned seniority-based layoff policies ("last hired, first fired") for ones that favor the retention of women and minorities (who tend to be the newest workers). What affect would such a change have on the likelihood of a firm successfully using a deferred compensation scheme?

Chapter 12
Gender, Race, and Ethnicity in the Labor Market

■ Summary

The discussion in Chapter 11 of the complex relationship between pay and productivity drew on a wide array of material from Chapters 5, 8, 9, and 10. In so doing, it significantly expanded the analytical framework available for thinking critically about labor issues. It is this analytical framework that allows one to strip away the rhetoric that often surrounds highly controversial labor market issues and see more clearly the consequences of various labor market practices and policies. Perhaps no topic is more controversial than that taken up in Chapter 12.

Issues related to gender, race, and ethnicity have come to play a more prominent role in labor market analysis because of the tremendous demographic changes that have taken place in the American labor force over the last 30 years. If the trends continue, white workers, 81% of the labor force in 1981, will comprise only 65% of the civilian labor force by the year 2012. The percentage of women in the work force continues to rise, while the percentage of Hispanic and Asian workers is growing so rapidly that the two groups are projected to comprise over 20% of the labor force by the year 2012, up from less than 9% in 1982. For the most part, the demographic groups growing most rapidly earn significantly less than white males. What is the source of these earnings differences? How much of the difference is attributable to discrimination? These are the questions taken up in the first part of Chapter 12.

Although the difference in earnings between men and women has been narrowing gradually, in 2000 full-time white women workers over the age of 18 still earned only 67% of what white males earned on average. The ratio is even smaller if just older workers are compared, but somewhat larger if younger and more educated workers are compared. Some of the difference is clearly due to the different occupational distributions of men and women, with women being more prevalent in traditionally lower-paying occupations. But women tend to be paid less then men even in the same occupation. One reason may be that women, on average, work fewer hours than men, and so men's higher wages may be a compensating differential for longer hours of work. Women also tend to have less work experience, and that experience may be interrupted by time out of the labor force. Thus they are less likely to be promoted.

However, even when differences in occupation, age, experience, and hours of work are considered, there is still unexplained variation between the earnings of women and men. It may be that the differences reflect something about the preferences of men and women, or other factors, such as differences in the productive characteristics with which the groups *enter* the labor market, **pre-market differences**. Or there may be **labor market discrimination**, differences in the way that the groups are treated *within* the labor market.

Wage discrimination exists when one group is paid less than another, given the same experience, working conditions, and productive potential. **Occupational discrimination** exists when members of one group are pushed into lower-paying jobs or positions of less responsibility by employers, again given the same experience and productive potential. **Occupational segregation** occurs when the distribution of occupations within one group is very different from the distribution in another. However, that may reflect preferences and not discrimination, unless occupational choices are directly limited. But preferences themselves may be the result of **premarket discrimination**, different societal treatments that may push one group toward certain pursuits and interests long before they actually enter the labor market.

One measure of the occupational differences between men and women is the **index of dissimilarity**. It is defined as the percentage of women (or men) that would have to change occupations in order for women to be distributed among occupations in the same proportions as men. Formally, the index (S) is computed using the summation formula

$$S = \frac{1}{2}\sum_{i=1}^{N}|M_i - F_i|,$$

where M_i is the percentage of the total population of male workers in occupation i, F_i is the percentage of the total population of female workers in occupation i, and N is the number of occupations. If men and women were distributed identically, the index would equal zero, while completely segregated occupations would have an index of 100.

The index of dissimilarity, which was 68 in 1970, has declined to 53 in 1990, which indicates that occupational segregation has decreased somewhat, though studies still find that there is a significant effect on the wages of women.

Example: Measuring Wage Discrimination

Consider a labor market where a worker's wage is a function of his or her work experience (EXP) and occupation (OC). Let the occupational variable OC take on a value of 1 if the person works in the "high-paying" sector of the labor market and 0 otherwise. Suppose the relationships between wages, experience, and occupation for males (M) and females (F) can be represented by the equations

$$W_M = 4 + 2\ OC + 0.75\ EXP,$$
$$W_F = 4 + 2\ OC + 0.5\ EXP.$$

Assuming women are employed only in the low-paying sector of the economy, these equations can be rewritten as

$$W_M = 6 + 0.75\ E,$$
$$W_F = 4 + 0.5\ E.$$

These equations are represented by lines M_1 and F_0 in Figure 12-1.

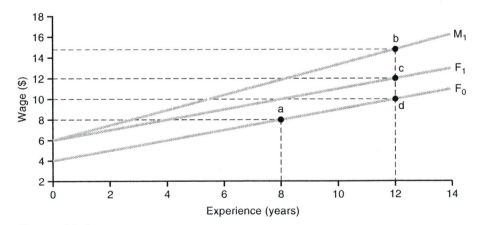

Figure 12-1

If EXP averages 12 years for men and only 8 years for women, then the average wages for each group will be

$$W_M = 6 + 0.75(12) = 15,$$
$$W_F = 4 + 0.5(8) = 8.$$

These wage levels are shown as points a and b in Figure 12-1. Note how the different productive characteristics (different occupations and experience levels), along with the payoffs to those characteristics, come together to determine the wages paid to each group. In this example, the average woman earns only 53% of what the average man does.

To measure the degree of wage discrimination, occupation and the level of experience must be held constant so that just the differences in labor market payoffs can be observed. In this case, we calculate what women would earn if they were employed in the same jobs and had the same experience levels as men. Substituting OC = 1 and EXP = 12 into the female wage equation yields

$$W_F = 4 + 2\,(1) + 0.5\,(12) = 12.$$

This is point c in Figure 12-1 (line F_1 represents the returns to experience for women assuming they were employed in the same jobs as men). After adjusting for the differences in occupation and experience, note that women still earn only 80% of what the average man does. The 20% difference in wages (the percentage difference between points b and c), which is due to differences in the payoff to experience, is a measure of the degree of wage discrimination. Notice that wage discrimination accounts for less than half of the 47% gap in wages that is actually observed.

If the different employment patterns of men and women are the result of occupational segregation, the total amount of current labor market discrimination is found by just controlling for the differences in experience and not the differences in occupation. Given the occupations of men and women, we calculate what women would earn if they had the same experience levels as men. Substituting EXP = 12 into the female wage equation yields

$$W_F = 4 + 0.5(12) = 10.$$

This is point d in Figure 21-1. Note that at point d, women earn only 67% of what men do. The 33% difference between points b and d is a measure of the current labor market discrimination. The difference between points c and d ($2 or 13% of the men's wage) represents the effects of occupational segregation. Note that the current labor market discrimination in this example can be decomposed into approximately 20% wage discrimination and 13% occupational segregation. Empirical studies using cross-section data suggest current labor market discrimination in the range of 15% to 20%. Recall that the total wage gap was 34% in 1993.

An ideal study of wage discrimination would of course include more than just experience and occupation as a measure of the worker's productive characteristics. For example, education and ability should also be included. But even if all measured productive characteristics were accounted for, some unmeasurable differences may still exist. These unmeasurable characteristics suggest that the estimate of the female to male wage ratio computed after controlling for all measured productive characteristics should be interpreted as an upper bound on the degree of wage discrimination.

In contrast, if past wage discrimination has reduced the incentive of women to make human capital investments, some of the differences in productive characteristics (premarket differences) may also reflect discrimination. Therefore, while the 33% gap between male and female earnings in the above example might be a good measure of *current* labor market discrimination, a measure of the differential due to both current and past discrimination would be larger since it would have to take into account the extent to which pre-market differences in productive characteristics reflect past discrimination. It is possible that pre-market choices are themselves significantly affected by labor market discrimination. If, for example, women believe that entry to some professions is more difficult due to labor market discrimination, they may avoid those occupations, and then occupational differences do not solely represent a difference in preferences between men and women.

However, it is frequently the case that data cannot be obtained on all of the pre-market variables that have an impact on wages, and thus it is possible that estimates of labor market discrimination are overstated. If, for example, differences in employment patterns represent voluntary differences in occupational choice instead of occupational segregation, the hypothetical 33% estimate in the above example would overstate the degree of current labor market discrimination.

While bearing in mind the limitations of such estimation, a variety of studies have found that while differences in labor market experience explain much of the gender gap in earnings, labor market discrimination could explain a small but significant portion of the gap.

The basic framework for analyzing earnings differences between men and women also applies when analyzing differences between blacks and whites, as well as differences between whites and various ethnic groups. The wage gap between white and black men (67% in 2003) is similar to that between men and women overall. Where blacks continue to differ most from whites, however, is in their unemployment and participation rates. For black men, participation rates are consistently lower than for white men, and unemployment rates are higher. There is also evidence that black males suffer disproportionately in recessions, suggesting that they are last hired and first fired. Participation rates for black women are higher than rates for white women, but the unemployment rate for black women again exceeds the rate for white women.

Studies measuring occupational segregation have found about half the dissimilarity found between men and women, but studies of wage discrimination have found about an 11% differential between the earnings of black and white men, all other things equal. Again, this may be due to unmeasured productive characteristics. One characteristic that is usually unmeasured is cognitive achievement. Scores on the Armed Forces Qualification test show lower levels of cognitive achievement for black Americans, which may be associated with poorer-quality schooling and effects of poverty. This difference alone may explain most of the wage differential.

Applying the wage discrimination methodology to data on other ethnic groups in the United States shows relatively higher earnings for white, Asian, and European ethnic groups, and lower earnings for Native American and Hispanic workers. Studies on Hispanic residents reveals that their earnings remain 3% to 6% below those of non-Hispanic whites after controlling for language proficiency and other productive characteristics.

Assuming that at least a significant portion of the unexplained earnings gaps that exist for women, blacks, and some ethic groups is attributable to current labor market discrimination, what is the source of the discrimination? What is the mechanism by which the discrimination affects labor market outcomes? These are the questions taken up in the second part of Chapter 12.

One possible source of discrimination is **personal prejudice**, which can be exhibited by employers, customers, or fellow employees. In the case of employer prejudice, the discrimination can be modeled as a shifting down of the marginal product curve pertaining to a particular group of workers as employers subjectively devalue their productivity. This downward shift leads to a reduction in employment opportunities and/or real wages for the group. For the market as a whole the size of the wage gap is ultimately driven by the number of prejudiced employers relative to the supply of the group's workers and the intensity of the discriminatory preferences. The subjective devaluation of the group's productivity also lowers profits for the employer. This suggests that prejudiced employers will not survive in a competitive market. Thus, employer prejudice seems like a plausible source of discrimination only if the firms are insulated from competition (e.g., by being in a regulated industry). Similarly, since discrimination based on customer or employee prejudice can cause a firm's costs to increase, such discrimination is likely to persist only if the firm finds that eliminating the discrimination is even more costly than catering to it.

Another possible source of discrimination is the hiring and screening process. In this process, firms try to evaluate an applicant's productivity using observable personal characteristics such as education, experience, and test scores. The problem is that while these variables tend to be correlated with productivity, they are not perfect predictors of it. Knowing this, firms sometimes supplement the information about personal characteristics with group information. For example, if black high school graduates tend to be less productive, on average, than whites because of differences in high school quality, employers may give preference to white applicants when all other personal characteristics are equal. Modifying individual data based on group characteristics is called **statistical discrimination**. Although such discrimination need not stem from malicious feelings towards any particular group, it can have the unfortunate side effect of limiting employment opportunities or reducing wages paid to those who do not fit the group profile. After all, even if schools in predominantly black neighborhoods are, on average, inferior to predominantly white schools, there will likely still be blacks that graduate from these schools who are at least as productive as any white applicant. Ultimately, as members of a particular group become more dissimilar (e.g., the number of excellent black schools increases) making judgments on the basis of group affiliation will actually hinder the firm's hiring process and lead to lower profits.

Occupational crowding and **dual labor market** theories of discrimination use lack of occupational mobility to explain wage differences between groups. The dual labor market theory, for example, postulates the existence of a **primary** sector of high-wage and stable jobs, and a **secondary** sector of undesirable jobs. Historically, women and minorities have been employed in the secondary sector, resulting in poor work histories that are then used to block breakthroughs into the primary sector. Another theory explains wage differences between different groups by pointing out that **search costs** will be higher for workers subject to discrimination. These higher search costs, in turn, give employers a greater degree of monopsony power over some groups, which then translates to lower wages for those groups. Another theory is that white employers collude in the hiring of certain groups and so effectively become monopsonists. This position enables them to dictate lower wages to women and certain minority groups.

While each theory that relies on noncompetitive forces to explain discrimination is in a way consistent with the data on wages, each version also raises more questions than it answers. For example, what caused women and minorities to be originally assigned to the secondary sector of the labor market? Why do the employers paying higher wages in male-dominated occupations not substitute less expensive female labor? How is the collusion against women and minorities by millions of employers maintained when each individual firm has an incentive to cheat on the agreement and hire members of the disfavored group to substitute for more expensive white male labor?

While none of the theories of discrimination outlined above is completely satisfactory, the discussion does suggest that discrimination cannot persist without imperfectly competitive markets or high adjustment costs. Can government play a role in helping to create an environment where discrimination can not persist? The third part of Chapter 12 reviews and analyzes public policy towards discrimination.

Employers are prohibited from discriminating with respect to compensation or employment opportunities by Title VII of the Civil Rights Act of 1964. However, the term *discrimination* means different things to different people, and it is ultimately up to the courts to define discrimination. Unfortunately, the courts have not always provided consistent answers. One definition of discrimination adopted by the courts has come to be known as the **disparate treatment** standard. Under this definition, a violation of Title VII occurs if individuals are intentionally paid different wages or denied certain employment opportunities because of characteristics like gender, race, or ethnicity. An alternative definition is known as the **disparate impact** standard. Under this definition, personnel policies that treat everyone the same, but impact certain groups (e.g., women or minorities) more than others, are illegal provided the policies do not relate directly to job performance and serve a business necessity. Under a disparate impact definition, seemingly neutral policies like word-of-mouth recruiting may be illegal since they can carry forward the effects of past discrimination. Layoffs in order of reverse **seniority**, however, are permitted under the law even though they may disadvantage women and minorities who tend to be the newest hires (perhaps because they were the victims of past discrimination). The disparate impact standard has also given rise to efforts to replace the free market setting of wages with a system of **comparable worth** pay in which workers are paid according to the skills, responsibilities, and working conditions involved in any particular job. Such a system is thought by some to help break down the effect of occupational segregation on wages, though critics suggest the employment ramifications of deviating from market-determined wages could harm many of those the system was intended to help.

Even under the disparate impact definition, Title VII is very clear in not requiring any party to grant preferential treatment to any group to make up for labor market imbalances. However, considerable tension exists between this principle and the **affirmative action** plans required of most federal contractors by the Office of Federal Contract Compliance Programs. Under an affirmative action plan, contractors must commit to a schedule for rapidly overcoming any less-than-proportional representation of women and minorities in the various levels of the firm. But what constitutes the proportional representation of women and minorities? To answer this question requires knowledge of the number of women or minorities that are available to the firm and what fraction of total available workers they constitute. Guidelines for defining the pool of available workers are vague but require the consideration of a number of factors. These factors include the geographic area from which employees can reasonably commute, the population percentage of women and minorities, the percentage that are actually in the labor force, the percentage that are unemployed, the percentage that have the necessary skills, the number of promotable women and minorities already in the firm, and the possibilities for training women and minorities in the necessary skills. Once the percentage goal is set, the key question is whether that percentage applies to new hires or whether the target group should constitute even a greater percentage of new hires. Hiring at a rate just equal to the percentage in the pool of available workers means that achieving the overall goal throughout the firm will be a slow process, whereas hiring women and minorities in greater-than-proportionate numbers would seem to violate Title VII's prohibition against requiring preferential treatment. Although studies of the contract compliance program show it has had little effect on raising the black-to-white earnings ratio, evidence also suggests that all federal antidiscrimination efforts taken together may account for up to one-third of the improvement in black-to-white earnings ratios that took place between 1960 and 1975.

The appendix to Chapter 12 discusses a simple estimation method for making comparable worth pay adjustments. Under the comparable worth system discussed in the appendix, jobs that are at least 70% male or female are rated by outside consultants as to the degree of know-how, problem-solving skills, and accountability the jobs require. These ratings, along with a rating of working conditions, are summed to create a total score for each job. Using the least squares regression technique discussed in Appendix 1A, the wages earned by male workers are then regressed on the scores associated with each male job. The estimated relationship between wages and scores is then used to predict the wage that should accompany any score. These predictions can then be compared to the wages earned in female jobs with the same overall score. Any gap that is observed can then be closed through future pay adjustments.

■ Review Questions

Choose the letter that represents the **<u>BEST</u>** response.

Defining and Measuring Labor Market Discrimination

1. Labor market discrimination towards women can be said to currently exist if
    a.   women, on average, are paid less than men for performing the same job.
    b.   men and women with identical productive characteristics are treated differently in the labor market simply because of gender.
    c.   women tend to be employed in a different set of occupations than men.
    d.   all of the above.

2. One form of current labor market discrimination toward women is wage discrimination. Which of the following factors must be controlled for before wage discrimination can be identified?

a. working conditions

b. occupation

c. experience

d. all of the above

3. One form of current labor market discrimination toward women is occupational segregation. This refers to a reduction in the relative wage of women caused by restrictions on the types of occupations open to women. Which of the following factors must be held constant before the effects of occupational segregation can be identified?

a. All productive characteristics except occupation

b. All productive characteristics including occupation

c. All productive characteristics except previous occupational training

d. All productive characteristics except previous work history

4. In the context of measuring gender discrimination, the term "premarket differences" refers to

a. the gap between the average wages of men and women.

b. differences in the current productive characteristics of men and women.

c. the effects on women of past discrimination.

d. differences between men and women regarding the "price" each productive characteristic brings in the labor market.

In answering Questions **5–10**, please refer to Figure 12-2 which assumes that the wage workers receive is a function of their occupation and experience. Line M_1 refers to the relationship between the wage and experience for men who are employed exclusively in the high-paying sector of the labor market. Line F_0 refers to the relationship between the wage and experience for women who are employed exclusively in the low-paying sector. Line F_1 refers to the relationship between the wage and experience for women if they were employed in the same occupations as men. Assume women average 2 years of work experience while men average 6 years.

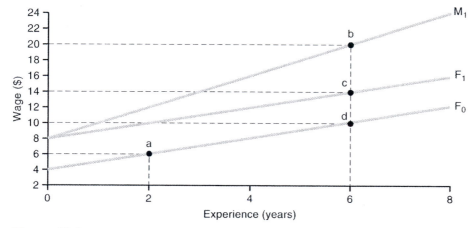

Figure 12-2

5. On average, how much will men's wages exceed women's?

a. $14

b. $10

c. $6

d. $4

6. How much of the gap between men's and women's wages could be attributed to current labor market discrimination?
    a. $16
    b. $10
    c. $6
    d. $4

7. How much of the gap between men's and women's wages could be attributed to current wage discrimination?
    a. $12
    b. $8
    c. $6
    d. $4

8. How much of the gap between men's and women's wages could be attributed to occupational segregation?
    a. $14
    b. $12
    c. $6
    d. $4

9. The estimate of current labor market discrimination will be overstated if
    a. there are unmeasurable productive characteristics that differ by gender.
    b. occupational choice is the result of preferences formed before labor market entry.
    c. women have experienced wage discrimination in the past.
    d. both **a** and **b**.

10. The index of occupational dissimilarity in the above example is 100 since the occupations are completely segregated. Suppose instead that 10% of all female workers were employed in occupation 1 and 90% in occupation 2, while 75% of male workers were employed in occupation 1 and 25% in occupation 2. The index of dissimilarity for this labor market would be
    a. 30.
    b. 35.
    c. 65.
    d. 80.

Theories of Market Discrimination

11. Assume all demographic groups have the same productive characteristics. An employer who is prejudiced against blacks will
    a. hire the same number of blacks and whites provided the wage paid to blacks is low enough.
    b. hire fewer blacks than whites.
    c. never hire blacks.
    d. either **a** or **b**.

12. Assume all demographic groups have the same productive characteristics. An employer who discriminates against blacks because of personal prejudice will
    a.   earn lower profits than employers who do not discriminate.
    b.   be less productive than those that do not discriminate.
    c.   earn higher profits through the exploitation of blacks.
    d.   have to charge higher prices.

13. Which of the following pieces of evidence would indicate that the source of discrimination against blacks was customer prejudice?
    a.   The existence of segregated workplaces in occupations with high customer contact
    b.   Differences in the average earnings of self-employed black and white workers after controlling for all premarket differences
    c.   Blacks who hold customer contact positions are found to be more qualified than whites holding those same positions
    d.   All of the above

14. If the source of discrimination against blacks is employee prejudice, one would predict that
    a.   whites with the same productive characteristics would be paid more if they worked in integrated workplaces.
    b.   firms that do not cater to discriminating employees would be more profitable than those that do.
    c.   there would be wide variations in the earnings of black employees.
    d.   both **a** and **b**.

15. The likelihood of a firm using statistical discrimination in its hiring and screening of women decreases as
    a.   the monopoly power of the firm decreases.
    b.   prejudice against women decreases.
    c.   women become less similar in their productive characteristics.
    d.   all of the above.

16. The major problem with the occupational crowding and dual labor market theories of discrimination is that
    a.   they are based on the notion of noncompeting groups.
    b.   they do not explain how the noncompeting groups were initially formed.
    c.   they are not completely consistent with the empirical facts of labor market discrimination.
    d.   they suggest discrimination is profitable for the firms.

17. Which of the following is a true statement concerning the collusive action model of discrimination?
    a.   The firms conspire to create prejudice.
    b.   Discrimination increases profits for all the firms.
    c.   Individual firms will be very reluctant to break the agreement.
    d.   All of the above.

Federal Programs to End Discrimination

18. Assuming the courts follow a disparate treatment definition of discrimination, which of the following personnel practices would be illegal under Title VII of the Civil Rights Act?
    a. Using seniority to allocate promotions and layoffs
    b. Comparable worth pay adjustments
    c. Deliberately granting preference in the hiring process to groups that are underrepresented in the workforce relative to their population percentages
    d. All of the above

19. Assuming the courts follow a disparate impact definition of discrimination, which of the following personnel practices would be illegal under Title VII of the Civil Rights Act?
    a. Using seniority to allocate promotions and layoffs
    b. Comparable worth pay adjustments
    c. Job related tests and standards that serve a business necessity
    d. Word-of-mouth recruiting

20. Affirmative action planning is required by the Office of Federal Contract Compliance Programs for most government contractors. It requires firms to commit to a schedule of hiring and promotion for certain demographic groups that is based on their percentage in the pool of "available" workers. Which of the following is not a factor that firms must take into account when deciding which workers are available for hire?
    a. The population of the targeted group within the area of reasonable commuting distance
    b. The unemployment rate of the targeted group within the area of reasonable commuting distance
    c. The interest people from the targeted group have in working at the firm
    d. The investment in training the firm is able to make

Estimating "Comparable Worth" Earnings Gaps

21. Which of the following is not a factor that is typically used in scoring jobs under a comparable worth pay system?
    a. working conditions
    b. problem-solving skills
    c. required training
    d. the worker's previous work history

22. Assume the relationship between monthly earnings and job evaluation scores (S) for male workers has been estimated by least squares regression to be

$$\text{Earnings} = 1000 + 5S.$$

If a woman works at a job where $S = 100$ and has monthly earnings of $1,200, what is the size of the comparable worth earnings gap expressed in percentage terms?
    a. 5%
    b. 20%
    c. 25%
    d. 80%

■ Problems

Measuring Labor Market Discrimination

23. Consider a labor market where a worker's wage is a function of his or her years of education past the compulsory level (*ED*), work experience (EXP), and occupation (OC). Let the occupational variable OC take on a value of 1 if the person works in the "high-paying" sector of the labor market and 0 otherwise. Suppose the relationships between wages, education, experience and occupation for males (*M*) and females (*F*) can be represented by the equations

$$W_M = 3 + 0.5 \, ED + 0.6 \, EXP + OC,$$
$$W_F = 3 + 0.4 \, ED + 0.5 \, EXP + OC.$$

Assume that, on average, *ED* = 4, and EXP = 10 for men, while for women the averages are *ED* = 3 and EXP = 6. Also assume that women are only employed in the low-paying sector of the labor market.

23a. Find the average wage of men and women. What is the ratio of women's to men's wages? What is the gap between women's and men's wages in percentage terms?

23b. What wage would women earn if they had the same premarket characteristics as men on average? What would be the ratio of women's to men's wages?

23c. Express the amount of current wage discrimination in percentage terms.

23d. Suppose that the differences in occupation do not reflect premarket choices but occupational segregation. What is the most women could earn even if all other productive characteristics were the same as men? What would be the ratio of women's to men's wages?

23e. Express the amount of current labor market discrimination in percentage terms. Express the wage reduction due to occupational segregation in percentage terms.

23f. Is the estimate of current labor market discrimination likely to understate or overstate the true impact of discrimination on labor market outcomes?

23g. An alternative way to compute the extent of wage discrimination would be to determine what men would earn if they had the same premarket characteristics (including occupation) as women. What would the ratio of women's to men's wages be under this approach? Is the measure of wage discrimination in percentage terms greater or less than the answer to 23c?

23h. An alternative way to see the effect of occupational segregation is to suppose that the segregation is broken down so that half of all women now work in the high-paying sector and half of all men work in the low-paying sector. Assuming this does not change the payoffs to education and experience that men and women receive in the labor market, compute the average wages that would be observed for men and women. Find the ratio of women's to men's wages.

Measuring the Degree of Occupational Segregation

24. Consider Table 12-1, which shows the total employment in each of four occupations as well as the percentage of each occupation that is staffed by male and female workers.

24a. Construct a table showing the actual number of male and female workers in each occupation.

24b. Construct a table showing the percentage of total male and female workers employed in each occupation.

24c. Compute the index of occupational dissimilarity.

Table 12-1

Occupation	% Male	% Female	Total Employment
A	20%	80%	50
B	40%	60%	50
C	80%	20%	50
D	60%	40%	50
			200

Changes in the Employment Ratio of Black Men

25. The employment to population ratio (*ER*) for any particular group can be expressed as a function of the group's labor force participation rate (LFPR) and unemployment rate (*UR*) using the formula

$$ER = \text{LFPR}\,(1 - UR).$$

According to data presented in Table 12.5 of the text, the employment ratio of black men was 71.9% in 1970. By 1997 the ratio had fallen to 61.4% because of an increase in the group's unemployment rate from 7.3% to 10.2% and a decrease in its labor force participation rate from 77.6% to 68.3%. If the labor force participation rate of black men could be increased to its 1970 level, how high could the unemployment rate be without the group's employment ratio falling further?

The Effects of Employer Prejudice

26. Consider a firm that hires both white and black workers. Each group of workers has an identical marginal product curve given by the equation

$$MP_L = 25 - 0.5L.$$

Suppose that the going real wage rate for each group of workers is 15.

26a. What is the optimal level of employment for each group of workers? How much profit does the employment of the black workers add to the firm?

*26b. Now suppose that the employer develops a prejudice against the black workers. This prejudice causes the employer to subjectively devalue the productivity of black workers. The result is that at any given level of employment, the employer will act as if the marginal product of black workers is 5 units less than it really is. Assuming the going wage rate for each group remains the same, what is the optimal level of employment for each group of workers? How much profit does the employment of black workers add to the firm now?

*26c. How low would the wage of black workers have to fall to keep the employment of black workers the same as it was originally? How much profit does the employment of black workers add to the firm now?

*26d. Given the new wage of black workers, what employment level would a non-prejudiced employer set? How much profit would this employment of black workers add to the firm?

Determinants of the Relative Wage Between Men and Women

27. Figure 12-3 shows the market demand curve for women expressed in terms of the ratio of women's to men's wages (W_F/W_M).

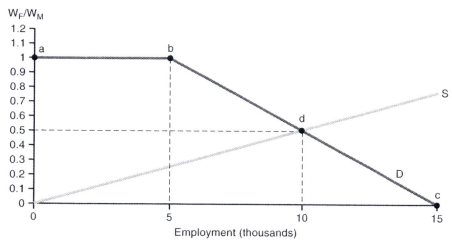

Figure 12-3

The figure assumes that there are enough nondiscriminating employers so that up to 5,000 women can be hired at a relative wage of 1. After that point, women will be hired by discriminating employers who demand a decrease in the relative wage to induce them to hire women. Assume that for every $1 decrease in the relative wage, the quantity of women demanded increases by 10,000. Therefore, if the relative wage fell to zero, 15,000 women would be hired. This combination of discriminating and non-discriminating employers leads to the market demand curve given by the line *abc*. The supply curve of women is represented by the line labeled *S*.

27a. What is the market-clearing value of the relative wage? How many women will be employed at this wage?

27b. Now suppose that the number of nondiscriminating employers increases in such a way that the number of women who can be hired at a relative wage of 1 increases to 10,000. At the same time, however, suppose that the discriminatory preferences of the other employers worsens so that for every $1 decrease in the relative wage, the quantity of women demanded increases by only 5,000. What will happen to the relative wage and employment of women?

Estimating "Comparable Worth" Earnings Gaps (Appendix 12A)

28. Assume the relationship between yearly earnings (Y) and job evaluation scores (S) for male workers has been estimated by least squares regression to be

$$Y = 20000 + 50\,S.$$

Suppose a woman works at a job where $S = 600$ and earns a salary of $40,000.

28a. What is the size of the comparable worth earnings gap expressed in dollar terms?

28b. What is the size of the comparable worth earnings gap expressed as a percentage of the wage earned by men?

■ Applications

Measuring Discrimination

29. Data presented in Table 12.6 of the text suggest that men of Russian ancestry earn 57% more than the U.S. average. Does this mean that there is no discrimination against Russians in the United States? If not, how could such discrimination be measured?

Effects of Unmeasurable Characteristics on Estimates of Discrimination

30. Consider a labor market where a worker's wage is a function of his or her years of work experience (EXP), occupation (OC), and attitude towards making money (Z). Let the occupational variable OC take on a value of 1 if the person works in the "high-paying" sector of the labor market and 0 otherwise. Similarly, the variable Z takes on a value of 1 if making money is high priority for the person, and 0 otherwise. Suppose the relationships between wages, experience, occupation, and attitude for males (M) and females (F) can be represented by the equations

$$W_M = 8 + 0.75 \text{ EXP} + 2 \text{ OC} + Z,$$
$$W_F = 8 + 0.5 \text{ EXP} + 2 \text{ OC} + Z.$$

Assume that, on average, EXP = 12 for men and 8 for women, and that women are only employed in the low-paying sector of the labor market. Also suppose that men tend to place a high priority on making money while women do not.

30a. Find the average wage of men and women. What is the ratio of women's to men's wages? What is the gap between women's and men's wages in percentage terms?

30b. What wage would women earn if they had the same premarket characteristics as men on average? What would be the ratio of women's to men's wages?

30c. Express the amount of current wage discrimination in percentage terms.

30d. In general, attitudes about making money may be very difficult to observe or measure. Find the wage that women would earn if all productive characteristics except Z were the same as men on average. What would be the ratio of women's to men's wages?

30e. What would be the estimate of current wage discrimination in percentage terms assuming Z is unmeasurable?

Social Losses from Occupational Segregation

31. Consider an economy with three sectors of employment. Table 12-2 shows the relationship between employment, total output, and the marginal product of labor in each sector. Suppose there are 6 male workers and 6 female workers in this economy. Due to occupational segregation, all 6 women work in sector A, while 3 of the men work in sector B and 3 men work in sector C.

31a. What is the real wage paid in each sector under occupational segregation?

31b. How much total output is produced given the segregated distribution of labor?

31c. Suppose discrimination in employment is eliminated and so one women flows from sector C to sector A, and another woman flows from sector C to sector A. What would be the real wage paid in each sector?

31d. How much total output is produced under the new distribution of labor? Is the new distribution of labor optimal?

Table 12-2

Employment	Output	Marginal Product
1	90	90
2	170	80
3	240	70
4	300	60
5	350	50
6	390	40
7	420	30
8	440	20
9	450	10
10	450	0

Effects of Affirmative Action Planning

32. Consider a government contractor with 1,000 employees, 100 (10%) of whom are black. Suppose that the yearly turnover rate at this firm is 20% and that the firm annually replaces anyone who leaves with a new hire. Suppose that in the pool of available workers, 20% are black.

32a. If this firm's affirmative action plan calls for the proportion of new hires that are black to be the same as their proportion in the pool of available workers, how many blacks will be hired in the first year? How many blacks will leave the firm during the first year?

32b. How many blacks will be employed at the firm one year into the affirmative action plan? What percentage of the total employment does this represent?

32c. Find the percentage of black workers at the firm 5 years into the affirmative action plan.

32d. Suppose the ultimate goal under the affirmative action plan is a workforce that is 20% black. Would an increase in the turnover rate increase or decrease the number of years that it would take to achieve this goal?

Chapter 13
Unions and the Labor Market

■ **Summary**

Chapter 12 introduced an objective framework for analyzing the earnings differences that accompany gender, race, and ethnicity. This framework was then used as the basis for a systematic inquiry into labor market discrimination, a frequently misunderstood topic where passions tend to run high. The topic of labor unions also stirs up strong feelings in many people. The purpose of this chapter is to provide a framework for objective and critical thinking about the role labor unions play in the labor market. This framework draws heavily on the discussion of the elasticity of labor demand presented in Chapter 4.

Labor unions are organized as either **industrial** or **craft** unions. An industrial union, like the United Steel Workers, represents most or all of the workers in a particular firm or industry regardless of the job they perform. A craft union, like the carpenters union, represents only workers performing a certain type of job. Bargaining on behalf of the collective membership can take place at the national or local level and often involves more than one employer. Subjects raised in bargaining sessions include wages and employee benefits, job security, safety, and workplace rules. Unions also play a role in enforcing the eventual agreement and in helping workers communicate with management.

The importance of unions varies a great deal internationally. The United States and Japan, for example, have relatively small percentages of workers that are covered by collective bargaining agreements. Some countries, such as France, have very low union membership but almost all workers are covered by a collective bargaining agreement. In Sweden, nearly all workers are union members and are covered by a collective bargaining agreement, but some unions are far stronger and have better bargaining power than others.

In the United States, unions faced a hostile legal environment throughout most of the 19th and early 20th centuries, and this helped to hinder their growth and development. Beginning in 1932, with the Norris-LaGuardia Act, the legal climate turned in organized labor's favor by banning the use of labor injunctions. In 1935 the Wagner Act established the **National Labor Relations Board** to conduct union elections and to stop employers from interfering with unions through unfair labor practices. Later laws focused on keeping unions from becoming too powerful. Under the 1947 Taft-Hartley Act, states were allowed to pass **right-to-work laws**. These laws prohibit agreements requiring employees to become union members. The 1959 **Landrum-Griffin Act** was directed towards increasing union democracy. Since 1962, federal government workers have also been allowed to organize, although laws for state workers vary.

Union membership in the U.S. peaked at about one-third of the labor force just after World War II. Since then it has steadily declined, standing at 13.7% in 2002. Unionized workers usually belong to a local union, which bargains at the firm level, but the local unions are generally part of a national or international union. In cases where wage agreements are industry-wide, the national union will bargain. Most of the national unions are affiliated with the AFL-CIO, a national association of unions that acts to coordinate initiatives between member unions, act as a unified political voice, and provide information and research. More men than women are unionized, and the highest rates of unionization are in manufacturing, construction, transportation, and public utility industries.

What do unions want, and how do unions and employers behave in their negotiations over wages and benefits? Unions clearly seek higher compensation for their members, a package that includes both wages and other benefits. But they face constraints. As unions raise the price of union workers, firms will be induced to substitute capital for labor, and thus the demand for labor decreases (as does the ability of unions to achieve higher wages). Increasing wages also reduces the quantity of workers demanded, all other things equal. In industries that are stable or declining and where the elasticity of demand for labor is high, unions will be weak because any increase in the wage will cause a sharp decrease in employment. In industries where demand for labor is inelastic and in industries that are growing, unions may be able to obtain higher wages without employment effects.

The traditional **monopoly** view of unions has been that unions bargain for higher wages and then the employer is free to determine the employment level that will maximize the firm's profits. This occurs at the point on the firm's demand curve consistent with the negotiated wage rate. The problem with this scenario is that if the union values both the wage and employment of its members, such an outcome is not economically efficient; in other words, there is a whole range of wage and employment combinations that still exist where at least one party can be made better off without hurting the other. Using indifference curves to represent union preferences and isoprofit curves to represent the firm's constraints, the **efficient contracts** model shows the set of combinations preferable to the monopoly outcome. Within that set, those combinations where it is impossible to make one party better off without making the other worse off form the **contract curve** or locus of efficient contracts. These wage and employment combinations are shown to lie to the right of the firm's demand curve for labor.

If the level of union membership is thought of as the result of the demand for, and supply of, union activity, what accounts for the decline in the percentage of the United States labor force that is unionized? Three factors have combined to shift the demand for union services to the left. The first is the substantial increase in the percentage of the labor force that is female. Seniority provisions, job security arrangements, and retirement plans are of little interest to any worker who expects to be with the firm for only a short period of time. However, these are some of the main issues for which unions typically fight. Historically, women had shorter attachments to the labor force than men, and were consequently less likely to demand union representation. More recently, however, women's attachment to the labor force has come to more closely parallel that of men, and it is not likely that increased labor force participation among women has been much of a factor in declining union membership for the past two decades.

The second reason is the change in the composition of private sector employment. Workers employed in the growing areas of wholesale and resale trade, finance, insurance, and other services have traditionally not joined unions because in these competitive areas labor demand tends to be very elastic. When labor demand is elastic, the ability of unions to bargain for higher wages is constrained by the large employment losses such wage increases bring. Historically, female employment has been much stronger in the service than in the production industries. This probably served to reduce the independent impact of growing female participation, since women were not entering (in very large numbers) markets where unions were strong.

The third reason has been overall increase in product market competition due to deregulation and foreign competition. As product markets become more competitive, labor demand becomes more elastic and the expected benefits from union membership decline.

Two factors have also combined to shift the supply of union services to the left. Regional shifts in employment opportunities to the South, due in part to increased product market competition, have made union organizing more difficult since most of these states have passed right-to-work laws. Faced with more competition and a rising union to non-union wage ratio, many employers have also increased their resistance to union organizing campaigns. Some forms of employer resistance are perfectly legal, but some have taken the form of unfair labor practices.

As noted previously, given the limits that large employment losses place on a union's ability to raise wages, unions are more likely to be successful when labor demand is **inelastic**. A growing demand for labor may also help to mask the reduction in employment opportunities brought about by higher wages. But what factors lead to an inelastic demand for labor? According to the Hicks-Marshall laws discussed in Chapter 4, labor demand elasticity decreases as the difficulty of substituting other inputs for labor in the production process increases, as the supply of other inputs becomes less elastic, as the demand for the product becomes less elastic, and as the share of total costs that are labor costs decreases. When these factors are not favorable to union success, unions can be expected to take steps to change them. For example, union support for a higher minimum wage, restrictions on immigration, staffing and subcontracting restrictions, strict specification of a worker's job function, and limits on the supply of skilled workers to a craft can be traced to the union's desire to limit the substitution possibilities for union labor. Similarly, support for import quotas or tariffs, domestic content legislation, and programs to "buy American" can be traced to the desire to stimulate the demand for union labor.

Given the elasticity and position of the labor demand curve, unions are able to secure higher wages for their members mainly because of their ability to impose costs on management through work slowdowns or **strikes**. While no single model of strike activity is completely satisfactory, a number of models exists to highlight different aspects of the process. According to Hicks' model of the bargaining process, the optimal strike length occurs at the intersection of the firm's upward-sloping **employer concession curve** and the downward-sloping **union resistance curve**. The employer concession curve slopes upward because longer strikes impose additional costs on the firm, creating an incentive to raise the wage offer. The union resistance curve slopes downward because strikes also impose costs on union members through lost income. As the strike lengthens, the income loss increases and union members reduce their wage demands. One problem with this framework is that if each side is aware of the other's schedule, there is no need for a strike since agreeing to the predicted wage increase before the strike would make each side better off. Hence, the credibility of this model depends on the existence of imperfect information or the ability of a strike to influence future negotiations.

For public sector unions, the collective bargaining situation may be substantially different since public sector unions are not allowed to strike in most states, and instead must deal with the possibility of some form of third-party arbitration. Chapter 13 discusses the incentives faced by each party in a collective bargaining situation when there is the possibility of having an arbitrator impose a settlement, and a formal model is presented in Appendix 13A. The model shows that the wider the range of **uncertainty** about the arbitrator's decisions and the greater the **risk aversion** of the parties, the greater is the range of acceptable settlements to both parties. Assuming the probability of reaching a negotiated settlement is positively related to the size of the acceptable range, increased uncertainty and risk aversion increase the likelihood that arbitration will not be necessary.

What effects do unions have on the labor market? The *absolute* effect that unions have on wages is impossible to determine since union wages can only be measured *relative* to non-union wages, and non-union wages are affected by union activities. Unions may have a positive or negative effect on non-union wages, so it is not always clear whether the relative wage advantages unions secure for their members overstate or understate the absolute wage effects of unions.

Example

Consider a labor market with union and non-union sectors. The demand and supply curves for union (U) labor are given by the equations

$$\text{Demand: } L_U^D = 20 - 0.5W,$$
$$\text{Supply: } L_U^S = 1.5W.$$

These curves are shown as lines D and S_0 in Figure 13-1a. The demand and supply curves in the non-union (N) sector are given by

$$\text{Demand: } L_N^D = 40 - 2W,$$
$$\text{Supply: } L_N^S = 2W.$$

These curves are shown as lines D and S_0 in Figure 13-1b. Note that the initial market-clearing wage in each sector is $10. The optimal employment level is 15 in the union sector and 20 in the non-union sector.

Now suppose that the union succeeds in raising the wage of its members to $12. This represents an **absolute wage effect** of 20%. What effect will this wage change have on the relative wages between the two sectors?

Note that the increase in the union wage reduces the quantity of union labor demanded to

$$L_U^D = 20 - 0.5(12) = 14,$$

while the quantity of labor supplied increases to

$$L_U^S = 1.5(12) = 18.$$

Together this creates a labor surplus in the union sector of 4 units.

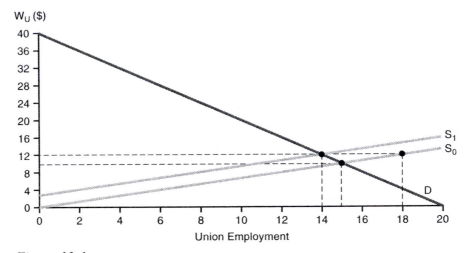

Figure 13-1a

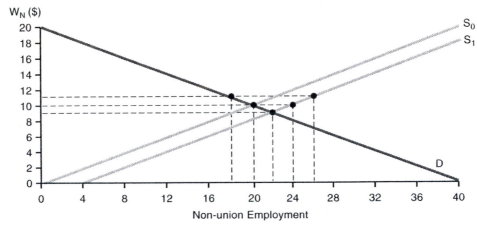

Figure 13-1b

How will these workers respond to the unemployment in the union sector? One possibility is that the 4 surplus workers may seek employment in the non-union sector. Suppose the workers **spill over** from the union to the non-union sector in such a way that the supply curve in the union sector becomes

$$L_U^S = 1.5W - 4,$$

while the supply curve in the non-union sector becomes

$$L_N^S = 2W + 4.$$

These curves are denoted by the lines labeled S_1 in Figures 13-1a and 13-1b. The supply shift in the union sector is just enough to eliminate the unemployment in that sector. The increase in supply in the non-union sector creates a surplus in that sector at the original wage of $10. However, since the wage is free to adjust in the non-union sector, the market will clear where

$$L_N^D = L_N^S$$
$$\Rightarrow 40 - 2W = 2W + 4$$
$$\Rightarrow W_N^* = \$9 \text{ and } L_N^* = 22.$$

Note that after the spillover adjustment is complete, the union wage ($12) exceeds the non-union wage ($9) by $3 for a **relative wage advantage** of 33%. Therefore, if labor market spillovers occur in response to union wages, the relative wage advantage will overstate the absolute effect of the union on its members' wages. However, such a spillover effect may not be the most likely response to the increase in the union wage.

Another possibility is that a wage increase in the union sector may actually trigger a wage increase in the non-union sector as employers move to head off union attempts to organize non-union workers and secure an even larger wage increase. The ability of a union wage increase to bring about a wage increase in the non-union sector is called a **threat effect**. In this example, the threat effect may result in the non-union employer raising the wage somewhere between the original wage of $10 and the union wage of $12. If, for example, the wage was raised to $11, note that this would create unemployment in the non-union sector. Given the supply curve S_1, the quantity of labor supplied would increase to

$$L_N^S = 2(11) + 4 = 26,$$

while the quantity of labor demanded would decrease to

$$L_N^D = 40 - 2(11) = 18,$$

creating a surplus of 8 units in the non-union sector. Note however, that the threat effect would lower the relative union wage advantage to one-eleventh or 9.1%. In this case the relative wage advantage understates the absolute effect of the union on member wages.

Another problem with the standard spillover scenario is that expected earnings are not equal at the new market-clearing wage and employment levels. Letting F stand for the fraction of each period that a person expects to be employed, expected earnings (Y) are given by the equation

$$Y = (W)(F).$$

Since there is no unemployment after the spillover is complete, F equals 1 in both sectors. However, since the union wage exceeds the non-union wage, expected earnings are greater in the union sector. This suggests that some workers may find it attractive to remain in the union sector even though they will be unemployed for at least part of the time. Such decisions lead to what is called **wait unemployment**.

For example, suppose one of the workers who spilled over to the non-union sector now returns to the union sector. Also suppose we adopt the simple rule that the fraction of time any individual will be employed is related to the unemployment rate (UR) in that sector according to the equation

$$F = 1 - UR.$$

Letting E be the number employed and U the number unemployed, the unemployment rate is given by the formula

$$UR = \frac{U}{U + E}.$$

If 3 workers return to the union sector, expected earnings in that sector would equal

$$Y_U = W_U F_U \Rightarrow Y_U = 12\left(1 - \frac{3}{3+14}\right)$$
$$\Rightarrow Y_U = (12)(0.823) = \$9.88.$$

The flow of workers out of the non-union sector would reduce the supply of non-union workers to

$$L_N^S = 2W + 1,$$

which means that the non-union sector clears where

$$40 - 2W = 2W + 1$$
$$\Rightarrow W_N^* = \$9.75 \quad \text{and} \quad L_N^* = 20.5.$$

Since there is no unemployment in the non-union sector, Y_N also equals \$9.75. Note that the migration of 3 workers back to the union sector has significantly reduced the expected earnings gap between the two sectors. To drive the expected earnings exactly into equality would require a movement of just over 3 units of labor back to the union sector. Moving all 4 units back to the union sector would result in a situation where

$$W_U F_U = (12)\,(0.778) = \$9.33 < \$10 = W_N F_N,$$

which is not an equilibrium allocation of labor.

Given that the amount of wait unemployment is just over 3 units of labor in this case, the wage in the non-union sector will remain slightly below the original level of \$10, meaning that again the relative wage advantage will overstate the absolute effect of the union on wages. Note that it is possible, however, for the final equilibrium to occur where the wage in the non-union sector is above its original level, meaning that the relative wage advantage will understate the absolute effect of the union. The comparison of relative and absolute union wage effects can be further complicated by outward shifts in the demand for union labor that may accompany union bargaining efforts. If such shifts come at the expense of non-union labor, they lead the relative wage to again understate the absolute wage effect of the union.

Empirical evidence places the union relative wage advantage in the range of 10% to 20%, with some evidence pointing to a decrease in non-union wages. This suggests that the spillover effects (along with the demand shift effects just mentioned) tend to outweigh the threat and wait unemployment effects illustrated in this example.

In interpreting the effects of unions on wages, it is important to keep in mind that wages are only part of the total compensation package received by workers. Evidence also suggests that union workers receive higher levels of employee benefits and that employee benefits account for a greater percentage of total compensation. However, union workers also tend to work under conditions that are more structured, inflexible, and involve a faster pace and greater risk of injury. Thus, some of the difference in compensation between union and non-union workers may reflect a compensating differential for the less desirable working conditions. This issue serves as a vivid reminder that the same sets of problems that hamper the measuring of discriminatory wage differentials also applies when measuring the returns to unionization. That is, to truly measure even the relative wage advantage due to unions one must be careful to control for differences in productive characteristics and working conditions. Even then, there may be unmeasurable or unobservable differences that account for some part of the gap, leading to an overstatement of the union relative wage advantage.

Perhaps the most controversial issue surrounding unions is their effect on productivity and output. Clearly, some union activities reduce productivity and output. The labor market spillovers that result from higher union wages lead to a lower total output than before the wage change. Restrictive work rules and staffing requirements secured by unions to make the demand for labor more inelastic serve to move the firm away from its cost-minimizing combination of inputs. If a firm wishes to stay at the original cost level it must then reduce its total output. In addition, there may be lost output from strikes.

An alternative view, however, stresses that unions can have positive effects on productivity and output by giving workers an avenue for communicating directly with management. In a perfectly competitive labor market, workers who are unhappy with their jobs communicate with management by quitting. If enough workers quit, ultimately management is forced to make changes to attract workers. Quits, however, tend to erode worker loyalty and morale, and cause firms to lose their hiring and firm-specific training investments. High turnover also makes it impossible for firms to use productivity-enhancing compensation policies like pay sequencing and efficiency wages that depend on the existence of internal labor markets. By providing workers with a way to speak with a **collective voice**, unions can serve as an alternative and less costly adjustment mechanism. Some empirical studies suggest that unions increase productivity enough to offset the increased costs that come from higher union wages. However, such findings conflict with observations of continued employer resistance to unions and unfavorable stock market reaction to unionization efforts. These observations are consistent with a belief that unions increase costs and reduce profitability.

From a normative point of view, the question is: do unions enhance or reduce social welfare? If there is lost production due to strikes and excessive hiring due to restrictive work rules, then clearly the outcome is not Pareto efficient. Also, if the marginal productivity of the last worker employed in each industry is not equal, greater output at lower cost could be achieved by reallocating workers. If unions raise wages and thus reduce employment in some sectors, this marginal productivity condition cannot be achieved, because they are preventing some lower-wage workers (who have lower productivity due to excess labor in the low-wage sector) from moving into the high-wage sector (where they would be more productive, because there is less labor).

Others argue that unions enhance social welfare by giving workers a collective voice in establishing working conditions. Individuals may find it too costly to speak out or to leave their job if they are unhappy, and thus there are Pareto-efficient transactions that may not take place. Secondly, as in the efficient-contracts section, if employers are monopolists, unionism may involve redistribution of some of the monopolist's profit (to the workers) rather than a reduction in employment. This is an equity issue but has no impact on overall allocative efficiency. Finally, better management-worker communications through the union's collective voice might lead to productivity increases.

■ Review Questions

Choose the letter that represents the **BEST** response.

Unions and Collective Bargaining

1. Which of the following is an accurate description of the nature of unions and collective bargaining in the United States?
   a. Unions tend to be intimately and uniformly associated with one political party.
   b. Bargaining must take place separately with each employer.
   c. Unions are organized as industrial or craft unions.
   d. Union bargaining positions tend to be controlled by the American Federation of Labor-Congress of Industrial Organizations (AFL-CIO).

2. Which of the following is not a role of the National Labor Relations Board (NLRB)?
   a. Conduct union representation elections.
   b. Conduct union decertification elections.
   c. Prevent employers from opposing union organizing campaigns.
   d. Investigate and rule on charges of unfair labor practices.

3. Under the 1947 Taft-Hartley Act, states were allowed to pass laws that have come to be known as right-to-work laws. These laws prohibit
   a. requiring a person to become a union member as a condition of employment.
   b. the permanent replacement of striking workers.
   c. employer interference in union elections.
   d. discrimination against union members.

4. Holding all else constant, which of the following changes would tend to decrease the demand for union activity?
   a. A decrease in the average job tenure
   b. The repeal of some right-to-work laws because of changing attitudes towards unions
   c. Increased use of tariffs and import quotas to restrict the flow of foreign imports
   d. Higher penalties for committing an unfair labor practice

5. Holding all else constant, which of the following changes would tend to decrease the supply of union activity?
   a. A decrease in the ratio of union to non-union wages
   b. Increased employer resistance to unions
   c. An increase in the number of regulated industries
   d. A decrease in the wage elasticity of demand for union labor

6. Union membership as a percentage of the labor force has declined steadily since 1954 when it reached a high of 25.4%. By 1997, only 11.8% of the individuals in the labor force were members of unions or employee associations. Which of the following factors has not contributed to this trend?
   a. New federal legislation unfavorable to union organizing efforts
   b. Deregulation of firms in the airline, trucking, and telephone industries
   c. Migration from the Northeast and Midwest to the South
   d. An increase in the fraction of the labor force that is female

"Monopoly Unions" or "Efficient Contracts"?

7. Which of the following is a characteristic of firm isoprofit curves drawn in the same space as the demand for labor?
    a. The curves must be downward sloping.
    b. Higher curves are associated with higher levels of profit.
    c. The curves reach their maximum when they intersect the demand curve.
    d. Both **a** and **b**.

8. An efficient contract between the union and the employer is reached when
    a. the parties explicitly bargain over both wage and employment levels.
    b. it is possible to make one party better off without hurting the other.
    c. it is impossible to make one party better off without making the other worse off.
    d. the firm maximizes its profits and the union maximizes its utility.

How Unions Achieve Their Objectives

9. Which of the following factors would contribute to union success in raising its members' wages without the occurrence of substantial employment losses?
    a. A rapidly growing product demand
    b. An inelastic supply of substitute inputs
    c. A high price elasticity of demand for the final product
    d. Both **a** and **b**

10. There are more constraints on union power in the long-run because
    a. the firm can substitute other inputs for union labor.
    b. in the long run the supply of substitute inputs may be more elastic.
    c. product markets become more competitive in the long run with the entry of new firms.
    d. all of the above.

11. Which of the following factors do unions usually try to limit in collective bargaining agreements?
    a. The number of apprentice workers that can be employed
    b. The firm's ability to subcontract work to other firms
    c. The firm's ability to substitute between capital and labor
    d. All of the above

12. Which of the following public policies are most likely to be supported by unions?
    a. The elimination of tariffs and import quotas
    b. A lower minimum wage for teenage workers
    c. Occupational licensing laws
    d. Higher ceilings on the number of immigrants allowed into the country

13. The Hicks model of the bargaining process predicts that a wage settlement will be made in advance of a strike provided that
    a. each side has perfect information about how the other's bargaining position will change over time.
    b. the union's threat to strike is credible.
    c. the union's resistance curve is always downward sloping.
    d. both **a** and **b**.

The Effects of Unions

14. Which of the following repercussions associated with a union wage increase could cause the relative union wage advantage to understate the absolute effect of the union on wages?
    a. The threat of unionization in the non-union sector
    b. Wait unemployment in the union sector
    c. Spillovers from the union to the non-union sector
    d. Both **a** and **b**

15. Assume that the ratio of union to non-union wages is 1.25 and that there is no unemployment in the non-union sector. What is the fraction of each time period that individuals in the union sector expect to be employed?
    a. 0.25
    b. 0.75
    c. 0.8
    d. 1.0

16. Suppose that the average union worker has wage earnings 15% more than the average non-union worker. Before this difference can be attributed to the monopoly power of unions, which of the following factors must be held constant?
    a. Working conditions
    b. Employee benefits
    c. Worker productivity
    d. All of the above

17. Unions have traditionally been thought to lower worker productivity by
    a. enabling workers to speak with a collective voice in the workplace.
    b. increasing quit rates.
    c. bargaining for rules that promote the use of internal labor markets.
    d. bargaining for limits on the substitution of capital for labor.

18. Which of the following is a likely consequence of a union's serving as an effective collective voice for its members?
    a. More strikes
    b. Longer job tenures
    c. Less firm-specific training
    d. More restrictive work rules

Arbitration and the Incentive to Bargain (Appendix 13A)

In answering Questions **19–21**, assume that two parties (call them A and B) negotiate over the share (*S*) of a fixed dollar amount that will go to each. If the parties can not agree, an arbitrated settlement will be imposed. Uncertainty exists as to the arbitrator's eventual decision and the two parties have identical risk averse preferences.

19. The lowest share that person A would voluntarily accept is the share that yields a utility level
    a. equal to the average utility from arbitration.
    b. equal to the utility associated with the average arbitrated settlement.
    c. slightly greater than the utility associated with the minimum share expected under arbitration.
    d. higher than the utility level achieved by person B.

20. The contract zone consists of those shares that
    a. both parties find preferable to going to arbitration.
    b. yield equal utility for both parties.
    c. are in between the minimum and maximum shares expected under arbitration.
    d. yield utility levels higher than the average utility from arbitration.

21. Assuming the probability of a voluntary settlement is positively related to the size of the contract zone, the probability of a voluntary settlement increases as
    a. the spread of possible outcomes under arbitration increases.
    b. preferences become more risk averse.
    c. the amount to be divided between the two parties increases.
    d. both **a** and **b**.

■ Problems

The Employment Effects of Unions

22. Suppose the demand curve for union labor is given by the equation

$$L = 100 - 2W.$$

Suppose the current wage is $10. Now suppose the union is successful in raising the wage of its members to $15. At the same time, it is able to shift the demand for labor out to

$$L = 120 - 2W.$$

22a. What was the original employment level? What is the new employment level?

22b. Has the higher wage negotiated by the union reduced the employment opportunities of its members? If so, by how much?

23. Consider a firm with a marginal revenue product (MRP_L) curve given by the equation

$$MRP_L = 40 - 4L.$$

Assume that the firm has monopsony power in the labor market and faces a market supply curve for labor given by the equation

$$W = 2L.$$

If the monopsonist pays the same wage to all its workers, the marginal expense of labor (ME_L) to the firm will be

$$ME_L = 4L.$$

23a. Graph the marginal revenue product curve, the labor supply curve, and the marginal expense of labor curve together on the same axes.

23b. Compute the optimal employment and wage levels for this monopsonist.

23c. Now suppose that a union organizes all the workers in this market and negotiates a wage of $16. What employment level will result? Has the union wage led to an increase or decrease in employment opportunities for the members?

23d. Assuming the union wants to raise the wage of its members (relative to what it was originally) and maximize member employment, what would be the optimal wage from the union's perspective? What employment level would be associated with this wage?

"Monopoly Unions" or "Efficient Contracts"?

*24. Consider a firm with a production function given by the equation

$$Q = 10L - 0.5L^2.$$

The resulting marginal product of labor expression is

$$MP_L = 10 - L.$$

Suppose the firm sells its output in a perfectly competitive market where the going price (P) is $5.

24a. Find the firm's marginal revenue product equation and graph it.

24b. If the going wage is $15, find the optimal employment level. What output level is associated with this level of employment?

24c. Given the wage of $15, verify that the profit associated with the optimal employment level is $122.50.

*24d. Find the equation for the isoprofit curve associated with a profit level of $122.50. That is, find an expression for the wage and employment combinations that yield the same profit level as the combination in **24b**. Express your answer with the wage on the left side of the equation and employment on the right.

*24e. Plot the isoprofit curve on the same graph as the marginal revenue product curve.

24f. Now suppose the union raises the wage to $30. Find the optimal employment level. What is the resulting output of the firm? Verify that the firm's profit falls to $40.

The Effects of Unions on Wages

25. Consider a labor market with union and non-union sectors. The demand and supply curves for union (U) labor are given by the equations

$$\text{Demand: } L_U^D = 30 - 0.5W,$$
$$\text{Supply: } L_U^S = W.$$

The demand and supply curves in the non-union (N) sector are given by

$$\text{Demand: } L_N^D = 60 - 2W,$$
$$\text{Supply: } L_N^S = W.$$

25a. Find the equilibrium wage and employment levels in each sector.

25b. Now suppose that the union succeeds in negotiating a wage for its members of $22. What is the absolute wage effect of the union in percentage terms? Compute the labor surplus that is created by the new wage.

25c. Suppose the labor surplus in the union sector spills over to the non-union sector. Assume the union supply curve shifts left by the amount of the surplus and the non-union supply curve shifts right by the amount of the surplus. Find the non-union wage and employment level. What is the relative union wage advantage in percentage terms?

25d. Find the expected earnings in each sector after the labor spillover. Is this situation likely to represent a labor market equilibrium?

25e. Suppose that the fraction of time any individual will be employed is related to the unemployment rate (UR) in that sector according to the equation

$$F = 1 - UR.$$

Letting E be the number employed and U the number unemployed, the unemployment rate is given by the formula

$$UR = \frac{U}{U + E}.$$

Find the expected wage in each sector if 2 of the workers who had previously sought work in the non-union sector return to the union sector to wait for a job opening. Does it make sense for a certain amount of wait unemployment to occur in this labor market?

25f. Find the expected wage in each sector if 3 of the workers who had previously sought work in the non-union sector return to the union sector to wait for a job opening. Will any wait unemployment that occurs in this market lead the relative union wage advantage to understate or overstate the absolute wage effect of the union?

26. Consider again the supply and demand curves initially given in the **Summary** section **Example** problem. As the union initially raises the wage to $12, suppose that it also succeeds in raising the demand for union labor to

$$L_U^D = 24 - 0.5W.$$

This increase comes at the expense of labor demand in the non-union sector which is now reduced to

$$L_N^D = 36 - 2W.$$

26a. What effect would the change in demand have on the wage and employment in the union sector?

26b. What effect would this change in demand have on the wage and employment in the non-union sector?

26c. Would this change in demand cause the relative union wage advantage to overstate or understate the absolute wage effect of the union?

Arbitration and the Incentive to Bargain (Appendix 13A)

27. Consider a situation where two parties (call them A and B) are negotiating about how to split a certain level of profit. The utility function for A and B are given by the equations

$$U_A = \sqrt{S_A} \quad \text{and} \quad U_B = \sqrt{S_B},$$

where S_A and S_B represent the share of total profits received by A and B. These shares must add to one. If the two sides can not agree on how to split the profits, the decision will be made by an arbitrator.

27a. How much utility would A derive if the arbitrator awarded him half of the profits with certainty?

27b. How much utility would A derive from receiving one-fourth of the profits? What about three-fourths?

27c. If the probability of A receiving a one-fourth share was 50%, and the probability of receiving a three-fourths share was also 50%, what is the average level of utility person A could expect? How does this average level of utility compare with the average level derived from receiving a 50% share with certainty? What does this say about A's attitudes toward risk?

27d. What is the minimum share A could receive with certainty that would yield the same average level of utility that is expected from arbitration?

27e. Assuming person A receives this minimum share, what is the maximum share B could receive?

27f. What is the minimum share B could receive with certainty that would be acceptable? What does that imply about the maximum share A could receive?

27g. What is the contract zone over which the two sides can bargain?

27h. Suppose that uncertainty about the arbitrator's decision decreases. Half of the time she is expected to award A a share of one-third, while the rest of the time she is expected to award A a two-thirds share. What happens to the size of the contract zone? Is a negotiated settlement more or less likely? State any assumption you make.

■ Applications

Comparing Private and Public Sector Unions

28. One of the unique characteristics of public sector labor markets is that the percentage of employees that are members of a bargaining organization increased throughout much of the 1960s and 1970s and has been roughly steady ever since. In contrast, the percentage of union members in the private sector has been steadily declining. At the same time, numerous studies also suggest that public sector unions have had less of an effect on their members' wages than private sector unions. If public sector unions have had less success raising wages, why have they been more successful attracting and retaining members?

"Monopoly Unions" or "Efficient Contracts"?

29. Figure 13-2 shows the demand curve (*D*) for union members. Suppose the preferences of union members concerning wage and employment combinations can be represented by the indifference curves labeled *U* where higher subscripts represent higher levels of utility. The curves labeled *I* represent employer isoprofit curves. Higher subscripts are associated with higher profit levels.

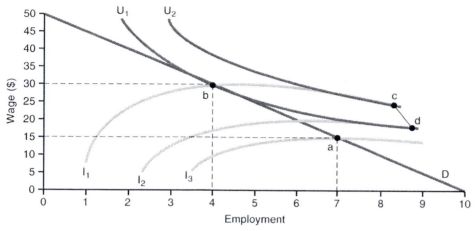

Figure 13-2

29a. Suppose the union is successful in raising the wage of its members from $15 to $30. The monopoly union model predicts that as a result of this, employment will fall from 7 to 4 (from point *a* to point *b*). Why is point *b* not an efficient contract?

29b. The set of points along the line *cd* represent the set of efficient contracts in this diagram. What characteristic does each point in this set share? Are each of the outcomes fair to the union and to the firm?

29c. Unlike the monopoly union model, the efficient contract model requires that the union and employer bargain over both wage and employment levels. However, according to data cited in the text, in 1980 only 11% of major private sector bargaining agreements had explicit provisions guaranteeing employment levels. Does this mean that the collective bargaining process rarely leads to efficient contract agreements?

Models of Strike Activity

30. One of the most widely discussed strikes of the 1990s was the United Auto Workers strike against Caterpillar Inc., a maker of heavy construction and farm equipment. The strike began on November 4, 1991, with the union pushing for a contract similar to that signed earlier with Deere & Co., Caterpillar's main domestic competitor. The company estimated that such a settlement would eventually raise wage and benefit costs 26% over three years. It countered with an offer of a 17% wage and benefit increase. After a five-and-a-half-month strike, members returned to work when the firm threatened to begin hiring permanent replacement workers. The firm imposed the terms of its last contract offer.

30a. Despite incurring the costs of a strike, union members were not able to secure a wage settlement above management's original offer. Keeping in mind the problems of asymmetric information and the distinction between union leaders and the rank-and-file members, explain how such an outcome could have come about.

30b. Caterpillar's argument throughout the strike was that a settlement in excess of management's offer would make the company noncompetitive with rivals in Japan and Europe. Assuming this is true, was there any other bargaining approach the union could have taken that would have helped to make the firm more competitive and at the same time increased its members' wages?

Effects of Unions on Output and Productivity

31. Consider an economy with a union and non-union sector. Suppose for simplicity that the relationship between employment, total output, and the marginal product of labor is the same in each sector. The relationship for each sector is shown in Table 13-1.

Table 13-1

Employment	Total Output	Marginal Product
1	50	50
2	95	45
3	135	40
4	170	35
5	200	30
6	225	25
7	245	20
8	260	15
9	270	10
10	275	5

31a. Suppose that the real wage in each sector is originally 25. What would be the quantity of labor demanded in each sector? Assuming the demand can be satisfied, how much total output would be produced?

31b. Now suppose the wage is increased in the union sector to 35. Find the employment level and total output in the union sector.

31c. Assuming the workers unemployed by the union wage spill over to the non-union sector, find the wage and total output in the non-union sector.

31d. Contrast the total output in the economy before and after the union wage increase. Is the new allocation of labor in the economy optimal?

31e. Suppose that instead of spilling over to the non-union sector, unemployed workers in the union sector waited for future openings in that sector. Contrast the total output in the economy before and after the union wage increase.

31f. The effect unions have on total output through the reallocation of labor can theoretically be offset if unions enhance worker productivity by functioning as a collective voice in the workplace. Why is it necessary for workers to speak with a collective voice in order to bring about change in the workplace? Why can't individual workers communicate with management directly?

Chapter 14
Unemployment

■ Summary

As will be discussed in Chapter 15, the widespread introduction of new technology has brought new employment opportunities and rising relative wages to those with the highest levels of human capital. However, this new technology has also helped to bring about higher than normal job losses, particularly among unskilled workers, and has put a premium on being able to adapt to new workplace challenges. The result has been that unemployment, or the fear of unemployment, has touched the lives of more and more people. While the national unemployment rate is often viewed as being determined solely by macroeconomic forces, it clearly has a number of important microeconomic determinants. The purpose of Chapter 14 is to present an analysis of the phenomenon of unemployment from a microeconomic perspective.

The national unemployment rate is one of the most visible and closely-watched indicators of aggregate economic well-being. To understand its microeconomic determinants, it is first necessary to understand how it is measured. As noted in Chapter 2, the population (POP) aged 16 or over can be divided into those in the labor force (L) and those not in the labor force (N). The **labor force** consists of all those who are employed for pay (E), actively seeking work, or waiting to be recalled from layoff. Those actively seeking work or waiting to be recalled from layoff are classified as unemployed (U). Therefore, if the population can be defined as the sum of L and N, the labor force can be defined as the sum of E and U. The **unemployment rate** (u) is defined as the ratio of U to L. The data on U and L come from the Current Population Survey, a national survey of over 60,000 households conducted monthly.

As a measure of economic hardship, the unemployment rate has a number of drawbacks, some of which have been discussed in previous chapters. For example, the unemployment rate actually decreases when those who search unsuccessfully for work give up the search. The rate also does not distinguish between part-time and full-time work, nor does it distinguish whether the unemployed person is the primary source of their family's income. The unemployment rate may also give very little indication as to the employment rate (e)—the fraction of the total population that is employed. The reason is that the employment rate is related to the unemployment rate via the equation

$$e = \mathbf{lfp}\,(1 - u),$$

where **lfp** denotes the **labor force participation rate**, the ratio of the labor force to the population. If the labor force participation rate is growing rapidly, the employment rate can increase at the same time the unemployment rate is rising. If one keeps in mind these limitations, the unemployment rate can still be a useful indicator of labor market conditions.

The microeconomic determinants of the unemployment rate are best understood within the context of the flows of people over any given period between different labor market categories. Letting P_{ij} represent the proportion of individuals in labor market state i that flow to labor market state j during the period, where the labor market states are employment (e), unemployment (u), and not in the labor force (n), under certain conditions the unemployment rate can be expressed as a function (F) of these flows where

$$u = F(\overset{+}{P}_{en}, \overset{-}{P}_{ne}, \overset{-}{P}_{un}, \overset{+}{P}_{nu}, \overset{+}{P}_{eu}, \overset{-}{P}_{ue}).$$

The sign over each proportion indicates the effect of an increase in that particular proportion on the unemployment rate, holding all else constant. An intuitive understanding for each of the effects can be obtained by using the definition of the unemployment rate. For example, an increase in the flow from e to n raises the unemployment rate because it leaves the numerator of the unemployment rate unchanged but reduces the denominator. The stock flow model shows that even when the unemployment rate is not changing, significant changes are still taking place in the labor market.

The values of P_{ij}, if computed using monthly data, are also referred to as average monthly transition probabilities. Data on the proportions for particular demographic groups can be useful in understanding why unemployment rates vary across groups. For example, the relatively high unemployment rate for teenagers is due to relatively high flows from e to n and from e to u. This suggests that the unemployment problem is not so much a lack of jobs but an inability or unwillingness to keep a job. By using the stock flow model to pinpoint the cause of a group's unemployment rate, it may be possible to design a more appropriate policy for lowering the group's unemployment rate. For example, since teenagers have trouble holding jobs, not finding them, a program of job search assistance would have little impact on that group. Such a program would be more appropriate for a group that has a relatively low probability of moving from unemployment to employment. Teenagers would be better served by attempts to promote on-the-job training (perhaps by lowering the minimum wage for teens).

The stock flow model can also be helpful in understanding the various types or categories of unemployment. **Frictional** unemployment occurs because labor market information is imperfect. Even when labor markets are in equilibrium, it may take time for job seekers to fill the available job vacancies. These market imperfections reduce the proportion of people flowing from u to e and so raise the unemployment rate.

Additional insights into the determinants of unemployment can be obtained using a model of the **job search** process. The following example illustrates one such model.

Example

Consider a labor market where employers differ in the level of skill (K) that they require, where K ranges from 1 to 3. Each employer then pays a wage equal to the skill level of the job multiplied by 10. Assuming for simplicity that there is an equal proportion of employers at every wage level, the distribution of wage offers can be represented by the function $f(W)$ in Figure 14-1. Such a probability distribution is called a **uniform distribution** since the wage offers are spread evenly over the range $10 to $30. A wage drawn at random from this distribution would be equally likely to take on any of the values between $10 and $30. Note that the height of the distribution is constant at $1/(30 - 10)$ or 0.05. This ensures that the area under the distribution equals one, a requirement of any probability distribution.

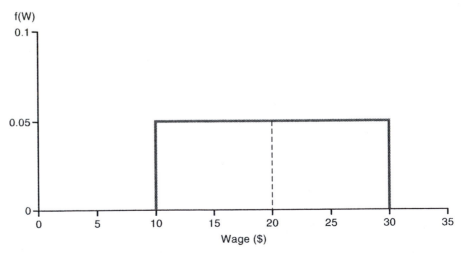

Figure 14-1

Note that the probability distribution need not (and is probably not) uniform; the text illustrates the same model with a non-uniform distribution. The uniform distribution is used in this example for simplicity.

Now consider an unemployed individual with a skill level of $K^* = 2$. Since no firm will hire a worker that does not meet its requirements, the highest wage this worker can expect to be offered is $20. This also means that if the person does not know the skill level associated with any particular employer, and instead searches randomly over all the firms in this labor market, the probability of receiving an offer is only 50%. The other 50% of the distribution (the area of the distribution to the right of $W = \$20$) represents positions that are unattainable. Note that the total or cumulative probability associated with any particular wage range on the graph can be found by computing the area under $f(W)$.

Given the applicant's situation, the ideal result would be to instantly receive a job offer of $20. In such a situation, the applicant would receive his or her highest attainable wage without incurring the costs associated with job search. But what if the first offer is not $20 but something lower? Assuming offers cannot be accumulated, rejecting the offer means that there is still the chance of receiving an offer closer to $20, but the person will have to bear the costs of additional job search for at least another period. One way to proceed in such a situation is to adopt a **reservation wage** strategy. In such a strategy, the person picks a lower bound below which any offers will be rejected. Note that deliberately ruling out a certain range of lower wage offers will further reduce the probability of receiving any offer, and so increase the likelihood a person would have to incur additional job search costs. However, such a lower bound will also increase the wage that that the person can eventually expect to receive. In general then, the reservation wage (W_R) should be set at the level where the expected benefit from additional job search just equals the additional cost.

Given the distribution of wage offers in Figure 14-1, what is the expected benefit from additional job search? The expected benefit can be thought of as the probability that a new offer will exceed WR multiplied by the average gain that can be expected when it does. Using WR as the reference point, what is the probability that a new offer will exceed WR? Note that if WR were set at $10, the probability of getting a better offer on the next job search attempt is 50%. On the other hand, if the reservation wage were set at $20, the probability of getting a better offer is zero (given the skill level of this individual). Hence, for reservation wages between $10 and $20 the probability ($P$) of getting a better offer can be written as

$$P = \frac{20 - W_R}{20}.$$

What is the average gain that can be expected from such an offer? Since the average wage in the interval between W_R and $20 can be written as $(W_R + 20)/2$, this wage would represent a gain (G) over W_R of

$$G = \frac{W_R + 20}{2} - W_R \Rightarrow G = \frac{W_R + 20 - 2W_R}{2} \Rightarrow G = \frac{20 - W_R}{2}.$$

Multiplying G by P yields the expected gain from additional job search (EG)

$$EG = (P)(G) = \frac{20 - W_R}{20} \frac{20 - W_R}{2} \Rightarrow EG = \frac{(20 - W_R)^2}{40}.$$

Assuming for simplicity that the marginal cost of an additional period of job search is constant at $2, the optimal value for the reservation wage occurs where

$$\frac{(20 - W_R)^2}{40} = 2 \Rightarrow W_R = 20 - \sqrt{80} = \$11.06.$$

A few implications follow directly from this exercise. Note that by setting a reservation wage of $11.06, the individual deliberately reduces his or her chances of a job offer from 0.5 to $(20 - 11.06)(0.05) = 0.447$. If everyone did this, it would reduce the proportion of people flowing from unemployment to employment in any period (lower P_{ue}) and so raise the unemployment rate. Once the reservation wage is set, the actual wage drawn from the acceptable range is a matter of luck. Virtually every individual, however, will ultimately be underemployed in the sense that the job offer accepted will involve a hiring standard less than the individual's skill level.

Anything that decreases the marginal cost of another period of job search will tend to increase the reservation wage and reduce the probability of a job offer. Hence **unemployment insurance** benefits can be expected to increase the duration of unemployment and slow the proportion of people flowing from u to e. On the other hand, an increased reservation wage does lead, on average, to higher post-unemployment wages less underemployment. Over time, better job matches help to reduce employee turnover and so reduce the proportion of people flowing from e to u, thus reducing the unemployment rate.

An increase in an individual's skill level will have an ambiguous effect on the probability of a job offer. On one hand, a higher skill level increases the proportion of jobs for which the individual is qualified. On the other hand, a higher skill level will also induce the person to raise the reservation wage. While higher skill levels clearly lead to higher expected wages, the effect on the probability of flowing from unemployment to employment is unclear.

The job search model serves as a reminder that a certain amount of unemployment is a normal part of any dynamic labor market where there is imperfect information.

The proportion of people flowing from u to e is also reduced in the case of **structural** unemployment. This type of unemployment stems from changing patterns of demand that occur in the context of both rigid real wages and high costs of occupational or geographic mobility. For example, if the demand for labor is high in one state and low in another, both wages and unemployment rates with vary between the states. Workers will eventually move in response to this wage gap, but this will take time. The same thing is true about demand for labor and wages between different industries. Workers will eventually retrain and "move" between industries, but it will take time.

Structural unemployment can also arise when some firms follow efficiency wage strategies. In such situations, some workers may choose to wait for jobs in the high-wage sector as opposed to filling vacancies in the low-wage sector. Empirical support for the efficiency wage theory can be found in the empirical finding known as the **wage curve**. This robust empirical relationship shows a negative relationship between local unemployment rates and the level of wages, not the positive relationship predicted by the standard supply and demand model. The efficiency wage theory is consistent with this finding because when unemployment is high, shirking tends to fall, thus reducing the need for wage premiums that exceed the market wage.

Demand deficient (cyclical) unemployment refers to the excess supply of labor that is created when the aggregate demand for labor declines and the real wage is inflexible downward. Note that as firms cut back on employment in response to the demand shift, the proportion of workers flowing from e to u in the stock flow model increases and the unemployment rate rises. As firms reduce the rate at which they replace those who quit and retire, the proportion flowing from u to e and from n to e will also be reduced, further increasing the unemployment rate.

While real wages will fall when prices rise, all other things equal, nominal wages tend to be very inflexible downward. This in turn means that if prices are not rising, the real wage cannot fall. There are many reasons why nominal wages are inflexible downward. Unions resist nominal wage cuts (and may be more concerned with **insiders**, those within the union or with seniority than **outsiders**, nonmembers or those who have been laid off). Firms have an incentive to lay off less-experienced workers rather than cut wages across the board and risk losing workers with more specific human capital. There is asymmetric information, and workers may view layoffs as a more credible signal that the firm is really in trouble than a claim by management that wages must be cut for the good of the firm. Risk aversion by workers may mean that they prefer a constant income stream with greater risk of layoffs to the variable income stream that would result from nominal wage cuts. Additionally, workers who care about status may prefer unemployment for some period to accepting a job at a low-wage firm, and thus there may not be downward pressure on wages.

Firms pay a payroll tax in order to finance unemployment insurance, and the tax payment is based on the worker's income, the state the firm is in, the industry the firm is in, and the firm's **layoff experience**. One reason employers may prefer temporary layoffs to wage reductions is the **imperfect experience rating** of the unemployment insurance (UI) payroll tax. Firms with a history of frequent layoffs would be expected to have to offer workers a compensating wage differential to equate their expected earnings with those from lower paying jobs that do not have frequent spells of unemployment. The availability of unemployment benefits helps fill this gap, reducing the necessary compensating differential. With imperfect experience rating—most notably, maximum tax rates—the unemployment taxes paid by employers who frequently lay off workers will be inadequate to cover benefit claims of their employees. In effect, these employers (and indirectly, their employees) are subsidized by those employers with less frequent layoffs. Therefore, the structure of the UI tax system enhances the attractiveness of layoffs and should be expected to increase the proportion of people flowing from e to u over any given period, thus increasing the unemployment rate.

Unemployment resulting from a demand decrease and downwardly rigid real wages is often categorized as **seasonal** unemployment if the decrease in demand follows a systematic and predictable pattern over the course of a year. If these periods of unemployment cause workers to consume more leisure than desired, Appendix 8A showed that firms using predictable but excessive temporary layoffs would have to pay a compensating differential to attract workers. Again, the size of those differentials is muted by the availability of unemployment insurance benefits. The existence of such differentials makes seasonal unemployment difficult to evaluate from a normative perspective since one could argue that it is the result of voluntary choice.

The level of unemployment that tends to prevail in "normal" times is called the **full-employment** or **natural** rate of unemployment. The full-employment rate refers to the rate of unemployment associated with zero excess demand for labor. The full-employment rate was considered to be in the 5.5% to 6% range until fairly recently. But recent experience with unemployment consistently below 5% and no significant inflation is causing economists to reconsider what the natural rate might be. Reasons for changes in the natural rate include demographic shifts, such as the number of teenagers in the work force, as well as institutional factors.

Unemployment rates above the full-employment rate lead to significant reductions in national output. One estimate, generally known as Okun's Law, states that every one percentage point decline in the aggregate unemployment rate is associated with a 3 percentage point increase in the output of the United States. More recent estimates suggest that a 2 percentage point increase in output is more accurate, but regardless, it is clear that unemployment results in a large cost due to forgone output.

■ Review Questions

Choose the letter that represents the **<u>BEST</u>** response.

The Measurement of Unemployment

1. If the number of unemployed workers equals 15 and the number of employed workers equals 135, the unemployment rate equals
   a.   10%.
   b.   11.1%.
   c.   12.5%
   d.   15%.

2. Which of the following is a reason that the unemployment rate may overstate the degree of economic hardship?
   a. The employment rate can be rising at the same time the unemployment rate is rising.
   b. The number of people classified as unemployed includes those not actively seeking work.
   c. Job seekers may become discouraged and drop out of the labor force.
   d. Both **a** and **b**.

A Stock-Flow Model of the Labor Market

3. If the labor market flow P_{ue} is found to equal 0.2 for a particular month, this means that
   a. 20% of the total adult population flowed from unemployment to employment during the month.
   b. 20% of the total labor force flowed from unemployment to employment during the month.
   c. 20% of those who were initially unemployed became employed during the month.
   d. 20% of those who were initially employed became unemployed during the month.

4. Holding all else constant, which of the following labor market flows would increase the unemployment rate if it increased?
   a. P_{en}
   b. P_{un}
   c. P_{ue}
   d. All of the above

Types of Unemployment

5. The level of frictional unemployment is determined by
   a. the flows of people into and out of employment.
   b. the duration of the spells of unemployment.
   c. the level of excess demand.
   d. both **a** and **b**.

6. Which of the following factors would tend to increase a person's reservation wage?
   a. An increase in the cost of job search
   b. An increase in the replacement rate of unemployment insurance benefits
   c. The imperfect experience rating of unemployment insurance
   d. A decrease in the person's skill level

7. Which of the following is an effect associated with a higher reservation wage?
   a. Decreased duration of unemployment
   b. Higher post-unemployment wages
   c. More underemployment
   d. All of the above

8. Structural unemployment is caused by
   a. changing patterns of labor demand.
   b. real wages being inflexible downward.
   c. high costs of occupational and/or geographic adjustment.
   d. all of the above.

9. A government policy likely to be helpful in dealing with structural unemployment is
   a. a requirement that firms give employees advance notice of plant closings.
   b. a minimum wage law.
   c. an increase in unemployment insurance.
   d. the creation of public sector jobs.

10. The payment of efficiency wages may result in higher rates of unemployment because
   a. firms will lay off workers once productivity increases.
   b. quit rates tend to be higher at firms paying efficiency wages since workers must work harder than at other firms.
   c. employees at low-wage firms may decide that expected earnings can be increased by searching for employment among employers paying efficiency wages.
   d. firms that pay efficiency wages work their existing workers longer hours.

11. The empirical relationship known as "the wage curve" says that
   a. high rates of unemployment tend to be associated with higher wages.
   b. high rates of unemployment tend to be associated with lower wages.
   c. high rates of unemployment tend to be associated with falling wages.
   d. high rates of unemployment tend to be associated with low rates of inflation.

12. A likely explanation for the empirical finding known as "the wage curve" is that
   a. wages are inflexible downward.
   b. a surplus of labor causes the wage to fall.
   c. employers do not feel as much of a need to pay an efficiency wage when the unemployment rate is high.
   d. higher reservation wages lead to higher levels of frictional unemployment.

13. Demand deficient unemployment results from
   a. a general slowdown in business activity.
   b. real wages being inflexible downward.
   c. changes in the skills required of workers.
   d. both **a** and **b**.

14. A social norm against undercutting the prevailing wage may develop because
   a. workers are concerned about the future level of wages.
   b. unions are likely to strike if wages fall too low.
   c. unemployment insurance exists to protect unemployed workers.
   d. worker mobility is not perfect.

15. The method of financing unemployment insurance benefits tends to
   a. increase the length of job search.
   b. increase frictional unemployment.
   c. create an incentive for firms to prefer layoffs to wage cuts.
   d. both **a** and **b**.

16. Under an unemployment insurance system that uses no experience rating, the cost to a firm in increased unemployment insurance taxes of laying off a worker would
    a. equal zero.
    b. equal the unemployment insurance benefits paid to the worker .
    c. equal approximately 50% of the benefits paid to the worker.
    d. equal approximately 50% of the worker's previous earnings.

17. Seasonal unemployment can be considered voluntary unemployment because
    a. it is caused by wages being inflexible downward.
    b. to attract workers to industries with well-known seasonal fluctuations in demand, employers may have to pay workers a compensating differential.
    c. workers are covered by unemployment insurance.
    d. all of the above.

When Do We Have "Full-Employment"?

18. Which of the following is not a commonly used definition of the full-employment (natural) rate of unemployment?
    a. The unemployment rate that prevails in normal times
    b. The unemployment rate where the number of job vacancies equals the number of new labor force entrants
    c. The unemployment rate associated with zero excess demand for labor
    d. The unemployment rate at which all unemployment is voluntary

19. Over the last fifteen years the full-employment rate of employment seems to be moving downward. Which of the following changes are consistent with this movement?
    a. A decrease in the share of teenagers in the labor force
    b. A decrease in the share of blacks in the labor force
    c. An increase in the share of women in the labor force
    d. All of the above

20. Recent estimates suggest that every one percentage point decrease in the unemployment rate raises national output by
    a. 2 percentage points.
    b. 3 percentage points.
    c. 5 percentage points.
    d. 10 percentage points.

■ Problems

The Measurement of Unemployment

21. Suppose that the population aged 16 or over in a particular area could be categorized as follows

    Not in the labor force = 150,

    Employed = 230,

    Looking for work = 15,

    Waiting to be recalled from a layoff = 5.

21a. Compute the unemployment rate.

21b. Compute the labor force participation rate.

21c. Compute the employment rate.

21d. If the unemployment rate rises 2 percentage points above its initial level, how much would the labor force participation rate have to increase to keep the employment rate constant?

Types of Unemployment

22. Consider a labor market with two sectors denoted by A and B. The demand and supply curves for labor in sector A are given by the equations

$$\text{Demand: } L_A^D = 20 - W,$$
$$\text{Supply: } L_A^S = W.$$

The demand and supply curves in sector B are given by the equations

$$\text{Demand: } L_B^D = 40 - 2W,$$
$$\text{Supply: } L_B^S = 2W.$$

22a. Find the market-clearing wage and employment level in each sector.

22b. Is it likely that the unemployment rate will be zero at the market-clearing value of the wage? If not, how would you categorize this unemployment?

22c. Suppose that the demand for the product produced in sector B increases at the expense of the product in sector A. As a result the demand for labor in sector A becomes

$$L_A^D = 15 - W,$$

while the demand in sector B becomes

$$L_B^D = 45 - 2W.$$

If W denotes the real wage, and the real wage in sector A is inflexible downward, how many workers will be unemployed in sector A? What will happen to the real wage and employment level in sector B?

22d. What adjustment in the supply of workers in each sector would eliminate the unemployment in sector A? How would this affect wages and employment in sector B?

22e. What factors tend to inhibit these adjustments?

22f. Assuming the necessary adjustments cannot be made, how would you classify this type of unemployment?

A Model of Job Search

23. Consider a labor market where employers differ in the level of skill (K) that they require, where K ranges from 1 to 6. Each employer then pays a wage equal to the skill level of the job multiplied by 10. Assuming for simplicity that there is an equal proportion of employers at every wage level, the distribution of wage offers can be represented by the uniform distribution

$$f(W) = 0.02.$$

Now consider an unemployed individual with a skill level of $K^* = 5$. Assuming that the person does not know the skill level associated with any particular employer, suppose that he or she searches randomly over all the firms in this labor market.

23a. Assuming the worker will accept any job that is offered, what is the probability that a job offer will be forthcoming at any particular employer?

23b. Now suppose that the worker plans to use a reservation wage strategy. What is the probability of the worker getting a better offer than the reservation wage?

23c. What is the wage gain that can be expected from such an offer?

23d. What is the expected gain from additional job search under the reservation wage strategy?

23e. Assuming for simplicity that the marginal cost of an additional period of job search is $1, what is the optimal value of the reservation wage?

23f. What is the probability of a job offer given the reservation wage strategy?

23g. Using the stock flow model of the labor market, explain how the use of a reservation wage strategy impacts the unemployment rate.

■ Applications

The Effects of a Government Training Program on Job Search

24. Consider the distribution of wages used in the **Summary** section **Example** problem. Suppose that a government-sponsored training program has increased the person's skill level to $K^* = 3$.

24a. Assuming the worker will accept any job that is offered, what is the probability that a job offer will be forthcoming at any particular employer?

24b. Now suppose that the worker plans to use a reservation wage strategy. What is the probability of the worker getting a better offer than the reservation wage?

24c. What is the wage gain that can be expected from such an offer?

24d. What is the expected gain from additional job search under the reservation wage strategy?

24e. Assuming for simplicity that the marginal cost of an additional period of job search remains at $2, what is the optimal value of the reservation wage? How does it compare with the value derived in the **Example** problem?

24f. What is the probability of a job offer given the reservation wage strategy?

24g. How will the training program affect the proportion of people flowing from unemployment to employment?

The Inter-industry Effects of Unemployment Insurance

25. If real wages are inflexible downward, workers employed in seasonal industries may be subjected to temporary layoffs as the demand for labor fluctuates over the course of the year. If these layoffs cause workers to consume more leisure than desired, the firm may be forced to pay a compensating wage differential to attract the needed workers during the rest of the year. In general, the greater the use of layoffs, the larger the compensating differential that must be paid. However, the existence of unemployment insurance would tend to reduce the size of the compensating differential since layoffs would not impose as large an income loss on workers.

25a. Consider a firm that never uses temporary layoffs. Describe how this firm's unemployment insurance tax would be computed.

25b. Consider a firm with a regular history of using large temporary layoffs to meet seasonal changes in demand. Suppose all the workers together receive a total of $100,000 in unemployment insurance benefits annually during the layoffs. Why is it likely that the firm has paid less than $100,000 in unemployment insurance taxes? Where did the system get the rest of the money it paid out to the workers?

25c. Assuming that the unemployment benefits paid to workers reduce the total amount of the compensating differential the firm must pay by $100,000, what effect does the manner of financing unemployment insurance have on the proportion of workers flowing from employment to unemployment?

The Tax Treatment of Unemployment Benefits

26. Since 1987 all unemployment insurance benefits have been subject to federal and state income taxation. However, recipients do not pay Social Security and Medicare taxes on the benefits. Consider the case of a worker earning a wage of $10 per hour for 40 hours a week. Assume the federal tax rate is 15%, the state tax rate is 3%, and the Social Security and Medicare tax rate is 7.5%.

26a. How much does this worker pay per week in taxes? What is his or her after-tax earnings per week?

26b. Suppose the unemployment insurance system replaces 55% of a worker's before-tax earnings. How much would this worker receive per week if unemployed? How much would the recipient pay per week in taxes? What would be the after-tax "pay" associated with not working?

26c. What is the marginal cost associated with being unemployed for a week? How will the tax treatment of unemployment benefits affect the duration of job search?

Social Norms and Unemployment

*27. One recent theory for why wages remain fixed in the face of declining demand is that the prevailing market wage becomes a social norm. If unemployed workers plan to remain in the labor force a number of periods, such a norm may be in the workers' best interest since offers to work for less than the going wage in the current period may lead employers to permanently cut wages in future periods as well. An individual may obtain a higher present value of compensation stream by remaining unemployed and waiting for a job at the current wage. The model is presented formally in Robert M. Solow's book *The Labor Market as a Social Institution* (Cambridge: Blackwell Publishers, 1990). The book demonstrates that the desirability of an unemployment strategy increases the longer the worker plans to remain in the labor force and the higher the probability of finding a job in future periods. This probability, in turn, is inversely related to the unemployment rate. Note that this explanation for wage rigidity is similar to the model of wait unemployment first introduced in Chapter 13.

Consider a labor market where the prevailing market wage is $10. There are many identical unemployed workers at this wage. Each worker values the sum of his or her unemployment benefits and household production time at $5. Each unemployed worker plans to remain in the labor force for 2 periods after the current one and each has a discount rate (r) of 6%. At the current market wage, the probability of employment in any future period is 0.6.

*27a Suppose an unemployed worker offers to work in the current period for $9.90, 10 cents below the going wage. If this wage cut leads firms and workers to bid the wage down to $5 in future periods, what is the present value of the earnings stream that the worker can expect from offering to work at the lower wage?

*27b. What is the level of expected earnings in any given period for a worker who will not accept less than the going wage?

*27c. What is the present value of the earnings stream associated with refusing to work for less than the going wage?

27d. Which strategy leads to the higher present value on average?

Chapter 15
Inequality in Earnings

■ Summary

The majority of the models presented so far in *Modern Labor Economics* relate in some way to the issue of wage determination. Wages, in turn, combine with hours worked to determine the **level** of earnings. Chapter 15 represents an extension of the wage determination discussion in that it takes up questions related to the **distribution** of earnings. Over the last decade, the study of the distribution of earnings has moved from a minor branch of labor economics to a major research area. The purpose of this chapter is to introduce the measurements and concepts that are central to this topic and to summarize the major research findings in this area. The forces behind the changes in the earnings distribution are then identified using previous models of wage determination.

The distribution of earnings has received considerable attention over the last decade because of the perception that the distribution of earnings has been growing more unequal. A more unequal distribution is one in which there is greater **dispersion** in earnings. To see if inequality has increased, it is first necessary to understand how income dispersion is measured. Common measures include the **variance** and the **coefficient of variation**. Other measures try to capture the range of earnings without looking at the actual distribution. The following example illustrates the computation of each of these measures for a very small data set. Most statistical computer programs, as well as most popular spreadsheet programs, contain commands that will perform these calculations for any number of observations.

Example

Consider a simple 5-person economy. Table 15-1 ranks the earnings from lowest to highest and shows the percentage of the total earnings accounted for by each worker.

Table 15-1

Worker	Earnings ($)	Percent
1	20	5
2	40	10
3	80	20
4	100	25
5	160	40
Total	400	100

The variance (σ^2) is computed using the formula

$$\sigma^2 = \frac{\sum_{i=1}^{n}(E_i - \bar{E})^2}{n},$$

where E_i is the earnings of the ith workers, $\bar{E}$ is the average (mean) earnings, and n is the number of workers. The intermediate calculations needed to compute the variance are shown in Table 15-2. Note that the mean earnings in the economy are $400/5 or $80. Taking the sum of the squared deviations from the mean and dividing by 5 yields a variance of 2,400 for this economy.

Table 15-2

E_i	$E_i - \bar{E}$	$(E_i - \bar{E})^2$
20	−60	3600
40	−40	1600
80	0	0
100	20	400
160	80	6400
Total		12,000

The coefficient of variation (CV) can be computed by taking the square root of the variance (called the standard deviation) and then dividing by the mean earnings.

$$CV = \frac{\sqrt{\sigma^2}}{\bar{E}} \Rightarrow CV = \frac{\sqrt{2400}}{80} = 0.61.$$

The range or spread of earnings can be measured by looking at the difference in earnings associated with certain percentiles. Assuming the earnings data have been arranged from smallest to largest, the term ith percentile refers to the earnings value at or below which i percent of the population falls. In this simple economy with only 5 workers, each worker represents one-fifth or 20% of the total population. Consequently, the lowest income level can be treated as the 20th percentile, the next lowest as the 40th percentile, and so on, with the top income representing the 100th percentile. In this example, the ratio of the earnings levels associated with the 80th and 20th percentiles is $100/$20 = 5. Because it is simple to compute and readily available, this **"80:20" ratio** (and/or the "90:10" ratio) is used throughout Chapter 15.

These measures of dispersion mean very little unless they are compared to measures derived from a different distribution. Notice also that each measure may respond in a different way to changes in the data. For example, if each earnings entry in Table 15-1 were multiplied by 1,000, none of the measures of dispersion would change except for the variance—which would increase from 2,400 to 2.4×10^9.

On one hand, one could argue that multiplying everything by 1,000 has not really changed the degree of dispersion since everyone has gained by the same percentage amount and there have been no changes in relative position. Notice that the coefficient of variation and the 80:20 ratio are measures that would support this argument. On the other hand, the person with the top income has gained much more in absolute terms than the person at the bottom. The variance is a measure consistent with this argument.

How would each of the measures of dispersion change if the earnings of each person increased by the same absolute amount? For example, suppose each person in the economy had $20 added to their earnings. On one hand, one could argue that this does not change the dispersion at all since everyone has moved up by the same amount. On the other hand, one could argue that it lowers the dispersion of earnings in the sense that person 1's earnings double, while person 5's only increase by 12.5%. How do the measures computed earlier respond to the change? Substituting the new values into the appropriate formulas yields

$$\sigma^2 = 2,400,$$
$$CV = 0.49,$$
$$\frac{\text{Earnings at 80th pecentile}}{\text{Earnings at 20th percentile}} = \frac{\$120}{\$40} = 3.$$

Note that in this case moving all the earnings up by the same amount does not change the variance. On the other hand, the coefficient of variation and the 80:20 ratio show a reduction in dispersion consistent with the fact that the lower wage workers have gained a greater percentage amount. So, depending on one's view of what constitutes a change in earnings inequality, there is a measure that is responsive to those concerns. The variance clearly captures changes in the absolute dispersion of earnings, while the coefficient of variation and the 80:20 (or 90:10) ratio capture changes in the relative dispersion of earnings.

How has the dispersion of earnings changed in recent times? As measured by the 80:20 ratio, the dispersion of earnings among men increased greatly over the period 1980–2005. For women, real earnings generally rose, but there was also an increase in the 80:20 ratio. Women in the 20th percentile had very low earnings and thus were unlikely to be full-time workers; thus it is difficult to infer much about what happened to women's wages. The increased dispersion for men took place within the context of generally falling real earnings, while the stability in the dispersion among women occurred while their real earnings were generally rising. Examining other ratios also shows that earnings in the lower part of the distribution generally became more even after 1990, while in the upper end of the distribution inequality increased.

How does a greater dispersion of earnings come about? There are really only two possibilities. The first is that the earnings distribution is "hollowing out," that is, those in the middle of the distribution are moving over time to either end of the distribution. The second is that individuals originally at the upper end of the distribution gain over time relative to those at the lower end. If this second explanation is true, it could be caused by rising relative wages or hours of work.

Although there is some evidence that the proportion of middle-income jobs has fallen while the proportion of high-paying jobs has risen, these changes have not been large enough to account for much of the rise in earnings inequality. Instead, evidence suggests that rising relative wages account for most of the increase in inequality. The rising relative wages, in turn, have resulted from large **increases in the payoff to additional education**, particularly in the 1990s. There has also been a slight increase in the payoff to experience among all educational groups. Relative hours of work between high- and low-paying occupations have not changed significantly. Results for **within-group** dispersion are less clear, increasing during the 1990s for college-educated men but changing little for high school graduates.

What has caused the rising payoff to higher education, the rising payoff to experience among the less educated, and the greater dispersion in wages between those with similar levels of human capital? There are three possible explanations. First, the supply of unskilled workers might have risen relative to the supply of skilled workers. This would cause wages of unskilled workers to fall both absolutely and relatively, all other things equal. Alternatively, the **quality** of unskilled labor might have declined relative to the quality of skilled labor. However, the data does not suggest that either explanation could be a primary cause of rising inequality.

Secondly, there may have been changes in institutional factors such as union coverage. Union membership has consisted largely of less-skilled workers. In such jobs, there was little return to education because of the effect of unions in compressing wage differentials among skill groups (see Chapter 13). With weakened unions, the returns to education should increase. However, the decline of unions in the U.S. began far earlier and did not change significantly in the 1980s. Another institutional factor that may well have played some role is the real value of the minimum wage, which has continued to decline in real terms, even after nominal increases in the 1990s.

However, the third explanation is far more strong. Evidence suggests that the rising payoff to education has been caused by **rising demand** for more educated workers. A small part of the demand increase has come from shifts in employment away from manufacturing towards the private service sector. Since the private service sector uses a greater proportion of highly educated workers than does manufacturing, the growth in the service sector leads to an increase in the demand for more highly educated workers.

Most of the increase in the demand for highly educated workers, however, has come from the rising demand for educated workers **within** industries. The rising demand within industries, in turn, has been caused by the introduction of **new technology**, especially computers, into the workplace. As discussed in Chapter 4, technological change is equivalent to a decrease in the price of capital, and will stimulate the demand for any category of labor that is a gross complement with capital. In general, capital and skilled labor tend to be gross complements, while capital and unskilled labor tend to be gross substitutes. Periods of rapid technological change also favor those workers who can learn quickly, and as discussed in Chapter 9, highly educated workers tend to find learning easier.

Technological change may also help to explain the rising payoff to experience among less-educated workers. As technological change causes firms to cut back on less-educated workers, it is usually the younger and less-experienced workers that lose their jobs. As a result, the wages of these workers were bid down more than the wages of older workers.

Although the driving forces behind increases in within-group earnings dispersion are not fully understood, some of the increased dispersion may be attributable to technological change. To the extent that technological advances brought job losses for some, they brought new opportunities for others. As the labor market was thrown into a state of flux, those lucky enough to find jobs in expanding sectors and/or firms did well, while those who lost their jobs did poorly. Also, even within the most narrowly defined groups, difficult-to-measure characteristics like adaptability are likely to differ, so changes brought about by new technology may have simply brought an increased demand (and ultimately higher wages) for those workers with the most adaptability. Evidence also suggests that within-group dispersion increased most for those in sales positions. Since sales workers are paid on a commission basis, a possible hypothesis is that the use of contingent or output-based pay may have contributed to increases in within-group dispersion.

The appendix to Chapter 15 explains how to construct and interpret two additional measures of earnings inequality—the **Lorenz curve** and the **Gini coefficient**. Unlike the 80:20 ratio that compares the level of earnings at different points in the distribution, the Lorenz curve employs data on the share of earnings accumulating to different proportions of the population. (When data are not readily available for earnings, Lorenz curves are constructed using income data.) For example, if the population is ranked according to earnings from lowest to highest and then divided into fifths, the first point on the Lorenz curve (after the origin) would be the share of total earnings accounted for by the lowest 20% of the population. The second point would be the share accounted for by the lowest 40% of the population, and so on. The last point always indicates that 100% of the population accounts for 100% of the earnings. If everyone in the economy had the same earnings, the Lorenz curve would be a straight line with a slope of one. This is called the **line of perfect equality**.

The Gini coefficient is an attempt to quantify the degree to which the Lorenz curve departs from the line of perfect equality. Using the formula for the area of a triangle, the area under the line of perfect equality is always 0.5. The area under the Lorenz curve must be some number between 0 and 0.5. Taking the difference between those two areas, the Gini coefficient is defined as the ratio of that difference to the area under the line of perfect equality (0.5). Note that the Gini coefficient will be a number between 0 and 1, with higher numbers suggesting greater inequality.

■ Review Questions

Choose the letter that represents the **BEST** response.

Measuring Inequality

1. The distribution of earnings refers to
   a. the number of people receiving each given level of earnings.
   b. the difference between the lowest and highest earnings level in a group.
   c. the overall level of earnings.
   d. the relative standing associated with any given level of earnings.

2. Which of the following characteristics of the earnings distribution are most closely associated with the degree of earnings inequality?
   a. The average level of earnings
   b. The dispersion of earnings
   c. The median level of earnings
   d. All of the above

3. Which of the following statistical measures best describes the absolute dispersion of earnings associated with a given earnings distribution?
   a. The mean
   b. The variance
   c. The coefficient of variation
   d. The ratio of earnings at the 80th percentile to earnings at the 20th percentile

4. Which of the following statistical measures associated with an earnings distribution would increase if everyone received an extra $1,000 in earnings?
   a. The median
   b. The standard deviation
   c. The variance
   d. The coefficient of variation

Descriptive Data on Earnings Inequality

5. As measured by the ratio of earnings at the 80th percentile to earnings at the 20th percentile, earnings inequality since 1980
   a. increased for both men and women.
   b. decreased for men and increased for women.
   c. decreased slightly for both men and women.
   d. increased for men and held constant for women.

6. The changes in earnings inequality that occurred during the 1980s took place within the context of
   a. generally falling real earnings for men and women in all percentiles.
   b. generally increasing real earnings for men and women in all percentiles.
   c. rising real earnings in the 20th percentile for women but not men, and rising real earnings in the 80th percentile for both men and women.
   d. rising real earnings in the 20th percentile for both men and women, but falling real earnings in the 80th percentile for both men and women.

7. Which of the following changes would be consistent with an overall increase in earnings inequality?
   a. The replacement of middle-income jobs by very low-or high-paying jobs
   b. An increase in the wage of high-paying jobs relative to low-paying jobs
   c. An increase in the hours worked by high-wage workers relative to the hours worked by low-wage workers
   d. All of the above

8. Consider the 80:50 and 50:20 ratios. Based on this measure, since the 1980s, income inequality has
   a. increased in only the upper range for both men and women.
   b. increased in only the lower range for both men and women.
   c. increased in the upper range but fell in the lower range for both men and women.
   d. not changed significantly in either range, for both men and women.

9. Which of the following is <u>most</u> responsible for the increases in the wages of high-paid workers relative to low-paid workers that took place since 1980?
   a. An increase in the returns to a college education
   b. An increase in the returns to a high school education
   c. An increase in the returns to a graduate education
   d. All of the above

10. Changes in the returns to a college education that occurred since 1980 took place within the context of
    a. slowly increasing real earnings for male college graduates.
    b. rapidly falling real earnings for male high school graduates.
    c. large increases in the real earnings of female college graduates.
    d. all of the above.

11. Which of the following is a correct statement about the returns to a college education?
    a. The relative return to a college education did not increase significantly from 1980–1990.
    b. The relative return to a college education did not increase significantly from 1990–2005.
    c. The relative return to a college education was comparatively greater over the 1990–2005 period because fewer college graduates entered the market.
    d. The relative return to a college education was comparatively less over the 1990–2005 period because more college graduates entered the market.

12. Since 1980, the earnings of workers with similar levels of education and experience tended to become more
    a. predictable.
    b. dispersed.
    c. similar.
    d. symmetric.

The Causes of Growing Inequality

13. Which of the following factors are capable, in theory, of widening the gap between the earnings of highly educated and less-educated workers?
    a. An increase in the supply of less-educated workers relative to the supply of highly educated workers
    b. An increase in the demand for highly educated workers relative to the demand for less-educated workers
    c. Institutional forces such as the decline of unionism
    d. All of the above

14. The widening gap between the wages of highly educated and less-educated workers that occurred over the past two decades is best explained by
    a. an increase in the supply of less-educated workers relative to the supply of highly-educated workers.
    b. an increase in the demand for highly educated workers relative to the demand for less-educated workers.
    c. institutional forces such as the decline of unionism.
    d. all of the above.

15. Which of the following factors are capable, in theory, of causing an increase in the demand for highly educated workers relative to less-educated workers?
    a. Shifts in product demand toward industries using a higher proportion of highly educated workers
    b. Substitution of highly educated workers for less-educated workers within industries
    c. Increases in the relative supply of less-educated workers
    d. Both **a** and **b**

16. Which of the following factors is most responsible for the increase in the demand for highly educated workers relative to less-educated workers that took place during the past two decades?
    a. Shifts in product demand toward industries using a higher proportion of highly educated workers
    b. Substitution of highly educated workers for less-educated workers within industries
    c. Increases in the price of capital
    d. Both **a** and **b**

17. Why would technological change be a plausible explanation for the demand-side increases in the returns to education that have taken place during the past two decades?
    a. Technological change is equivalent to a decrease in the price of capital.
    b. Capital and skilled labor tend to be gross complements.
    c. There were significant differences in the growth rate of earnings inequality across industrialized countries.
    d. Both **a** and **b**.

18. Technological change may have led to an increase in the returns to experience among high school graduates because
    a. technological change is equivalent to a decrease in the price of capital.
    b. capital and unskilled labor tend to be gross substitutes.
    c. seniority rules assure that the brunt of any decline in the demand for unskilled workers is borne by younger workers.
    d. both **a** and **b**.

Lorenz Curves and Gini Coefficients (Appendix 15A)

19. Which of the following is a valid statement if two Lorenz curves cross?
    a.   The two earnings distributions have the same degree of inequality.
    b.   The Gini coefficient associated with each curve will be the same.
    c.   The Gini coefficient associated with each curve may be the same.
    d.   Both **a** and **b**.

20. If over time the Lorenz curve moves closer to the line of perfect earnings equality, one can infer that
    a.   earnings inequality must have been reduced.
    b.   the Gini coefficient will be smaller.
    c.   earnings have increased by some constant percentage.
    d.   both **a** and **b**.

■ Problems

Measures of Earnings Dispersion

21. Consider the data from Table 15-1 in the **Summary** section **Example** problem. Note that the variance was originally computed as 2,400, the coefficient of variation as 0.61, and the 80:20 ratio as 5.

21a. Suppose $20 is redistributed from worker 5 to worker 1. Compute the new variance and coefficient of variation.

21b. Suppose $20 is redistributed from worker 5 to worker 4. Compute the new variance and the coefficient of variation.

21c. Intuitively, which redistribution brings about more income equality? Which measure of dispersion changes in a way that corresponds to your intuition?

21d. For the two redistributions described above, what happens to the 80:20 ratio? For each case, does the change in the ratio correspond with your intuition about what constitutes more income equality?

22. One of the key pieces of descriptive data presented in this chapter is that earnings within narrowly defined human capital groups also became more dispersed since 1980. The point of this exercise is to show how this increased dispersion affects the overall dispersion of earnings. The questions that follow pertain to Table 15-3 which shows the individual earnings associated with members of two distinct human capital groups. Group A is assumed to be the high human capital group while group B denotes the low human capital group.

Table 15-3

Group A		Group B	
Person	**Earnings**	**Person**	**Earnings**
1	$70	1	$10
2	$80	2	$20
3	$90	3	$30

22a. Compute the mean earnings in each group. Compute the variance and coefficient of variation for each group.

22b. Compute the variance and coefficient of variation for the entire population.

22c. Suppose that the earnings distribution changes. In group A, the earnings are now $65, $80, and $95, while in group B, the earnings are $5, $20, and $35. Compute the mean earnings in each group. Compute the variance and coefficient of variation for each group.

22d. Compute the variance and coefficient of variation for the entire population. How has the change in the within-group dispersion affected the dispersion of the entire population?

Changes in the Relative Demand for Educated Workers

23. The change in employment between periods i and j for a particular category of labor (C) in a certain industry can be found using the equation

$$\Delta C = E_j \Delta k + k_i \Delta E,$$

where E refers to the total employment in the industry, k refers to the proportion of total employment in the industry comprised by category C workers, and Δ refers to any change that occurs between period i and period j. This equation was derived in a footnote of the text to make the point that even small increases in the proportion of college-educated workers employed by particular industries could have a large effect on the demand for college-educated workers.

23a. Suppose that over the last decade, the proportion of group C workers in a particular industry increased 50% from 0.2 to 0.3. Assuming total industry employment remained constant at 1,500, what is the change in the employment of group C?

23b. Suppose that over the last decade, the proportion of group C workers in a particular industry remained constant at 0.2. Assuming that total industry employment increased 50% from 1,000 to 1,500, what is the change in the employment of group C?

23c. Suppose that over the last decade, the proportion of group C workers in a particular industry rose from 0.2 to 0.3. At the same time, total industry employment fell from 1,000 to 800. What is the change in the employment of group C?

The Skewness of Earnings

*24. Another issue related to earnings inequality is the skewness of the distribution. An earnings distribution is said to be skewed when the dispersion of earnings is not symmetric. If earnings are distributed in such a way that individuals are bunched at the lower end of the distribution, while a few individuals have high earnings, the distribution is said to be skewed to the right. If most individuals are bunched at the high end of the distribution, while a few have low incomes, the distribution is said to be skewed to the left. Some statisticians measure skewness (g) using the formula

$$\gamma = \frac{3(\bar{E} - E_M)}{\sigma},$$

where $\bar{E}$ is the mean earnings, E_M the median earnings, and s is the standard deviation. The median earnings is the earnings value that falls exactly in the middle of the list when earnings are ranked from lowest to highest. If γ is positive, the distribution is skewed right. If γ is negative, the distribution is skewed left. The greater the magnitude of g, the greater the degree of skewness.

*24a. For the data in Table 15-1 in the **Summary** section **Example** problem, compute the skewness measure. Is the distribution skewed left or right?

*24b. Now suppose that $20 is transferred from person 3 to person 1. Has the variance increased or decreased? Has the skewness increased or decreased?

*24c. Does increased earnings equality necessarily mean less skewness?

*24d. Why might an earnings distribution that is skewed to the right be considered unfair?

Lorenz Curves and Gini Coefficients (Appendix 15A)

25. Consider the data from Table 15-1 in the **Summary** section **Example** problem.

25a. Draw the Lorenz curve consistent with the data. Be sure to indicate the line of perfect equality.

*25b. Compute the Gini coefficient associated with this earnings distribution.

25c. Now suppose the distribution of earnings changes so that the earnings levels are now $32, $48, $60, $80, and $180. Total earnings are still $400. Draw the new Lorenz curve.

25d. Is it clear from the Lorenz curves which distribution is more equal?

*25e. Compute the Gini coefficient associated with the new earnings distribution.

■ Applications

Popular Perspectives on Inequality

26. A perspective shared by many Americans is that the economy is essentially a "zero-sum" game, i.e., when those at the upper end of the earnings distribution gain, the gain comes at the expense of those at the bottom. Some would go so far as to say that what the rich gain is taken from the poor.

26a. Did higher-earning men actually "gain" in an *absolute* sense during the period 1975–1997? Did higher-earning women?

26b. Data suggest that higher wage earners of both genders did gain *relative* to lower wage earners during the period 1975–1997. What was the major reason for this gain? Did this gain result from the rich exploiting the poor?

26c. Explain why shifts in the relative supply of less-educated workers could not have caused the decrease in relative wages experienced by those workers.

26d. Explain why changes in the relative quality of labor supplied by less-educated workers could not have caused the decrease in relative wages experienced by those workers.

26e. Explain why institutional changes like declining union membership could not have been a major factor in the rising return to education seen during the 1980s.

The Superstar Effect

27. Consider the situation of two lawyers with the same education, age, and experience. Lawyer A is just slightly more proficient under pressure than lawyer B. You are involved in a major lawsuit where the loser must pay the winner $1 million. The case is very close and sure to be decided in favor of the side with the better lawyer.

27a. How much would you be willing to pay lawyer A in this situation? How much would you be willing to pay lawyer B?

27b. What is the relationship between worker productivity and earnings in this example? What is it about the nature of the contest that makes for this relationship?

27c. What effect would such contests have on the dispersion of earnings within narrowly defined human capital groups? What effect does such dispersion have on the overall dispersion of earnings in the economy?

27d. Review the hypothesis about the effects of relative standing concerns discussed in Question **27d** in Chapter 1. If this hypothesis is true, what effect would it have on the inequality of earnings?

Effects of Income Maintenance Policies on the Earnings Distribution

28. Review **Example 2** from the **Summary** section of Chapter 6 on labor supply.

28a. For the person with preferences given by the utility function

$$U = L^{\frac{3}{4}}Y^{\frac{1}{4}},$$

find the total wage earnings before and after the development of the welfare program described in the example.

28b. For the person with preferences given by the utility function

$$U = L^{\frac{1}{4}}Y^{\frac{3}{4}},$$

find the total wage earnings before and after the development of the welfare program described in the example.

28c. What effect does the welfare program described in this example have on the dispersion of earnings?

Lorenz Curves and Gini Coefficients (Appendix 15A)

29. Consider the data from Table 15-1 in the **Summary** section **Example** problem. The Lorenz curve and Gini coefficient for this data were computed in Problem **25**.

29a. How would the Lorenz curve change if all earnings levels were multiplied by 1,000?

*29b. Suppose each worker in the economy received an additional $20 in earnings. Draw the new Lorenz curve and compute the new Gini coefficient.

29c. Lorenz curves can be drawn to represent the distribution of earnings or income. In this example, since there is no nonlabor income or taxes, the two curves would be the same. In general, this would not be true. Would you expect the distribution of earnings to be more or less equal than the distribution of income?

Chapter 16
The Labor Market Effects of International Trade and Production Sharing

■ Summary

Freeing up resources so that they can be used more productively in other industries is the logic behind **international trade**. As trade protection has decreased and telecommunications and shipping technologies have improved, the movement of goods, services, and information across national borders has increased significantly. However, this has also led to increased competition between American workers and foreign workers as jobs are outsourced to other countries.

The basis for trade lies in differences in the internal costs of producing goods or services without trade, and this same logic applies whether we consider individuals or countries. Individuals must decide every day about which items to produce themselves versus purchasing, essentially "outsourcing" household tasks to others. Individuals, like countries, engage in trade, specializing in one or more activities and using the income obtained to purchase other goods and services through the market. For both individuals and countries, there are two types of costs involved in the decision to make something (produce something domestically) versus purchase it (trade for it). First, neither individuals nor firms are specialists in everything, and thus cannot produce all goods as efficiently or as well. Secondly, use of time or resources in the production of a good has an opportunity cost, the other goods that could be produced instead, or other ways in which the time could be spent. These opportunity costs arise because the same resources, whether time or production inputs, can only be used once.

Resources used to grow food, for example, are then no longer available to produce clothing, and the cost of the food is best measured by the amount of clothing the same resources could have produced. The relative costs of each good can be represented by the slope of each country's production possibilities curve. Such a curve shows (for two goods) all the different combinations of goods that can be produced when a country efficiently uses all of its resources. Trade will cause shifts in employment between industries, but countries with high living standards and high wages need not fear permanent employment losses because of trade. While shifts in employment opportunities associated with free trade can cause temporary unemployment and hardship for those workers producing goods that will no longer be produced domestically, the overall effects of trade are higher living standards for both trading partners. The reason for this gain, and the irrelevance of a country's internal wage rates to the process of trade, is explored in the following example.

Example

Suppose the United States is endowed with resources and technology such that producing an additional 1 unit of food (F) means that it must give up producing 1/3 a unit of clothing (C). Conversely, an additional 1 unit of clothing would require giving up 3 units of food. Furthermore, suppose the maximum amount of clothing that can be produced is 300 million units, and the maximum amount of food production is 900 million units. Provided the tradeoff between food and clothing is constant, this **production possibilities curve** can be represented by the equation

$$C = 300 - (1/3)F.$$

This curve is shown as line *ab* in Figure 16-2a.

In comparison, suppose Mexico can only produce a maximum of 200 units of clothing or 200 units of food. Its production possibilities curve can then be represented by the equation

$$C = 200 - F.$$

This curve is shown as line *vw* in Figure 16-2b. This curve implies that the real cost of an additional 1 unit of clothing is 1 unit of food, and an additional 1 unit of food involves a real cost of 1 unit of clothing.

From these production possibilities frontiers, we can infer the **comparative advantage** of each nation. Note first that the United States has an **absolute advantage**; the United States can produce absolutely more of both goods. But both nations are still able to gain from trade due to the difference in their opportunity costs of production. To find the opportunity costs of production, consider the slope of the production possibilities frontiers. The United States can produce 300 unit's of clothing or 900 units of food or any combination in between. Thus for every unit of food that the United States produces, it gives up 1/3 unit of clothing. This is the opportunity cost of <u>food</u> production in the United States. Similarly, Mexico can produce 200 units of clothing or 200 units of food or any combination in between. For every unit of food produced, Mexico gives up 1 unit of clothing; the opportunity cost of food production in Mexico is 1. Since the U.S. opportunity cost of food production is less than the Mexican opportunity cost of food production, we say that the United States has a comparative advantage in food. Similarly, we can show that Mexico's opportunity cost of clothing is 1, while the U.S. opportunity cost of clothing is 3. Mexico has a comparative advantage in clothing production.

Both nations can thus gain from trade, regardless of initial wage levels. Suppose that before trading, the United States devoted two-thirds of its resources to food and one-third to clothing, producing the combination $F = 600$, $C = 100$ (point *c*). As a starting point for Mexico, suppose three-fourths of the resources are devoted to food and one-fourth to clothing, resulting in an initial combination of $F = 150$, $C = 50$ (point *x*). If we assume there are 100 million workers in the United States and 50 million in Mexico, then it is clear that living standards (i.e., real consumption per capita) would be higher in the United States than in Mexico. United States workers would average 6 units of food and 1 unit of clothing compared to 3 units of food and 1 unit of clothing for Mexican workers. Another way of interpreting this is to say that real wage rates are higher for American workers (since real per capita consumption is closely connected to real per capital income, which in turn reflects the real wages of the workers). Do these higher real wage rates pose a problem for American workers if the two countries now decide to trade?

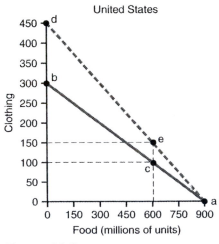

Figure 16-2a

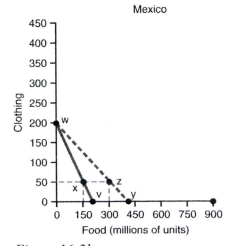

Figure 16-2b

The answer is clearly no. Since it does not have unlimited resources, Mexico must make choices. If it chooses to produce more clothing and export some to the United States, it will be giving up the chance to produce food. The only way it makes sense for Mexico to export clothing to the United States is if it can replace the food production it is giving up by purchasing it more cheaply from the United States. Does such an opportunity exist in this example? Recall that 1 additional unit of food costs 1 unit of clothing in Mexico, while in the United States 1 additional unit of food costs only 1/3 unit of clothing. If, for example, the **terms of trade** were set at 1 unit of food for 1/2 unit of clothing, then indeed Mexico could obtain food more cheaply than it could produce itself. Similarly, the United States would benefit through the purchase of the clothing exports from Mexico. At the stated terms of trade, 1 unit of clothing only costs the United States 2 units of food, whereas every unit of clothing the United States produces on its own costs 3 units of food. But will not importing clothing from Mexico result in lost jobs? It is true that jobs in the clothing industry will be lost, but at the same time, those resources will be needed to produce the food that will be exported to Mexico. The result will be a transfer of jobs out of clothing production and into food production, not a permanent loss of overall jobs as is commonly assumed.

What benefits will result from this transfer of resources? Assume each country first **specializes** in the good for which they are the low-cost producer (United States in food and Mexico in clothing), and assume again the terms of trade are set at 1 unit of food for 1/2 unit of clothing, or conversely, 2 units of food for 1 unit of clothing. Depending on exactly how many units of food are traded, the United States now can consume along the line *ad* in Figure 16-2a. Point *a* represents the point of specialization in food production, point *d* the amount of clothing attainable if all the food were traded away. Similarly, Mexico now sees its consumption possibilities as lying along the line *wy*. Point *w* represents its point of specialization in clothing production, point *y* the maximum it could attain in food if all the clothing were traded away. If the actual amount traded were 150 units of clothing for 300 units of food, the United States would move to point *e* and Mexico would move to point *z*. Notice Mexico now consumes the same amount of clothing as it did at the start, but now has 150 more units of food. The United States has the same amount of food as at the start, but now has 50 more units of clothing. Living standards as indicated by per capita consumption levels (real wage rates) have gone up in each country as a result of trade. Each country has had to undergo a transformation in terms of the type of work its people do, but each country has continued to utilize all its resources. The shifting out of the production possibilities curve is analogous to what would happen if the United States experienced a technological improvement in clothing production, and Mexico experienced technological improvement in food production.

In practice, it is difficult to determine whether international trade increases the output of a country, and, due to data collection and measurement issues, it is even difficult to determine whether countries that are more open to trade have faster growth rates. We will also see that, although the theoretical effects are clear, it is also difficult to determine the effect on the demand for labor due to trade.

In theory, the effect of international trade on the demand for labor is very similar to the effects of technological change, discussed in Chapter 4. Greater international trade generally means that a nation's imports and exports will expand. Thus the demand for labor will tend to increase in export industries, and wages will rise, and the demand for labor will fall in import industries, and wages will fall. To the extent that international trade also increases income, it will also increase the demand for goods and services overall.

The mix of these influences will have both wage and employment effects and will also be likely to influence the price level and real wages. For example, suppose that demand expands in an export-related industry. The increase in the demand for labor will tend to increase employment and raise wages, but the relative size of the employment and wage effects will depend, all other things equal, on the elasticity of labor supply in the market. Where labor supply is relatively elastic, employment will expand considerably with little increase in the wage, but in markets where labor supply is inelastic, the wage will rise considerably with little effect on employment. In import-related markets, labor demand will fall, so the effects will be similar but will involve falling wages and employment. Additionally, since international trade tends to lower the prices of at least some goods and services, real wage changes will be less than nominal wage changes in declining industries (and greater than nominal wage changes in expanding industries).

In recent years, trade has also meant the relocation of American production facilities to lower-wage countries, essentially bringing American workers into direct competition with lower-wage foreign workers. When the cost of an alternative factor of production falls, there is a **cross-wage effect**. This effect is the sum of the income and substitution effects of the wage change. The substitution effect of lower wages depends not on the wage alone but on the **ratio of wages to marginal productivity** in both countries. For it to be cost-effective to relocate to another country, the ratio of wages to marginal productivity in that country must be *lower* than in the United States.

If that is the case, the size of the substitution effect depends on the laws of derived demand. First, it must depend on the supply response of American workers (the shape of the U.S. supply of labor in this particular market). If the U.S. labor supply curve is relatively inelastic, then a fall in the demand for labor will also reduce wages considerably, offsetting some of the substitution effect. The second important factor is the elasticity of substitution between U.S. and foreign workers. Where workers can easily be substituted, or in other words, where it is easy to produce and transport goods in another country, and where relative skill levels are comparable, substitution effects will be large. But where skill levels are very different or transportation costs are very high, substitution is limited.

The scale effect depends on the reduction in production costs from relocating production. Decreases in costs will tend to increase supply and lower price, thus increasing the quantity demanded and the scale of production. The increase in the scale of production will tend to offset some of the substitution effect, so the overall effect on the number of jobs in the industry is unclear and depends on the size of both effects. Again, the size of the scale effect depends on the laws of derived demand. Where the elasticity of demand for the final product is high, the scale effect will be large, as a small fall in price will lead to a relatively large change in the quantity of output demanded. Where the share of foreign labor in total cost of production is high, the effect on product price will be more significant, and the scale effect will be relatively large.

Trade also tends to increase the elasticity of labor demand and the elasticity of final product demand by making more substitutes available at both stages of production. The net effect of all these factors on labor demand is difficult to quantify, although there are factors that are more likely to indicate winners or losers from trade. Losses are most likely to occur in industries with less specialized labor and in cases where product demand is relatively inelastic, so cost differences do not impact the quantity demanded very much. Displaced workers are likewise most likely to suffer when it is difficult for them to switch jobs or industries. Winners occur in output sectors and in sectors where jobs are complements to foreign production.

Empirical estimates of the effect of trade on employment have shown relatively small percentage losses in affected industries, although these estimates vary and do not show the total effect of trade, since they consider only declining and not expanding industries. Much of the net effect depends on the flexibility of the labor market. If wages adjust rapidly and displaced workers can move easily, then spells of unemployment are likely to be short.

However, even if markets adjust rapidly, displaced workers have losses due to the costs of finding and qualifying for new jobs and may experience falling wages, particularly if they had above-market wages to begin with. Empirical estimates again suggest that wage effects in the United States have been small as compared to other influences (such as technological change) on wages. Others find that trade has increased wages for skilled labor and decreased wages for unskilled labor.

In principle, the absence of trade barriers might cause wages between all nations to converge eventually, as firms move production to lower-wage countries, increasing the demand for labor in those countries (and reducing demand for labor in high-wage countries). This could only happen completely if the ratio of wages to marginal productivities were equal throughout the world, or in other words, if workers everywhere were equally productive. This is unlikely to occur, due to a variety of difference's, from capital stocks and the availability of resources to education and cultural differences. Also, lower wage to marginal productivity ratios may cause firms to consider relocation, but there are a variety of other factors that influence that decision, including the higher cost of trading across international borders.

Overall, we can conclude that expanded trade is likely to increase national income and consumption but impose costs on some segments of society, often the least skilled and least able to easily adjust. Normative considerations imply that it may be desirable for the government to implement policies that reduce the costs to these groups. These policies include subsidizing human capital investment by displaced workers, encouraging displaced workers to attempt to become reemployed quickly through earned income tax credits, and subsidizing employment through payroll subsidies. Since the costs of international trade are not born solely by displaced workers and others directly affected, a broad "safety net" of policies may be selected in order to reduce risks and enhance gains from growing trade opportunities.

■ Review Questions

Choose the letter that represents the **BEST** response.

International Trade and Comparative Advantage

In answering Questions **1–7**, please refer to Figure 16-3. The production possibilities curve for wheat (W) and corn (C) facing the United States is the line ab, and the production possibilities curve for Canada is the line vw.

1. What is the internal tradeoff between wheat and corn facing the United States?
    a.   1 unit of wheat costs 5 units of corn
    b.   1 unit of wheat costs 1/5 unit of corn
    c.   1 unit of corn costs 5 units of wheat
    d.   both **b** and **c**

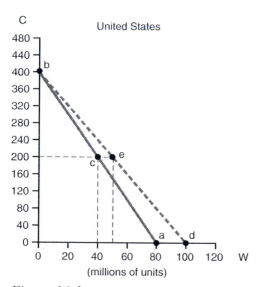

Figure 16-3a   Figure 16-3b

2. What is the internal tradeoff between wheat and corn facing Canada?
    a.   1 unit of corn costs 1/2 unit of wheat
    b.   1 unit of wheat costs 2 units of corn
    c.   1 unit of corn costs 1/2 unit of wheat
    d.   both **b** and **c**

3. Suppose that the initial production levels in each country are represented by points c ($W = 40, C = 200$) and x ($W = 45, C = 150$). Also suppose that the number of workers in the United States is 100 million, and the number of workers in Canada is 50 million. If per capita consumption levels can be taken as indicators of the real wage rate in each country then
    a.   real wages are higher in the United States.
    b.   real wages are higher in Canada.
    c.   real wages are the same in both countries.
    d.   real wages are higher in the United States for corn producers, but lower for wheat producers.

4. Terms of trade acceptable to both countries would be
    a.   1 unit of wheat for 4 units of corn.
    b.   1 unit of corn for 1/3 a unit of wheat.
    c.   1 unit of wheat for 2-1/2 units of corn.
    d.   all of the above.

5. Suppose the actual terms of trade agreed to by both countries are reflected in the lines *bd* and *vy*. The actual terms of trade are
    a.   1 unit of corn for 4 units of wheat.
    b.   1 unit of wheat for 1/4 a unit of corn.
    c.   1 unit of wheat for four units of corn.
    d.   both **b** and **c**.

6. Suppose the final consumption combinations of the two countries are point e ($W = 50, C = 200$) and z ($W = 70, C = 200$). The actual trade that took place must have been
    a.   70 units of wheat for 200 units of corn.
    b.   50 units of corn for 70 units of wheat.
    c.   20 units of wheat for 240 units of corn.
    d.   50 units of wheat for 200 units of corn.

7. The effect on employment and wages of international trade between the two countries has been
    a.   lower real wages and job losses in the country that initially had the highest wages.
    b.   higher real wages in both countries.
    c.   a change in the mix of employment opportunities.
    d.   both **b** and **c**.

International Trade Effects on the Demand for Labor

8. Suppose that the wage of foreign workers falls. Which of the following best describes the **scale** effect on the demand for U.S. labor?
    a.   Lower foreign wages mean that U.S. companies will substitute foreign workers for U.S. workers, decreasing the U.S. demand for labor.
    b.   Lower foreign wages mean that U.S. companies will substitute foreign workers for U.S. workers, increasing the U.S. demand for labor.
    c.   Lower foreign wages mean that U.S. companies will have lower production costs, increasing output and thus increasing the U.S. demand for labor.
    d.   Lower foreign wages mean that U.S. companies will have lower production costs, increasing output but decreasing the U.S. demand for labor.
    e.   Lower foreign wages will not shift the U.S. demand for labor.

9. Suppose that the wage of foreign workers falls. Which of the following best describes the **substitution** effect on the demand for U.S. labor?

   a. Lower foreign wages mean that U.S. companies will substitute foreign workers for U.S. workers, decreasing the U.S. demand for labor.

   b. Lower foreign wages mean that U.S. companies will substitute foreign workers for U.S. workers, increasing the U.S. demand for labor.

   c. Lower foreign wages mean that U.S. companies will have lower production costs, increasing output and thus increasing the U.S. demand for labor.

   d. Lower foreign wages mean that U.S. companies will have lower production costs, increasing output but decreasing the U.S. demand for labor.

   e. Lower foreign wages will not shift the U.S. demand for labor.

10. A fall in the wage of foreign workers would be likely to increase the demand for U.S. labor under which of the following conditions?

   a. Skill levels of domestic and foreign workers are similar.

   b. Foreign labor is a large share of the total cost of production.

   c. The goods produced by domestic and foreign workers are substitutes in production.

   d. The elasticity of demand for the final product is very small (inelastic).

Effects on Employment and Wages of International Trade

11. Most empirical studies suggest that the <u>overall</u> effects of international trade on domestic employment are

   a. positive and large.

   b. positive but small.

   c. zero.

   d. negative but small.

   e. negative and large.

12. If the wage to marginal productivity ratio in another country is lower than in the domestic country, firms will

   a. move production to the other country.

   b. move production to the other country only if the benefits outweigh the higher transactions costs from foreign production.

   c. move production from the other country to the domestic market.

   d. move production from the other country to the domestic market only if there are tariffs and other trade barriers.

13. Wage convergence is most likely for

   a. occupations with very similar skill levels.

   b. products that are bulky and hard to transport.

   c. service and other occupations that need to be located near the end user.

   d. high-skilled, specialized labor.

Policy Issues

14. Which of the following is a good argument for using government policies to assist workers harmed by trade?
    a. International trade reduces total social welfare.
    b. International trade lowers wages for workers, which is unfair.
    c. International trade reduces the efficiency of the economy.
    d. The least-skilled workers are most at risk of losing from trade.

15. An argument for broad government policies that assist workers and citizens in all areas, not just those directly displaced by trade is that
    a. to be fair, the government should assist all workers.
    b. governments of other countries assist workers, so it is necessary to level the playing field.
    c. the costs of trade are also borne by workers not directly affected, due to increased uncertainty and other factors.
    d. the efficiency of society will be increased by increasing benefits to all workers.

■ Problems

International Trade and Comparative Advantage

16. Suppose the following equations represent the production possibilities curves for food (F) and clothing (C) in the United States and China. Both C and F are measured in millions of units.

$$\text{United States:} \quad C = 100 - 0.25F,$$
$$\text{China:} \quad C = 300 - 0.5F.$$

Suppose there are 100 million workers in the United States and 600 million in China. The initial production combinations are $F = 240$, $C = 40$ in the United States, and $F = 120$, $C = 240$ in China.

16a. What is the cost in the United States of 1 unit of food? Of 1 unit of clothing?

16b. What is the cost in China of 1 unit of food? Of 1 unit of clothing?

16c. Which country is the low-cost producer of food? Of clothing?

16d. What are the effective real wage rates in each country as indicated by the per capita consumption of its workers?

16e. How should each country allocate its capital and labor resources in order to maximize its future gains from trade?

16f. What are the limits of the terms of trade (i.e., what is the maximum amount of clothing a unit of food could trade for, what is the minimum amount clothing a unit of food could trade for)?

16g. Consider a trade of 150 units of food for 50 units of clothing. Show the effects of the trade on living standards in each country.

17. Despite the advantages that free trade offers, why do so many countries construct barriers to free trade like import quotas?

18. How are the employment effects of technological change like those associated with international trade?

International Trade Effects on the Demand for Labor

19. While a number of factors may be part of this empirical observation, it is generally true that in the United States, manufacturing industries have had greater job losses than service industries since the expansion of international trade.

19a. Why in general would you expect manufacturing industries to be more vulnerable to job losses due to trade than service-related industries?

19b. Using the concepts of substitution and scale effects, explain why the clothing industry in the United States has suffered large job losses due to trade.

Effects on Employment and Wages of International Trade

20. In an article published in *The Wall Street Journal* shortly before the 1992 presidential election, economist Robert J. Barro made the following statement:

   "The prize for poor economic analysis must surely go to Ross Perot. [H]is theory of international trade goes something like this: Wage rates in the United States are $15 per hour, whereas those in Mexico are $1 per hour. If we eliminated all barriers to trade, the U.S. businesses would move to Mexico to take advantage of the cheap labor; in the end, wage rates in the two countries would stabilize at about $7 to $8 per hour."

   Source: *The Wall Street Journal*, October 29, 1992 (p. A14).

20a. Assuming this is an accurate portrayal of Mr. Perot's view, why is this a poor economic analysis of the effects of free trade among countries?

20b. Do trade barriers such as import quotas really help American workers?

Answers To Chapter 1

■ Review Questions

1. **Answer d.** In product markets, firms sell and individuals buy. Also, human beings are not as intimately involved in the transactions, so nonpecuniary factors are less important.

2. **Answer d.** If people strive to make themselves as happy as they can (i.e., maximize their utility), and a human being is "attached" when labor market transactions take place, it seems likely that feelings, emotions, personalities, and working conditions will play a role in determining the nature of these transactions. All these factors seem to play an important role in determining a human being's happiness.

3. **Answer b.** This is the only statement that refers to "what is" true about the labor market. All the others, either explicitly or implicitly, make reference to "what should be" true about labor market outcomes.

4. **Answer a.** This statement makes reference to "what should be," while all the others refer to how labor market variables are actually linked.

5. **Answer a.** A model is useful precisely because it is abstract. If it accurately captured all of the complexity of the real world or people's actual thought processes, it would be so intricate that no patterns or principles could be discerned. Models can be used not only to predict behavior but also to illustrate the kind of behavior that should take place to reach certain goals.

6. **Answer d.** Individuals or households are assumed to maximize utility, while firms are assumed to maximize profits.

7. **Answer d.** The two most fundamental assumptions of positive economics are scarcity (people can not get everything they want) and rationality (people consistently weigh costs and benefits).

8. **Answer c.** Utility maximization means people strive to be as happy as possible, and that happiness may depend in part on how other people are doing, not solely on an individual's own circumstances. The concept of mutually beneficial transactions is a normative one, unrelated to what actually happens in some instances. Positive models refer to actual links between economic variables, and these links can only be exposed by holding other factors constant.

9. **Answer b.** The test of a positive economic model is how well it predicts average tendencies. It does not have to capture everyone's idiosyncrasies all the time. Normative models, on the other hand, relate to standards that someone feels should be attained.

10. **Answer b.** Normative statements are frequently connected to mandated transactions, not just voluntary transactions. These mandates can be driven by the quest for mutually beneficial gain, but they need not be. Other ethical principles or goals like fairness may be the driving force behind normative statements.

11. **Answer d.** If one person gains and no one else loses, that is a transaction that seemingly could be supported by unanimous consent. Therefore, if such a transaction can still be made, a Pareto efficient outcome has not been achieved.

12. **Answer b.** In most situations there are many different Pareto efficient outcomes, but many of these outcomes would probably be considered unfair. The outcome that is finally achieved may be arrived at voluntarily or by government mandate.

13. **Answer d.** Moving from one Pareto efficient outcome, even if it is to another Pareto efficient outcome, will make one person worse off at the same time it makes someone else better off. Deciding among Pareto efficient outcomes, therefore, involves some assessment of the fairness or equity of the outcomes. These judgments have traditionally been made in the political arena and are often influenced by each party's initial income or wealth position. Most political systems have been willing to support at least some redistribution of wealth from the rich to the poor.

14. **Answer d.** Other reasons include price distortions caused by government taxes or the lack of a market where the transaction can be worked out.

15. **Answer d.** Also, in some instances, government action is the impediment to the Pareto efficient outcome. In these instances the government must get out of the way before the transaction can be completed.

16. **Answer c.** Least squares regression makes no assumptions with respect to the relationship between independent variables (those on the right side of the equation) or the size of the coefficients attached to these variables. For the estimated parameters to be unbiased estimates of the true values, however, the error term must be random.

17. **Answer b.** One can reject the hypothesis that the true value of a particular coefficient is zero only if the estimated parameter is more than twice the size of its standard error (the *t*-statistic will then be greater than 2). A small standard error is no guarantee of a non-zero parameter if the estimated parameter is also very small. A random error term helps to ensure that the estimates are as precise as possible, but the existence of a random error term does not have any bearing on the existence of a relationship between the independent and dependent variables.

18. **Answer b.** A coefficient in a multiple regression indicates the effect on the dependent variable, on average, of a one-unit change in the independent variable, assuming the other variables are held constant. A non-zero estimate for the coefficient does not ensure that the true value of the parameter is different from zero. In this case, however, a parameter estimate four times as large as its standard error allows us to reject the hypothesis of a "true" value of zero.

19. **Answer d.** The relatively small value of the standard error means the coefficient on the W variable has been measured with a relatively small margin of error. Also, since the coefficient is 2.5 times its standard error, the hypothesis that the true value of the coefficient is zero can be rejected. However, a relationship that is significant in a statistical sense is not necessarily significant in an economic sense. Holding all else constant, in this equation, every \$1 increase in the wage is accompanied by just a one-half hour reduction in total annual hours, a very insignificant amount.

20. **Answer a.** Since W and V are positively correlated, the coefficient on W would pick up some of the negative effect V exerts on H, making the coefficient on W smaller.

■ Problems

21a. The drawing is a model because it is a deliberate abstraction designed to illustrate certain key characteristics of human beings.

21b. The model highlights that human beings walk upright on two legs. It also highlights the relative size of the head and limbs. It pushes all the details of our appearance, particularly things like the shape of our hands and feet, into the background. It also says nothing about the mental capacities that distinguish us from other animals. There are, of course, other characteristics that it doesn't capture either.

21c. A simple drawing was easy to make. Anything more involved would require some artistic skill. Also, such a simple drawing highlights the idea that models are abstract. A more realistic drawing would not have gotten across the idea that "humans walk upright on two legs" any better than this simple drawing. In fact, a more realistic drawing might have obscured this point by focusing attention on other features.

21d. This is a positive model since it attempts to show "what is" true about human beings. It does not attempt to assess our bodily design or illustrate "what should be."

22a. The person is being inconsistent. If it is worth taking 30 minutes to save \$5 in the first situation, it should also be worth it in the second situation. However, he may be acting like this because the percentage savings is much smaller in the second case. Studies of perception have revealed that the larger or more intense the stimulus (in this case the original expenditure on insurance), the larger any change (in this case the cost savings) has to be before it will be recognized.

22b. No, a model with poor predictive power may still be useful in a normative sense, in this case as a guide to more rational decision making. In this example, if confronted with his inconsistency, the worker may realize that his choice in the second instance was obscured by the large dollar amounts. As a result he may be able to avoid similar mistakes in the future.

23a. The outcome is Pareto efficient because there is no way any of the remaining firms or workers can reach an agreement that is mutually beneficial. For example, firm 9 will only benefit from a wage below \$360, but worker 9 will not benefit from anything below \$400. Since all the mutually beneficial deals have already been made, the outcome is Pareto efficient.

23b.   With deals below $480 prohibited, only firms 1, 2, and 3 will be interested in hiring. On the other hand, all 10 workers would be willing to work. Suppose for simplicity that workers 1, 2, and 3 are hired. Worker 4, who has been shut out of the market, could easily strike a mutually beneficial deal with firm 4 by offering to work for, say, $400, but the law prohibits this. Since mutually beneficial deals can still be made, the outcome under the legislated wage is not Pareto efficient.

23c.   The three workers who continue to be hired each gain $100 (the difference between the legislated wage of $480 and the wage of $380 that would have emerged if all mutually beneficial trades were allowed). The three firms that hire them each lose $100 relative to what they would have gained under the lower wage. The five workers who would have been hired under the lower wage also lose. Assuming workers 4 through 8 have been shut out, the total loss to these workers is $200 ($80 + $60 + $40 + $20). Combining the worker and firm losses yields a total loss of $500.

23d.   The winners do not gain enough ($300) to compensate the losers (−$500) and still come out ahead. Such a law can only be justified using principles developed outside of economics. For example, those who gain might have been very poor to begin with, while those who lost might have been well off. In such a situation, the redistribution might be justified by appealing to notions of equity or fairness.

23e.   Eight workers would be hired, the same outcome as in **23a**.

23f.   This is a Pareto efficient outcome since no mutually beneficial deals still exist. Even if person 9 were paid his minimum acceptable wage of $400, the firm would not gain by hiring him. While the outcome is Pareto efficient, it is not necessarily equitable since the firm has reaped all the benefits.

24a.   See the scatter of points in Figure 1-2.

24b.   See the straight line in Figure 1-2.

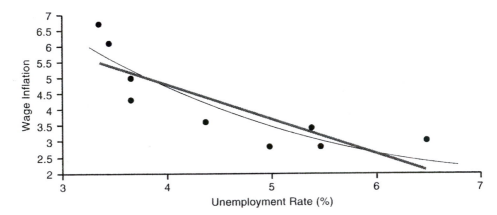

Figure 1-2

*24c. See Table 1-5 and the points plotted as squares in Figure 1-3.

Table 1-5

UR	Actual %ΔW	Predicted %ΔW	Residual
5.4	3.4	3.3	0.1
6.5	3.0	2.1	0.9
5.4	3.4	3.3	0.1
5.5	2.8	3.2	−0.4
5.0	2.8	3.7	−0.9
4.4	3.6	4.4	−0.8
3.7	4.3	5.2	−0.9
3.7	5.0	5.2	−0.2
3.5	6.1	5.4	0.7
3.4	6.7	5.5	1.2

*24d. The residuals do not seem random. They tend to be positive when the unemployment rate is relatively high or relatively low, and negative otherwise. From the scatter of points in Figure 1-2, it appears a convex curve would fit the data better.

*24e. See the solid curve in Figure 1-2.

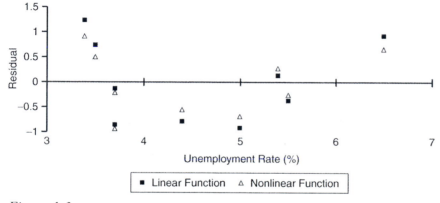

Figure 1-3

*24f.   See Table 1-6 and the points plotted as triangles in Figure 1-3. For six of the ten years the fit improved. There were two years where it worsened slightly and two years where it was essentially unchanged. The fit improved most at the lowest and highest values of the unemployment rate. For both values, the residual was 0.3 units less when the nonlinear function was used.

Table 1-6.

UR	Actual %ΔW	Predicted %ΔW	Residual
5.4	3.4	3.1	0.3
6.5	3.0	2.4	0.6
5.4	3.4	3.1	0.3
5.5	2.8	3.0	−0.2
5.0	2.8	3.5	−0.7
4.4	3.6	4.2	−0.6
3.7	4.3	5.2	−0.9
3.7	5.0	5.2	−0.2
3.5	6.1	5.6	0.5
3.4	6.7	5.8	0.9

24g.   See the scatter of points in Figure 1-4.

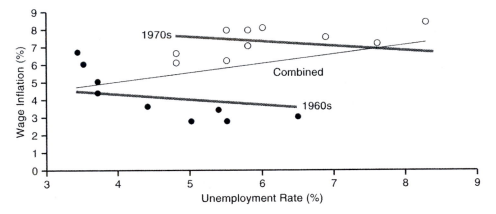

Figure 1-4

24h.   See the lines labeled "1960s" and "1970s" in Figure 1-4. The 1970s line lies 3.7 units above the 1960s line at every value of the unemployment rate.

24i.   See the line labeled "Combined" in Figure 1-4. The omission of the $D70$ variable severely biases the coefficient on the unemployment variable in an upward direction. The $D70$ variable normally would exert a positive effect on the dependent variable. However, since $D70$ and the unemployment rate are positively correlated (notice that both unemployment and inflation were higher in the 1970s), when the $D70$ variable is omitted, most of its positive effect on the dependent variable will be attributed to the unemployment rate variable. Notice that omitting a variable is a problem here because the omitted variable and the remaining variable are correlated. Omitting a variable that is not correlated with the independent variable would not create bias in the estimated coefficient.

*24j.   To allow both the position and slope of the curve to be different, estimate the equation

$$\%\Delta W_t = a_0 + a_1 UR_t + a_2 D70_t + a_3 D70 \ UR_t + e_t.$$

For the 1960s, the vertical intercept would be given by the estimate of a_0, while for the 1970s it would be given by $a_0 + a_2$. Similarly, for the 1960s, the slope would be given by the estimate of a_1, while for the 1970s it would be given by $a_1 + a_3$.

■ Applications

25a.   The notion of exercising a preferential option for the poor is very different from promoting the norm of Pareto efficiency. Under Pareto efficiency, only mutually beneficial changes should be undertaken. But when exercising a preferential option for the poor, some parties may be called upon to sacrifice so that the poor can advance.

25b.   When the goal is to promote Pareto efficient outcomes, the government mainly plays a facilitating role. Its task is to promote voluntary exchange based on accurate and complete information. When barriers to such transactions exist, however, the government sometimes can act in a way to overcome these barriers. Some examples of these actions include providing for the production of public goods, eliminating capital market imperfections, or establishing substitutes for the market.

Pope Leo XIII sees the task of government as promoting and protecting the interests of the poor and disadvantaged. Government need not act on behalf of all members of a society. Rather, government actions must be judged by their impact on the poor, even when these actions require sacrifice by others.

26a.   The survey suggests people care about where their income stands relative to others in the population.

26b.   The norm of Pareto efficiency says that all mutually beneficial changes should be undertaken. In this case, many people disagree that the program should be enacted, even though everyone gains. Therefore the responses are inconsistent with the norm of Pareto efficiency.

26c.   It appears that the premise of the question would have to have everyone gaining by roughly the same amount for the reform to be supported unanimously.

27a.   Estimating the parameters α_0 and α_1 would require cross-sectional data on earnings and employee-generated revenues for a number of workers at one or more firms. Estimates of the parameters would be derived by choosing values for α_0 and α_1 such that the squared differences between the actual and predicted values of employee earnings were minimized. Most statistical and spreadsheet programs have commands that will use this criterion to find the parameter estimates.

27b.   The precision of an estimate is indicated by its standard error. If the estimated parameter is approximately twice the value of its standard error, it is possible to reject with reasonable confidence the hypothesis that the true value of the parameter equals zero.

*27c.   If the hypothesis is that parameter α_1 equals one, rather than zero, then the value of the estimated parameter, minus one, must be approximately twice the standard error of estimated parameter.

*27d.   Frank's hypothesis implies that the relationship between earnings and productivity is much flatter than the standard theory predicts. For a graphical depiction of this effect, see Figure 1-5. Line *ab* represents the relationship between E and R implicit in the standard model, while line *cd* would be consistent with Frank's hypothesis. Consequently, the prediction would be that α_0 would be much greater than it is in the standard model, while the value of α_1 would be much less (and definitely less than one).

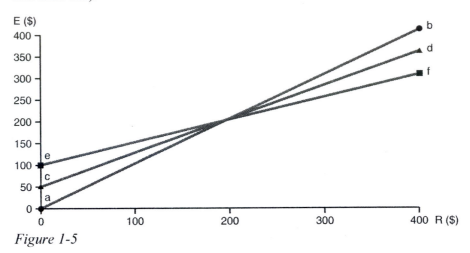

Figure 1-5

*27e.   The equation to be estimated is

$$E_i = \alpha_0 + \alpha_1 R_i + \alpha_2 D_i + \alpha_3 D_i R_i + e_i.$$

This equation allows both the intercept and slope to change as the degree of employee interaction increases. Since the hypothesis is that relationship between earnings and productivity flattens out as the degree of interaction increases, the expectation would be that the estimate of the parameter α_2 would be greater than zero and the estimate of the parameter α_3 would be less than zero. The effect of increased interaction is also shown in Figure 1-5. Line *cd* represents a possible relationship between E and R when there is modest worker interaction, while line *ef* represents a situation of more extensive interaction.

*27f.   It seems unlikely that D is correlated with the level of employee productivity (R) since high-productivity people can be found in all types of work environments. Therefore, eliminating D should not bias the estimates of the remaining parameters α_0 and α_1.

Answers To Chapter 2

■ Review Questions

1. **Answer a.** To be classified as in the labor force, an individual must be employed, actively seeking work, or waiting to be recalled from a layoff. However, those actively seeking work or waiting to be recalled from a layoff are called unemployed. Hence, the labor force can be defined as those employed plus those unemployed.

2. **Answer a.** The labor force participation rate is defined as those in the labor force divided by the population. The labor force is those employed plus those unemployed.

3. **Answer d.** The unemployment rate is defined as the number unemployed divided by the labor force, but recall that the labor force is the number employed plus the number unemployed.

4. **Answer c.** The index of nominal wages for 1996 is the nominal wage in 1996 expressed as a percentage of the nominal wage in the base year.

$$\frac{\$11.18}{\$9.54} \times 100 = 117.$$

5. **Answer b.** The index of real wages is the index of nominal wages divided by the price index (with the result multiplied by 100).

$$\frac{117}{127} \times 100 = 92.$$

6. **Answer b.** Since the index of real wages declined from 100 to 92, the real wage declined by 8% over the period.

7. **Answer d.** Although the words income, earnings, and wage are often used interchangeably in the English language, in this chapter they each refer to a different measure. The wage is defined as the payment per unit of time, while earnings equal the wage multiplied by the units of time worked. Adding employee benefits to earnings yields a worker's total compensation. Total compensation plus any unearned income yields total income. Therefore, even if the real wage falls, total income may not fall if the time spent working increases, benefits increase, or unearned income increases.

8. **Answer d.** The demand curve represents the relationship between the wage and quantity of labor firms wish to hire provided all the other things that can influence the quantity of labor demanded are held constant. Responses **a** and **b** are examples of non-wage determinants of the total demand for labor in the market. Note that the demand curve is constructed independently of the supply curve.

9. **Answer d.** The demand curve slopes downward in the long run because of the substitution and scale effects associated with a wage change. Answer **a** describes the substitution effect, and answer **b** describes the scale effect. Note that answer **c** simply repeats, using different words, the idea that the demand curve is downward sloping. It does not answer the question since it does not give an economic reason for the relationship.

10. **Answer d.** The demand curve as shown on the graph has a vertical intercept of 36 and a slope of −3, which implies that the equation is

$$W = 36 - 3L \implies L = 12 - \frac{1}{3}W.$$

11. **Answer c.** When the price of capital rises, the firm will substitute relatively cheaper labor for capital (substitution effect). The optimal output of the firm will also fall, however, leading the firm to use less of all its inputs (scale effect). As long as the substitution effect dominates the scale effect, the quantity of labor demanded will increase and the demand curve for labor will shift to the right. (Note that **a** reflects a change in the quantity of labor demanded, or a movement along the curve, not a shift in the curve.)

12. **Answer b.** The market supply curve is drawn holding working conditions and wages in other occupations constant. Wages in other occupations need not be at any particular level for the supply curve to be drawn. The presence of a union may mean that not all of the *S* curve will be relevant, but it would not change the fact that the market supply curve shows the number of workers willing to work at all the various wage levels.

13. **Answer b.** The supply curve as shown on the graph has a vertical intercept of 6 and a slope of 2, which implies that the equation is

$$W = 6 + 2L \implies L = \frac{1}{2}W - 3.$$

14. **Answer b.** Individual firms offering comparable jobs in a competitive labor market will be constrained to pay the market clearing wage. In this case, an individual firm will be able to hire as much or as little labor as it wants at a wage of $18.

15. **Answer d.** At any wage other than the market clearing wage, a shortage (excess demand) or a surplus (excess supply) will create a tendency for the wage to change. Also, when the wage is not at its market clearing value, an opportunity for mutually beneficial exchange between workers and firms will exist. Hence once the market clearing wage has been attained, all the mutually beneficial deals will have been made, and it will only be possible to make someone better off by making someone else worse off.

16. **Answer b.** Economic rent is the triangular area *abc* in Figure 2-5. The area of a triangle is given by the formula

$$\text{Area} = \frac{1}{2}(\text{base}) \times (\text{height})$$

$$\Rightarrow \text{Economic Rent} = \frac{1}{2}(6,000)(\$12) = \$36,000.$$

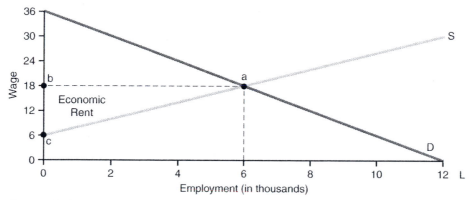

Figure 2-5

17. **Answer c.** With the wage fixed at $24, the supply curve effectively becomes a horizontal line at $24 and the quantity of labor demanded will fall to

$$L = 12 - \frac{1}{3}(24) = 4.$$

Note that the surplus will actually be 5 since the quantity supplied will increase to 9.

18. **Answer d.** If the wage is originally at the market clearing level, then quantity demanded will equal quantity supplied. When demand increases, quantity demanded will now be greater than quantity supplied at the market clearing wage. This means that there is a shortage of labor and upward pressure on the wage. As the wage rises, the shortage is eliminated and a new higher market clearing wage is established.

19. **Answer b.** When demand increases, upward pressure is put on the wage and the employment level. When supply increases, downward pressure is put on the wage, and upward pressure is put on the employment level. As long as both supply and demand increase by the same amount, the pressures put on the wage will tend cancel out, while the pressures put on the employment level will reinforce. Thus employment will increase, but the effect on the wage depends on which shift is larger. If the shift in supply is greater than the shift in demand, wages will fall. If the shift in demand is greater than the shift in supply, wages will rise.

20. **Answer b.**

$$L_D = L_S \Rightarrow 13 - \frac{1}{3}W = \frac{1}{2}W - 2$$

$$\Rightarrow \frac{5}{6}W = 15 \Rightarrow W^* = \$18.$$

$$W^* = \$18 \Rightarrow 13 - \frac{1}{3}(18) = 7.$$

■ Problems

21a. Unemployment rate $= \dfrac{U}{E + U} \times 100$

$$\Rightarrow \dfrac{10}{125} \times 100 = 8\%.$$

21b. While an 8% or higher unemployment rate is not unusual during economic downturns (e.g., 1982–83), it is fairly high by historical standards. Of course, it is nowhere near the peak unemployment of 24.9% experienced during the Great Depression!

21c. While the unemployment rate has tended to fluctuate less in recent years, the average unemployment rate seems to be slowly climbing.

21d. If the labor force (L) equals $E + U$, and the population (POP) equals $L + N$, then the labor force participation rate ($LFPR$) is

$$LFPR = \dfrac{L}{POP} \times 100$$

$$\Rightarrow \dfrac{10 + 115}{10 + 115 + 75} \times 100 = 62.5\%.$$

21e. No, this is not an unusually high labor force participation rate. Throughout the 1980s and 1990s the rate has been higher.

21f. Since 1950 the overall labor force participation rate rose modestly from about 60% in 1950 to the just over 67% in 2000, but fell to 66% by 2004. Over this period, however, the labor force participation rate of men dropped significantly from nearly 87% to 73%, while the rate for women increased from 34% to about 60%.

21g. The type of work has been changing steadily from goods producing to private-sector services.

22a. The reason for computing an index of real wages is to make it easier to compare the real purchasing power of a worker's wage when product prices are changing. The steps carried out in computing the index essentially hold prices constant. Hence any change in the index reflects a real change in the worker's command over goods and services, purchasing power. Also, by expressing purchasing power as a percentage of the purchasing power enjoyed in the base year (which is then standardized to 100%) the index makes it easy to compute the percentage change in buying power over time.

22b. See Table 2-6 for the index of real wages computed using 1980 as the base year.

Table 2-6

Year	Index of Nominal Wages	Price Index	Index of Real Wages
1945	14	22	64
1980	100	100	100
1997	184	195	94

22c. Over the period 1980 to 1997, real wages declined by 6%.

22d. This change understates the change in real compensation per worker since compensation includes both wages and employee benefits. Increases in employee benefits could easily offset the decline in real wages and make for an increase in real compensation per worker. Additionally, the price index may overstate the rate of inflation by ignoring substitution and changes in the quality of goods.

23a. Equilibrium $\Rightarrow L_D = L_S$

$$\Rightarrow 10 - \frac{1}{2}W = \frac{1}{2}W \Rightarrow W^* = \$10.$$

$$W^* = \$10 \Rightarrow L^* = 10 - \frac{1}{2}(10) = 5.$$

23b. See the curves labeled D and S in Figure 2-6. The equilibrium wage and employment occur at point a.

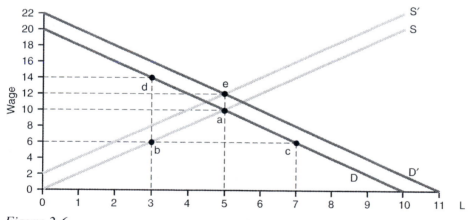

Figure 2-6

23c. At a wage of $6, the quantity supplied equals 3 (point b in Figure 2-6), while quantity demanded equals 7 (point c in Figure 2-6). The shortage of 4 units means that the market does not clear and that there will be upward pressure on wages.

*23d.   Note that at a wage of $6, firms would like to hire a total of 7 workers, but only 3 individuals are willing to work. Suppose that one of the firms shut out of the market offers to hire an additional worker at a wage of $10. The demand curve indicates that firms would be willing to pay up to $12 for a fourth worker, so this firm would still gain $2 by the offer. On the other hand, from the supply curve it is clear that it would take only a wage of $8 to get the fourth worker, so this worker earns economic rent of $2.

23e.   No, economic rent refers to the difference between what the worker actually earns and the minimum he or she would be willing to accept. A worker is only considered overpaid in an economic sense if the actual wage is above the equilibrium wage in the market.

*23f.   With the union restricting labor supply to 4 units, the supply curve becomes a vertical line at 4. This is line S' in Figure 2-7.

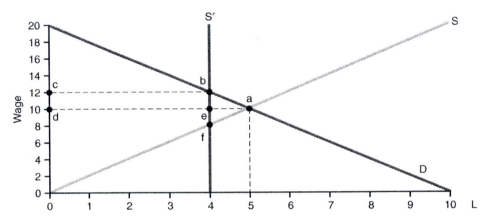

Figure 2-7

Equilibrium occurs where

$$L_D = L_S$$

$$\Rightarrow 10 - \frac{1}{2}W = 4 \Rightarrow W^* = \$12.$$

The equilibrium is point b in Figure 2-7. Since the equilibrium wage and employment level in the absence of the union was point a, the four members of the union who continue to be employed gain the area of the rectangle *bcde* for a total of ($2) × (4) = $8. This gain comes at the expense of the firms. However, since one more worker could have been hired if the wage stayed at $10, there is also a loss of economic rent equal to the area of triangle *aef*. This area is equal to $1 (0.5 × $2 × 1).

23g.   The market demand for labor increases, for example, when the demand for the product the firm produces increases, when labor becomes more productive, when the price of capital falls and the scale effect dominates the substitution effect, when the price of capital rises and the substitution effect dominates the scale effect, or when the number of firms increases. The market supply of labor decreases, for example, when wages in other occupations increase relative to the occupation being considered, when working conditions in the occupation worsen, or when the number of workers in the area decreases.

■ Applications

24a. The unemployment rate decreases. Suppose that initially the number of unemployed workers is 3 and the number of people in the labor force is 9. Since the unemployment rate is the number unemployed divided by the labor force, the unemployment rate is 33.3%. If one of the unemployed workers drops out of the labor force, then the number unemployed would be 2 and the size of the labor force would be 8. Consequently, the unemployment rate drops to 25%.

24b. When the unemployment rate drops, as it would in this case, it usually indicates the labor market is getting tighter; that is, employers are finding it harder to fill positions, and prospects are improving from the workers' perspective. In this case, however, even though the unemployment rate is going down, the labor market is actually getting looser. Workers' prospects are declining and employers would be able to draw on an increasingly desperate pool of workers.

*25a. No, it is not plausible to think that firms would desire to hire more workers at higher wage rates. An alternative conclusion is that the data reflect a series of equilibrium points (that is, both supply and demand are changing, or that demand is shifting, and thus the demand curve cannot be identified from the data).

*25b. If the demand curve for this category of labor shifted to the right over time along a stable supply curve, one would observe the wage and employment level rising together. Such a situation is shown in Figure 2-8.

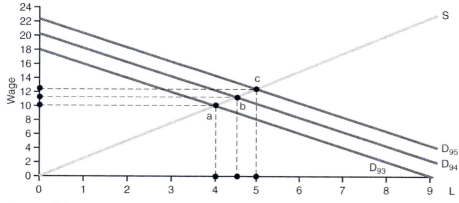

Figure 2-8

26. Since the net effect of the reduction in computer prices is projected to be a decrease in employment, the decrease in employment coming about through the substitution effect must be larger in magnitude than the increase coming about through the scale effect.

27a. An investment tax credit would have an ambiguous effect on employment opportunities in the industries where it applied. When the price of capital is reduced, firms have an incentive to substitute the relatively cheaper capital for labor (substitution effect). On the other hand, the reduction in the price of capital leads to a reduction in the firm's cost of producing another unit of output. This creates an incentive to expand output, and when a firm expands output, it uses more of all its inputs, including labor.

27b. Workers would see increased employment opportunities only if the positive scale effect associated with the investment tax credit exceeded the negative substitution effect.

28a.   This statement confuses a shift in the position of the demand curve (a change in demand) with movement along the demand curve (a change in quantity demanded). An increase in the supply of labor will cause the wage to fall, but this will lead to an increase in the quantity of labor demanded as the new equilibrium is established. The reduction in the wage will not cause a shift in demand as the statement suggests.

28b.   Assuming the market is originally in equilibrium, when the supply of labor increases, an excess supply of labor is created at the current wage. This excess supply will put downward pressure on the wage. As the wage falls, the quantity of labor demanded by firms increases, and the quantity of labor supplied by individuals is reduced. The wage will stop falling when the excess supply has just been eliminated. At this new market clearing wage, the total level of employment will be greater than it was when the scenario began.

The market supply of labor will increase, for example, when working conditions in the occupation improve or wages in other occupations fall relative to this one. Also, as the number of workers in a particular area increases the supply curve will shift to the right.

Answers To Chapter 3

■ Review Questions

1. **Answer d.** Competition ensures that the firm will be a wage taker. If the firm pays less than the going wage, no one would work for the firm. If the firm pays more, it will be at a cost disadvantage relative to rivals that did pay the going wage, and as a result the firm will be forced to close. Since the wage does not change as employment changes, the additional cost associated with hiring an additional worker is just the going wage that the firm pays.

2. **Answer d.** Competition ensures that the firm will be a price taker. If the firm sells for more than the going price, no one would buy the product. If the firm sells for less, it will not be taking in the amount of revenue it could and so earns less than comparable firms. If this continues the firm will be forced to close. Since the price does not change as output changes, the additional revenue associated with an additional unit of output is just the going price that the firm receives.

3. **Answer d.** Answers **a** and **c** simply repeat the premise of the question, they do not give any economic reasons for the relationship. Answer **b** has the relationship backwards. A decrease in the wage will trigger a higher level of employment and, in turn, a lower marginal product since a larger number of workers will be spread over a fixed capital stock.

4. **Answer b.** When the MR_L gets very close to the ME_L, all the moves that add to profit have been made.

5. **Answer a.** Recall that a monopsonist chooses a wage and labor combination below its MRP_L curve. Monopoly in the output market would only affect whether the MRP_L expression could be simplified to $P \lozenge MP_L$. The expression $MRP_L = MR \lozenge MP_L$ is a definition and is always true.

6. **Answer b.** To survive in a competitive market, a firm must maximize profits. How it gets to that point (e.g., trial and error, luck, etc.) does not matter. However, since the $MRP_L = ME_L$ rule does lead to maximum profits, a firm that is maximizing profits is acting as if it did follow that rule. Thus, even if no firm understands or actually follows the rule, it is useful to consider because it has predictive power. In the end we should see firms operating at this point because if they do not, they will not be maximizing profits, and can be driven out by firms that do.

7. **Answer b.** To find the market demand, add the individual quantities that are demanded at the real wage of 10. Since $L_1 = 2.5$, $L_2 = 5$, and $L_3 = 10$, the market quantity is 17.5.

8. **Answer a.**

$$\frac{W}{MP_L} = \frac{\$10}{5} = 2 < \frac{C}{MP_K} = \frac{\$36}{12} = 3.$$

The firm should increase L and decrease K to bring about an equality. As L increases, MP_L will fall, increasing the left side of the equation. As K decreases, MP_K will rise, decreasing the right side of the equation. Currently, the marginal cost of output produced by capital is $3, and only $2 for that produced by labor. Alternatively, an additional dollar spent on labor currently yields one-half unit of additional output, but the same dollar spent on additional capital only increases output by one-third unit.

9. **Answer a.** As C falls, the MC of the firm falls and the output of the firm increases. As output increases, the firm will use more of both capital and labor. This is called the scale effect of the price change. As long as this effect dominates the tendency of the firm to substitute capital for labor, the quantity of labor demanded should increase.

10. **Answer d.** In this question, capital and labor are used in fixed proportions in the production process. For example, if a firm uses one unit of labor and one unit of capital, it may be able to produce one unit of output, but if it adds another unit of capital without adding another unit of labor, output will not increase. In such a situation, the firm cannot substitute capital for labor when the price of capital falls, since this would take it away from the required proportion of labor and capital. The reduction in the price of capital, however, will reduce the marginal cost of production, leading to an increase in output (a scale effect) and an increase in the usage of both labor and capital. When the price of capital falls and labor usage increases, labor and capital are called gross complements.

11. **Answer d.** When the price of capital rises, in the long run the substitution and scale effects will combine to reduce the quantity of capital demanded. If the demand for labor shifts right as a result, that means labor usage is increasing. This occurs if the substitution effect of the capital price increase dominates the scale effect. In such a situation, labor and capital are called gross substitutes.

12. **Answer d.** The tax is the amount by which the demand curve is shifted down.

13. **Answer c.** As a result of the 4-unit tax, the equilibrium wage has been driven down by 2 (from 10 to 8). Therefore, the workers bear 50% of the tax in this example.

14. **Answer a.** In addition to the wage burden, workers see employment opportunities reduced by 1 (from 5 to 4) because of the tax.

15. **Answer d.** Who bears the burden of the tax is determined by which side of the market is least responsive to changes in the wage. When supply is perfectly vertical, the downward shift of the demand curve causes the wage to fall by the same amount.

16. **Answer a.** At the cost-minimizing combination of L and K, the isoquant is tangent to, and hence has the same slope as, the isoexpenditure line. Note that the slope of the isoexpenditure line is $W/C = \$16/\$25 = 0.64$.

17. **Answer a.** $TC = \$16(125) + \$25(80) = \$4,000$. Notice also that the vertical intercept equals TC/C and the horizontal intercept equals TC/W.

18. **Answer d.** If C increases to $40 holding all else constant, the isoexpenditure line would connect 250 on the labor axis with 100 on the capital axis. This would make an output of 100 unattainable. To produce along the old isoquant, the isoexpenditure line would have to move out parallel, reflecting an increase in cost. If it did so, notice that a tangency would occur with the $Q = 100$ isoquant at a point that involved less capital and more labor.

■ Problems

19a. MR is the change in total revenue (R) associated with a one-unit change in output (Q), holding all else constant. More formally, if ΔQ represents a small change in output, and ΔR represents the resulting change in revenue, then

$$MR = \frac{\Delta R}{\Delta Q}.$$

Similarly, MP_L is the change in output associated with a one-unit change in labor, holding all else constant. Formally, the MP_L can be written as

$$MP_L = \frac{\Delta Q}{\Delta L}.$$

By definition, $MR \lozenge MP_L$ is the marginal revenue product (MRP_L). Substituting the above expressions for MR and MP_L yields

$$\frac{\Delta R}{\Delta Q} \times \frac{\Delta Q}{\Delta L} = \frac{\Delta R}{\Delta L},$$

which is by definition MR_L, the additional revenue associated with a one-unit change in labor.

19b. If there is perfect competition in the output market, MR simplifies to P in the MRP_L expression. With P constant, the MRP_L slopes downward because MP_L is assumed to diminish. With P constant, MRP_L reaches zero when the MP_L reaches zero. When the firm has monopoly power in the output market, the MRP_L is downward sloping because both MR and MP_L diminish as L increases. (For a monopoly, MR falls as Q increases, and Q increases as L increases.)

20a. The new MRP_L (demand) curve has the equation $MRP_L = 40 - L$. It is shown as curve D_2 in Figure 3-7. Notice that the shift is not parallel, since the curve reaches zero when the MP_L reaches zero (at $L = 40$). If W stays at $10, the optimal level of labor to demand is 30.

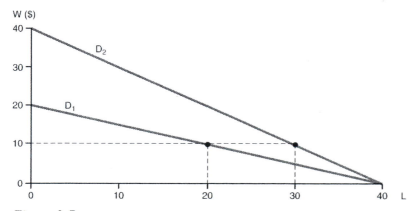

Figure 3-7

20b.   The changes are identical to those in **25a**.

20c.   The changes are identical to those in **25a** and **25b**.

21a.   See Figure 3-8.

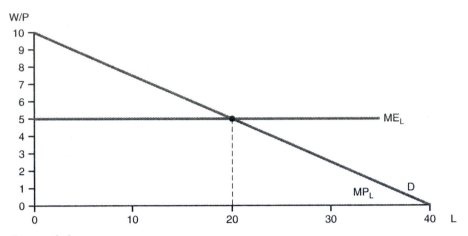

Figure 3-8

21b.   The marginal product of labor curve now serves as the firm's demand curve for labor.

22a.   See Figure 3-9.

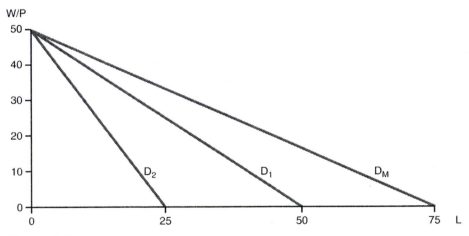

Figure 3-9

22b.   Let L standard for the total quantity demanded in the market. Then, $L = L_1 + L_2 = 50 - (W/P) + 25 - 0.5(W/P) = 75 - 1.5(W/P)$ or $W/P = 50 - (2/3)L$.

23.   The inequality suggests that if the firm produced one less unit of output by using less capital, its total cost of production would go down by $5. If the firm then proceeded to produce that same unit of output using labor, its total costs would only go up by $4. In other words, the firm could produce the same total output by changing its mix of labor and capital. If the firm can produce the same output at a lower cost with a different input mix, it could not have been at the optimal mix of labor and capital.

*24a.   If $P = 56 - 2Q$, then $MR = 56 - 4Q$. As W increases from \$4 to \$9 again, the MC will still rise from \$16 to \$24. What will be the change in optimal output? Originally, $MR = MC \Rightarrow 56 - 4Q = 16 \Rightarrow Q^* = 10$. After the rise in MC, $MR = MC \Rightarrow 56 - 4Q = 24 \Rightarrow Q^* = 8$. So originally, with an output of 10, $L^* = 20$ and $K^* = 5$. Holding output constant at 10, the change in W will lead to $L^* = 13.33$ and $K^* = 7.5$. Allowing output to adjust downward to 8 yields $L^* = (4/3)8 = 10.67$ and $K^* = (3/4)8 = 6$.

The net result of W increasing from \$4 to \$9 was that L^* fell from 20 to 10.67 (a reduction of 9.33 units), and K^* rose from 5 to 6 units (an increase of one unit). This net result, however, can be explained by a substitution effect where L^* fell from 20 to 13.33 (a reduction of 6.67) and a scale effect where L^* fell even further from 13.33 to 10.67 (an additional reduction of 2.67). Similarly, the increase in K^* can be explained by a substitution effect where K^* increased from 5 to 7.5 (a 2.5 unit increase), and also a scale effect where K^* fell from 7.5 to 6 (a 1.5 unit decrease).

24b.   Since the substitution effect on capital of the wage increase dominated the scale effect, labor and capital are gross substitutes, and the demand for capital will shift right (increase) as the wage increases.

*25a.   Originally, $L^* = 20$ and $K^* = 5$. After the change in C, the expressions for the optimal levels of L and K become $L^* = 3Q$ and $K^* = (1/3) Q$. If the original output level of 10 were maintained, the firm would substitute labor for capital so that $L^* = 30$ and $K^* = 3.33$. However, output does not remain at 10 since MC rises from \$16 to \$24. As the MC rises to \$24, output falls to $Q^* = 6$. At the new level of output, $L^* = (3)6 = 18$ and $K^* = (1/3) 6 = 2$.

The net result of C increasing from \$16 to \$36 was that L^* fell from 20 to 18 (a reduction of 2 units), and K^* fell from 5 to 2 (an decrease of 3 units). This net result can be explained by a substitution effect where L^* rose from 20 to 30 (an increase of 10) and a scale effect where L^* fell from 30 to 18 (a reduction of 12). Similarly, the decrease in K^* can be explained by a substitution effect where K^* fell from 5 to 3.33 (a 1.67-unit decrease), and also a scale effect where K^* fell from 3.33 to 2 (a 1.33-unit decrease).

25b.   Since the scale effect on labor of the capital price increase dominated the substitution effect, labor and capital are gross complements, and the demand for labor will shift left (decrease) as the price of capital increases.

26a. MP_L is the change in output associated with a one-unit change in labor, holding all else constant. More formally, if ΔL represents a small change in labor, and ΔQ represents the resulting change in output, then

$$MP_L = \frac{\Delta Q}{\Delta L}.$$

Using this formula, the movement from point a to b implies $MP_L = 2/4 = 0.5$. For the movement from b to c, $MP_L = 2/5 = 0.4$.

26b.   The diagram does show a diminishing marginal product of labor. It does not help to explain why the MP_L falls, however. The diagram is drawn assuming a diminishing MP_L and so simply reflects that assumption.

27a.   The substitution effect is zero on both inputs, since holding output constant, the increase in the price of capital has no effect on the optimal input mix. The firm will remain at point *a* as long as it wishes to produce 70 units of output.

27b.   The scale effect is a reduction in 20 units of both labor and capital. The firm moves from point *a* to point *b*.

27c.   Labor and capital are gross complements since labor has been reduced in response to an increase in the price of capital.

27d.   The total cost level has increased. Originally $TC = \$5(70) + \$10(70) = \$1,050$. After the price change and the adjustment in the input mix, $TC = \$5(50) + \$20(50) = \$1,250$. Without the scale adjustment, however, the increase in cost would have been much worse.

■ Applications

28a.   Equilibrium occurs where $W_D = W_S$.

$$30 - 0.04L = 0.05L - 15 \Rightarrow 0.09L = 45$$

$$\Rightarrow L^* = 500 \Rightarrow W^* = \$10.$$

28b.   The $9 per unit payroll tax shifts the demand curve down vertically by $9.

$$30 - 0.04L - 9 = 0.05L - 15 \Rightarrow 0.09L = 36$$

$$\Rightarrow L^* = 400 \Rightarrow W^* = \$5.$$

The cost of labor (per unit) to the employer is the $5 wage plus the $9 tax for a total of $14.

28c.   Since workers see their wage reduced from $10 to $5, they bear five-ninths of the tax. The firm sees its labor costs per unit rise from $10 to $14, so they bear the remaining four-ninths of the tax.

28d.   Like the payroll tax, mandated benefits impose real per-unit labor costs on firms. The effect of such costs would be to shift the demand for labor down and thereby reduce wages and employment levels. When all adjustments required by the market have been made, workers are likely to have borne a significant share of the cost of such programs.

*29a.   The demand curve is the MRP_L curve.

$$MRP_L = MR \Diamond MP_L.$$

$$K = 16 \Rightarrow Q = 4\sqrt{L}.$$

$$MR = 20 - Q = 20 - 4\sqrt{L}.$$

$$MRP_L \left(20 - 4\sqrt{L}\right) \frac{2}{\sqrt{L}} = \frac{40}{\sqrt{L}} - 8.$$

29b.   Profit maximization occurs where $MRP_L = W$.

$$\frac{40}{\sqrt{L}} - 8 = 10 \Rightarrow L^* = 4.94$$

$$Q^* = 4\sqrt{4.94} = 8.89 \Rightarrow P^* = \$15.56.$$

*29c. $MRP_L = 15\dfrac{2}{\sqrt{L}} = \dfrac{30}{\sqrt{L}}$

$$\text{Profit maximization} \Rightarrow \frac{30}{\sqrt{L}} = 10$$

$$\Rightarrow L^* = 9 \Rightarrow Q^* = 12.$$

*29d.   See Figure 3-10.

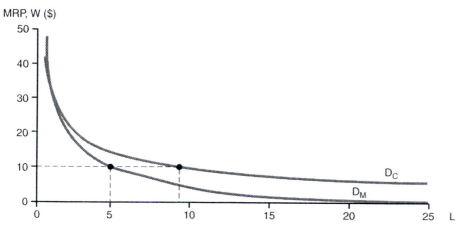

Figure 3-10

29e.   In the long run the increase in output should lead to a scale effect that would increase the usage of both capital and labor.

29f.   Regulations usually allow the firm a normal rate of return over its costs. As a result it has no incentive to control costs. If the firm pays higher wages, workers will be happier and the best new workers can be hired, making life smoother for the mangers of the firm, and the firm's rate of return will not be affected.

30a.   At $W = \$4$, $L = 120$. See the line ab in Figure 3-11 for a plot of the original demand curve.

*30b.   The subsidy is 50% of the difference between the target wage ($8) and the actual wage ($4). Therefore, the subsidy is $2 for each eligible worker. The effective cost to the firm of a new worker is $4 – $2 = $2.

*30c.   Since the effective cost of new labor is $2, the firm should be willing to hire out to $L = 140$. It is as if the firm is moving to the employment level associated with point e while the wage remains at $4. The intersection of the $4 wage and the new employment level creates the point f. Repeating this process for wage rates other than $4 creates the line segment dg. The new demand curve in its entirety would be the line bdg.

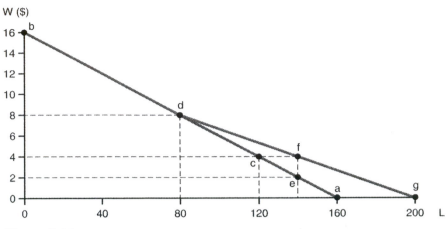

Figure 3-11

*30d.   At a wage of $4, the new demand curve is flatter (the slope as it appears on the graph changes from −0.1 to −0.067). The curve would be even flatter if the percentage of the subsidy increased to 75%. Point *f* would lie further to the right at *L* = 150 (and the slope would become −0.057).

*30e.   The total payment would be $2 times the number of new hires (20) for a total of $40. If the subsidy applied to all workers, the payment would be $2 times 140 for a total of $280.

*30f.   If the original demand were steeper, the subsidy would have a smaller effect on employment. If the demand were steeper, point *e* would lie to the left of its current position. Since the employment level associated with point *e* determines the employment level associated with point *f*, point *f* would lie to the left of its current position.

*30g.   Targeted programs like this do not always work as well as the model predicts because there may be a stigmatizing effect associated with being eligible for the subsidy. The employer may feel there is something wrong with a worker who needs the government's help to be hired, and so judge the worker's marginal revenue product to be even lower than it actually is. If the employer devalues the employee's worth as much as the subsidy reduces the employer's cost of hiring this worker, there may be no increase in employment.

Answers To Chapter 4

■ Review Questions

1. **Answer b.**

$$\eta_{ii} = \frac{\%\Delta E_i}{\%\Delta W_i} = \frac{-5.25}{3.5} = -1.5.$$

2. **Answer b.**

$$\eta_{ii} = \frac{\%\Delta E_i}{\%\Delta W_i} \Rightarrow \%\Delta E_i = (\eta_{ii})(\%\Delta W_i) \Rightarrow \%\Delta E_i = (-.5)(3.5) = -1.75.$$

3. **Answer c.** The expression for η_{ii} simplifies to

$$\eta_{ii} = \frac{\Delta E_i}{\Delta W_i} \frac{W_i}{E_i} = (-5)\frac{7}{25} = -1.4.$$

4. **Answer b.** Expenditures on labor fall from $175 to $160, a change of −$15. If demand is elastic, expenditures on labor always fall as the wage rises.

5. **Answer d.** According to the Hicks-Marshall laws, demand is less elastic when it is difficult to substitute capital for labor (answer **a**), product demand is less elastic (answer **b**), and the supply of capital is inelastic (answer **c**).

6. **Answer d.** The demand curve facing an individual firm will always be more elastic than the market demand curve since from the point of view of any individual firm, consumers have many substitution possibilities. If consumers do not like the prices at one airline, they can often choose another. But from the point of view of the market as a whole, the only alternatives to air travel are the train, bus, or automobile, each considerably more time consuming for long trips.

7. **Answer d.** When labor and capital are used in fixed proportions, they can not be substituted for one another. Holding all else constant, the smaller the substitution effect of a wage change, the more inelastic the demand for labor.

8. **Answer a.** Letting (t) stand for teenagers and (a) for adults

$$\eta_{at} = \frac{\%\Delta E_a}{\%\Delta W_t} = \frac{1}{-5} = -0.2.$$

9. **Answer a.** If the cross-wage elasticity is negative, a rise in the price of teenage labor should reduce adult employment. Since teenage labor will also be reduced, teenagers and adults are gross complements.

10. **Answer c.** Adults and teenagers will be gross complements if the scale effect associated with the rise in teenage labor dominates the substitution effect. Answers **a** and **b** make for a large substitution effect, while **d** makes for a small-scale effect. When the cost of teenage labor accounts for a large share of total costs, a rise in teen wages will lead to a large increase in the marginal cost of production. The larger the increase in marginal cost, the larger the reduction in output and the more employment in both categories of labor will fall.

11. **Answer d.** As long as the labor demand curve is downward sloping, an increase in the minimum wage should move the firm up the demand curve, resulting in a lower employment level. The only way the actual level of employment can increase is if the curve also shifts out at the same time the movement along the curve is taking place. In this case, the employment increase would have been even larger had the minimum wage not been imposed.

12. **Answer b.** Because the share of total costs attributable to low-wage workers varies across firms, increases in the minimum wage affect some firms more than others, and this can lead to significant changes in the relative prices of the goods sold by these firms. These relative price changes can in turn cause changes in consumer buying patterns (intersectoral shifts in demand) and result in some firms actually seeing an increase in the demand for their product. The scale effect of this demand increase can lead to employment increases for some firms even though their costs are higher. Consequently, looking at the employment effects on individual firms may give a misleading impression of the overall employment effects of the minimum wage. For this reason, it is better to look at the employment effects on broader groupings of firms serving many different industries (e.g., the retail sector of the economy).

13. **Answer d.** In addition to the demand shifts, technological change makes for a more elastic labor demand because product demand will become more elastic as the number of substitution possibilities for consumers increase.

14. **Answer b.** A reduction in the price of capital stimulates the demand for labor only if there is a large-scale effect associated with the price decrease. A more elastic product demand contributes to a large-scale effect.

15. **Answer c.** While some industries and jobs are eliminated through technological change, the efficiency and competition it promotes tends to open up new consumption and employment possibilities. The increased productivity and technological change have helped to bring about higher real wages.

■ Problems

16a.   The slope is −2. For every one unit change in W, L changes by 2. This slope is the same for a wage change between $20 and $21 as it is for a change between $5 and $6. (Note that the slope as it appears on the graph is actually −0.5. Notice that when W is plotted on the vertical axis and L on the horizontal, the slope as it appears on the graph is actually $\Delta W/\Delta L$.)

16b. $\eta_{ii} = \dfrac{\Delta E_i}{\Delta W_i} \dfrac{W_i}{E_i}.$

For a change in the wage from \$5 to \$6,

$$\eta_{ii} = (-2)\frac{5}{40} = -0.25.$$

For a change in the wage from \$20 to \$21,

$$\eta_{ii} = (-2)\frac{20}{10} = -4.$$

16c.   While the slope remains constant as the wage increases, note that the absolute value of the elasticity gets larger. See Figure 4-5 for a plot of this curve.

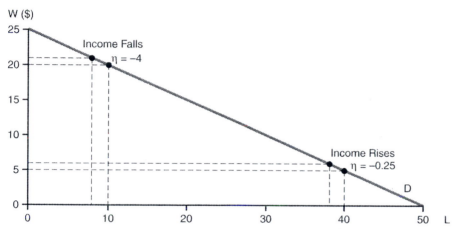

Figure 4-5

16d.   When the wage rises from \$5 to \$6, the firm's total expenditures on labor rise from \$200 to \$228, a change of +\$28. But when the wage rises from \$20 to \$21, total expenditures fall from \$200 to \$169, a change of −\$31.

16e.   When demand is inelastic, increases in the wage lead to increases in total expenditures. When demand is elastic, increases in the wage lead to decreases in total expenditures.

16f.   The slope is now −80, and the elasticity is

$$\eta_{ii} = (-80)\frac{5}{1600} = -0.25.$$

Changing the units in which labor is measured, in this case from number of workers to number of hours, changes the slope of the relationship but not the elasticity.

16g.   Elasticity is preferred to the slope as a measure of responsiveness because it is insensitive to changes in the units used to measure W and L. Defined as the ratio of two percentage changes, elasticity is a unit-free measure of responsiveness. Also, along a linear demand curve, slope is constant but elasticity is not. Thus elasticity shows the change in responsiveness at different prices (wages) whereas the slope does not.

*17a. As the wage changes from $5 to $10, the slope decreases in magnitude from −4 to −1. (Note that the slope as it appears on the graph changes from −0.25 to −1. Since W is plotted on the vertical axis and L on the horizontal, the slope as it appears on the graph is actually $\Delta W/\Delta L$.)

*17b. As the wage changes from $5 to $6, elasticity remains constant at −1. Any demand curve that can be written in the form

$$L = KW^{\eta},$$

where K is any constant, has a constant elasticity equal to η.

*17c. See Figure 4-4.

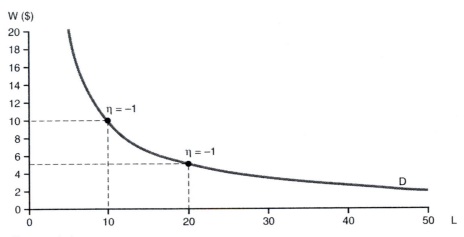

Figure 4-4

18a. Demand 1 is more elastic at any given price. For example, at $P = \$20$, demand 1 yields $\eta_{QP} = (-1)(20/16) = -1.25$, while demand 2 yields $\eta_{QP} = (-0.5)(20/16) = -0.625$.

18b. Use the $MR = MC$ rule to find the optimal output. With demand 1, optimal output is reduced from 10 to 6, while with the more inelastic demand 2, optimal output is reduced from 10 to only 8.

18c. The scale effect would be larger with the more elastic product demand (demand 1). Holding all else constant, the larger the scale effect, the more elastic the long-run labor demand.

19a. According to this study, as the wage of teenagers falls (because of the youth subminimum), the quantity of teenagers demanded increases and the quantity of adults demanded decreases. Since the quantity demanded of teenagers and adults moves in opposite directions, teenagers and adults are gross substitutes and the cross-wage elasticity would have a positive sign.

19b. For teenagers and adults to be gross substitutes, the substitution effect must dominate the scale effect.

19c. If teenagers and adults are gross substitutes, then the demand for adults would shift left as the teenage wage falls.

■ Applications

20.   The total income flowing to labor is the wage multiplied by the quantity of labor hired. When demand is elastic, small percentage increases in the wage cause large percentage reductions in the quantity of labor demanded. With the quantity of labor demanded falling faster than the wage is increasing, total income falls as the wage increases.

21a.   An airline pilot has a job that requires rather specialized knowledge, and so it is difficult to substitute other types of labor for the pilots. It is also rather difficult to substitute any kind of capital for the pilots, although running fewer flights with larger planes is one way to do this. Firms that try this latter approach, however, may require new planes. The supply of such planes is likely to be inelastic, since planes are complex items not quickly produced. In the airline industry, the labor costs associated with pilots are a small share of total costs, with fuel being one of the largest. Finally, before deregulation, the number of competitors was tightly controlled, making the product demand facing individual firms more inelastic.

Garments workers, on the other hand, are unskilled labor, and so it is relatively easy for firms to find other labor to substitute. Also the firm can probably hire as much or as little of this substitute labor as necessary at a constant price. It does not have to worry about the price of the substitutes being bid up significantly. Garment work like cutting and sewing fabric is labor intensive, and overseas competition tends to make for elastic product demand.

21b.   Airline deregulation has tended to increase competition, making product demand more elastic. As the product demand becomes more elastic, so does labor demand. Similarly, reducing tariffs and import quotas on textiles and apparel should increase product demand elasticity and make the demand for garment workers even more elastic.

22a.   Plan B should have the least impact on employment since it involves a change in the price of capital. As C increases (holding output constant), there is a tendency for the firm to substitute labor for capital. There will also be a scale effect pushing both labor and capital down, but this scale effect is also present in Plan A and Plan C. Plan A has a substitution effect that will reinforce the reduction in L coming through the scale effect, not counteract it as in B. Plan C has no substitution effect.

22b.   Plan A would lead to a large reduction in employment if there were a large substitution effect and a large-scale effect associated with the increased labor cost. There would be a large substitution effect if it were easy to substitute capital for labor and if the supply of capital were elastic. There would be a large-scale effect if labor costs were a large share of total costs and if the product demand were elastic.

Plan B would lead to a large reduction in employment if there were a small substitution effect and a large-scale effect associated with the capital price increase. There would be a small substitution effect if it were difficult to substitute labor for capital and if the supply of labor were inelastic. There would be a large-scale effect if capital costs were a large share of total costs and if the product demand were elastic.

Plan C is a direct increase in the marginal cost of production. It reduces labor only through a scale effect. This scale effect would be large if the product demand were elastic.

23a.   At $W = 4$, the original employment level would have occurred where

$$4 = 25 - 0.5L \Rightarrow L^* = 42.$$

When W increases to 6, employment occurs where $6 = 25 - (1/3)L \Rightarrow L^* = 57.$

23b.   Without the minimum wage, employment would have occurred where

$$4 = 25 - (1/3)L \Rightarrow L^* = 63.$$

Therefore, even though employment increased from 42 to 57, it would have increased to 63 had it not been for the minimum wage. (Similarly, one could argue that it would have fallen from 42 to 38 had it not been for the demand shift.)

24a.   A better indicator of a country's standard of living would be its per capita output and consumption levels.

24b.   At the same time that technology destroys jobs, it also opens up new opportunities. Instead of automatically becoming farmers, young people are now free to become doctors, teachers, engineers, computer programmers, and so on.

24c.   Making plant closings more difficult is like banning farm machinery in that both policies are attempts to stop the transfer of resources out of obsolete or inefficient uses into new and more efficient uses. Some of these new uses may not be currently envisioned.

Answers To Chapter 5

■ Review Questions

1. **Answer d.** This is the best response since it is the broadest true statement. Answers **a** and **c** are too broad since these categories include some costs that are not also quasi-fixed. Answer **b** gives an example of quasi-fixed costs, but there are others.

2. **Answer a.** The hourly wage is not a quasi-fixed cost because the total amount paid varies directly with hours worked (and thus with output). Defined benefit plans obligate the firm to make certain payments to retirees. All retirees with a certain number of years of service may receive the same amount, regardless of how many hours they actually worked for the firm, and thus this is likely to be a quasi-fixed cost. Both defined benefit and Social Security programs have elements that are quasi-fixed and elements that do vary with hours worked. Defined contribution plans are usually based on an employee's total earnings, and hence their cost will be partially a function of how many hours the retiree worked for the firm. Social Security contributions are a percentage of total earnings, provided the earnings are less than some maximum amount.

*3. **Answer d.** Given the benefits are prorated based on hours worked, these contributions do not qualify as quasi-fixed costs, but rather will vary both as the number of workers changes and as hours change.

4. **Answer c.** The total cost of training includes the explicit costs of training (3,000) plus the implicit opportunity cost of the trainees time (3,500 – 2,000 = 1,500), for a total cost of 4,500.

5. **Answer c.** ME_H = (wage + variable benefits per hour) × number of workers = $[10 + (50/40)]$ 500 = 5,625.

6. **Answer b.** ME_H = [(1 + overtime premium) wage + variable benefits per hour] × number of workers = $[(1.5)10 + (50/40)]500 = 8,125$.

7. **Answer c.** ME_M = weekly wages + weekly employee benefits and quasi-fixed costs = $[10(40) + 200] = 600$.

8. **Answer a.**

$$\frac{ME_M}{MP_M} = \frac{600}{50} = 12 < \frac{ME_H}{MP_H} = \frac{8,125}{625} = 13.$$

The firm should *increase M* and decrease *H* to bring about an equality. As *M* increases, MP_M will fall, increasing the left side of the equation. As *H* decreases, MP_H will rise, decreasing the right side of the equation.

9. **Answer d.**   Another possibility is that there will be a decrease in the straight-time wage to the level needed to keep total compensation unchanged.

*10. **Answer d.**   Such a law would increase both ME_M and ME_H. Without knowing the specific ME and MP figures, an increase in both ME values leads to an ambiguous change in the cost-minimization equation.

*11. **Answer a.**   Such a law would raise the ME of part-time workers, causing the firm to substitute full-time workers for part-time workers. Even though part-time workers may still be cheaper than full-time workers, a change in the relative cost of each type of input should bring about a change in the input mix.

12. **Answer a.**   This law would increase quasi-fixed costs, thus raising the ME_M but not the ME_H associated with part-time workers. The ratio of ME to MP for the M input would rise, forcing the firm to decrease M and increase H to restore the cost-minimization equality. There would be fewer part-time workers employed, but those that were still employed would be working longer hours.

13. **Answer a.**   While the effects of this law on the employment/hours mix would be different from the version where benefits are prorated, the laws would have very similar effects on the mix of part-time and full-time workers. Again, as in Question **11**, the law would increase the ME of part-time workers, causing the firm to substitute full-time workers for part-time workers.

14. **Answer a.**   The present value of the bonus is the 250,000 received in the current period plus the discounted value of the future payments.

$$250,000 + \frac{250,000}{1.06} + \frac{250,000}{(1.06)^2} + \frac{250,000}{(1.06)^3} = 918,253.$$

15. **Answer b.**   As the interest rate falls, dollars received in the future are not discounted as much, hence the gap between the post-training wage and the marginal product does not have to be as large for the firm to recover the full value of its training investment.

16. **Answer d.**   If workers paid entirely for the training in the initial period (as is the case with general training), the wage during training would have to be much lower, and then there would be no gap between the wage and marginal product in future periods to protect workers from temporary layoffs. The present value of the total compensation package is unaffected, however, by the way in which the training costs are recovered.

17. **Answer d.**   If the firm had to pay the entire cost of training during the initial period then they would have a bigger investment to recover in future periods, causing a bigger gap between the wage and the marginal product. If the gap grows so large that the wage slips below the worker's inherent marginal product, the worker will have an incentive to quit. In either case, however, the firm recovers in present value terms the entire training investment.

18. **Answer c.**   Whether the firm can attract workers to its training program and keep them will depend on how the present value of the entire compensation stream compares with what can be earned elsewhere. To recover its training costs, however, the firm must pay the workers less than their marginal product at the firm.

19. **Answer d.** When a firm invests a large sum in its workers, it should be expected to try to recover those investments or take steps to minimize the size of the investment. Thus large investments are consistent with a large gap between the wage and the marginal product, as well as statistical discrimination and internal labor market strategies.

20. **Answer d.** If the firm attributes shorter job tenures to women, it will probably try to pay them less so as to recover the hiring and training investments over the shorter period. If for some reason they must pay the same, the firm will either invest less in its women workers or simply not hire them in the first place.

21. **Answer b.** In a monopsonistic labor market, the firm faces an upward-sloping supply curve for labor because either it is the only firm in the market, or because mobility costs limit the willingness of workers to leave if other firms offer higher wages.

22. **Answer b.** Higher mobility costs mean that workers are less likely to leave. Thus a given percentage change in the wage will lead to a relatively smaller change in the quantity of labor supplied (than if mobility costs were lower), and the supply of labor will be relatively less elastic.

*23. **Answer d.** If a monopsonist faces a market supply of labor $W = a + bL$, then the ME_L will equal $a + 2bL$. The reason the ME_L lies above the wage is that when the firm faces an upward-sloping market supply curve, to attract additional workers it must pay a higher wage, but this higher wage applies to all workers previously hired at the lower wage (assuming it pays a single wage to all workers). This means that the cost of an additional worker to the firm is more than just the wage paid to that worker. The intercept is the same, however, because hiring just one worker does not require any wage changes.

24. **Answer d.** Setting a minimum wage above the monopsony wage creates a horizontal segment to the marginal expense of labor curve. If this segment lies below the point where the original ME_L intersects the MRP_L, the optimal employment level will rise. If it intersects the MRP_L above that point, employment will fall. It is also possible for the minimum wage to be set exactly at the level where the original ME_L intersects the MRP_L. In that case, there would be no change in employment.

■ Problems

25a. The typical worker is employed for 2,000 hours and earns $25,000. The firm must contribute 5% of this, or $1,250, to the fund. For each additional worker hired (with the same hours and wage), the firm's contribution will go up by $1,250. However, if existing workers were required to work one hour longer per week (50 per year), earnings would rise to $25,625 and hence the firm's contribution would also rise to $1,281.25. Since the cost varies with the number of workers and with the number of hours worked, it is not a quasi-fixed cost.

25b. Holding hours and the wage base constant, if the typical worker earned $25 per hour then the contribution would be a quasi-fixed cost. Each worker would earn $50,000 and the firm would contribute $2,500 for each employee. However, if the employees worked more hours and increased their earnings, the firm would not have to increase its contribution. On the other hand, given the typical workweek and wage at this firm, a wage base of only $25,000 would also transform this contribution into a quasi-fixed cost.

26a.   The cost of checking new hires for legal residency (and the fines levied if a violation is detected) would represent an increase in hiring costs, and hence an increase in quasi-fixed costs. This raises ME_M and will lead the firm to substitute a longer workweek for more workers.

26b.   An increase in quasi-fixed costs raises ME_M and hence the relative cost of employing additional workers. This induces a substitution of hours for workers. However, it will also raise the marginal cost of production, which in turn should lead the firm to choose a lower output level. This lower output level triggers a scale effect in which the firm will have an incentive to cut back on its use of both workers and hours. Therefore, whether the workweek actually increases depends on whether the substitution effect dominates the scale effect (whether hours and employment are gross substitutes).

27.   The inequality suggests that if the firm produced one less unit of output by using fewer workers, its total cost of production would go down by 2. If the firm then proceeded to produce that same unit of output using a longer workweek, its total cost of production would only rise by 1.5. In other words, the firm could produce the same total output at a lower cost by changing its mix of employment and hours. If the firm can produce the same output at a lower cost with a different input mix, it could not have been at the optimal mix of workers and hours.

28a.   The post-training wage will be set at 240.

$$(MP_0 - W_0) + (MP_1 - W_1) + \ldots + (MP_{15} - W_{15}) = Z.$$

Assuming for simplicity $W_1 = \ldots = W_{15} = W$, then

$$200 - 150 + 15(250 - W) = 200 \Rightarrow 15W = 3600 \Rightarrow W = 240.$$

Under this plan, workers pay for 50 of the 200 in training initially, and then the firm recovers 10 per month over the next 15 months. Workers will find this position attractive since the total payment stream over the entire length of employment is greater than what they could have earned elsewhere based on their inherent marginal product.

$$150 + 15(240) = 3750 > 16(225) = 3600.$$

28b.   The firm would have to recover its full 200 in training expenses over the 15 post-training periods. This implies a wage of 236.67. While this is still above the worker's inherent marginal product, the protection the firm has against quits has shrunk. The more the workers pay for their training in the initial period, the more protection the firm has against quits.

28c.   There would be no gap between the post-training wage and the marginal product. Workers want the firm to bear some of the initial cost so that there is a gap, and hence some protection from temporary layoffs.

28d.   This would reduce the post-training wage to 235 and increase the gap between the wage and the marginal product to 15.

28e.   The firm can recover its costs over 5 periods if

$$MP_0 - W_0 + MP_1 - W_1 + \ldots + MP_5 - W_5 \geq Z.$$

Given the constraint $W_0 = \ldots = W_5 = 225$, then

$$200 - 225 + 5(250 - 225) = 100 < Z = 200.$$

Therefore, the firm could not recover its training costs. The shortest time of recovery (n) can be determined by solving the equation

$$200 - 225 + n(250 - 225) = 200,$$

which implies $n = 9$ months (after training).

28f. The inherent MP sets a lower bound for the wage in the post-training periods. To find the highest this boundary could be, solve the equation

$$200 - 150 + 15(250 - MP^*) = 200,$$

which implies the maximum MP^* equals 240.

29a. The post-training wage will be set at 402.5.

$$MP_0 - W_0 + \frac{MP_1 - W_1}{1+r} = Z \Rightarrow 400 - 375 + \frac{535 - W_1}{1.06} = 150$$

$$\Rightarrow 535 - W_1 = 132.5 \Rightarrow W_1 = 402.5.$$

29b. Although the inherent MP is not given in the problem, the lowest it could be is 400, the marginal product during training. Using this value as a lower bound, the firm's training program is not attractive since the present value of the total compensation stream is less than what can be earned elsewhere.

$$375 + \frac{402.5}{1.06} = 754.72 < 400 + \frac{400}{1.06} = 777.36.$$

30a. The firm more than recovers its training investment on a present value basis.

$$1800 - 1600 + \frac{2500 - 2200}{1.06} + \frac{2800 - 2600}{(1.06)^2} = 661 > Z = 500.$$

30b. This training program is not likely to persist since other firms could offer the workers the same kinds of specific training opportunities at higher wages and still make a profit.

31a. Since this is general training, the firm will offer a wage of $W_0 = MP_0 - Z = 5.50 - 3 = 2.50$ during training. In the post-training periods the wage will equal the marginal product of 9.

31b. Although it would appear a post-training wage of 7.5 would enable the firm to recover its general training investment, such a wage could not be sustained since the typical worker's marginal product of 9 will be observed by all firms. Other firms would be willing to bid up to 9 for these workers.

31c. Since the training period wage could not fall to 2.50, the firm would have to cut back the amount of training it offers to only 1.50. If this is not possible, then either no training will be offered, or the workers will not be hired.

*32a.   The optimal employment level (L^*) occurs where $W/P = MP_L$ (P represents the price of the firm's output). Substituting the given information yields

$$40/2 = 50 - 2L^* \Rightarrow 2L^* = 30 \Rightarrow L^* = 15.$$

*32b.   Employing the $W/P = MP_L$ rule again yields

$$40/1 = 50 - 2L^* \Rightarrow 2L^* = 10 \Rightarrow L^* = 5.$$

Assuming no training investment, the firm cuts employment from 15 to 5 when the product price falls.

*32c.   At $L = 15$, $MP_L = 20$. If the firm sets W at only 20 and the product price is 2, then at that employment level the MP exceeds the real wage ($MP_L = 20 > 10 = W/P$). If the product price now falls to 1 (say, because the demand for the product falls), the gap will be eliminated, but W/P will now be exactly equal to the MP_L and there will be no need to change the employment level. The gap that existed between the wage and the marginal product insulated the workers from the reductions in employment that usually accompany reductions in P.

■ Applications

33a.   Robin would be offered a post-training wage of 15,122.

$$MP_0 - W_0 + \frac{MP_1 - W_1}{1+r} + \frac{MP_2 - W_2}{(1+r)^2} = Z,$$

$$\Rightarrow 11,000 - 10,500 + \frac{16,000 - W_1}{1.06} + \frac{17,000 - W_2}{(1.06)^2} = 3,000.$$

Assuming for simplicity $W_1 = W_2 = W$, then

$$\frac{(1.06)(16,000 - W) + (17,000 - W)}{(1.06)^2} = 2,500 \Rightarrow \frac{16,690 - 1.06W + 17,000 - W}{1.1236} = 2,500$$

$$\Rightarrow 33,960 - 2.06W = 2,809 \Rightarrow 2.06W = 31,151$$

$$\Rightarrow W = W_1 = W_2 = 15,122.$$

33b.   The program is attractive since the present value of the total compensation stream exceeds that associated with the alternative offers.

$$10,500 + \frac{15,122}{1.06} + \frac{15,122}{(1.06)^2} = 38,225$$

is greater than

$$11,500 + \frac{11,500}{1.06} + \frac{11,500}{(1.06)^2} = 32,584.$$

33c.   Ann would be offered a lower post-training wage of 13,350.

$$11,000 - 10500 + \frac{16,000 - W_1}{1.06} = 3,000 \Rightarrow 16,000 - W = 2,650 \Rightarrow W = 13,350.$$

33d.   The firm's training program should be attractive since the present value of the total compensation stream is more than what can be earned elsewhere.

$$10,500 + \frac{13,350}{1.06} = 23,094$$

is greater than

$$11,500 + \frac{11,500}{1.06} = 22,349.$$

33e.   Assuming the firm must pay Ann the higher wage, then they would not be able to recover the 3,000 training investment over her shorter job tenure. As a result, either Ann would not be hired or the firm would not invest as much in her training.

34a.   The subminimum wage should increase the likelihood that teens would receive on-the-job training of all types, but especially general training. In the training investment model discussed in this chapter, the minimum wage serves as a floor beneath which the wage cannot fall, but in so doing, it sometimes results in a gap between the wage and the marginal product that is too small for the firm to recover its training investment. (Recall Problem **25e.**) This situation is most likely to arise in the case of general training because general training must be recovered during the training period, and so often necessitates a large gap between the wage and the marginal product. This in turn may necessitate a wage so low that it is below the minimum wage.

34b.   Using the example given in the **Summary** section of this chapter, suppose instead the training is general and there is a minimum wage of 425. The firm would like to set a wage of 400 during period zero, but would be prohibited from doing so. The firm would be unable to recover its training investment, and as result, the worker would not be hired or less training would be offered. A subminimum wage of, say 390, would allow the firm to hire the worker and offer the full amount of training.

35a.   Using the cost-minimization framework, subsidizing training costs should lead to a reduction in the ME_M term, setting off adjustments that would increase the number of workers demanded. (It would also result in a different mix of workers, with a higher percentage of workers from disadvantaged groups being hired.) Holding output constant, as the number of workers demanded increases, the number of hours worked by existing employees will probably go down unless other inputs like capital are adjusted downward instead. This reduction in hours would be called a substitution effect, and it takes place because workers are now relatively cheaper than they were before. A complete analysis should also allow for the possibility of output changing. An increase in output is to be expected here since a decrease in ME_M will drive down the MC of production and lead to an increase in output. As output increases, typically both employment and hours rise. This increase in the demand for both inputs would be called a scale effect. If the scale effect dominates the substitution effect, hours could actually increase. In such a situation, hours and workers would be called gross complements in the production process.

35b.   Since the program is targeting employer expenditures on training, assume that the training being offered is firm-specific. (Recall that with general training the worker typically pays for the training in the initial period.) As mentioned in the answer to **31a**, the program should result in an increase in the number of workers from disadvantaged backgrounds being hired. For those disadvantaged workers who would have been hired and trained anyway, protection against temporary layoffs is reduced since there is now likely to be a smaller gap between the post-training wage and the workers' marginal product. The wage should exceed the workers' inherent marginal product by more than before, however, providing the firm more of a buffer against quits. For those workers who would not have been hired and trained except for the program, job stability is clearly increased since they now have a job where the post-training wage will be set such that $MP^* < W < MP$.

*36a. $MRP_L = MR * MP_L$.

$$K = 3 \Rightarrow Q = 3L \Rightarrow MP_L = 3.$$
$$MR = 64 - 2Q = 64 - 2(3L) = 64 - 6L.$$
$$MRP_L = (64 - 6L)\,3 = 192 - 18L.$$

*36b.   In this problem, the marginal product of labor is constant; it does not diminish as L increases. This assumption is made to make the algebra of the problem simpler.

*36c.   If $W = a + bL$, then $ME_L = a + 2bL$

$$\Rightarrow ME_L = 6L.$$

36d.   Profit maximization occurs where $MRP_L = ME_L$.

$$192 - 18L = 6L \Rightarrow L^* = 8.$$

36e. $W^* = 3(8) = \$24$, $Q^* = 3(8) = 24$, $P^* = 64 - 24 = \$40$, Profit $= PQ - WL - CK = 40(24) - 24(8) - 5(3) = \$753$.

36f. $W_{min} = 30 \Rightarrow ME_L = 30$ (provided $L < 10$) $\Rightarrow$ profit maximization occurs where

$$192 - 18L = 30 \Rightarrow L^* = 9.$$

In this case, the minimum wage leads to an increase in employment opportunities.

$W_{min} = 66 \Rightarrow ME_L = 66$ (provided $L < 22$) $\Rightarrow$ profit maximization occurs where

$$192 - 18L = 66 \Rightarrow L^* = 7.$$

In this case, raising the minimum wage too high leads to a decrease in employment opportunities.

Answers To Chapter 6

■ Review Questions

1. **Answer d.** Individuals can also affect their hours through working more than one job, vacations, and leaves of absence.

2. **Answer d.** Typically when one observes indifference curves crossing on a graph, for example in Figure 6-4, they represent the preferences of different individuals. If they pertain to the same person, than the point of intersection simultaneously yields two different levels of happiness, which violates the basic notion that the person can consistently rank different combinations of leisure and income. Steep indifference curves indicate a high value for leisure, since the person requires a large amount of income to offset a small sacrifice of leisure.

3. **Answer a.** The wage rate is reflected in the slope of the constraint. Note that nonlabor income is $200 and the optimal number of hours to supply is 100.

4. **Answer d.** When indifference curves are drawn with a convex shape, it ensures that when one moves from an extreme combination (one where there is a lot of one good but not much of the other) to one where the goods are more evenly consumed, a higher indifference curve will be attained. In other words, the convex shape of the indifference curves is a way to make the statement that people prefer variety to extremes.

5. **Answer c.** The objective of the consumer is not to maximize income or leisure but to find that combination of income and leisure that is consistent with the budget constraint and leads to the highest level of utility. Since higher indifference curves represents higher levels of utility, maximizing utility can be thought of as trying to get on the highest attainable indifference curve. Note that it is impossible for both leisure and income to be maximized at the same point.

6. **Answer d.** When this condition holds, a window of opportunity exists for the individual to attain a higher level of utility by moving to a point involving less than the maximum leisure time. Very steep indifference curves can result in a corner solution.

7. **Answer c.** When work is viewed as something good, leisure implicitly becomes something bad. Leisure is bad here when it exceeds 350 hours: when one gets more of it, income must go up, not down, to keep the person at the same level of satisfaction. This creates the upward slope to the indifference curves.

8. **Answer c.** Usually when the budget constraint has a flat segment, representing a guaranteed income, the optimum occurs at the point of maximum leisure. But because after a point, leisure is viewed as bad, the optimum occurs at 50 hours of work. The market wage is $4, with an implicit tax of 100% on the first $400 of earnings, zero thereafter.

9. **Answer b.** For a person working zero hours, an increase in the wage cannot lead them to reduce hours even further. So, although there is theoretically an income effect—if the person makes any changes, her income will rise—in practical terms it **must** be dominated by the substitution effect.

10. **Answer a.** If leisure were an inferior good, then the income effect associated with the wage increase would actually cause the person to cut back on leisure. This, together with a positive substitution effect, would ensure work hours would go up.

11. **Answer d.** Typically, goods do not switch from being normal to inferior, but even if they did, the curve described in answer **c** could never turn back, since leisure being inferior guarantees that portion of the curve would be upward sloping.

12. **Answer a.** Hours supplied should go up because such a change creates a pure substitution effect. The lower marginal tax rate is like an increase in the wage, but the assumption that the total taxes paid by workers remains constant means that income remained constant.

13. **Answer a.** A lump sum payment unrelated to earnings is an increase in nonlabor income that shifts the budget constraint out parallel to the old constraint, thus creating a pure income effect.

14. **Answer b.** Scheduled benefits unrelated to earnings create a parallel shift of the constraint. Hence, the opportunity cost of leisure remains the market wage rate, and so an incentive to work is preserved.

15. **Answer d.** The maximum subsidy (S) is $600, and the breakeven income (S/t) is $1,200. Therefore, the value of t must be 0.5. With an implicit tax rate of 0.5, the initial subsidy will be completely "taken away" by the time earnings reach $1,200.

16. **Answer d.** The new optimum occurs at $L = 350$ ($H = 50$). The actual subsidy equals $S - t(WH) =$ $600 - .5(\$200) = \$500$.

17. **Answer b.** The substitution effect is the movement from the point ($L = 247$, $Y = \$990$) to the point ($L = 350$, $Y = \$700$).

18. **Answer b.** The income effect is the movement from the point ($L = 200$, $Y = \$800$) to the point ($L = 247$, $Y = \$990$).

19. **Answer b.** As the implicit tax rate increases, the effective wage rate decreases, lowering the opportunity cost of leisure, and reducing work incentives for most individuals. An exception to this tendency is exhibited in Problem **30**.

20. **Answer d.** While reducing the implicit tax rate tends to preserve work incentives, it extends the reach of the program (potentially to everyone if $t = 0$). As more people are eligible for the program, the cost of the program tends to go up.

21. **Answer c.** The lowest income recipients actually face an above-market wage, creating a substitution effect in favor of working, working against the income effect allowing more leisure. Without knowing about preferences, one cannot predict the net response. For higher income eligibles, either a zero implicit tax, or a positive implicit tax on earnings exists, so there is nothing to counteract the income effect, and a substitution effect may even reinforce it, reducing work effort.

22. **Answer d.** Many who work for minimum wages do not live in low-income households, and although their impact on work incentives may be positive (they are theoretically ambiguous), they may result in reduced hours because of employer cutbacks. As noted in the text, subsidies given to employers to hire low-income workers have not been very successful, and in some cases appear to have worsened the target population's chances of finding employment by identifying them as potential problem employees.

■ Problems

23a. See the solid line in Figure 6-9.

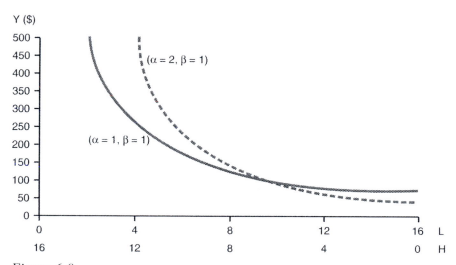

Figure 6-9

23b. See the dashed line in Figure 6-9.

23c. Increased appreciation for leisure relative to income tends to make the indifference curves steeper. It takes larger amounts of income to compensate for a given sacrifice of leisure.

24a. See the solid line in Figure 6-10.

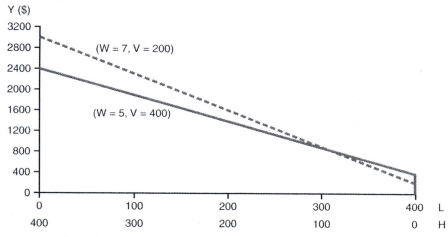

Figure 6-10

24b. See the dashed line in Figure 6-10.

25a. Full income ($WT + V$) for the original budget line is $2,700. Noticing that $V = \$300$ and $T = 400$, the original wage was $6. Similarly, after the wage decrease the new level of full income is $1,500, which implies a wage of $3, given the same values of V and T.

25b. The income effect is the movement from the point ($L = 225$, $Y = \$1350$) to the point ($L = 177$, $\$Y = 1061$), a decrease of 48 leisure hours. The substitution effect is the movement from the point ($L = 177$, $Y = \$1061$) to the point ($L = 250$, $Y = \$750$), an increase of 73 leisure hours.

25c. The two points would be ($W = \$6$, $H = 175$), and ($W = \$3$, $H = 150$). The curve is positively sloped. The substitution effect is stronger than the income effect in **25b**.

26a. Given that preferences are represented by the Cobb-Douglas utility function, the expression for the optimal level of leisure is

$$L^{*} = \frac{\alpha}{\alpha + \beta} \frac{WT + V}{W}.$$

Substituting the values that apply before the injury yields $L = 8$ ($H = 8$), $Y = \$40$, and $U = 320$.

26b. If all the income is replaced after an injury, then $L = 16$, $Y = \$40$, and $U = 640$, a higher level of utility than that attained while working.

26c. To keep the worker at $U = 320$, solve the equation $(16)(Y) = 320$. This implies $Y = \$20$. Therefore, to keep utility constant, only 50% of the original income needs to be replaced. This whole analysis, of course, assumes that all leisure time is identical. That is, leisure time obtained through injury yields the same utility as leisure time taken while healthy. This may not be the case, for example, if the injury is painful or limiting.

27a. Given that preferences are represented by the Cobb-Douglas utility function, the expression for the optimal level of leisure is

$$L^{*} = \frac{\alpha}{\alpha + \beta} \frac{WT + V}{W}.$$

(Note that both α and $\beta = 1$ in this example.) Substituting the values that apply before the welfare program, the original optimum is 200 leisure hours (200 work hours).

With $t = 1$, the effective wage, given by the expression $(1 - t)W$, becomes zero and while we cannot divide by zero, the optimum occurs at the maximum of 400 leisure hours (zero work hours).

With $t = 0.5$, the effective wage rate is $2. Combining this with $500 in nonlabor income yields an optimum of 325 leisure hours (75 work hours).

With $t = 0$, the effective wage remains the market wage of $4. Combining this with the nonlabor income of $500 yields an optimum of 262.5 leisure hours (137.5 work hours).

Summarizing, $t = 1$ implies H falls by 200, $t = 0.5$ implies H falls by 125, and $t = 0$ implies H falls by 62.5.

27b. An implicit tax rate of zero preserves work incentives the best since the opportunity cost of leisure remains the market wage. Hours of work still fall under such a program because of the income effect of the subsidy, but there is no reinforcing substitution effect if implicit taxes do not reduce the effective wage rate.

28a. The breakeven income occurs at the value S/t. So for constraint acdb we have $350/t = 350$, which implies $t = 1$. For the constraint aceb we have $350/t = 1400$, which implies $t = 0.25$. Note that when we can view the breakeven point graphically, the tax rate can be calculated as $S/B = t$, or in the two cases here, $350/350 = 1$ and $350/1400 = 0.25$.

28b. For these preferences, $t = 1$ provides the strongest work incentives. The reason for this somewhat unusual result is that when t is reduced, the reach of the program (as illustrated by the breakeven point) is expanded dramatically. In this case, the person would not even have been affected by the program with the high implicit tax rate. The lower rate, however, enables the person to be eligible for the program and experience the income and substitution effects it creates.

29a. See Figure 6-11. The breakeven point occurs at $L = 1,600$ ($H = 1,200$) and $Y = \$6,000$.

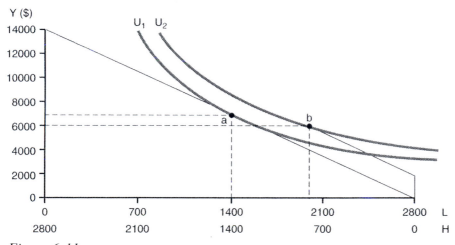

Figure 6-11

29b. Given that preferences are represented by the Cobb-Douglas utility function, the expression for the optimal level of leisure is

$$L^* = \frac{\alpha}{\alpha + \beta} \frac{WT + V}{W}.$$

Substituting the values that apply before the program is enacted yields an optimum of $L = 1,400$ ($H = 1,400$) and $Y = \$7,000$. This is point a in Figure 6-11. The level of utility (denoted by U_1) is 9,800,000.

29c. Using the graph as a guide, it appears likely that the individual will be pulled into the program, even though they are currently above the breakeven point. The optimal point appears to be the corner of the constraint which occurs at $L = 2,000$, $Y = \$6,000$. Notice that the level of utility at this point is 12,000,000. This represents an improvement over the original point. The optimum is identical to that which would have been achieved if benefits were simply cut off once earnings reached $4,000. No one who values both leisure and income would want to locate along the horizontal segment of the constraint when moving to the corner of the constraint is possible.

■ Applications

30a. See Figure 6-12. The breakeven point occurs at $L = 175$ ($H = 225$), $Y = \$900$. The value of $S/t = 200/0.4 = \$500$ in this case represents the additional income needed to reduce the subsidy to zero once the person qualifies for the program. Note that in this case, however, the person does not qualify for the program immediately, but rather works 100 hours, and hence earns $400, before the usual type of income maintenance program begins.

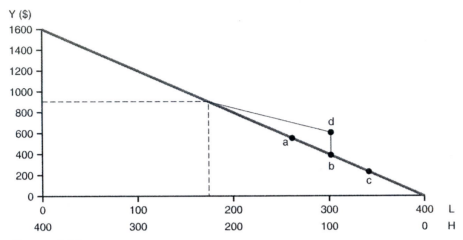

Figure 6-12

30b. Given that preferences are represented by the Cobb-Douglas utility function, the expression for the optimal level of leisure is

$$L^* = \frac{\alpha}{\alpha + \beta} \frac{WT + V}{W}.$$

For $\alpha = 0.65$, $\beta = 0.35$, the optimal combination before the program was $L = 260$ ($H = 140$), $Y = \$560$. This is point a in Figure 6-12. After the program, the person should end up at the corner of the new constraint (point d). Since the corner point has coordinates $L = 300$ ($H = 100$), $Y = \$600$, this represents a reduction in work hours of 40.

For $\alpha = 0.75$, $\beta = 0.25$, the optimal combination before the program was $L = 300$ ($H = 100$), $Y = \$400$. This is point b in Figure 6-12. After the program, the person should also end up at the corner of the new constraint (point d). There will be no reduction in work hours.

For $\alpha = 0.85$, $\beta = 0.15$, the optimal combination before the program was $L = 340$ ($H = 60$), $Y = \$240$. This is point c in Figure 6-12. After the program, the person should also end up at the corner of the new constraint (point d). This represents an increase in work hours of 40.

30c. While some people will reduce their work hours due to the income and substitution effects such programs can create, the possibility of such individuals dropping out of the labor force is very remote. Also, some individuals will actually increase their hours just enough to cross over the threshold and qualify for the program's maximum benefit. Such thresholds seem like a sensible way to preserve at least some minimal work incentives.

31a. See Figure 6-13. The original earnings constraint is line *ab*. Under this EITC, the maximum
subsidy first occurs where earnings equal $9,000. This occurs where $L = 1,500$ ($H = 1,500$). This
is point *c* in Figure 6-13. The level of total income (including the government payment) will be
$Y = $11,700$ (point *d*). The maximum subsidy continues to be received until earnings = $12,000
(point *e*). This occurs where $L = 1,000$ ($H = 2,000$). Factoring in the subsidy, total income is
$14,700 at $L = 1,000$ (point *f*). The breakeven point occurs when earnings equal $18,000 (point *b*).
Once the person has reached point *e*, an additional $6,000 in earnings at an implicit tax rate of 0.45
just eliminates the $2,700 subsidy ($6,000 × 0.45 = $2,700). To achieve the additional $6,000 in
earnings, the person must increase work hours (reduce leisure) by 1,000 hours.

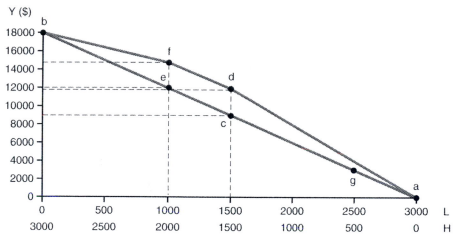

Figure 6-13

31b. To the right of point *d*, the individual is accumulating income according to the formula

$$\text{income} = WH + .3(WH),$$

which makes the effective wage rate (the absolute value of the slope of the constraint) $(1.3)(W)$
which equals 7.8. To the left of point *f*, the effective wage rate is $(1 − t)W$, where $t = 0.45$. This
means that the absolute value of the slope is 3.3.

31c. A person originally at point *g* will experience both an income effect and a substitution effect. The
substitution effect will push the person in the direction of more work, while the income effect will
tend to counteract this. At low levels of work hours, however, the income effect tends to be
relatively small, and so it is likely that the substitution effect will dominate the income effect and
the person will work more.

31d. A person originally to the left of point *c* will tend to reduce work hours. The extent of the reduction
depends on whether the person originally worked more or less than 2,000 hours. If the person
worked more than 1,500 hours but less than 2,000 hours, he will experience just a pure income
effect. If the person worked in excess of 2,000 hours, he will experience reinforcing income and
substitution effects. Note for $H > 2,000$, the position of the constraint moves out at the same time
that it becomes flatter. This creates a strong incentive to work less, and many workers are likely to
end up near point *f*.

*32a. See Figure 6-14.

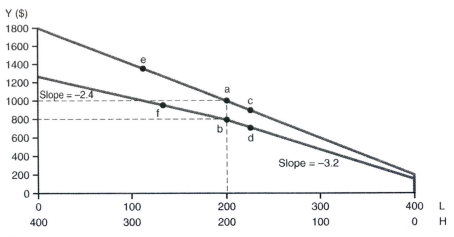

Figure 6-14

*32b. The 40% marginal tax rate applies after $1,000 in total income is reached. With nonlabor income of $200, that income level is reached when $L = 200$ ($H = 200$). This is point a in Figure 6-14. The tax reduces total income by 20 percent to a total of $800 (point b). The effective wage rate (the slope of the constraint) is now $(1 - t)W$, where t is the marginal tax rate. To the right of point b, the slope is $(1 - .2)4 = 3.2$. To the left of point b, the slope is $(1 - .4)4 = 2.4$.

*32c. Given that preferences are represented by the Cobb-Douglas utility function, the expression for the optimal level of leisure is

$$L^* = \frac{\alpha}{\alpha + \beta} \frac{WT + V}{W}.$$

Substituting the appropriate values leads to an optimum of $L = 225$ ($H = 175$), $Y = \$900$ (point c) before the tax. After the tax, the level of nonlabor income falls to $160 and the effective wage rate is 3.2. Substituting into the L^* expression again yields $L = 225$ ($H = 175$), but Y is now lower at $720. There is no change in labor supply since the income and substitution effects of the tax change have exactly canceled one another. This combination is point d. The person has paid $180 in taxes, making for an average tax rate of $180/$900 = 20%$.

*32d. What is the value of Y on the after-tax constraint when $H = 400$? $H = 400$ implies $Y = \$1800$. When total income is $1800, the person pays $200 on the first $1,000 he earned, plus $320 on the next $800, for a total after-tax income of $1,280. If $WT + V = \$1,280$, and W is $2.4 and T is 400, the implicit value of V is $320.

*32e. Making the appropriate substitutions into the L^* expression yields $L = 112.5$ ($H = 287.5$), $Y = \$1,350$ before the tax program (point e). After the tax program, substitute $W = \$2.4$ and $V = \$320$ into the L^* expression to find $L = 133.33$, ($H = 266.67$), $Y = \$960$ (point f). Hours of work are reduced modestly because of the stronger substitution effect of the higher marginal tax rate. The total tax paid is 20% of $1,000 plus 40% of $350, for a total of $340. Note that this is not the difference between $1,350 and $960, since the $960 reflects the lower level of work hours that the tax induced. The average tax rate is $340/$1,350 = 25.19%$.

*32f. Significantly higher marginal tax rates can result in appreciable reductions in the work hours of higher-income individuals.

33a. Given that preferences are represented by the Cobb-Douglas utility function, the expression for the optimal level of leisure is

$$L^* = \frac{\alpha}{\alpha + \beta} \frac{WT + V}{W}.$$

With both fixed monetary and time costs of working it is as if V is only $100 and T is 370 hours. This leads to an optimum at $L = 197.5$ ($H = 172.5$) and $Y = 790. This yields a utility level of 156,025. This does exceed the utility associated with not participating in the labor force since the combination $L = 400$, $Y = 200 yields a utility level of 80,000.

33b. Telecommuting would return V to $200 and T to 400, leading to an optimum at $L = 225$ ($H = 175$) and $Y = 900. Utility would now be 202,500. In this example, telecommuting leads to higher levels of leisure, work, income, and utility.

Answers To Chapter 7

■ Review Questions

1. **Answer d.** In the household production model, income is assumed to be spent on market-purchased goods and services. Time spent in home production yields commodities that the individual or family consumes, and leisure is also a consumption good. Thus three types of goods enter the utility function: market goods, household goods, and leisure.

2. **Answer a.** Each indifference curve represents a tradeoff between income (market goods) and household production time (time spent producing household goods or consuming leisure).

3. **Answer a.** The magnitude of the slope is given by the wage rate, and the height of the constraint at the maximum amount of time available equals the level of nonlabor income.

4. **Answer c.** The income effect of the wage increase creates an incentive to spend more time in household production (and leisure consumption), while the substitution effect creates an incentive to spend less time in household production activities.

5. **Answer d.** An increase in the wage increases the opportunity cost of both household production and leisure time, creating an incentive to reduce both. On the other hand, for any given amount of work (except zero hours) an increase in the wage leads to an increase in income. This allows an individual to buy more of all goods, including leisure and any commodities produced at home. The greater the demand for household-produced commodities, the greater the incentive to spend time in home production.

6. **Answer c.** If **a** were true, household production time would have decreased. If **b** were true, leisure time would have decreased.

7. **Answer d.** In addition, for women's total market work hours to have increased, the net effect on market work hours resulting from **a** must have been strong enough to overcome the net effect on work hours resulting from **b**.

8. **Answer a.** When time and goods are easily substitutable, the substitution effect of a wage change tends to be large. When time and goods are used complementarily or in fixed proportions, the substitution effect of a wage change tends to be small.

9. **Answer c.** A household's total production will be maximized when the spouse with the lowest **net gain** from market work stays home. For example, suppose spouse A can earn $12 per hour in the market and produce the equivalent of $6 per hour at home, while spouse B can earn $15 per hour in the market and produce the equivalent of $10 per hour at home. Even though spouse B can earn more in the market, the net gain to the household of having B work is only $5, while the net gain to having A work is $6. For every hour A works and B stays at home, the household produces the equivalent of $22, while having B work and A stay at home would result in only $21.

10. **Answer d.** This condition ensures that the household will attain at least the same level of utility as before the extra hour of work.

11. **Answer c.** If the wife's increase in work hours increases the husband's marginal productivity at home, the net gain to the husband from working will decrease and the incentive to substitute household production for market work will increase.

12. **Answer d.** If the husband's marginal productivity at home does not decrease because of the health problem, the drop in the wage will make him relatively more productive at home, increasing his incentive to work at home. If the husband's time at home is a substitute for the wife's, this would decrease her marginal productivity at home and increase the net gain associated with her market work.

13. **Answer d.** The expected wage $E(W)$ is given by the equation $E(W) = \pi W$ where π is the probability of finding a job and W is the wage of the job. During a recession p falls, reducing the expected wage of the unemployed person. The change in the expected wage lowers the expected gain from job search. This lowers the opportunity cost of time at home and creates a substitution effect that can cause the person to stop allocating any time to job search activities.

14. **Answer d.** The reduction in the effective wage and the increase in family income creates reinforcing income and substitution effects that will cause more total time to be allocated to household production. However, it is at least possible that with more total time devoted to household production, the husband's household marginal productivity may increase so much that the wife's net gain from market work may exceed his. This would create a situation where she would be the one to work for pay, provided the family continues to have an incentive to supply hours to the market.

15. **Answer b.** Although the other factors would also tend to increase the labor force participation rates of married women, those factors have been changing rather steadily, and hence could not explain the large increase observed after age thirty.

16. **Answer c.** If the path of wages is anticipated, workers can form an estimate of lifetime wealth. Then, as anticipated wage changes occur, there will be no change in the estimate of lifetime wealth and no income effect will be experienced. Higher wages do, however, change the opportunity cost of leisure, resulting in a substitution effect in favor of more hours of work.

17. **Answer d.** If lifetime benefits remained constant as the retirement age increased, remaining lifetime earnings would rise at a constant rate as the retirement age increased. In terms of Figure 7-1 from the **Summary** section, the budget constraint connecting points *a* through *f* would now be a straight line rather than a concave curve. Although point *a* would remain the same, the rest of the curve would rotate outward slightly and straighten as the vertical intercept rose from $195,000 to $220,000. This would create opposing income and substitution effects. The retirement age would decrease only if the increase in the demand for leisure resulting from the change in the position of the constraint (the income effect) dominated the increased incentive to work coming from the higher effective wage rate (the substitution effect).

Problems

18a. Notice that the isoquant for family 2 is drawn with less convexity than the one for family 1. This means that for family 2, household goods and market goods are traded off at roughly a constant rate. This means that family 2 sees household goods and purchased goods as easily substitutable. On the other hand, the isoquant for family 1 is relatively convex. This means that family 1 sees household goods and purchased goods as not as easily substitutable.

18b. See Figure 7-5. The substitution effect can be observed by allowing the budget constraint to rotate outward in response to the higher wage, and then pulling it back so the family just attains its old level of utility. The movement along the original indifference curve will reflect the family's response to just the change in the opportunity cost of time, and therefore can be interpreted as the substitution effect of the wage change.

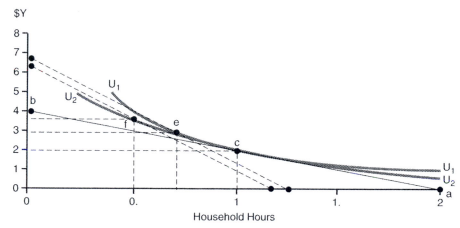

Figure 7-5

In Figure 7-5, the substitution effect for family 1 is the movement from point *c* to point *e*, while the substitution effect for family 2 is the movement from point *c* to point *d*. Since family 2 sees time and goods as more substitutable, it is not surprising that the change in the opportunity cost of household time resulted in a larger decrease in household hours.

19a. $H = 4 \Rightarrow N = 12$ and $Y = (\$10)(4) = \$40$. $N = 12$ and $Y = 40 \Rightarrow U = 480$.

19b. Y rises to $80 for an increase of $40.

19c. With H increasing to 8 hours, N falls to 8 hours. To keep U at 480, Y would have to rise to $60. This represents an increase in income of $20.

19d. Since income would only have to rise by $20 to compensate for the decrease in household hours, the increase of $40 that actually takes place will make the family better off.

19e. Under the new ranking formula, the original combination of $N = 12$ and $Y = \$40$ yields a utility level of $(12^2)(40)$ or 5760. When H rises to 8 and N falls to 8, Y must rise to $90 to keep U at 5760. This represents an increase of $50. Since the increased work hours bring in only $40, this move would make the family worse off. Given the presence of the child, the extra hour of work makes the family worse off.

19f. If H equals 8, then N equals 8 and Y equals $80. This means that the original level of utility is now 640. If H increases to 9, N decreases to 7 and Y increases to $90. Under this utility function, this combination receives a lower ranking of 630.

19g. Under the new ranking formula, the original combination of $N = 8$ and $Y = \$80$ yields a utility level of $(8)(80^2)$ or 51,200. When H rises to 9 and N falls to 7, Y rises to $90, and the new ranking rises to 56,208. Given the new technology, the extra hour of work makes the family better off.

20a. A household's total production will be maximized when the spouse with the highest net gain from market work is the one who works for pay. Even though the wife is more productive at home than the husband, the net gain to the household of having the wife work is $5, while the net gain to having the husband work is $3. For every hour the wife works and the husband stays at home, the household produces the equivalent of $32, while having the husband work and the wife stay at home would result in only $27.

20b. Yes, since an extra hour of market work allows each to buy at least enough goods and services to compensate for the hour of lost production time at home.

20c. An increase in the wife's wage would decrease her work hours if the income effect of the wage increase dominated the substitution effect. On the other hand, work hours would increase if the substitution effect of the wage increase dominated the income effect. Empirical studies suggest that the latter is the more common occurrence for women. The income effect associated with the wife's wage increase reduces the husband's incentive to work for pay provided there are no cross effects on the husband's household marginal productivity or the marginal utility that the husband derives from household consumption.

20d. If the husband and wife are substitutes in household production, an increase in the wife's work hours will increase her household marginal productivity, creating an incentive for the husband to spend more time in household production and less time in market work.

20e. If the husband and wife are complements in the consumption of household commodities, an increase in the wife's work hours will decrease the utility the husband derives from the additional consumption of household commodities and create an incentive to spend more time in market work.

21a. $H = 7 \Rightarrow N = 9$ and $Y = (\$5)(7) + \$10 = \$45$. $N = 9$ and $Y = \$45 \Rightarrow U = 405$.

21b. $H = 0 \Rightarrow N = 16$ and $Y = \$10$. $N = 16$ and $Y = \$10 \Rightarrow U = 160$.

*21c. The return to taking an hour away from household production activities to look for work is the expected wage $E(W) = \pi W$ where π is the probability of finding a job.

*21d. One hour of job search yields an expected payoff of $(0.5)(\$5) = \$2.50$, which raises the expected income to $Y = \$2.50 + \$10 = \$12.50$. The level of utility associated with $N = 15$, and an expected value of $Y = \$15$ is $(15)(15) = 225$. When compared to the utility associated with not looking for a job $(U = 160)$, one hour of job search is a good move. When a person is unemployed but looking for a job, he is a member of the labor force.

*21e. One hour of job search now yields an expected payoff of $(0.1)(\$5) = \$0.5$, which raises the expected income to $Y = \$0.50 + \$10 = \$10.50$. The level of utility associated with $N = 15$, and an expected value of $Y = \$10.50$ is $(15)(10.50) = 157.5$. When compared to the utility associated with not looking for a job $(U = 160)$, one hour of job search is not a good move. When a person drops out of the labor force because of the reduced probability of finding a job, she is categorized as a discouraged worker.

*21f. One hour of job search yields an expected payoff of $(1/3)(\$2) = \$0.667$, which raises the expected family income to $Y = \$0.667 + \$10 = \$10.667$. The level of utility associated with $N = 15$, and an expected value of $Y = \$10.667$ is $(15)(10.667) = 160$. Since the utility associated with not looking for a job $(U = 160)$ is the same, the person will be completely indifferent about looking for a job.

■ Applications

22a. See Figure 7-6. The substitution effect can be observed by allowing the budget constraint to rotate outward in response to the higher wage (line ad), and then pulling it back (line ef) so the individual just attains his or her old level of utility. The resulting movement along the original indifference curve will reflect the individual's response to just the change in the opportunity cost of time, and therefore can be interpreted as the substitution effect of the wage change. In Figure 7-6, there is no response to the change in slope since the optimum remains at point c. The substitution effect is zero.

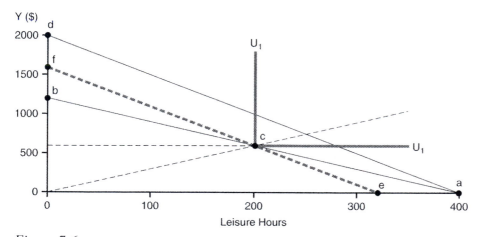

Figure 7-6

22b. See Figure 7-7.

The substitution effect can be observed by allowing the budget constraint to rotate outward in response to the higher wage (line *ac*), and then pulling it back (line *de*) so the individual just attains his or her old level of utility. The resulting movement along the original indifference curve will reflect the individual's response to just the change in the opportunity cost of time, and therefore can be interpreted as the substitution effect of the wage change. In Figure 7-7, the individual moves from point *a* to point *e* in response to the change in slope. The substitution effect is a reduction in household work of the full 400 hours available.

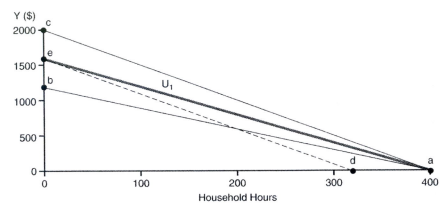

Figure 7-7

22c. Figure 7-3 is a better model of the choice between market work and leisure because the tradeoff between income (purchased goods) and leisure that underlies the choice is inherently one where the substitution possibilities are limited. Purchased goods and leisure are usually utilized in a complementary manner.

22d. Figure 7-4 is a better model of the choice between market work and household production time because the tradeoff between purchased goods and household production time that underlies the choice is one where goods and services can be readily substituted for household time.

22e. If purchased goods and household production time are highly substitutable, Figure 7-7 shows that wage increases can be associated with very large substitution effects that lead to household production time being reduced dramatically in favor of market work. Since women have traditionally been responsible for most household production activities, it seems likely that as their wages have increased over time, they may have experienced these rather large substitution effects that could easily dominate any income effect associated with the wage increase. For men, who have traditionally been primarily consumers of household production, the wage increases would create primarily an income effect that would lead them to consume, and perhaps help supply, more household production.

At the same time, Figure 7-6 shows that wage increases may be associated with very small substitution effects from the point of view of the labor/leisure choice. For this choice, the income effect will almost surely dominate the substitution effect leading to more leisure and less market work. This should probably be true for both men and women. However, since the increase in market work that comes from the substitution away from household production will be so large for women, it could easily overcome the tendency toward less market work that comes out of the choice between market work and leisure. Given this strong tendency to reduce household work, it seems very clear that women could increase their leisure time and at the same time still increase their market work substantially. For men, however, the income effect appears likely to dominate the substitution effect in the context of both choices, thereby leading to more leisure and household production, and less market work.

23a. The curve is concave because lifetime Social Security benefits do not remain constant as the retirement age increases. Yearly benefits increase with retirement age, but not enough to overcome the reduced number of years over which the benefits will be received, so that older retirees are penalized with lower lifetime benefit levels.

For the points a through f in Figure 7-1 to lie along a straight line, yearly Social Security benefits would have to be set at the levels listed in Table 7-3.

Table 7-3

Retirement age	Yearly social security	Lifetime social security	Lifetime earnings	Total lifetime income
65	8	120	0	120
66	8.57	120	20	140
67	9.23	120	40	160
68	10	120	60	180
69	10.91	120	80	200
70	12	120	100	220

Plotting the retirement age against the total remaining lifetime income figures in the last column of the table would then yield a straight line. Point a would retain its current position and the vertical intercept (point f) would increase to $220,000.

23b. The rotation of the constraint described in the answer to **23a** would create opposing income and substitution effects. The retirement age would decrease only if the increase in the demand for leisure resulting from the change in the position of the constraint (the income effect) dominated the increased incentive to work coming from the higher effective wage rate (the substitution effect). Using the same ranking formula as in the Example, Table 7-4 was constructed.

Table 7-4

Retirement age	Leisure years (L)	Lifetime income (Y)	Utility ranking (U = LY)
65	15	120	1,800
66	14	140	1,960
67	13	160	2,080
68	12	180	2,160
69	11	200	2,200
70	10	220	2,200

Table 7-4 shows that the optimal retirement age increases to 69 (or 70), indicating that the substitution effect of the change dominated the income effect. (If it were possible to retire at half-year increments, the optimal retirement age would be 69.5 since 11.5 remaining years and a remaining income of $210,000 would yield a ranking of 2,415.)

24a. See the line *adefb* in Figure 7-8. The person receives no benefits when he or she works 1,610 hours (1,390 hours allocated to household production) and earns a total of $32,200 (point *f*).

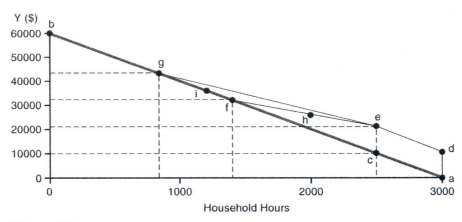

Figure 7-8

24b. See the line *adegb* in Figure 7-8. The person receives no benefits when he or she works 2,160 hours (840 hours allocated to household production) and earns a total of $43,200 (point *g*).

24c. For a person working 1,000 hours (point *h*) the reduction in the implicit tax rate would create counteracting income and substitution effects. The person would receive a higher benefit, creating an income effect which would reduce the incentive to work. However, the effective wage would also rise, creating a substitution effect which would increase the incentive to work. For a person working 1,800 hours (point *i*), the reduction in the implicit tax rate would make the person eligible to receive benefits. This in turn would create reinforcing income and substitution effects. The person would receive a higher benefit, creating an income effect which would reduce the incentive to work. In addition, the effective wage would also be reduced, creating a substitution effect which would further decrease the incentive to work.

24d. Reducing the rate at which benefits are scaled back increases the amount of benefits paid out and so most likely would require increased payroll taxes on all those working. For a worker like the one at point *h*, the increase in taxes should roughly offset the increase in benefits so that lifetime wealth will remain unchanged. The payroll tax, however, decreases the effective wage during the working years, while the reduction in the implicit tax rate increases the wage after retirement. With expected lifetime wealth constant, this should lead the person to reduce market work during their younger years and increase market work after retirement.

Answers To Chapter 8

■ Review Questions

1. **Answer a.** Worker utility is a function of both the pecuniary and nonpecuniary aspects of the job. However, with the nonpecuniary characteristics held constant, the level of utility will be determined by the level of monetary compensation.

2. **Answer c.** The whole point of a compensating wage differential is to make sure that even firms with undesirable working conditions can obtain workers. It will also be true that workers who are indifferent about the adverse conditions will work for the higher-paying firm, but this will occur even before the equilibrium compensating differential is reached. Compensating differentials do not represent so much an incentive to improve conditions as they do a way firms can avoid making improvements in their working conditions.

3. **Answer b.** The compensating differential framework assumes that people choose the wage/risk combinations that best suit their preferences. This results in those doing dangerous work being better paid than those in comparable jobs working under safer conditions. While those who choose dangerous jobs will generally be less averse to risk, the model in no way assumes that danger is a good. Also, the model explicitly assumes that people do have other employment opportunities.

4. **Answer b.** A compensating differential represents the payment needed to attract the borderline or marginal worker. There will always be some workers who would work under the adverse conditions for less than the equilibrium differential, and some workers who probably could never be induced to work under the adverse conditions.

5. **Answer d.** It is important to realize that the theory only predicts higher wages will be associated with less desirable conditions if all the other things that influence wages are held constant. In answer **c**, wages are the same even though some workers are experiencing more desirable conditions. This does not contradict the theory, however, since these workers are more highly skilled. They normally would be paid more than their less skilled counterparts. All that is important is that here the more desirable conditions still exert a dampening effect on wages.

6. **Answer a.** The theory assumes workers try to maximize their utility, not their level of compensation.

7. **Answer c.** Indifference curves are typically drawn downward sloping since a "good" appears on each axis. In this case, however, a "bad" (risk of injury) appears on the horizontal axis. While **b** may be true, it does not impact the shape of the indifference curves, which only reflect worker preferences.

8. **Answer d.** The slope of the indifference curve indicates the willingness of the person to give up wages for a given reduction in risk. As one moves up a given indifference curve, the slope increases and so the willingness to pay for a given risk reduction increases.

9. **Answer a.**   Isoprofit curves represent all the wage/risk combinations that yield a certain profit level. Since making the workplace safer is costly, the firm stays at the same profit level only if it reduces the wage.

10. **Answer d.**   The slope of the isoprofit curve indicates the rate at which a firm must reduce wages for a given reduction in risk. As one moves up a given isoprofit curve, the slope decreases and so the rate at which the firm must reduce wages for a given risk reduction is lower. If the firm can reduce wages at a lower rate for a given risk reduction, that risk reduction must be less costly.

11. **Answer b.**   Since the isoprofit curves shown in Figure 8-3 are assumed to be wage/risk combinations associated with zero economic profits, the offer curve also represents actual wage/risk offers consistent with zero economic profits, not positive economic profits.

12. **Answer d.**   In the hedonic theory of wages, workers like B who experience undesirable conditions do so voluntarily as part of a mutually beneficial arrangement between themselves and firm Y.

13. **Answer d.**   By forcing risk exposure down to 4 deaths per 10,000 workers, person B will be forced to a lower indifference curve. The reduction can be minimized by switching to employer X (i.e., moving to point *a*), but this will still represent a lower level of utility for B.

14. **Answer c.**   When imperfect information exists, Figure 8-3 may no longer be an accurate depiction of the matching process between employers and employees. Such imperfect information often leads to a window of opportunity for regulation to make workers better off provided the worker's willingness to pay for a certain risk reduction does not exceed the cost. If it does, the person will actually end up on a lower indifference curve because of the mandated risk reduction.

15. **Answer d.**   Estimates of the benefits of a regulation typically focus on the current willingness to pay values of those directly affected by the regulation. This is a fairly narrow perspective that is often criticized for the reasons listed in responses **a** through **c**.

16. **Answer a.**   As income tax rates increase, the benefits of receiving compensation in the form of wages decreases, and so the willingness to give up wages for a given increase in employee benefits should increase. This increased willingness to pay shows up as an increase in the slope of the indifference curve.

17. **Answer b.**   Answer **a** would be true if it stated that taxes and insurance contributions were based on a percentage of the firm's cash payroll. Answer **c** is a true statement but does not relate to the slope of the firm's isoprofit curve.

18. **Answer b.**   The hedonic wage theory of employee benefits is based on the same assumptions as the hedonic wage theory relating to risk of fatal injury. Workers (not firms) are assumed to have complete information and are assumed to be mobile enough to have access to various employment opportunities. Although workers being free to determine their own mix of wages and benefits would make it easier for workers to achieve their optimal mix, it is typically the firms that set the compensation mix. Workers must then match themselves with the firms that best satisfy their preferences.

19. **Answer d.** When workers have steeper indifference curves, the optimal compensation mix will include a higher proportion of employee benefits. Workers have steeper indifference curves, in turn, when they are willing to give up a significant amount in wages for a given increase in benefits. This willingness is usually displayed by older workers with higher incomes, since the tax advantages associated with receiving compensation in the form of benefits are likely to be more substantial. Younger workers are typically more in need of discretionary income to facilitate the purchase of things like homes and automobiles.

20. **Answer d.** The mandated provision of benefits, like mandatory risk reduction, only increases worker well-being if worker willingness to pay for the benefit exceeds the cost to the firms of providing it.

21. **Answer a.** The unconstrained choice of 200 leisure hours may involve a job with a layoff since layoffs are one way for a worker to obtain more leisure time. Two hundred work hours may constitute a part-time or full-time job depending on the time period being considered and the work hours that are customary for that occupation. Since the choice is unconstrained, however, any layoff implicit in this level of hours will not be considered an undesirable characteristic and so need not be accompanied by a compensating differential.

22. **Answer a.** To attain an income of $500 when working only 80 hours requires a wage of $500/80 or $6.25. Since the original wage was $4, the new wage reflects a compensating differential of $2.25.

23. **Answer d.** The vertical intercept of the budget line represents the level of income attained if the person works the maximum number of hours. (This is often called the level of full income.) If the wage is $6.25 and the maximum number of work hours is 400, the maximum level of income is ($6.25)(400) or $2,500.

24. **Answer a.** The person experiences a utility level of 10 half of the time, and a utility level of 30 the other half of the time, so the average level of utility is 20.

25. **Answer d.** A job that involves 250 hours all of the time will yield a utility level between 20 and 25 all of the time, which means that the average level of utility will exceed the average level associated with the uncertain schedule. This preference for the certain situation is called risk aversion. The only way the uncertain schedule could yield the same average level of utility would be if the wage associated with this job was higher.

■ Problems

26a. The lack of alternative offers means that person A ends up on the indifference curve A₁ that goes through point *a* instead of being able to reach a higher indifference curve. Given the shape of A's indifference curve, it appears A's maximum utility would be attained near point *c*. To reach point *c*, however, A would have to be able to move and work for employer X.

26b. Such a regulation would make the immobile person A better off by allowing A to attain the level of utility associated with point *b*.

26c. The regulation would make person B worse off by forcing B to point *c*, a point associated with a lower indifference curve. The regulation, however, would be even worse if B was constrained to work for employer Y since that would require a movement to point *b*.

27a. The optimal level of risk is that level associated with point *c* (4 deaths per 10,000 workers). The wage rate, however, would fall from somewhere between $10 and $11 to $8.

27b. The lowest level of risk is that associated with point *d* (approximately 1.6 deaths per 10,000 workers).

27c. No, person A would not be in favor of such a regulation since A perceives that he or she is on indifference curve A$_3$. In this case, however, movement to point *e* does also lead to a lower actual level of utility.

27d. Under perfect information and mobility, person A should choose point *c* where the wage is $8 and the risk of fatal injury is 4 deaths per 10,000 workers.

27e. No, regulation to any risk level lower than 4 deaths per 10,000 workers would make a fully informed and mobile worker worse off.

28a. Person A would be willing to see the wage reduced from $8 to just under $6 (from point *a* to point *c*).

28b. The cost of reducing risk can be seen in the wage reductions necessary to keep the firms competitive. In this case, the wage must fall from $8 to $4 (from point *a* to point *b*) for a cost per hour of $4.

28c. No, since the cost ($4) exceeds the worker's willingness to pay (slightly over $2), the regulation fails a benefit/cost test. When this happens, note that the worker will be forced to a lower indifference curve.

28d. The slope of the dashed line is −1. At point *a*, the tradeoff between wage and risk is such that every one-unit reduction in risk must be accompanied by a one-dollar reduction in the wage.

28e. Based on the rate of change at point *a*, one would predict that person A would be willing to give up $3 in wages for a reduction in risk from 4 deaths per 10,000 to 1.

28f. The extrapolation overstates A's willingness to pay for risk reductions. This occurs because the extrapolation ignores the convexity of A's indifference curves. This convexity reflects a decreasing willingness to pay for risk reductions as the workplace becomes safer. This means that benefit/cost studies of risk reductions may be slightly biased in favor of finding that the benefits exceed the costs.

29a. Such a weighting occurs when the spending flexibility that wage income provides is more important than the tax advantages of receiving compensation in the form of employee benefits.

29b. Originally $E = \$40$ and $W = \$60 \Rightarrow U = (40)(60)^2 = 144,000$.

29c. To keep utility constant as E rises by $20 to $60, the wage can fall to

$$W = \sqrt{\frac{144,000}{60}} = \$48.99.$$

This means the person is willing to give up $11.01 in wages for the $20 increase in benefits. However, since every $1 increase in benefits costs the firm 75 cents, a $20 increase in benefits costs the firm $15. Since the willingness to pay for the increased benefits is lower than the cost, the change in the compensation mix would make the worker worse off.

29d. Originally $E = \$40$ and $W = \$60 \Rightarrow U = (40)(60) = 2,400$.

To keep utility constant as E rises by $20 to $60, the wage can fall to

$$W = \frac{2,400}{60} = \$40.$$

This means the person is willing to give up $20 in wages for the $20 increase in benefits. However, since every $1 increase in benefits costs the firm 75 cents, a $20 increase in benefits costs the firm $15. Since the willingness to pay for the increased benefits is greater than the cost, the change in the compensation mix would make the worker better off.

30a. Originally $L = 200$ and $Y = \$400 \Rightarrow U = (200)^2(400) = 16,000,000$.

See the indifference curve labeled U_1 in Figure 8-10. The original budget line is the line ab and the original optimum is point c.

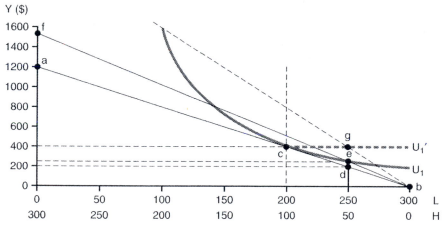

Figure 8-10

30b. To find the income level needed to keep utility constant, solve the equation

$$(250)^2(Y) = 16,000,000 \Rightarrow Y = \$256.$$

See point e in Figure 8-10. At $L = 250$, however, the person only earns $200 (point d).

30c. If leisure increases to 250 hours, then work hours decrease to 50. To earn $256 when H is only 50, the wage must rise to

$$W = \frac{256}{50} = \$5.12.$$

Since the original wage was $4, this new wage represents a compensating differential of $1.12. The budget line consistent with this new wage is line bf in Figure 8-10.

*30d. If, at the original equilibrium, the person saw leisure and income as perfect complements, the original indifference curve would be represented by curve U_1' in Figure 8-10. Therefore, to keep utility constant as leisure increases to 250, income would have to stay at $400 (point g). This would require a wage of $400/50 or $8. This means the compensating differential is now $4. This new wage is represented by the dashed budget line connecting points b and g in Figure 8-10.

*30e. The change in preferences raised the compensating differential that is required. With the new preferences, the extra leisure that is forced upon the worker has no value, whereas with normal downward-sloping indifference curves it does. So to keep utility constant, income (and hence the wage) must be higher in the perfect complement case.

*31a. When work hours $(H) = 5$, then Y is $25 and U is 5. If U is always equal to 5, then the average level of utility is also 5.

*31b. The average work hours is given by the equation

$$\text{Average Hours } = \frac{1}{2}(2) + \frac{1}{2} 8 = 5.$$

*31c. When $H = 2$, $Y = \$10$. When $H = 8$, $Y = \$40$. The average level of utility is given by the equation

$$\text{Average } U = \frac{1}{2}\sqrt{10} + \frac{1}{2}\sqrt{40} = 4.74.$$

*31d. The worker will prefer job A, the job with the certain schedule since the average level of utility is higher.

*31e. The compensating differential can be inferred from the wage that is necessary to make the average level of utility from job B equal the average level of utility from job A. This wage can be found by solving the equation

$$\frac{1}{2}\sqrt{2W} + \frac{1}{2}\sqrt{8W} = 5 \Rightarrow 2.121\sqrt{W} = 5 \Rightarrow W = \$5.56.$$

Since the original wage was $5, the compensating differential for the less desirable schedule is 50 cents.

■ Applications

32a. The law would force the non-union worker (person A) away from the point a to point c. This point would be associated with a lower indifference curve.

32b. Person A will now try to move from point c to point b since b will be associated with a higher level of utility. The problem is that all the B workers will still be at point b as well. With all the workers preferring firm U, the firm will be able to be more selective in its personnel decisions and so will end up with the most skilled and productive workers among this general class of workers.

32c. Although the wage will be the same for all workers, the more skilled and productive workers at firm U will also be enjoying better working conditions than those workers at firm NU. This situation is consistent with theory of compensating differentials. More productive workers typically will be paid more, so here the better working conditions are still exerting a dampening effect on the wage.

32d. The argument about the effects of the minimum wage is identical to that observed in this problem. A higher minimum wage should cause firms to move up along their isoprofit curve, offsetting the increased wage costs with reductions in costs obtained by increasing the pace of work and decreasing other desirable conditions and benefits such as job training. Among all the firms paying the minimum wage, workers will seek out those with the best conditions. Those firms can then be more selective in their personnel decisions. The result will be that the least skilled workers will end up working at the minimum wage firms offering the least desirable working conditions.

*33a. In Table 8-1, U_A and U_B represent the levels of utility attained by persons A and B under each of the 4 possible scenarios. The utilities were computed as follows.

Safe for A/Safe for B

$$\Rightarrow U_A = 200 + 200 + 0 = 400,$$
$$U_B = 200 + 200 + 0 = 400.$$

Unsafe for A/Safe for B

$$\Rightarrow U_A = 300 + 0 + 200 = 500,$$
$$U_B = 200 + 200 - 250 = 150.$$

Safe for A/Unsafe for B

$$\Rightarrow U_A = 200 + 200 - 250 = 150,$$
$$U_B = 300 + 0 + 200 = 500.$$

Unsafe for A/Unsafe for B

$$\Rightarrow U_A = 300 + 0 + 0 = 300,$$
$$U_B = 300 + 0 + 0 = 300.$$

Table 8-1

Person A/Person B	Safe conditions	Unsafe conditions
Safe conditions	$U_A = 400$ $U_B = 400$	$U_A = 150$ $U_B = 500$
Unsafe conditions	$U_A = 500$ $U_B = 150$	$U_A = 300$ $U_B = 300$

*33b. Regardless of person B's choice, person A always does better by choosing the unsafe conditions. Similarly, regardless of A's choice, person B always does better by choosing the unsafe conditions.

*33c. Forcing the workers to the safe conditions makes each worker better off.

*33d. Norms and standards play an important role in shaping our behavior and influencing our level of satisfaction. While a fifty-degree day seems delightful if it occurs in January, that same temperature seems uncomfortably cold in July. It is not so much the absolute temperature that is important but what we are accustomed to. In much the same way, material satisfaction depends on the amount of goods one has relative to the amount needed or desired. These needs and desires in turn are largely determined by the way in which one observes other members of the society living. As the obligations and expectations of individuals change, the goods they consume change and people's perceptions of what they need change. For example, the average family in the United States today does not consider itself wealthy even though they live in a way only the wealthy did 200 years ago. Our consumption standards are not those of the colonial days but those of a much more complex society. In addition it is important to recognize that concern about relative standing may be instrumental in helping to achieve certain absolute goals. In general, any winner-take-all competition or auction system makes it imperative for people to be concerned about relative standing. When viewed in this way, it seems clear that concern about relative income can be something perfectly consistent with the assumption of rational consumers.

34a.   The premise of the proposed change is essentially the theory of compensating differentials presented in this chapter. Regulations to reduce risk force costly adjustments upon firms, and the result is lower wages. When individuals earn lower incomes, their spending on health care may be reduced, leading to more illness and earlier deaths. While it may sound insensitive to refer to a tradeoff between wages and risk, the fact is that safety cannot be achieved without cost. This forces workers to balance the desire for more safety against their desire for more income.

34b.   Benefit computations often do not take into account the benefits from increased safety that would accrue to people not directly affected by the regulation, including those workers who will be employed in helping to make the workplace safer. Also, the computations typically take worker willingness to pay for increased safety as a given. This ignores the convexity of indifference curves as well as changes in preferences and attitudes such regulations can bring about over time. Also, one could argue that regulations leading to increased health and safety will help to raise productivity and income since healthier and safer workers may work harder and have better morale.

35a.   Increased administrative costs should rotate the isoprofit curve for the firm inward. For example, in Figure 8-11, the firm initially is willing to tradeoff $500 in wages for $750 in benefits (line *ab*). However, if the benefits become more costly to administer, the firm may be willing to trade $500 in wages for only $500 in benefits (line *ad*).

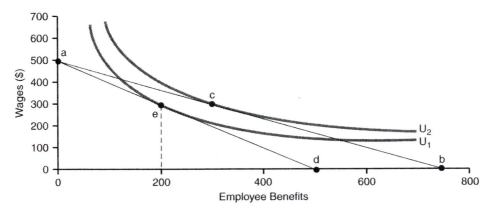

Figure 8-11

35b.   An increase in administrative costs should lead to a reduction in employee benefits. In Figure 8-11 the level of benefits falls from $300 to $200 (point *c* to point *e*).

36a.   Taxing health care benefits should lead to a flattening of the indifference curves in the hedonic wage model as the willingness to give up wages for additional dollars of benefits should decrease. This is shown in Figure 8-12 as a change in the shape of the indifference curves from U_1 to U_1'.

36b. Allowing firms to deduct only part of their health care expenses would increase the cost of providing benefits relative to the cost of providing wages. This should lead to steeper isoprofit curves for firms. For example, in Figure 8-12, the isoprofit curve is shown rotating from line *ab* to line *ad*. Previously, the firm could trade off, say, $500 in wages for $750 in benefits. With the change in policy, however, the firm may be able to trade off $500 in wages for only $500 in benefits.

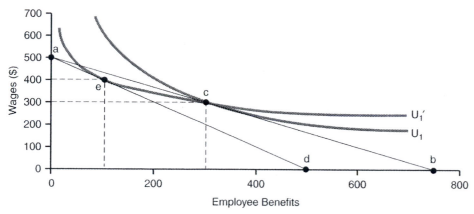

Figure 8-12

36c. Taken by itself, the flattening of the indifference curve should lead to more wages and fewer benefits. The steepening of the isoprofit curve should lead to fewer benefits (and perhaps more wages). Taken together, the prediction would be for fewer benefits and more wages. This is illustrated in Figure 8-12 as a movement from point *c* to point *e*. In this movement, benefits decrease from $300 to $100 and wages increase from $300 to $400.

37a. Firms make changes such as these so that they can attract the type of workers they feel will be best for the firm. In this case, offering more work at home and family leave policies means that the firm is strategically trying to attract older workers with families. Perhaps they feel these workers will be more reliable, dependable, and productive, and that they will stay with the firm for longer periods.

37b. While such compensation packages will be attractive to many workers, the provision of such benefits will be costly and will cause the firm to reduce wages below what they would otherwise be. Mandating such a move for all workers would make workers who preferred to take more of their compensation in the form of wages worse off.

38a. This unemployment insurance payment will allow the worker to attain point *e* ($L = 250$, $Y = \$256$) in Figure 8-10. No compensating differential will be required.

38b. By not having to pay the compensating differential of $1.12 on the 50 hours the person works, the firm saves $56. However, since the firm has paid only $30 into the fund, the unemployment insurance program effectively subsidizes this firm by $26. Firms subsidized in this way will tend to thrive and grow, and so the program is promoting the growth of firms that rely on temporary layoffs.

Answers To Chapter 9

■ Review Questions

1. **Answer d.** Other benefits include a more stable employment situation, more interesting and challenging work, and access to occupations with more prestige and more desirable working conditions.

2. **Answer d.** The costs associated with education include direct expenses, forgone earnings, and psychic losses.

3. **Answer d.** While discounting will also adjust for differences in purchasing power if the discount rate includes a premium for expected inflation, it is also possible to adjust for inflation using a price index for different years. Even if all the benefits are expressed in real terms, it would still be necessary to discount future benefits.

4. **Answer a.**

$$\frac{\$1,000}{(1+0.06)^{10}} = \$558.39.$$

5. **Answer a.** Substituting $B = \$10,000$, $r = 0.06$, and $T = 40$ into the annuity formula yields

$$PVB = \$10,000 \frac{1 - \dfrac{1}{(1+0.06)^{40}}}{0.06} \Rightarrow PVB = \$150,462.97$$

6. **Answer b.** Setting the present value of the benefits equal to the costs

$$\Rightarrow \frac{\$2,500}{(1+r)^2} = \$2,000 \Rightarrow (1+r)^2 = \frac{2,500}{2,000}$$

$$\Rightarrow 1+r = \sqrt{1.25} \Rightarrow r = 0.118 \Rightarrow r = 11.8\%.$$

7. **Answer c.** An increase in the retirement age effectively increases T, the length of time over which the benefits to education can accrue, raising the present value of the benefit stream. On the other hand, an increase in r would lower the present value of the benefit stream. The higher wages and decreased aptitude associated with high school graduates will tend to raise the costs of additional educational investments by increasing the forgone earnings and raising the psychic costs of education.

8. **Answer b.** Even if the value of B were falling for most individuals, an increase in T could more than compensate, thus raising the present value of the benefit stream.

9. **Answer a.**   The net gain from education is greatest at 12 years. The net gain, represented by the distance between points *a* and *b*, equals $1,000,000 and is greater than that attained at any other education level. For example, at 14.5 years, the net gain is zero, while at 16 years the net gain is only $200,000 (the distance between points *e* and *d*). At 20 years of education, the costs actually exceed the benefits.

10. **Answer c.**   At 16 years, the net gain is $1,600,000 (the difference between points *e* and *c*), while at 12 years the net gain is only $1,000,000. At 14.5 the net gain is something less than $1,000,000 because additional costs have been incurred, but no additional benefits. Likewise, at 20 years, there are additional costs but no added benefits, leaving net benefits less than $1,600,000.

11. **Answer c.**   Since only the higher-productivity individuals (the type B individuals) will have an incentive to attain 16 years of education, this level of achievement will be an effective way to distinguish between types of workers. The reason the low-productivity individuals voluntarily choose the lower education level is because of the higher costs they face for attaining a given level of education.

12. **Answer b.**   The socially optimal level of education to use as a screening device would be that level just slightly past point *f* (14.5 years). This is the lowest threshold that firms could set and still have type A workers choose less than the threshold amount and type B workers above the threshold amount. In a world where education's only value is as a signal, it does not make sense from the point of view of society as a whole to devote any resources to education beyond that level needed to maintain the signaling function.

13. **Answer d.**   Answers **b** and **c** account for the steepening of the age-earnings profile, while Answer **a** accounts for the flattening of the profile as age increases.

14. **Answer b.**   Age-earnings profiles steepen when an individual receives more on-the-job training. On-the-job training, in turn, is more likely to be acquired by those for whom the costs of training are lower, holding all else constant. Those who have completed higher levels of schooling have shown that they can learn more quickly, which implies that the cost of educational investments will be lower for these individuals.

15. **Answer d.**   Steepening of the age-earnings profile is usually attributable to on-the-job training. Such training becomes a better investment for women as their worklives increase (*T* increases).

16. **Answer b.**   The higher wages attained by those completing higher levels of education are, for the most part, the benefits to investing in human capital. However, these benefits must be weighed against the costs. For the investment to be worthwhile, not only must the internal rate of return be positive, but it must also exceed the person's discount rate.

17. **Answer c.**   High-ability people typically earn more than lower-ability people, holding all else constant. Since education and ability are positively correlated, measures of the rate of return to education that ignore ability may attribute all of the earnings gap to education itself, when in fact some of the difference is due to the higher ability of the more educated person.

18. **Answer d.**   For those who actually made the investment, the return may be understated since they probably would have been a worse than average worker in the unskilled profession. On the other hand, for those who did not make the investment, the potential return is overstated since they may be a worse than average worker in jobs requiring greater skill.

19. **Answer a.** If a certain level of education already has signaling value, higher levels of education may actually destroy the signaling value of education. Answer **b**, far from being a sign of wasted resources, represents a situation where the level of education has reached its optimal social level. Answer **c** is a sign that the investment is acceptable since the investor will earn just a normal rate of return.

20. **Answer b.** The initial shortage is the difference between the quantity demanded off the new demand curve (28) and the quantity supplied (18).

    For readers wishing to derive these answers more precisely, note that the equations underlying Questions **20–24** are

    $$\text{Demand 1: } L_D = 30 - W,$$

    $$\text{Demand 2: } L_D = 40 - W,$$

    $$\text{Supply: } L_S = 1.5W.$$

21. **Answer b.** With the quantity of labor supplied fixed at 18, the wage must rise to $22 to clear the market.

22. **Answer d.** When the labor supply plans of all workers have been realized, the surplus will be the difference between the quantity supplied and quantity demanded at the wage of $22.

23. **Answer a.** With the quantity of labor supplied now at 33, the wage must fall to $7 to clear the market.

24. **Answer d.** The magnitude of the slope of the demand curves (as it appears on the graph) is one, while the slope of the supply curve is two-thirds. If workers had rational expectations there would be no boom-and-bust cycle. If workers were adapting their expectations based on the past behavior of wages, the cycle would tend to diminish.

25. **Answer b.** Indifference curves represent the education and wage combinations that keep worker utility constant at a particular level, not what firms have to do to attract workers. In this case, since higher wages accompany higher levels of education, the implicit message is that higher levels of education are perceived by workers as a *bad* since they are costly. Therefore, in order to keep workers at the same level of utility the wage, a *good*, must rise. Note that with this kind of preference structure, workers prefer movements toward combinations that involve a higher wage and less education.

26. **Answer d.** An isoprofit curve is a constraint from the firm's point of view. It represents what the firm is willing and able to pay workers with different levels of education, not what workers demand. If the firm perceives that workers with higher levels of education are more productive, either because education makes them more productive or because it identifies workers who are inherently more productive, it should be willing and able to pay them a higher wage and still stay at the zero (normal) profit level.

27. **Answer d.** The steeper the indifference curve, the more averse the person is to additional years of education. On the other hand, the steeper the isoprofit curve, the more the firm is willing to pay for additional years of education. The matching of person B with firm Z suggests that the person least averse to additional schooling is matched with the firm most willing to pay for additional education. Since each individual is free to choose from the combinations offered by both firms Y and Z, the implicit assumption must be that *A* and *B* are mobile enough to be able to accept either employment opportunity. Such a matching process also typically assumes that workers are accurately informed about the wage and education combinations offered by the different firms.

Problems

28. Substituting $B = \$3,000$, $r = 0.06$, and $T = 10$ into the annuity formula yields a total present value of benefits equal to

$$PVB = \$30,000\frac{1-\dfrac{1}{(1+0.06)^{10}}}{0.06} \Rightarrow PVB = \$22,080.26$$

The total cost of the investment is the \$2,000 for tuition and books plus \$20,000 in lost earnings for a total cost of \$22,000. The costs need not be discounted since they all occur in the current year (year 0). Since the present value of the benefits exceeds the present value of the costs, this is a good investment.

*29a. Setting the present value of the benefits equal to the present value of the cost yields

$$\Rightarrow \frac{\$2,000}{1+r} + \frac{\$2,000}{(1+r)^2} = \$3,500$$

$$\Rightarrow \frac{2,000 + 2000r + 2000}{(1+r)^2} = 3,500$$

$$\Rightarrow 4,000 + 2,000r = 3,500(1+r)^2$$

$$\Rightarrow 4,000 + 2,000r = 3,500(1 + 2r + r^2)$$

$$\Rightarrow 3,500r^2 + 5,000r - 500 = 0$$

$$\Rightarrow 35r^2 + 50r - 5 = 0.$$

Applying the quadratic formula yields

$$r = \frac{-50 \pm \sqrt{50^2 - (4)(35)(-5)}}{2(35)} \Rightarrow r = 0.0938 \text{ or } 9.38\%.$$

29b. Since the internal rate of return exceeds the interest rate on alternative investments, the training program is a good investment for the worker.

29c. Any discount rate that is less than or equal to the internal rate of return would still make this a worthwhile investment. A person may have a higher discount rate than the market interest rate if he or she is very present-oriented. For example, a person may discount future benefits at a very high rate because of a fear that he or she may not live long enough to enjoy the benefits.

29d. Since older workers have a shorter time period over which to reap the benefits of the investment, the present value of the entire benefit stream will be lower, holding all else constant. Also, since older workers typically receive a higher wage than younger workers, the earnings that they forgo during training are higher, raising the cost of the investment. The tendency of on-the-job training to diminish with age leads to a flattening out of the age-earnings profile, thus contributing to its concave shape.

30a. Since the costs occur in the current period they are not discounted. The present value of the benefits equals

$$PVB = \frac{\$6,000}{1+0.06} + \frac{\$2,000}{(1+0.06)^2} = \$11,000.40.$$

Therefore, the present value of the benefits exceeds the present value of the costs by $1,000.40.

30b. Substituting $r = 0.06$ and $p = 0.04$ into the formula for the real interest rate (i) yields

$$i = \frac{0.06 - 0.04}{1+0.04} = 0.01923 \quad \text{or} \quad 1.923\%$$

30c. To convert nominal values to real values, divide the nominal value by the price index and multiply the result by 100. This yields

Real cost in year $0 = 10,000$,
Real benefit in year $1 = 5,769.23$,
Real benefit in year $2 = 5,547.34$.

30d. Since the costs occur in the current period they are not discounted. The present value of the real benefits equals

$$PVB = \frac{5,769.23}{1.01923} + \frac{5,547.34}{(1.01923)^2} = 11,000.40.$$

Therefore, the present value of the benefits exceeds the present value of the costs by 1,000.40 in real terms.

30e. Comparing the Answers to **30a** and **30d** suggests that discounting nominal values by the market interest rate is the same as converting nominal values to real and then discounting by the real interest rate. Because the market interest rate adjusts to reflect anticipated inflation, it is not necessary to deflate future benefits by the anticipated price indices.

31a. For those who have actually made the educational investment, selection bias leads to an understatement of the true return, which suggests that the upper end of the range of estimates is more appropriate. On the other hand, for those who have not made the investment, selection bias tends to overstate the rate of return that is possible on educational investments. This suggests that the lower end of the range of estimates would be more appropriate.

31b. Selection bias and ability bias are both examples of the omitted variable problem discussed in the appendix to Chapter 1. Selection bias is a problem that stems from a failure to account for the comparative advantage people have in different occupations. For example, someone who successfully completes a college education probably has a set of interests and abilities that would not be well utilized in a work environment suitable for the typical high school graduate. That is presumably part of the reason the person chose to attend college in the first place. Therefore, simply comparing the average earnings of high school and college graduates understates the benefits to the person choosing to attend college. Such a simple comparison does not account for the fact that the person would probably not have been as successful as the typical high school graduate had he or she not attended college. If one could control for the different aptitudes and interests of each individual, there would be no selection bias. The problem is that these differences are very difficult to observe and measure and so in some studies their effects go unaccounted for. In the same way, ability bias is simply a failure to control for the differences in ability that occur between those achieving different levels of education. Since ability is difficult to define and measure, it often goes unaccounted for. To do so, however, overstates the return to education provided individuals attaining higher levels of education also have more general ability. The increase in wages earned by the more educated and more able workers is all attributed to education if measures of ability are not also included in the analysis.

32a. For a type A person, the net benefit from 12 years of education is $1,000,000 (distance *ab*), while the net benefit from 16 years of education is $800,000 (distance *ed*). The optimal level of education is 12 years.

32b. For a type B person, the net benefit from 12 years of education is $1,000,000 (distance *ab*), while the net benefit from 16 years of education is $1,200,000 (distance *ec*). The optimal level of education is 16 years.

32c. Since only type B workers have an incentive to acquire 16 years of education, that level of education could be used to distinguish high productivity workers from low-productivity workers.

32d. Figure 9-10 shows the new wage schedules given the decrease in the hiring standard.

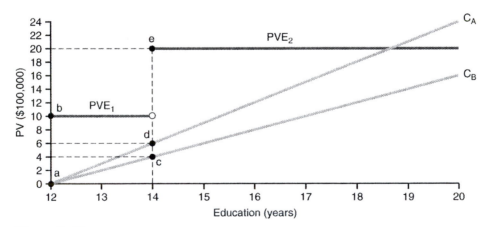

Figure 9-10

Note that type A individuals will now have an incentive to attain 14 years of education since the net gain of $1,400,000 (distance *ed*) exceeds the $1,000,000 return on 12 years of education (distance *ab*). Type B individuals will also have an incentive to attain 14 years of education since the net gain of $1,600,000 (distance *ec*) exceeds the $1,000,000 return on 12 years of education. Since both types of workers would have an incentive to acquire 14 years of education, that threshold would be an ineffective signal of worker productivity.

32e. Figure 9-11 shows the new wage schedules given the increase in the hiring standard. Note that type A individuals will now have an incentive to attain only 12 years of education since the net gain of $1,000,000 (distance *ab*) exceeds the $200,000 return on 18 years of education (distance *ed*). Type B individuals will also have an incentive to attain just 12 years of education since the net gain of $1,000,000 exceeds the $800,000 return on 18 years of education (distance *ec*). Since both types of worker would have an incentive to acquire just 12 years of education, that threshold would be an ineffective signal of worker productivity.

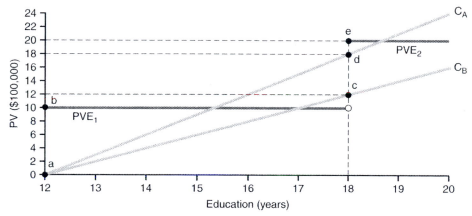

Figure 9-11

33a. Equilibrium $\Rightarrow L_D = L_S$

$$\Rightarrow 10 - 0.5W = 0.5W$$

$$\Rightarrow W^* = \$10 \Rightarrow L^* = 5.$$

The initial equilibrium is represented by point *a* in Figure 9-12.

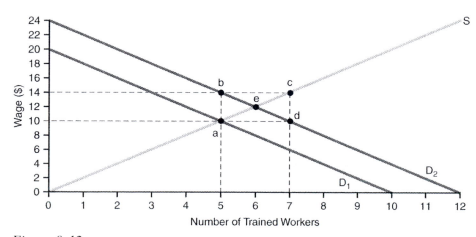

Figure 9-12

33b. Equilibrium $\Rightarrow L_D = L_S$

$$\Rightarrow 12 - 0.5W = 0.5W \Rightarrow W^* = \$12 \Rightarrow L^* = 6.$$

The new equilibrium is represented by point *e* in Figure 9-12.

33c. With the quantity of labor supplied fixed temporarily at 5, the market clears where

$$12 - 0.5W = 5 \Rightarrow W^* = \$14.$$

This outcome is represented by point *b* in Figure 9-12.

33d. With the wage rising to $14, an incentive will be created for the quantity of labor supplied to increase to

$$L_S = 0.5W = 0.5(14) \Rightarrow L_S = 7.$$

This outcome is represented by point *c* in Figure 9-12.

33e. With the quantity of labor supplied fixed temporarily at 7, the market will clear at

$$12 - 0.5W = 7 \Rightarrow W^* = \$10.$$

This outcome is represented by point *d* in Figure 9-12.

33f. With the wage at $10, there will be an incentive to supply labor to the point where

$$L_S = 0.5W = 0.5(10) \Rightarrow L_S = 5.$$

This outcome is represented by point *a* in Figure 9-12.

33g. The market is not moving closer to the market-clearing values associated with the demand curve D_2. Rather, the market continues to cycle around the true equilibrium value.

33h. The cycle will not converge to the true equilibrium since the magnitude of the slope of the demand curve (as it appears on the graph) is the same as the slope of the supply curve. For this model to converge, the demand curve must be flatter than the supply curve.

34a. Provided person B were willing and able to switch to employer Z (i.e., move from point *a* to point *b*), the 4-year increase in education would result in a wage increase of slightly over $4.

34b. Given the initial indifference curve B_1, the person would require an increase in the wage of just over $2 to undertake the costs of an additional four years of education. This difference of just over $2 represent the difference in the wage between points *a* and *c*.

34c. The additional years of education would be a good investment for person B since the benefits exceed the minimum necessary to keep utility constant. The result is an increase in utility as B moves from point *a* to point *c*, and from indifference curve B_1 to indifference curve B_2. On the other hand, person A is already at his or her optimum wage and education combination. Any increases in education beyond point *a* will result in a lower level of utility since the increases will result in a smaller increase in the wage than is necessary to compensate person A for the increased costs.

■ Applications

35. The simplest explanation is that enrollment rates were rising, despite the cost increases, because the benefits of a college education were also rising. (According to the article, male college graduates earned on average 23.8% more than high school graduates in 1979, but by 1986 the difference had risen to 39.2%. For women, the difference rose from 27.9% to 40.5% over the same period.) Human capital investment decisions are made by comparing costs *and* benefits.

36. This explanation is very plausible and highlights the uncertain nature of the benefits associated with educational investments. Decisions about particular educational investments are based on expectations of future earnings, formed largely through contacts with friends, family, neighborhood acquaintances, and other role models. It seems very plausible, given the small percentage of women with graduate degrees in business in the early 1970s, that information on future career and earnings prospects would have been relatively hard to come by. Recent experiences suggest that the initial estimates made by many women of the benefits of an M.B.A. degree may have been overly optimistic. As this information has circulated to younger women, it apparently has had the dampening effect on enrollment rates that the human capital investment framework would predict.

*37a. The parameter r could be estimated using least squares regression analysis. Letting S be the independent variable, $\ln Y_S$ the dependent variable, and $\ln Y_0$ the constant (or intercept) term, an estimate of r could be derived by fitting a least squares regression line to cross-section data on schooling and earnings.

*37b. A large number of variables that can influence earnings have been left out of this model. For example, the amount of ability, on-the-job training, experience, and employee benefits a person receives all influence earnings. However, these omitted variables only bias the estimate of r if they are correlated with the level of education. For example, some measure of individual ability must be included in the regression (making this a multiple regression analysis). Since education and ability are most likely positively correlated, failure to include a measure of ability would bias the estimate of r upward.

*37c. Unless the regression included a good measure of individual interests and aptitudes, the estimate would suffer from selection bias. The estimate of r would overstate the rate of return that could be expected by someone who has not invested in additional years of schooling, and would understate the return attained by those who already have invested in additional years of schooling.

*37d. The rate of return would be 8.4%.

$$r = \frac{\ln 35{,}000 - \ln 25{,}000}{4} = 0.084$$

*37e. Education would be a good investment provided this rate of return exceeded the rate of return available on other comparable investments.

38a. For a type A person, the net benefit from 12 years of education is $1,000,000 (distance *ab*), while the net benefit from 16 years of education is $1,400,000 (distance *ed*). The optimal level of education is 16 years.

38b. For a type B person, the net benefit from 12 years of education is $1,000,000 (distance *ab*), while the net benefit from 16 years of education is $1,600,000 (distance *ec*). The optimal level of education is 16 years.

38c. Since both types of workers have an incentive to acquire 16 years of education, that level of education could not be used to distinguish high-productivity workers from low-productivity workers. Lowering the cost of education has increased the incentive to invest in education, but in so doing it has taken away education's signaling value, thus eliminating the social benefit society derives from education in this model.

38d. Grade inflation may lower the cost of education perceived by individuals, particularly the psychic costs, by reducing the difficulty and anxiety associated with schooling. As shown in the previous questions, however, lowering the cost of education can destroy the ability of education to function as an effective signal of the most productive individuals.

39a. The law would force person A to move from point *a* to point *b*. This would force person A to a lower indifference curve. Person B would not be affected.

39b. If person A is restricted to employer Y, the law would force person A to move from point *a* to point *c*. This would lead to a greater reduction in utility than in the previous problem. Person B would not be affected.

Answers To Chapter 10

■ Review Questions

1. **Answer c.** Note that answer **a** ignores the possibility of psychic costs or benefits as well as the timing of costs and benefits. Answer **b** does not address the costs of mobility.

2. **Answer b.** The present value of the benefit stream is

$$PVB = \frac{100{,}000}{1+.06} + \frac{100{,}000}{(1+.06)^2} + \frac{100{,}000}{(1+.06)^3} \Rightarrow PVB = \$267{,}301.$$

   Assuming there are no other benefits associated with the move, and the costs of moving all occur in the current period, the total costs could not exceed this amount.

3. **Answer c.** Access to information about job opportunities is easier for educated workers to obtain since they tend to participate in regional and national labor markets. This reduces the costs associated with mobility. Older workers have too little time to recover the costs of mobility and their psychic costs tend to be high. Psychic costs may also be high for married couples, and if both spouses work, it may be difficult for both to find good job matches.

4. **Answer d.** Education, not age, tends to determine whether a person participates in a local or national labor market.

5. **Answer b.** Age tends to be more closely connected to the psychic costs of moving, while education influences the cost of obtaining information about employment opportunities.

6. **Answer b.** When the earnings distribution is compressed in the sending country, human capital investments by skilled workers have little payoff, and so these workers may seek out an environment where they can reap the rewards of their investments.

7. **Answer a.** Given the low standards of living from which many immigrants come, an earnings level even close to that of native-born Americans means that their investment in mobility has resulted in a very high stream of benefits. Individual outcomes, of course, depend on the individual circumstances. The evidence does not necessarily demonstrate that immigrants are more productive than native-born workers, however, since such a relationship may simply result from a failure to account for change in the productive quality of immigrants over time.

8. **Answer a.**   Note that the human capital investment framework utilizes *expectations* of future benefits and costs. Given incomplete information and uncertainty about future events, it is easy to see how mistakes could be made in evaluating mobility investments. Even though migration appears to be a good investment on average, that does not mean that it will be a good investment for all individuals. Regarding family mobility decisions, evidence indicates that while family income rises, one of the spouses may see their earnings fall.

9. **Answer a.**   Note that while traditionally viewed as something voluntary, quits can also be seen as a form of employer-induced mobility since the firm did not raise the wage high enough to keep the worker.

10. **Answer b.**   Quit rates decrease when the probability of quickly finding another job decreases. This happens when the unemployment rate and layoff rate rise. Such a situation is considered a loose labor market in the sense that many job seekers exist at the same time there are fewer jobs.

11. **Answer c.**   Mobility investments, including quits, are less likely for older workers since the benefits accrue for a shorter time (the value of T is lower). The lower quit rates, in turn, translate into longer job tenures for older workers.

12. **Answer a.**   The costs of quitting are likely to be higher since changing jobs frequently requires a change of residence given that there are fewer job opportunities in rural areas. Note also that if rural residents did have lower discount rates this would tend to increase the likelihood of voluntary turnover, since the present value of the future benefit stream would be higher.

13. **Answer b.**   If immigration were prohibited, the market equilibrium would result in the employment of 8 native-born workers at a wage of $8. With immigration, total employment is 12 at a wage of $4. Native-born workers fill 4 of those jobs, while immigrants fill the other 8.

14. **Answer c.**   The total real income of native-born workers falls from 64 (area $dbi0$) to 16 (area $efh0$) for a decrease of 48.

15. **Answer d.**   Total profits increase from 32 (area abd) to 72 (area ace) for an increase of 40.

16. **Answer c.**   Total output increases from 96 (area $abi0$) to 120 (area $acj0$) for an increase of 24.

*17. **Answer b.**   At any given employment level, immigrants should be willing to give up the difference between the wage they actually receive and the minimum they would be willing to accept in return for supplying that quantity of labor. This latter value can be read off the immigrant supply curve at any given employment level. Summing up these differences for the eight units of labor supplied by immigrants yields area $eg0$ (or equivalently, area $fc0$), which is the area of economic rent. It has a value of 16. Immigrants could pay just up to this amount and still have some incentive to supply labor in this market.

18. **Answer d.**   It is not necessary that immigrants be denied all government assistance, rather they must pay more in taxes than they receive in subsidies so that there is a net transfer of income from immigrants to native workers. Denying all assistance would also accomplish this, but denying it just to illegal immigrants would not be sufficient since illegal immigrants are only a small subset of the total immigrant work force.

19. **Answer d.**   Note that Figure 10-2 is a single-market analysis and so ignores the effects of immigration on other markets.

■ Problems

20a. The benefits of the move are the increases in combined salary for each year. The present value of the benefit stream is

$$PVB = \frac{3,000}{1+.06} + \frac{5,000}{(1+.06)^2} + \frac{7,000}{(1+.06)^3} \Rightarrow PVB = \$13,157.51.$$

The costs of $10,000 need not be discounted because they occur in year 0. Therefore, the present value of the benefits exceeds the present value of the cost and the investment is worthwhile.

20b. Assuming there are no other benefits associated with the move, and the costs of moving all occur in the current period, the total costs could not exceed $13,157.51.

20c. Although the psychic costs of leaving friends, family, coworkers, and familiar surrounding will be greatest initially, such feelings will continue into the future and can intensify in the future. For example, the events connected to the illness or death of an aged parent can be very stressful when they have to be handled from a long distance.

20d. The benefits of moving may extend well beyond monetary improvements in employment opportunities. The opportunity to leave problems behind and experience new challenges and people are very important to some families. Migration to new areas of the country may also allow for lifestyle changes or access to leisure activities that yield more enjoyment.

*20e. The first year wage in the new job (call it W) must be high enough to just keep the present value of the benefits equal to the present value of the costs

$$\Rightarrow \frac{W - 80,000}{1.06} + \frac{5,000}{1.06^2} + \frac{7,000}{1.06^3} = 10,000$$

$$\Rightarrow \frac{W - 80,000}{1.06} = -327.32$$

$$\Rightarrow W - 80,000 = -346.96$$

$$\Rightarrow W = \$79,654.04.$$

20f. It is unlikely that both spouses would gain equally. Evidence suggests that while family income rises because of migration, one of the spouses may actually see his or her income decline because of the move.

21a. Table 10-3 shows the marginal product of labor schedule for market A.

Table 10-3

Labor Market A		Labor Market B	
Labor	MP_L	**Labor**	MP_L
1	12	1	17
2	8	2	13
3	5	3	10
4	3	4	8
5	2	5	7

21b. See Figure 10-5.

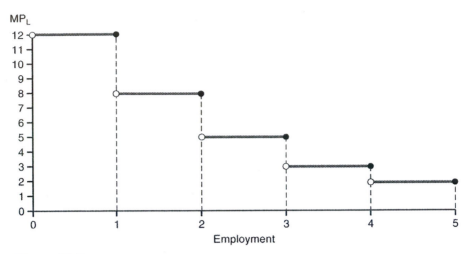

Figure 10-5

21c. The area under the marginal product schedule consists of the area of the 5 rectangles that can be seen in Figure 10-5. The height of each rectangle is the marginal product, while the width is one unit

$$\Rightarrow \text{Area} = 12(1) + 8(1) + 5(1) + 3(1) + 2(1).$$

Note that this computation is the same as summing the marginal product values. Note that the area equals 30, the total output associated with 5 units of labor in market A.

21d. See Table 10-3.

21e. The wage rate will be 5 in market A and 10 in market B. The total output from this allocation of labor will equal 65 (25 + 40).

21f. Given the higher wage rate in B, workers would be expected to migrate from A to B. If one worker migrates so that now A has 2 workers and B has 4, the total output increases to 68. If an additional worker migrates, however, output falls to 67. There would not be an incentive for the second worker to migrate, however, since after the first worker migrates, the marginal product, and hence the real wage, equals 8 in both markets. The output of this economy is maximized when labor is allocated in such a way that the marginal product is equal across the markets.

22a. If immigration were totally prohibited, the market-clearing wage and employment level would occur where

$$L_D = L_N$$

$$\Rightarrow 20 - 2W = 2W$$

$$\Rightarrow W^* = 5 \Rightarrow L^* = 10.$$

See point *b* in Figure 10-6. Allowing immigrants to enter this labor market would create a total supply curve given by the equation

$$L_T = L_N + L_I \Rightarrow L_T = 2W + W \Rightarrow L_T = 3W.$$

Given the two groups of workers, the market-clearing wage occurs where

$$L_D = L_T$$

$$20 - 2W = 3W$$

$$\Rightarrow W^* = 4 \Rightarrow L^* = 12.$$

See point c in Figure 10-6. Substituting this wage back into the supply equations for each group reveals that the employment of native-born workers will be 8 (point g) and the employment of immigrants will be 4 (point f). Therefore, immigration has reduced native employment from 10 to 8. Note that this reduction of 2 is less than the number of immigrants employed.

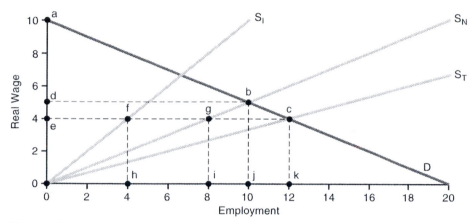

Figure 10-6

22b. Real income for native-born workers has fallen from 50 (area $dbj0$) to 32 (area $egi0$) for a total reduction of 18.

22c. Total profits increase from 25 (area abd) to 36 (area ace) for an increase of 11.

22d. Total output increases from 75 (area $abj0$) to 84 (area $ack0$) for an increase of 9.

*22e. Immigrants should be willing to give up area $ef0$ (or equivalently, area $gc0$) which equals 8, the area of economic rent.

*22f. Native-born workers have lost 18 in income but the firms have gained 11 in profits and immigrants have earned 8 in economic rent. So, for example, if the increased profits of 11 plus 7 of the "surplus" earned by immigrants were transferred to the native-born workers, their income would be the same as before immigration. The other two groups are also the same or better off than before immigration.

22g. This problem is a single-market analysis and so ignores the effects of immigration on other markets. For example, the wage reduction brought about by immigration in this market will help to put downward pressure on consumer prices The income earned by immigrants will also translate into increased demand for products. The scale effect that this creates will lead to employment and wage gains for those categories of labor that are gross complements with the labor in this market. Also, the change in employment opportunities that occur in this market may create a situation where native-born workers will migrate away from the geographic areas experiencing the influx of immigrants.

■ Applications

23.   This example does not contradict the notion that mobility is an investment undertaken when the present value of the benefits is expected to exceed the present value of the costs. In this case, the choice is no longer between the $60,000 salary and the $50,000 salary. Rather the choice is between the $50,000 salary and whatever the best opportunity is in the New England area. Perhaps because of the increased unemployment in this area, the only other alternative was a $40,000 salary. Given that scenario, it is easier to see the payoff to mobility.

*24a.   If women are perceived to have shorter work lives because of traditional child rearing responsibilities, firms may feel that there is not sufficient time to recover their investment in firm-specific training. As a result, women may not be hired for jobs involving training or may be offered less extensive training opportunities.

*24b.   When a firm invests in firm-specific training for the worker, it tries to recover the investment in the post-training periods by offering a real wage that is less than the worker's marginal product but above what the worker can get elsewhere. If no such training is offered, there will not be a gap between the wage the worker is receiving and his or her alternative offers. In this situation, the worker has little incentive to stay with the firm. Eliminating general training opportunities does not create the same kind of change since workers pay for the cost of general training in the form of lower wages during the training period. As a result, the real wage and the marginal product (which in this case also represents the worker's alternative offers) are already equal in the post-training period. Eliminating general training would not change the relationship between the wage the worker receives and the worker's alternative offers.

25a.   Recall from problem 24 that the market-clearing wage was 4 if immigration was allowed and 5 if it was not. In either situation, a minimum wage of 6 will be binding.

25b.   Substituting $W = 6$ into the demand equation yields

$$L_D = 20 - 2(6) = 8.$$

See point *a* in Figure 10-7.

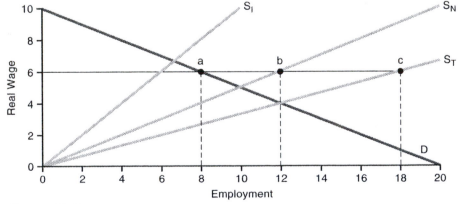

Figure 10-7

25c. Substituting $W = 6$ into the equation for the total supply curve yields

$$L_T = 3(6) = 18.$$

See point c in Figure 10-7. Of these 18, 12 are native-born workers (point b) and 6 are immigrants.

25d. There is no way of determining how the 8 jobs will be split between immigrants and domestic workers. It could be that all 6 immigrants will be hired along with 2 natives, or perhaps only 8 natives will be hired, or anywhere in between. Native workers may have an advantage over immigrants, because of proficiency with the language and other local knowledge. On the other hand, an unscrupulous employer might try to exploit immigrants—especially if they lack legal status and hence would be afraid to complain—by paying them less than the minimum wage that would be demanded by native-born workers.

25e. When the minimum wage is binding, native workers will replace immigrants on a one-to-one basis. For example, suppose the 8 available positions were filled by 4 illegal immigrants and 4 native-born workers. Under the 1986 law, the 4 illegal residents could not be hired and so the firm would hire native-born workers for all 8 positions. Note that this relationship holds only when the minimum wage is set above the intersection of demand and the supply of native-born labor. Note that in problem 25 where there was no minimum wage, eliminating the 4 immigrants that were hired would only increase native-born employment by 2. (The cost of determining whether workers are legal residents is an example of a quasi-fixed cost.)

25f. Such an amnesty program could increase the flow of immigrants by raising the potential benefits associated with immigration. Those contemplating illegal entry may be encouraged by the hope that a similar amnesty program would be offered in the future. (Also, once the immigrants become U.S. citizens, immediate family members are eligible to enter the country as well.)

25g. The expansion of welfare eligibility increases the chances that immigration will lead to a reduction in the aggregate income of native-born workers. For the native-born population not to be hurt by immigration, it is necessary that immigrants pay more in taxes than they receive in government assistance.

*26a. Since the 20-year-old will be from group C, the 40-year-old from group B, and the 60-year-old from group C, the cross section will consist of the points (20,10), (40,13), and (60,16). The points are connected by the dashed line labeled E in Figure 10-8. Note that these three points imply that each additional 20 years of experience increases the logarithm of earnings by 3. This translates into a rate of return of 0.15 per year.

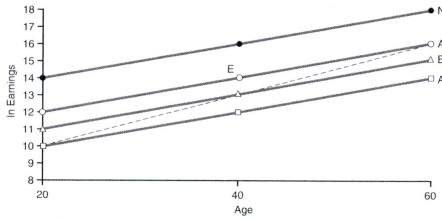

Figure 10-8

*26b. The estimated rate of return will give a misleading impression. Even though the growth rate of immigrant earnings is the same as that of native-born workers (*r* was set at 0.1 for all workers), the cross-section estimate yields a rate of increase of 0.15 for immigrants. Given this steeper estimated age-earnings profile for immigrants, it would be tempting to conclude that immigrants are more productive than native-born workers.

*27a. Since the 20-year-old will be from group C, the 40-year-old from group B, and the 60-year-old from group C, the cross section will consist of the points (20,14), (40,14), and (60,14). The points are connected by the dashed horizontal line labeled *E* in Figure 10-9. Note that these three points imply that additional years of experience do not change immigrant earnings. This translates into a rate of return of zero.

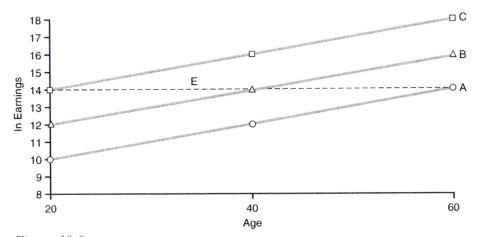

Figure 10-9

*27b. The key to eliminating the bias in the estimated age-earnings profile is to control for quality differences in immigrants over time. It is the omission of this variable that causes the bias. Instead of performing a simple least squares regression with the logarithm of earnings on the left side of the equation and time spent in the country on the right, it is necessary to perform a multiple regression where both time spent in the country and some measure of immigrant ability are included as independent variables. Simple regression would be appropriate only if panel data on immigrant earnings were available. Panel data is collected by following the fate of a particular group of immigrants over time.

*27c. All three biases are examples of the omitted variable problem discussed in the appendix to Chapter 1. The problem of cohort quality change is almost identical to the problem of ability bias discussed in Chapter 9. In each case, ability differences are not controlled for. However, since ability and the remaining explanatory variable (education in Chapter 9, age in Chapter 10) are correlated, the effects of the ability differences are attributed to the other variable, thus biasing the true relationship. Selection bias is also an omitted variable problem that stems from failure to account for hard-to-measure aptitudes and interests for particular occupations. In the same way, the bias resulting from cohort quality change arises in large part because such differences are difficult to observe and measure.

Answers To Chapter 11

■ Review Questions

1. **Answer c.** Although it would be possible for even non-union employers and employees to draw up formal employment contracts that precisely specify the obligations of each party in a way that would be legally enforceable, such agreements would be costly to form and would limit the flexibility of employers in responding to new situations. As a result, most employment contracts take the form of implicit and incomplete understandings. These characteristics, however, also make employment contracts difficult to enforce.

2. **Answer a.** Answers **b** to **d** are the characteristics that create the necessity for self-enforcing contracts.

3. **Answer d.** Employment contracts that are implicit and incomplete can be very vague and difficult to enforce. These problems are compounded when information is asymmetric since the likelihood of being able to successfully cheat on the employment contract increases.

4. **Answer d.** When employment contracts contain precise promises, formal financial penalties may be helpful in ensuring compliance. When contracts are not precise, compliance becomes a matter of contracting with the "right" person. How can you tell the kind of person with whom you are contracting? Information about an individual's characteristics can often be inferred through choices individuals make. For example, in Appendix 9A, it was shown that under certain conditions, different levels of education can serve as reliable signals of individual ability. While that information **might** be acquired through better interviewing and screening of applicants, **b** (and hence **d**) is a better answer.

5. **Answer b.** When the worker's marginal revenue product exceeds the alternative offers, the employment relationship can be said to generate a surplus that is capable of making each party better off—even when it is not divided evenly. It is the fear of losing one's share of the surplus that assures compliance. Firm-specific training is only one example of an investment that generates such a surplus.

6. **Answer d.** While close supervision and pay for performance are not feasible options for all firms, fair treatment is a principle that can be adopted at any firm to help increase productivity.

7. **Answer c.** Although most workers are concerned about their treatment relative to others in the firms, they also place some value on seeing the group as a whole succeed. The more workers are willing to work for group success, the less likely they are to shirk.

8. **Answer d.** Under output-based pay, external factors can have a significant effect on the pay received in any one period. The fluctuations in income, in turn, produce lower average levels of utility if the worker is risk averse. Answer **c** essentially repeats the question.

9. **Answer d.** Output-based pay leads to higher levels of pay because of quality differences between workers, risk-averse preferences, and the productivity increases caused by the pay scheme.

10. **Answer a.**   Firm profits are more stable under an incentive-pay scheme. If workers do not exert their best efforts and output falls, the compensation per worker also falls, helping to lower costs below what they would be under time-based pay. This additional cost reduction would help to offset losses in revenue caused by the lower output.

11. **Answer b.**   Group incentive-pay plans are more likely when it is difficult to measure individual output. When employees work interdependently in teams, it is difficult to decide how much of the group's output is attributable to each member. Answers **a** and **c** would make group incentive pay less likely.

12. **Answer b.**   Stock prices can fluctuate considerably over time due to factors beyond an executive's control. This variability in earnings would be viewed as an undesirable job characteristic by an executive having risk-averse preferences. Note that when executives are employed under these terms, evidence suggests that the stock market performance of the firm is superior to that of other firms. Incentives for managers to emphasize short-run profits tend to be created only when pay is tied to short-run measures of profitability, not to the firm's stock market performance.

13. **Answer c.**   Saying that individual output is highly correlated with individual effort is the same as saying that external factors do not play a significant role in determining output. It is in these situations that merit-pay plans have the most potential for motivating workers. Unfortunately, such situations are relatively rare. While relative rankings of workers help to create a sense of fairness and acceptance for the outcomes, if rankings are subjective and not based on readily identifiable individual performance that can be observed by all, they will typically be very unpopular among those being rated.

14. **Answer d.**   Although it would seem in the firm's interest to set the wage so as to keep as much of the surplus as possible, the higher turnover and reduced motivation that may result can actually lead to increases in the firm's total costs.

15. **Answer a.**   The tendency of workers to undercut rivals and invest time trying to win over supervisors is more a function of how the pay is based rather than the level of pay. Such problems are especially likely when merit-pay raises are based on a supervisor's ranking of a worker's relative performance.

16. **Answer b.**   This is the most specific correct answer. Answers **a** and **d** are really subsets of Answer **b**. The situation in **c** would make an efficiency wage strategy impossible.

17. **Answer d.**   If output were easily measurable, the firm could use an individual incentive-pay plan to increase worker motivation, and paying an efficiency wage would not be necessary. Efficiency wages are most likely when the firm anticipated a long-term attachment with the worker and other ways of increasing effort (e.g., increased supervision) are not feasible.

18. **Answer c.**   Setting the present value of the underpayment equal to the present value of the overpayment yields

$$5 + \frac{5}{1+.06} = \frac{W_2 - 20}{(1+.06)^2} + \frac{10}{(1+.06)^3} \Rightarrow \frac{W_2 - 20}{(1+.06)^2} = 1.32$$

$$\Rightarrow W_2 = (1.32)(1.06)^2 + 20 \Rightarrow W_2 = 21.48.$$

19. **Answer c.** Note that the firm just breaks even over the time period since at the end of period 3, the present value of the total compensation just equals the present value of the marginal product values. If workers continue to be paid more than they contribute, the firm will eventually go out of business. On the other hand, if workers had left before period 3 was complete, the firm would have made positive economic profits.

20. **Answer d.** If the firm develops a reputation for treating the losers poorly, it will not be able to attract enough entrants to make the tournament possible. Also, since the winner will be the one with the best relative performance, some effort may be diverted to undercutting rivals instead of enhancing the interests of the firm. The willingness of the firm to tolerate "deadwood" is one of the factors that make such tournaments possible.

■ Problems

21a. If the owners cooperate, the workers attain a higher level of utility by shirking. If the owners shirk, the workers again attain a higher level of utility by shirking.

21b. If the workers cooperate, the owners attain a higher level of utility by shirking. If the workers shirk, the owners again attain a higher level of utility by shirking.

21c. The employment contract is not self-enforcing since both parties have an incentive to shirk (i.e., not exert their best efforts). Note that when both parties shirk, however, they each end up with a lower level of utility than if they both cooperated.

21d. Knowing that the other party plans to shirk does not change the outcome. Each party perceives it to be in their self-interest to shirk regardless of the decision made by the other.

21e. Note that the payoffs from cooperation have all been increased, while the payoffs from shirking have all been reduced. Perhaps this occurred because each party developed a sense of loyalty to the group, and so feels bad when cheating on the employment contract.

21f. The employment contract is now self-enforcing. Regardless of the choice made by the owners, workers attain a higher level of utility by cooperating. Similarly, regardless of the choice made by workers, owners attain a higher level of utility by cooperating.

*22a. To make the compensation per worker (Y) under the profit sharing scheme equal to what the workers can attain elsewhere, the guaranteed wage and the profit sharing parameter must be set such that Y in long-run equilibrium equals the market clearing wage of $9. Substituting the appropriate values into the expression for Y yields

$$Y = 7 + \frac{1}{11} \frac{(38)(20) - (7)(20) - (9)(20)}{20}$$

$$\Rightarrow Y = 7 + \frac{1}{11} \frac{440}{20} = 7 + \frac{1}{11} 22 = 9.$$

*22b. Since the compensation per worker will be more variable under profit sharing, risk-averse workers will prefer a time-based wage. They will require a compensating differential to work at firms offering profit sharing. In other words, W_g and s must be set in such a way that they yield a compensation per worker slightly above $9.

*22c. Substituting the long-run equilibrium values into the marginal revenue and marginal product expressions yields

$$MR = 58 - 2(20) = 18,$$

$$MP_L = \frac{1}{2}\sqrt{\frac{20}{20}} = \frac{1}{2}.$$

Substituting these values into the marginal expense of labor expression yields

$$ME_L = 7 + \frac{1}{11}[(18)(.05) - 7] = 7.18.$$

*22d. Since $MRP_L = 9 > 7.18 = ME_L$, the firm has an incentive to increase employment.

*22e. Substituting $L = 21$, $K = 20$ into the production function yields

$$Q = \sqrt{21}\sqrt{20} = 20.494$$
$$\Rightarrow P = 58 - 20.494 = 37.506.$$

*22f. Substituting into the profit pool expression yields

$$\pi = (37.506)(20.494) - (7)(21) - (9)(20)$$
$$\Rightarrow \pi = 768.648 - 147 - 180 = 441.648.$$

*22g. Compensation per worker (Y) falls from 9 to

$$Y = 7 + \frac{1}{11}\frac{441.648}{21} = 7 + 1.912$$
$$\Rightarrow Y = 8.912.$$

Since the compensation per worker is less than what workers can attain elsewhere, the firm would not be able to retain 21 workers.

*22h. Although profit sharing will not lead to a higher level of employment in this example, it should lead to a more stable employment relationship because a gap exists between what the marginal worker contributes to the firm ($9) and what the marginal worker costs the firm ($7.18). If the MRP_L falls because of a decline in the demand for the product, but stays above $7.18, the firm does not have an incentive to lay off workers. Although workers do not have any incentive to quit the firm, the firm does not really have any protection against quits since the compensation per worker is just comparable to what workers can attain elsewhere (plus a compensating differential if workers are risk averse).

23a. At a wage of $50, 9 workers would be needed to produce 36 units of output since each worker only produces 4. Total labor costs will be ($50)(9) = $450. At a wage of $100, only 4 workers will be needed since each worker produces 9. As a result, total labor costs fall to $400. Since total revenue should be the same in each case, paying the higher wage will actually increase profits.

23b. This move would be consistent with an efficiency wage strategy. Whether $100 could actually be considered the efficiency wage depends on whether further increases in the wage continue to increase profits. If they do, then $100 is not the efficiency wage.

24a. Setting the present value of the underpayment equal to the present value of the overpayment yields

$$3 + \frac{2}{1.06} + \frac{1}{(1.06)^2} = \frac{W_4 - 16}{(1.06)^4}$$

$$\Rightarrow \frac{W_4 - 16}{(1 + .06)^4} = 5.78$$

$$\Rightarrow W_4 = (5.78)(1.06)^4 + 16$$

$$\Rightarrow W_4 = 23.29.$$

Given this value of W_4, note that both the marginal product and wage schedules yield identical present values of 52.27 even though the marginal product values sum to 60 and the wage values sum to 61.29. The underpayment (6) must be less than the overpayment (7.29) to compensate workers for the time value of money.

24b. A necessary condition for such a deferred payment scheme is a long-term relationship between workers and the firm. Internal labor market strategies promote long-term attachments by filling upper-level positions with workers from within the firm.

24c. A deferred payment scheme is thought to increase productivity for two reasons. The first is that such a scheme will appeal mainly to those types of workers who anticipate staying with the firm and working hard enough to avoid being fired before the deferred compensation is completely recovered. Thus such a scheme may be a way for a firm to attract workers with above average commitment and motivation. The second reason is that such a scheme provides an incentive for all employees to work hard since the penalty for shirking and being fired can be very large. Knowing that workers have less incentive to shirk, the firm can devote fewer resources to supervision.

24d. The prohibition of mandatory retirement means that the firm cannot prohibit workers from staying past period 4. In this example, workers who stay past period 4 will receive a deferred payment that exceeds, in present value terms, the earlier underpayment (assuming the firm cannot lower the wage to older workers). This means that firm will not be able to earn even a normal profit.

■ Applications

25a. Under such a "piece-rate" scheme, doctors have an incentive to see many patients quickly. The fear is that doctors provided with this type of incentive may not provide quality care to all patients, particularly those who need a great deal of attention.

25b. A flat fee system may help to keep costs down by taking away the incentive to provide excessive treatment.

25c. The fee must be set in such a way that it provides long-run compensation consistent with what the doctors can earn elsewhere. If the compensation elsewhere involves more certainty, a compensating differential will also be required to make the more variable income stream yield the same level of utility as the certain one.

25d. The advantage of such an incentive-pay plan is that it should make doctors more accountable to their patients, provide an incentive for them to keep careful records, and give those who work hard a chance to get ahead. Such plans also tend to appeal to those who have above-average ability and motivation. On the other hand, the plans may cause doctors to focus excessively on the aspects of the doctor-patient relationship asked about in the questionnaire. Also, the systems may be perceived as unfair since often patients are not in a position to understand the quality of the care they are receiving. Differences in pay can also cause resentment because of concern about relative standing. The questions used in measuring quality should ultimately be things that are under the doctor's control and not influenced by external factors. Also, the questions should relate to qualities that further the organization's overall objectives (e.g., providing quality care at a reasonable cost).

25e. The incentive-pay plans should work better with those who have private practices. Since the doctors do not interact with one another, differences in pay will not generate resentment due to concern about relative standing or status.

25f. To the extent that performance ratings are influenced by external factors, merit-pay plans may create little incentive for the doctors to exert extra effort. If the performance ratings are based on relative success, doctors may be less cooperative with one another and divert extra effort into ingratiating themselves with their supervisors.

25g. If measures of individual output cannot be constructed, it may make sense to base a portion of an individual's pay on the group success. Since most HMOs are non-profit organizations, however, some measure of success other than profits must be used. For example, the extent to which the organization can keep costs down may be an alternative measure. Such group incentives may be relatively ineffective, however, if the efforts of the typical doctor have little influence on the attainment of the goal. In those situations, individuals have an incentive to free ride on the efforts of others.

25h. While time-based pay is preferred by workers with risk-averse preferences, it provides little incentive for individuals to exert their best efforts and so may require increased supervision.

26a. The idea behind an efficiency wage strategy is that if workers are receiving more than they can earn elsewhere, they will avoid shirking so as to reduce the risk of being fired and losing the surplus they are accumulating. If a worker is planning on leaving the job anyway, the fear of being fired is not an effective deterrent to shirking. Also, workers with broader career concerns are less likely to shirk since being fired may affect opportunities at other firms. If workers are not likely to shirk, there is little reason to pay an efficiency wage.

26b. The argument that large firms are more likely to pay efficiency wages stems from the fact that large firms present employees with a wide variety of job options and so there is likely to be a longer-term attachment between employer and employee. Such long-term attachments increase the likelihood of efficiency wages. The highly interdependent production processes at large firms also require that firms take steps to stop shirking. To the extent that monitoring worker effort is more costly at a large firm, efficiency wages may be an effective alternative to motivate workers to exert their best efforts.

27. Layoff policies that do not protect those with longer job tenures inhibit the use of deferred payment schemes. Workers will not be willing to be paid less than their marginal product early in their career if they are likely to be laid off during the period when they are receiving the deferred payment.

Answers To Chapter 12

■ Review Questions

1. **Answer b.** Although Answer **a** is a true statement, the wage gap could be the result of differences in productive characteristics (premarket differences). Labor market discrimination focuses on differences in labor market payoffs to productive characteristics. Answer **c** is also a true statement but such segregation could be voluntary (i.e., represent premarket choices).

2. **Answer d.** Differences in any of the factors might justify differing wages between male and female employees.

3. **Answer a.** Holding occupation constant takes away its affect on wages, making it impossible to see the impact that restricting employment opportunities has on women's relative wages.

4. **Answer b.** Note that some of these differences may not be measurable or observable, making it impossible to hold them constant. Also, the current values of these productive characteristics may have been influenced by past discrimination. Answer **d** describes the goal in measuring wage discrimination.

5. **Answer a.** The observed wages are represented by Points *a* and *b*.

6. **Answer b.** Since some current labor market discrimination may take the form of occupational segregation, it is important not to control the occupation. Given the occupational differences, women would earn $10 (point *d*) if they had the same experience as men. That leaves a gap between men's and women's wages of $10 (the difference between points *b* and *d*).

7. **Answer c.** When measuring wage discrimination, all premarket factors, including occupation, must be held constant. This leaves the gap between points *b* and *c* ($6) unexplained.

8. **Answer d.** Assuming women's employment options are limited to the low-paying sector because of discrimination, this leads to a reduction in wages of $4, even if women had the same experience as men. Occupational segregation can be represented by the gap between points *c* and *d*.

9. **Answer d.** Note that if women experienced wage discrimination in the past, some of the premarket differences could be attributable to discrimination. Hence, holding them constant would understate the effect of discrimination on wages.

10. **Answer c.**

$$S = \tfrac{1}{2}\,(\,|\,75 - 10\,| + |\,25 - 90\,|\,) = 65.$$

11. **Answer d.** Prejudiced employers will act as if the marginal product of blacks has been shifted down. If black and white wages are equal this will lead to a reduction in employment for blacks. If blacks and whites are hired in the same numbers, blacks will be paid less since their marginal product will be subjectively devalued.

12. **Answer a.** If the employer's prejudice causes a reduction in employment, this reduces the area under the marginal product curve. Recall that this area represents output (real income) to the firm. If the firm reduces wages paid to blacks instead of black employment, note that the lower wage would lead a nondiscriminating firm to an even higher employment and output level. See **Problem 26** for numerical examples of these points.

13. **Answer d.** By segregating blacks away from customer contact positions, the firm can avoid losing prejudiced customers. On the other hand, allowing blacks in such positions may be worth it if they are more qualified, and hence more productive, than whites. This higher productivity presumably makes up for the lost customers. Since self-employment takes away the possibility of employment prejudice, an earnings gap between equally productive black and white entrepreneurs points to customer prejudice.

14. **Answer d.** Prejudiced white employees would have to be paid a compensating differential to work in an integrated group. This creates a window of opportunity for a firm to lower costs and increase profits by substituting less expensive black workers for whites.

15. **Answer c.** Firms use statistical discrimination as a way to identify the most productive workers while avoiding the cost associated with a careful investigation of each worker. The more diverse a group becomes in their productive characteristics, the less reliable is group affiliation as an indicator of productivity. Statistical discrimination does not stem from prejudice or monopoly power.

16. **Answer b.** The notion of noncompeting groups is a plausible one if firms exercise monopsony power over women and minorities. The problem is that theories do not give any reason for the lack of competition. The theories fit the facts, but are based on assumptions and premises that seem difficult to support.

17. **Answer b.** Firms do not necessarily create prejudice in the monopoly power models, but they are assumed to profit from its existence. However, such scenarios are unlikely to persist since there will be strong incentives for individual firms to cheat on the agreement.

18. **Answer c.** Disparate treatment occurs if individual workers are intentionally treated differently with respect to wages and employment opportunities because of the demographic group to which they belong.

19. **Answer d.** Although word-of-mouth recruiting may not intentionally disadvantage any group, it can have a disparate impact over time since it can carry forward the effects of past discrimination. The same is true of seniority systems, but such systems are explicitly allowed under Title VII.

20. **Answer c.** One shortcoming of standards used in calculating the pool of available applicants is the interest people in the targeted groups have in working at the firm. Because of commuting distance or the mix of compensation offered at a particular firm, all workers in a particular area may not be equally interested in working for the firm. By ignoring worker interest, affirmative action goals may be set beyond the firm's immediate reach.

21. **Answer d.** Comparable worth pay systems attempt to make pay a function of the job that is performed, rather than a function of a worker's personal characteristics.

22. **Answer b.** A job score of 100 would lead to $1,500 in earnings for a man. A salary of $1,200 represents only 80% of what a man earns. Therefore, the women's pay represents a 20% comparable worth earnings gap.

■ Problems

23a. Substituting the appropriate values into the wage formulas yields

$$W_M = 3 + 0.5(4) + 0.6(10) + 1 = 12,$$

$$W_F = 3 + 0.4(3) + 0.5(6) = 7.2$$

$$\Rightarrow \frac{W_F}{W_M} = \frac{7.2}{12} = 0.6 \Rightarrow 40\% \text{ earnings gap}$$

23b. Substituting $ED = 4$, EXP = 10, and $OC = 1$ into the women's wage equation yields

$$W_F = 3 + 0.4(4) + 0.5(10) + 1 = 10.6$$

$$\Rightarrow \frac{W_F}{W_M} = \frac{10.6}{12} = 0.883$$

23c. After controlling for all premarket characteristics, women still earn 11.7% less.

23d. Substituting $ED = 4$, EXP = 10 into the women's wage equation yields

$$W_F = 3 + 0.4(4) + 0.5(10) = 9.6 \Rightarrow \frac{W_F}{W_M} = \frac{9.6}{12} = 0.8$$

23e. After adjusting for all productive characteristics except occupation, women earn 20% less than men in this example. This gap can be attributed to current labor market discrimination because it reflects different employment opportunities and different labor market payoffs to the various productive characteristics. The occupational segregation costs women an extra $1 in wages and so widens the wage gap by 8.3%.

23f. If the premarket differences in education or experience are the result of past discrimination, the estimate of current labor market discrimination understates the influence of discrimination on labor market outcomes. On the other hand, if unmeasurable or unobservable differences exist in the productive characteristics of men and women, the estimate of current labor market discrimination overstates the problem.

23g. Substituting $ED = 3$, EXP = 6, and $OC = 0$ into the men's wage equation yields

$$W_M = 3 + 0.5(3) + 0.6(6) = 8.1 \Rightarrow \frac{W_F}{W_M} = \frac{7.2}{8.1} = 0.89$$

This approach yields a slightly smaller discriminatory wage gap (11%) than in **23c**.

23h. Half of the women would earn 7.2, while half would earn 8.2, for an average wage of 7.7. Similarly, half of the men would earn 12, while half would earn 11, for an average wage of 11.5. This change in the occupational distribution increases the relative wage of women from 0.6 to 0.67 (7.7/11.5).

24a. See Table 12-3. The number in each occupation can be found by multiplying the percentage male or female (expressed as a fraction) by the total employment.

Table 12-3

Occupation	#Male	#Female	Total
A	10	40	50
B	20	30	50
C	40	10	50
D	30	20	50
	100	100	200

24b. The percentage of the total male or female workers in each occupation can be found by dividing the number of males or females in each occupation by the total male or female population. In this example, the total population is 100 for each sex. The results are presented in Table 12-4. The last column computes the absolute value of the difference between the total male and female percentages in each occupation.

Table 12-4

Occupation	% Male	% Female	| % M-% F |
A	10%	40%	30
B	20%	20%	10
C	40%	10%	30
D	30%	20%	10
			80

24c. The index of dissimilarity is 40.

$$S = \tfrac{1}{2}\,(30 + 10 + 30 + 10) = 40.$$

This indicates that 40% of the women (or men) would have to change occupation in order to make the occupational distribution of women the same as men. For example, 30% of the women would have to move from A to C, and 10% of the women would have to move from B to D. The main point of this exercise was to show that the index of dissimilarity is computed using the percentage of the total male and female population in each occupation, not the percentage of each occupation that is male and female.

25. Substituting $ER = 0.608$ and $LFPR = 0.776$ into the employment rate expression yields

$$0.614 = 0.776(1 - UR) \Rightarrow UR = 0.209 \quad \text{or} \quad 20.9\%.$$

26a. Profit maximization occurs at that level of employment where the marginal product of labor equals the real wage

$$W = MP_1 \Rightarrow 15 = 25 - 0.5L$$

$$\Rightarrow L^* = 20 \text{ for each group.}$$

This equilibrium is shown as point c in Figure 12-4.

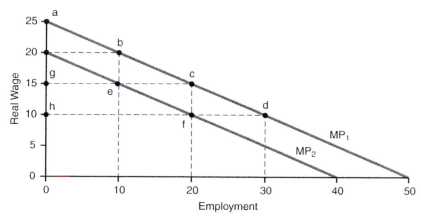

Figure 12-4

Ignoring the cost of capital, profit is represented by the area under the marginal product curve and above the wage line. Thus the employment of 20 blacks results in a profit (π) denoted by the area of triangle acg. This area has a value of

$$\pi = \frac{1}{2}(20)(10) = 100.$$

*26b. A prejudiced employer acts as if the marginal product of blacks is 5 units less than whites at any given employment level.

$$W = MP_1 \Rightarrow 15 = 25 - 0.5L - 5$$

$$\Rightarrow L^* = 10 \text{ for blacks.}$$

The new employment of blacks is represented by point e. White employment remains at 20. Profit from black employment is now given by the area of trapezoid $abeg$, which has an area of

$$\pi = \frac{1}{2}(10)(5) = (10)(5) = 75.$$

*26c. To keep black employment at 20 requires that the wage fall to

$$W = MP_1 \Rightarrow W = 25 - 0.5(20) - 5 \Rightarrow W^* = 10 \text{ for blacks.}$$

This equilibrium is denoted by point f. Profit from black employment is now given by the area of the trapezoid $acfh$ which has an area of

$$\pi = \frac{1}{2}(20)(10) + (20)(5) = 200.$$

*26d. At $W = 10$, an unprejudiced employer would hire blacks up to the point where

$$W = MP_1 \Rightarrow 10 = 25 - 0.5L \Rightarrow L^* = 30 \text{ for blacks.}$$

This equilibrium is represented by point d. Profit from back employment is now given by the area of the triangle adh which has an area of

$$\pi = \frac{1}{2}(30)(15) = 225.$$

Therefore, whether the prejudiced employer adjusts wages or employment, the prejudiced employer can always earn a higher profit.

27a. The market-clearing relative wage will be 0.5 and 10,000 women will be employed. This equilibrium is represented by point d in Figure 12-5.

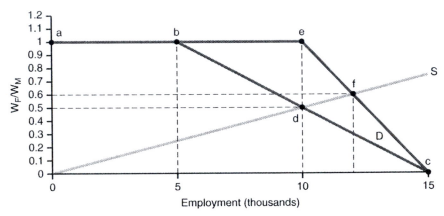

Figure 12-5

27b. The increase in the number of non-discriminating employers together with the worsening of discriminatory preferences creates the new market demand curve shown as line aec in Figure 12-5. This new demand curve leads to an increase in the relative wage and an increase in employment. The new equilibrium is point f.

28a. A job score of 600 would lead to $50,000 in earnings from a man. Therefore, the women's salary reflects a $10,000 comparable worth earnings gap.

28b. A salary of $40,000 represents only 80% of what a man earns. Therefore, the woman's salary represents a 20% comparable worth earnings gap.

■ Applications

29. Demographic groups that earn more than the U.S. average may still experience discrimination. Recall that wages can be thought of as a function of an individual's personal productive characteristics and the payoff that each characteristic brings in the labor market. Even though the payoffs may be reduced because of the group an individual belongs to, if the person has highly productive characteristics, the wage that is actually received may still be well above average. To measure the discrimination, one could estimate what Russians would earn if they had the same productive characteristics as native-born white Americans. If the estimate reveals Russians would earn less, this would be evidence supporting the hypothesis of discrimination.

30a. Substituting the appropriate values into the wage formulas yields

$$W_M = 8 = 0.75(12) + 2(1) = 20,$$
$$W_F = 8 + 0.5(8) = 12$$
$$\Rightarrow \frac{W_F}{W_M} = \frac{12}{20} = 0.6 \Rightarrow 14\% \text{ earnings gap.}$$

30b. Substituting EXP = 12, OC = 1, and Z = 1 into the women's wage equation yields

$$W_F = 8 + 0.5(12) + 2(1) = 17 \Rightarrow \frac{W_F}{W_M} = \frac{17}{20} = 0.85$$

30c. After controlling for all premarket characteristics, women earn 15% less than men.

30d. After Substituting EXP = 12, and OC = 1 into the women's wage equation yields

$$W_F = 8 + 0.5(12) + 2(1) = 16$$
$$\Rightarrow \frac{W_F}{W_M} = \frac{16}{20} = 0.8.$$

30e. After controlling for all pre-market characteristics except attitude, women appearing to be experiencing a 20% discriminatory earnings gap.

31a. Profit maximization requires that firms pay a real wage equal to the marginal product of labor in each sector

$$\Rightarrow W_a = 40, W_b = 70 = W_c.$$

31b. Total output = 390 + 240 + 240 = 870.

31c. The real wage would equal 60 in each sector.

31d. Total output = 3(300) = 900. the new distribution of labor is optimal since the marginal product of labor is equal across the sectors. This means that there is no way to reallocate labor and get a higher output.

32a. A 20% turnover rate in a firm with 1,000 employees means that the firm must replace 200 workers annually. If 20% of the new hires are black, the firm will be hiring 40 blacks annually. Provided the turnover rate applies equally across all demographic groups in the firm, 20% of the 100 black workers will leave the firm for a total loss of 20 black workers.

32b. If 20 blacks leave the firm during the first year and 40 are hired, there will be a net gain of 20. Therefore, at the end of year 1, there will be 120 black workers. This represents 12% of total employment, up from 10% at the start of the year.

32c. The computations in Table 12-5 show that 16.7% of total employment will be black after 5 years of affirmative action.

Table 12-5

	Year				
	1	**2**	**3**	**4**	**5**
#					
Loss	20	24	27	30	40
New Hires	40	40	40	40	40
Net Gain	20	16	13	10	8
Total	120	136	149	159	167
Percent Black	12	13.6	14.9	15.9	16.7

32d. An increase in turnover would reduce the number of years needed to achieve the goal. For example, if the turnover rate increased from 20% to 30%, 300 new workers would be hired in year 1, 60 of whom would be black. At the same time, 30 blacks would leave the firm in year 1, for a net gain of 30. When the turnover was 20%, the net gain in year 1 was only 20 black workers.

Answers To Chapter 13

■ Review Questions

1. **Answer c.** Note that bargaining often takes place simultaneously with a number of employers. The AFL-CIO is largely a political action group. It is not involved directly in the collective bargaining process.

2. **Answer c.** It is perfectly legal for employers to explain to employees why joining a union is not in their best interest, but they cannot threaten or discriminate against those that do.

3. **Answer a.** The replacement of striking workers (**b**) is legal. Answers **c** and **d** are examples of unfair labor practices.

4. **Answer a.** Workers with short job tenures are less likely to join unions since many of the things unions bargain for (seniority rules, job security arrangements, pensions) are of little benefit to someone who does not expect to stay with the firm.

5. **Answer b.** Increased employer resistance raises the cost of union organizing activity and shifts the supply curve to the left.

6. **Answer a.** Although the Reagan administration's replacement of striking air traffic controllers is often cited as an action of the federal government that contributed to the decline of unions, this action was taken under existing federal law and did not represent new legislation against unions. Growing female participation in the labor force was probably more of a factor in the first half of this period than it has been in the second half.

7. **Answer c.** Every point on the demand curve is a point of profit maximization. To stay at the same profit level as one moves to alternate levels of employment, wages must fall to keep profits at the specified level. Note that profits fall as the firm is forced up its labor demand curve by higher union wages.

8. **Answer c.** If it is possible to make someone better off without hurting anyone else, then it makes sense to move away from the current combination. An efficient contract has been reached only when these kinds of moves are no longer possible. Note that the firm's profits serve as a constraint on the union's ability to maximize utility.

9. **Answer d.** A rapidly growing product demand should translate into a growing demand for labor that can be used to mask the adverse employment effects of union wage increases. An inelastic supply of substitute inputs reduces the incentive of a firm to substitute other inputs for labor. Note that a highly elastic product demand leads to a more elastic labor demand.

10. **Answer d.** According to the Hicks-Marshall laws presented in Chapter 4, all of these factors should lead to a more elastic labor demand.

11. **Answer d.** All of these factors limit the firm's ability to substitute other inputs for union labor and so make the demand for labor more inelastic.

12. **Answer c.** Occupational licensing laws restrict entry into a profession and so limit a firm's ability to find substitutes for union labor.

13. **Answer d.** The Hicks bargaining model predicts that settlements will be made in advance when both parties are aware of how the other's bargaining position will change over time and that the union is not using the strike to strategically enhance its bargaining power in future negotiations. See Figure 13.6 in the text for an example of a union resistance curve that is not always downward sloping.

14. **Answer d.** Note that wait unemployment can cause the relative wage advantage to understate or overstate the absolute union wage effect.

15. **Answer c.** Expected earnings in each sector are equal when

$$W_U F_U = W_N F_N$$

$$\Rightarrow F_U = \frac{W_N}{W_U} F_N \Rightarrow F_U = \frac{1}{1.25}(1) = 0.8.$$

16. **Answer d.** All factors that can influence wages must be held constant before the relative union wage advantage can be identified.

17. **Answer d.** Limits on the substitution of capital for labor mean that the firm may not be able to produce using the most efficient combination of inputs. Note that empirical evidence associates unions with lower quit rates, which would likely increase productivity.

18. **Answer b.** If unions allow workers to communicate more effectively with management, workers may be able to resolve problems without quitting. Lower quit rates lead to longer job tenures.

19. **Answer a.** Person A should voluntarily accept only those shares that yield a higher level of utility than the level that is expected to result from arbitration. Note that if the person is risk averse, the expected, or average, utility from arbitration will be less than the utility level associated with the average arbitration settlement.

20. **Answer a.** The contract zone, like the contract curve in the efficient contract model, is where the parties should move in order to make themselves better off.

21. **Answer d.** Increasing the arbitrator's range of possible outcomes and/or increasing the curvature of the utility function lowers the average utility associated with the arbitrated outcome. The lower the average utility associated with the arbitrated outcome, the lower the share that will be needed from a voluntary settlement to make any individual better off.

■ Problems

22a. Substituting $W = \$10$ into the original demand yields an employment level of 80. Substituting $W = \$15$ into the new demand equations yields an employment level of 90.

22b. If the wage had remained at $10, the demand shift would have increased employment to 100. Alternatively, one could argue that without the demand shift, the increase in the wage would have reduced employment to 70. Either approach suggests that the union wage increase reduced employment by 10 relative to what it could have been.

23a. See Figure 13-3.

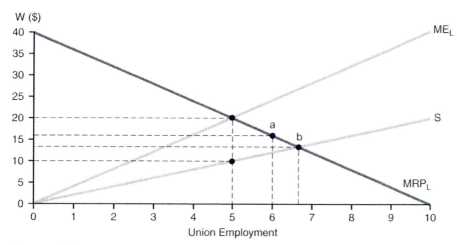

Figure 13-3

23b. Profit maximization occurs at the employment level where $MRP_L = ME_L$.

$$\Rightarrow 40 - 4L = 4L \Rightarrow L^* = 5.$$
$$L^* = 5 \Rightarrow W^* = 2(5) = 10.$$

23c. The firm now faces a fixed ME_L of $16 and so profit maximization occurs where

$$40 - 4L = 16 \Rightarrow L^* = 6.$$

See point *a* in Figure 13-3. In this case, the higher wage is associated with a higher employment level.

23d. Employment is maximized at the point where the labor supply curve intersects the MRP_L curve. See point *b* in Figure 13-3.

$$40 - 4L = 2L \Rightarrow L^* = 6.67.$$
$$L^* = 6.67 \Rightarrow W^* = 2(6.67) = 13.33.$$

24a. For a firm that sells its output in a perfectly competitive market

$$MRP_L = (P)(MP_L)$$
$$\Rightarrow MRP_L = 5(10 - L) = 50 - 5L.$$

This curve appears as the line labeled *D* in Figure 13-2 in the **Applications** section.

24b. Profit maximization $\Rightarrow$ MRP$_L = W$

$$\Rightarrow 50 - 5L = 15 \Rightarrow L^* = 7.$$

See point *a* in Figure 13-2.

$$L^* = 7 \Rightarrow Q^* = (10)(7) - (0.5)(49) = 45.5.$$

24c. $\pi = PQ - WL \Rightarrow \pi = (5)(45.5) - (15)(7) = \$122.5.$

*24d. To find the isoprofit curve expression, find those combinations of W and L that yield a profit level of $122.50. Substituting the production function and the price of output into the profit expression yields

$$122.5 = (5)(10L - 0.5L^2) - WL \Rightarrow 122.5 = 50L - 2.5L^2 - WL$$

$$\Rightarrow WL = 50L - 2.5L^2 - 122.5$$

$$\Rightarrow W = 5 - 2.5L - \frac{122.5}{L}.$$

*24e. See the isoprofit curve labeled I_3 in Figure 13-2.

24f. Profit maximization $\Rightarrow$ MRP$_L = W \Rightarrow 50 - 5L = 30 \Rightarrow L^* = 4.$

See point *b* in Figure 13-2.

$$L^* = 4 \Rightarrow Q^* = (10)(4) - (.5)(16) = 32.$$
$$\pi = PQ - WL$$
$$\Rightarrow \pi = (5)(32) - (30)(4) = \$40.$$

25a. Equilibrium in the union sector

$$\Rightarrow 30 - 0.5W = W \Rightarrow W^* = 20.$$
$$W^* = 20 \Rightarrow L^* = 20.$$

Equilibrium in the non-union sector

$$\Rightarrow 60 - 2W = W \Rightarrow W^* = 20.$$
$$W^* = 20 \Rightarrow L^* = 20.$$

25b. An increase in the union wage from $20 to $22 represents an absolute wage effect of 10%. Note that the increase in the union wage reduces the quantity of union labor demanded to

$$L_U^D = 30 - 0.5(22) = 19,$$

while the quantity of labor supplied increases to

$$L_U^S = 22.$$

Together this creates a labor surplus in the union sector of 3 units.

25c. The new supply curve in the union sector becomes

$$L_U^S = W - 3,$$

while the supply curve in the non-union sector becomes

$$L_N^S = W + 3.$$

The supply shift in the union sector is just enough to eliminate the unemployment in that sector. The increase in supply in the non-union sector creates a surplus in that sector at the original wage of $20. However, since the wage is free to adjust in the non-union sector, the market will clear where

$$60 - 2W = W + 3$$
$$\Rightarrow W_N^* = \$19 \quad \text{and} \quad L_N^* = 22.$$

Note that after the spillover adjustment is complete, the union wage ($22) exceeds the non-union wage ($19) by $3 for a relative wage advantage of 15.8%.

25d. Since there is no unemployment in either sector after the spillover, expected earnings equal $22 in the union sector and $19 in the non-union sector. This should lead to a movement of some workers back to the union sector.

25e. The unemployment rate in the union sector will be

$$UR = \frac{2}{2+9} = 0.095$$

$$\Rightarrow F_U = 1 - 0.095 = 0.905$$

$$\Rightarrow W_U F_U = (22)(0.905) = \$19.9.$$

In the non-union sector, the market will clear where

$$60 - 2W = W + 1$$
$$\Rightarrow W_N^* = \$19.67 \quad \text{and} \quad L_N^* = 20.67.$$

Since there is no unemployment in the non-union sector, expected earnings equal $19.67. Wait unemployment is rational here since workers should continue to flow back to the non-union sector as long as expected earnings there are greater than in the non-union sector.

25f. The unemployment rate in the union sector will be

$$UR = \frac{3}{3+19} = 0.136$$

$$\Rightarrow F_U = 1 - 0.136 = 0.864$$

$$\Rightarrow W_U F_U = (22)(0.864) = \$19.$$

In the non-union sector, the market will clear at the original wage and employment levels

$$\Rightarrow W_N^* = \$20 \quad \text{and} \quad L_N^* = 20.$$

Since there is no unemployment in the non-union sector, expected earnings equal $20. This suggests that the optimal amount of wait unemployment in this example is under 3 workers. As a result the wage in the non-union sector will be less than $20. If the non-union wage is less than $20, then the relative union wage advantage will overstate the absolute wage effect of the union.

26a. Equilibrium in the union sector

$$\Rightarrow 24 - 0.5W = 1.5W \Rightarrow W^* = 12.$$
$$W^* = 12 \Rightarrow L^* = 18.$$

Note that in this example the demand shift does not raise the wage but it does eliminate the excess supply associated with the union wage.

26b. Equilibrium in the non-union sector

$$\Rightarrow 36 - 2W = 2W \Rightarrow W^* = 9.$$
$$W^* = 9 \Rightarrow L^* = 18.$$

In the non-union sector, the demand decrease lowers the wage from \$10 to \$9 and decreases employment from 20 to 18.

26c. Ignoring any wait unemployment effects, the relative wage advantage of 33% overstates the absolute union wage effect of 20%.

27a. $S_A = 0.5 \Rightarrow U_A = \sqrt{0.5} = 0.707.$

27b. $S_A = 0.25 \Rightarrow U_A = \sqrt{2.5} = 0.5.$

$S_A = 0.75 \Rightarrow U_A = \sqrt{.75} = 0.866.$

27c. Expected utility from arbitration is

$$\frac{1}{2}(0.5) + \frac{1}{2}(0.866) = 0.683$$

Since receiving a share of 0.5 with certainty yields a higher level of utility (0.707) than receiving a share of 0.5 on average (0.683), the person exhibits risk-averse preferences.

27d. $\sqrt{S_A} = 0.683 \Rightarrow S_A = 0.47.$

A share of 0.47 received with certainty yields the same level of utility that can be expected from arbitration.

27e. Since the shares must add to one, the maximum share B could receive is 0.53.

27f. Since B has the same preferences as A, the minimum share B would accept is 0.47 and the maximum A could receive is 0.53.

27g. The contract zone consists of those shares between 0.47 and 0.53.

27h. $S_A = \dfrac{1}{3} \Rightarrow U_A = \sqrt{\dfrac{1}{3}} = 0.577,$ and $S_A = \dfrac{2}{3} \Rightarrow U_A = \sqrt{\dfrac{2}{3}} = 0.816.$

Expected utility from arbitration is

$$\frac{1}{2}(0.577) + \frac{1}{2}(0.816) = 0.697.$$

$$\sqrt{S_A} = 0.697 \Rightarrow S_A = 0.486$$

The contract zone consists of those shares between 0.486 and 0.514. Notice that a smaller spread between the arbitrator's settlements reduces the contract zone. Assuming the size of the contract zone is directly related to the probability of a voluntary settlement, the chances for a voluntary settlement have been reduced.

■ Applications

28. This paradox can be resolved by noting that wages are only a part of total compensation. Evidence suggests that public sector unions have had a larger effect on employee benefits than on wages since employee benefits are not as readily observed and their full costs can often be deferred. As a result, is not clear that public sector unions have had a smaller effect on the total compensation of their members.

29a. Point b is not efficient since it is possible to make one party better off without hurting the other. For example, by moving to point c, the union is better off and the firm is still at the same profit level. On the other hand, moving to point d increases firm profits while leaving the union at the same level of utility.

29b. Each point along the line cd is a point of tangency between a union indifference curve and a firm isoprofit curve. However, the outcomes are not necessarily equitable. Points closer to c are better for the union and worse for the firm, while points closer to d are better for the firm and worse for the union. Regardless of which party gains the most, all the points along cd are better than point b.

29c. While there may be few explicit agreements on employment, Chapter 11 pointed out that provisions of an employment contract are often implicit.

30a. In the asymmetric information model, union leaders, through their involvement with management during the bargaining process, may become well informed about the firm's true financial position and the maximum wage offer the firm can make. If this offer is less than what the membership expects, union leaders may recommend a strike even though they know it will not change the firm's wage offer. Such a strike will gradually serve to moderate the members' wage demands while at the same time allowing the union leaders to appear to be strong and decisive leaders.

30b. Perhaps the firm would have been more receptive to productivity bargaining. Under this type of bargaining, the union and employer explicitly agree to certain increases in compensation contingent on work rule changes and productivity increases.

31a. Workers will be demanded up to the point where the real wage equals the marginal product of labor. Therefore, a real wage of 25 translates into an employment of 6 workers in each sector. Output in each sector will be 225 for a total output of 450.

31b. A wage increase to 35 in the union sector should reduce employment to 4 and output to 170.

31c. An employment of 8 in the non-union sector should drive the wage down to 15 and increase output to 260.

31d. Total output after the labor spillover is 430 compared to 450 before the union wage increase. The allocation of labor is not optimal since the marginal product of labor is higher in the union sector than in the non-union sector.

31e. Assuming no spillovers, output would be 170 in the union sector and 225 in the non-union sector for a total output of 395. This represents a decline of 55 units from the original level.

31f. A collective voice is necessary since many improvements in the workplace can be likened to public goods. A public good is something that no one can be excluded from once it is provided. A good example is national defense. If workplace changes are like public goods, individuals may not come forward to bring about change, reasoning that if they wait for someone else to come forward, they will share in the benefits without bearing the costs. Individuals may also not come forward out of fear of retaliation by the firm.

Answers To Chapter 14

■ Review Questions

1. **Answer a.**

$$u = \frac{U}{U+E} = \frac{15}{15+135} = 0.10.$$

2. **Answer a.** The degree of economic hardship is clearly influenced by the percentage of the population that is employed, and yet the unemployment rate does not provide a reliable guide to how the employment rate is changing. If the labor force participation rate is growing fast enough, the employment rate will rise even if the unemployment rate is rising.

3. **Answer c.** The proportions can also be viewed as transition probabilities—in this case, the probability of moving from unemployment to employment during the month.

4. **Answer a.** As people flow from e to n, the numerator of the unemployment rate stays constant, but the denominator decreases, raising the entire fraction.

5. **Answer d.** Labor markets are inherently dynamic, resulting in continual flows between the various labor market states. Because information is imperfect, it may take workers and firms some time to match up.

6. **Answer b.** An increase in the replacement rate should increase unemployment benefits and lower the marginal cost associated with job search.

7. **Answer b.** A higher reservation wage means that more low-wage offers are ruled out, thus raising the expected wage.

8. **Answer d.** Structural unemployment results in a mismatch of workers and jobs in different occupations and geographic areas.

9. **Answer a.** Advance notice of a plant closing gives the workers time to consider geographic changes or human capital investments that will allow them to be employed in other sectors of the labor market.

10. **Answer c.** The unemployment associated with efficiency wages is similar to the phenomenon of wait unemployment discussed in Chapter 13.

11. **Answer b.** The supply and demand model suggests that unemployment (a surplus of labor) occurs when wages are too high, but the wage curve highlights the fact that high unemployment is associated with low wages.

12. **Answer c.** When unemployment is high, workers are less likely to shirk, and so firms need not pay a high efficiency wage premium.

13. **Answer d.** A change in required skills is more likely to result in structural unemployment.

14. **Answer a.** By collectively not undercutting the prevailing wage, workers may end up with a higher present value of earnings stream.

15. **Answer c.** An imperfect experience rating system increases the benefits to firms of laying off workers.

16. **Answer a.** No experience rating means that the tax rate paid by firms would be independent of the number of workers laid off.

17. **Answer b.** Note that **a** and **c** are also true for demand deficient unemployment and yet that does not make such unemployment voluntary.

18. **Answer b.** New entrants are only one part of the unemployed "pool" every month.

19. **Answer d.** Teenagers and blacks traditionally have above-average unemployment rates. Therefore, if their proportions in the labor force fall, the unemployment rate should fall. An increase in women does not counteract this trend because the unemployment rate for women now tends to be closer to that for men.

20. **Answer a.** This relationship was originally known as Okun's law.

■ Problems

21a. $u = 20/250 = 0.08$.

21b. **lfp** $= 250/400 = 0.625$.

21c. $e = 230/400 = 0.575$.

21d. Substituting $u = 0.1$ and $e = 0.575$ into

$$e = \mathbf{lfp}(1 - \mathbf{u}) \Rightarrow 0.575 = \mathbf{lfp}(0.9) \Rightarrow \mathbf{lfp} = 0.639.$$

Therefore, given that the unemployment rate rose to 0.1, the labor force participation rate must rise to 0.639 (an increase of 1.4 percentage points) if the employment rate is to remain constant.

22a. Sector A: $20 - W = W \Rightarrow W_A^* = \$10 \Rightarrow L_A^* = 10$.

Sector B: $40 - 2W = 2W \Rightarrow W_B^* = \$10 \Rightarrow L_B^* = 20$.

22b. Because of the time needed to make job matches, there will still be some positive rate of unemployment even when markets are in equilibrium. This is the idea behind frictional unemployment.

22c. Substituting $W = 10$ into the supply and demand equations

$$\Rightarrow L_A^D = 15 - 10 = 5 \text{ and } L_A^S = 10.$$

Therefore, there are 5 workers unemployed in sector A.

Solving for the new equilibrium in sector B

$$\text{Sector B: } 45 - 2W = 2W$$
$$\Rightarrow W_B^* = \$11.25 \Rightarrow L_B^* = 22.5.$$

22d. If the 5 unemployed workers were subtracted from the supply in A and added to the supply in B, a new equilibrium would occur where

$$\text{Sector A: } 15 - W = W - 5 \Rightarrow W_A^* = \$10 \Rightarrow L_A^* = 5.$$
$$\text{Sector B: } 45 - 2W = 2W + 5 \Rightarrow W_B^* = \$10 \Rightarrow L_B^* = 25.$$

22e. The costs of occupational and geographic mobility restrict these adjustments.

22f. If the adjustments could not be made, the unemployment could be classified as structural.

23a. The area of the distribution to the left of 50 is $(50 - 10)(0.02) = 0.8$. Therefore, if any offer in that range is acceptable, the person has an 80% chance of receiving a job offer.

23b. Note that if W_R were set at $10, the probability of getting a better offer is 80%. On the other hand, if the reservation wage were set at $50, the probability of getting a better offer is zero (given the skill level of this individual). Hence, for reservation wages between $10 and $50 the probability ($P$) of getting a better offer can be written as

$$P = \frac{50 - W_R}{50}.$$

23c. Since the average wage in the interval between W_R and $50 can be written as $(W_R + 50)/2$, this wage would represent a gain (G) over W_R of

$$G = \frac{W_R + 50}{2} - W_R \Rightarrow G = \frac{W_R + 20 - 2W_R}{2} \Rightarrow G = \frac{50 - W_R}{2}.$$

23d. Multiplying G by P yields the expected gain from additional job search (EG)

$$EG = (P)(G) = \frac{50 - W_R}{50} \frac{50 - W_R}{2} \Rightarrow EG = \frac{(50 - W_R)^2}{100}.$$

23e. Assuming for simplicity that the marginal cost of an additional period of job search is constant at $1, the optimal value for the reservation wage occurs where

$$\frac{(50 - W_R)^2}{100} = 1 \Rightarrow W_R = 50 - \sqrt{100} = \$40.$$

23f. Note that by setting a reservation wage of $40, the individual deliberately reduces his or her chances of a job offer from 0.8 to $(50 - 40)(0.02) = 0.2$ (from 80% to 20%). The dramatic reduction occurs because of the low marginal cost associated with additional periods of job search.

23g. A reservation wage strategy is a deliberate and purposeful restriction of the probability of flowing from unemployment to employment. If everyone does this, it lowers P_{ue} in the stock-flow model and so raises the unemployment rate.

■ Applications

24a. Since the person now has the highest skill level, he or she has a 100% chance of receiving a job offer.

24b. Note that if W_R were set at $10, the probability of getting a better offer is 100%. On the other hand, if the reservation wage were set at $30, the probability of getting a better offer is zero (given the skill level of this individual). Hence, for reservation wages between $10 and $30 the probability (P) of getting a better offer can be written as

$$P = \frac{30 - W_R}{20}.$$

24c. Since the average wage in the interval between W_R and $30 can be written as $(W_R + 30)/2$, this wage would represent a gain (G) over W_R of

$$G = \frac{W_R + 30}{2} - W_R \Rightarrow G = \frac{W_R + 30 - 2W_R}{2} \Rightarrow G = \frac{30 - W_R}{2}.$$

24d. Multiplying G by P yields the expected gain from additional job search (EG)

$$EG = (P)(G) = \frac{30 - W_R}{20} \frac{30 - W_R}{2} \Rightarrow EG = \frac{(30 - W_R)^2}{40}.$$

24e. Assuming for simplicity that the marginal cost of an additional period of job search is constant at $2, the optimal value for the reservation wage occurs where

$$\frac{(30 - W_R)^2}{40} = 2 \Rightarrow W_R = 30 - \sqrt{80} = \$21.06.$$

24f. Note that by setting a reservation wage of $21.06, the individual deliberately reduces his or her chances of a job offer from 1.0 to $(30 - 21.06)(0.05) = 0.447$ (from 100% to about 45%).

24g. Note that the increase in skill level has raised the reservation wage substantially, from $11.06 in the **Summary** section **Example** problem to $21.06 here. However, note that the probability of a job offer has remained at 0.447. Thus the proportion of people flowing from unemployment to employment should be unchanged.

25a. This firm would face the minimum unemployment insurance (UI) tax rate. Its tax payment for each worker is computed by multiplying the tax rate by the worker's earnings if the earnings are less than the specified taxable wage base (e.g., $10,000). If earnings exceed the base, the tax payment for the worker is the tax rate times the wage base.

25b. The firm would have contributed less because of the imperfect experience rating of the UI tax rate. This refers to the tendency of the UI tax rate to rise with layoff experience at a lower rate than is necessary to make the employer's marginal cost of layoff equal to the marginal UI benefits paid out to laid-off workers. Note that the tax rate also has a ceiling so that at some point additional layoffs have no effect on the UI tax rate. The rest of the money paid out to unemployed workers comes from the firms that conducted no layoffs but still paid their UI taxes.

25c. Since low-layoff firms are essentially subsidizing high-layoff firms, the high-layoff firms are more likely to survive and grow, thus increasing the incentive to use layoffs. More widespread use of layoffs increases the proportion of people flowing from employment to unemployment.

26a. Earnings = $400, taxes paid = 0.255(400) = $102, after tax earnings = $298 ($7.45 per hour).

26b. UI benefits = $220, taxes paid = 0.18(220) = $39.6, after tax benefits = $180.4 ($4.51 per hour).

26c. The marginal cost of being unemployed is only $117.6 per week ($2.94 per hour). If UI benefits were subject to Social Security and Medicare taxes, the marginal cost of unemployment would be higher, raising the cost of job search, and lowering the duration of job search unemployment.

*27a. $PV_{Cut} = 9.9 + \dfrac{5}{1.06} + \dfrac{5}{1.06^2} = 19.07.$

*27b. Expected wage = 0.4(5) + 0.6(10) = 8.

*27c. $PV_{Wait} = 5 + \dfrac{8}{1.06} + \dfrac{8}{1.06^2} = 19.67.$

27d. On average, the person is better off holding out for the prevailing wage even if it means a spell of unemployment.

Answers To Chapter 15

■ Review Questions

1. **Answer a.** The distribution can also be described by the percentage of people falling within specified earnings ranges.

2. **Answer b.** The average (mean) and median earnings are measures of the central location of the distribution.

3. **Answer b.** The variance is the only dispersion measure listed that would increase if all earnings were multiplied by some constant number.

4. **Answer a.** The median would increase. The standard deviation and variance would stay the same. The coefficient of variation would fall since its denominator, the standard deviation, is unchanged, and its numerator, the mean, will rise.

5. **Answer a.** According to Table 15.1 in the text, the 80:20 ratio for men rose from 3.08 in 1980 to 3.41 in 2005, a 10% increase. Over the same time period, the ratio for women increased by about 6%, from 3.70 to 3.94.

6. **Answer c.** According to Table 15.1 in the text, real earnings for men at the 20th percentile fell and the 80th percentile rose over the period 1980–2005. Over this same period, the earnings of women at the 20th and 80th percentiles rose, with the largest increases being at the top of the distribution.

7. **Answer d.** Mathematically, each of these changes would lead to the distribution of earnings becoming more stretched.

8. **Answer c.** According to Table 15.2 in the text, the 80:50 ratios increased over this period for both men and women, showing worsening inequality. At the same time, the 50:20 ratios improved for both groups, showing slightly improving inequality.

9. **Answer a.** These trends are clearly indicated in Table 15.3 of the text. Note the significant increases in the returns to education for both men and women. For women, the average earnings of college graduates relative to high school graduates rose from 1.36 to 1.85 over the period 1980–2005, a 36% increase; the increase for males, from 1.41 to 1.91, was 35%. Returns to other types of education also generally increased, but not by as much.

10. **Answer d.** See Table 15.3 in the text. The gain in relative earnings for college-educated men is due both to the falling earnings of high school graduates and to rises in their own earning. In contrast, the gain in relative earnings for women were due exclusively to the rising earnings (over 26%) of college-educated women; earnings of high school–educated women actually rose slightly over the period.

11. **Answer d.** Returns to a college education increased in both periods, but higher returns also encourage entry into the market, so the supply of college graduates also increased. This lowered the return to a college education relative to what it would have been without the increase in supply.

12. **Answer b.** Note that in Table 15.3 of the text, the ratio of earnings at the 80th and 20th percentiles rose for each male human capital group over the period 1980–2005.

13. **Answer d.** Note that each of these factors would increase earnings inequality by affecting relative wages.

14. **Answer b.** If supply shifts had been the cause, the share of aggregate employment accounted for by less-educated workers would have grown. However, just the opposite change took place, supporting the hypothesis of relative demand shifts in favor of more-educated workers. Explanations related to institutional factors such as the declining share of unionism are flawed for several reasons. For example, union membership has been declining steadily since the mid-1950s, yet the increases in earnings inequality have not occurred until more recently.

15. **Answer d.** Answer **a** corresponds to a scale effect favoring more-educated workers, while Answer **b** refers to a substitution effect in favor of more-educated workers.

16. **Answer b.** Several studies cited in the text suggest that shifts in employment across industries played a relatively small role in raising the relative wage of college-educated workers.

17. **Answer d.** Recall that when two inputs are gross complements, a reduction in the price of one leads to an increase in the demand for the other. While the rising wage inequality in other countries is consistent with the technological change explanation, the differences in rates have focused attention on factors other than the demand side of the labor market.

18. **Answer c.** Note that Answers **a** and **b** together simply ensure a decrease in the demand for unskilled labor. Without seniority rule, there would not necessarily be a larger decrease in demand for younger unskilled workers.

19. **Answer c.** When the Lorenz curves cross, it is possible for the area between each curve and the line of perfect equality to be the same. Since the Gini coefficient is this area divided by 0.5, the same Gini coefficient can be associated with two different Lorenz curves.

20. **Answer d.** Note that if all earnings increase by the same proportion, the Lorenz curve will be unchanged.

■ Problems

21a. The variance is reduced to 1,440 and the coefficient of variation is reduced to 0.47.

21b. The variance is now 2,080 and the coefficient of variation is 0.57.

21c. Many people would view the first redistribution as bringing about greater equality since it brings the ends of the distribution closer. Note that both measures show a larger decrease for the first redistribution.

21d. In the first case, the 80:20 ratio would fall to $100/40 = 2.5$. In the second case, the ratio would actually rise to $120/20 = 6$. The response in the first case seems consistent with the reduced inequality. The response in the second case seems to indicate more inequality, even though earnings have been redistributed away from the richest person.

22a. In group A the mean is $80, the variance is 66.67, and the coefficient of variation is 0.10. In group B the mean is $20, the variance is 66.67, and the coefficient of variation is 0.41.

22b. For the entire population, the variance is 966.67 and the coefficient of variation is 0.62.

22c. The mean earnings for group A are still $80, but the variance has increased to 150 and the coefficient of variation has increased to 0.15. The mean earnings for group B are still $20, but the variance has increased to 150 and the coefficient of variation has increased to 0.61.

22d. For the entire population, the variance has increased to 1,050 and the coefficient of variation has increased to 0.65. The increased within-group dispersion had increased the inequality measures for the entire group. The increased within-group dispersion is consistent with the earnings patterns observed in the United States. The difference is that the increased within-group dispersion in the United States has also been accompanied by a rise in across-group dispersion as the earnings of more-educated workers have risen relative to the earnings of less-educated workers. In this example, the ratio of average earnings in group A to average earnings in group B remained constant.

23a. $\Delta C = 1500(0.1) + 0 = 150$.

23b. $\Delta C = 0 + 0.2(500) = 100$.

23c. $\Delta C = 800(0.1) + 0.2(-200) = 40$.

*24a. Since the mean and the median earnings are both $80, $\gamma = 0$.

*24b. This redistribution lowers the variance from 2,400 to 2,080. Given that the median earnings is now $60, while the mean is $80, and the standard deviation is 45.61, γ is computed as 1.32. Since $\gamma > 0$, the distribution is skewed to the right.

*24c. Note that in this example, increased equality was accompanied by increased skewness. This serves as a reminder that dispersion and skewness are separate and distinct characteristics of any earnings distribution.

*24d. Recall that an earnings distribution that is skewed to the right means that individuals are bunched at the lower end of the distribution, while a few individuals have high incomes. This type of distribution violates many people's sense of fairness.

25a. See curve L_1 in Figure 15-1.

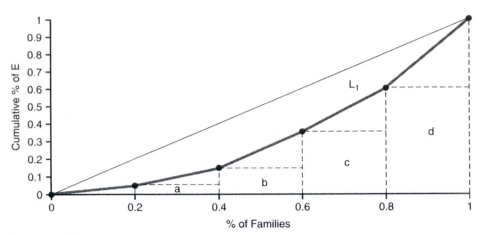

Figure 15-1

The coordinates of the points on the Lorenz curve are (0,0), (0.2,0.05), (0.4,0.15), (0.6,0.35), (0.8,0.6), and (1,1).

*25b. To find the area under the Lorenz curve, add the areas of rectangles *a*, *b*, *c*, and *d*, for a total area of 0.23. The remaining triangles have an area of 0.1 since each has a base equal to 0.2 and their height sums to one. Given that the total area under the Lorenz curve is 0.33, the Gini coefficient is given by

$$\text{Gini} = \frac{0.5 - 0.33}{0.5} = 0.34.$$

25c. See curve L_2 in Figure 15-2. The coordinates of the points on the new Lorenz curve are (0,0), (0.2,0.08), (0.4,0.2), (0.6,0.35), (0.8,0.55), and (1,1). Curve L_1 is repeated for comparison purposes.

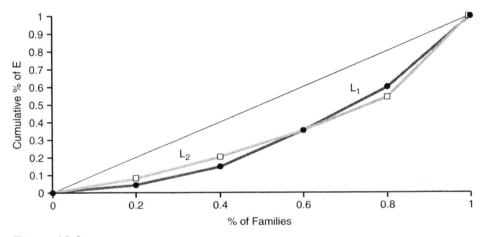

Figure 15-2

25d. Since the Lorenz curves cross, a conclusion about which represents the greater equality is not possible.

*25e. Using the same method as before, the area under L_2 is computed as 0.336. This yields a Gini coefficient of 0.328, slightly smaller than the previous one. This suggests that the second distribution displays more earnings equality.

■ Applications

26a. The growing inequality for men took place in the context of falling real earnings along all points in the earnings distribution. Hence, the higher earnings group simply declined less than the rest. For women, real earnings rose along all points on the earnings distribution.

26b. The gain in relative position was largely determined by increasing returns to education. It is hard to see how this could be construed as the rich exploiting the poor for material gain.

26c. Such supply shifts would have led to an increase in the share of aggregate employment accounted for by low-skilled workers. However, just the opposite happened.

26d. On tests of cognitive achievement, the scores of high school graduates actually rose relative to those of college graduates during the 1980s (even though the scores for both groups were falling). Since the relative quality of labor supplied by high school graduates seemed to be rising, this can not explain the rising wage gap between more- and less-educated workers.

26e. Union membership as a percentage of the labor force peaked in 1954, and has been declining steadily since then. If this decline were the major factor explaining the increasing returns to education, it would be very difficult to explain why the returns to education **dropped** significantly during the 1970s. As noted in the text, women have traditionally been less unionized than men, so declining unionization should not have had as much impact on their rate of return from education. That the returns to education for women rose as fast as or faster than those for men during the 1980s does not appear to have any relationship to the decline in unionization.

27a. I would be willing to pay up to $1 million for A, but nothing for B.

27b. In this example, very slight differences in productivity are translated into very large differences in earnings because of the winner-take-all nature of the contest.

27c. Such contests would increase the within-group dispersion of earnings significantly. This, in turn, would increase the inequality of the overall population.

27d. According to the hypothesis presented in Chapter 1, concern for relative standing tends to flatten the relationship between wages and productivity. This would tend to reduce the dispersion of earnings both within and across groups.

28a. Originally, the person worked 100 hours at $4 per hour for total earnings of $400. After the welfare program, work hours were cut back to 53.125 for total earnings of $212.5.

28b. This person was not affected by the program. Earnings remained constant at $1,200.

28c. The welfare program increased the dispersion of earnings by leading the lower earnings person to cut back on his or her work hours.

29a. The Lorenz curve is unchanged since the share of earnings going to any particular group has not changed.

*29b. See curve L_3 in Figure 15-3. The coordinates of the points on the Lorenz curve are (0,0), (0.2,0.08), (0.4,0.2), (0.6,0.4), (0.8,0.64), and (1,1). Curve L_1 is repeated for comparison purposes. The new Gini coefficient is 0.27. In this case, both the Lorenz curve and the Gini coefficient reflect increased earnings equality.

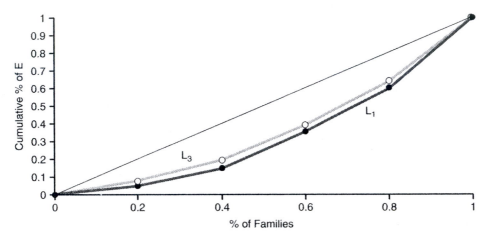

Figure 15-3

29c. The after-tax income distribution tends to be more equal than the earnings distribution because of government transfers to the poor and higher tax rates for the rich.

Answers To Chapter 16

■ Review Questions

1. **Answer a.** The production possibilities curve has a slope of −5. This tells how much corn must be given up to attain an additional unit of wheat.

2. **Answer d.** If 1 unit of wheat costs 2 units of corn as the slope of the production possibilities curve indicates, then it is possible to express that same tradeoff as 1 unit of corn for 1/2 unit of wheat.

3. **Answer b.** Per capita consumption in the U.S. is 0.4 units of wheat and 2 units of corn. In Canada, per capita consumption is 0.9 unit of wheat and 4.8 units of corn. Canada has the higher real wage rates in this case.

4. **Answer d.** The limits of the terms of trade are between 2 and 5 units of corn for a unit of wheat, or conversely, between 1/2 and 1/5 unit of wheat for one unit of corn. All the answers fall in this range.

5. **Answer c.** The new "trading possibilities curve" has a slope of −4. This tells how much corn must be given up to attain an additional unit of wheat.

6. **Answer d.** After specialization, the U.S. will have 400 units of corn and no wheat (point *b*), and Canada will have 120 units of wheat and no corn (point *v*). To get from these points to the final allocations, Canada must have traded 50 units of wheat to the U.S. for 200 units of corn.

7. **Answer d.** While both countries still fully employ their resources, all farmers in the U.S. now produce corn, while all Canadian farmers produce wheat. Before trade, there used to be some of both in each country. Note however, that per capita consumption levels have risen, indicating higher real wages through the shifting out of the production possibilities curve for each country.

8. **Answer c.** Lower wages abroad mean that total production costs for U.S. firms (that have overseas facilities) will fall. This decreases firm costs and increases supply (in a competitive market). Thus the price of the final product will fall, and output will increase as quantity demanded rises. At a higher scale of production, firms will demand more of all types of workers, increasing the U.S. demand for labor.

9. **Answer a.** Lower wages abroad make the ratio of wages to marginal productivity abroad lower than it was previously and encourages substitution of foreign labor for domestic labor. The demand for U.S. labor falls.

10. **Answer b.** Where foreign labor is a large part of the cost of production, a fall in its price will lead to a large decrease in total costs, which will make the scale effect relatively larger, and thus it is more likely that the demand for labor will increase.

11. **Answer d.**   Although empirical studies show mixed results, on average the consensus seems to be that current effects of international trade have reduced employment greatly in some sectors, but since labor is relatively mobile, overall effects have been slightly negative but small.

12. **Answer b.**   A lower wage to marginal productivity ratio will cause firms to consider moving. However, the costs of moving and trading across borders are generally very high, and thus firms are only likely to move if the cost savings is large enough to outweigh the additional costs of relocating production.

13. **Answer a.**   Wage convergence is most likely when workers have similar skill levels and the location of production relative to the end user is not very important, as with telecommunications and many manufactured goods.

14. **Answer d.**   The least-skilled and thus least able to adapt workers are most likely to be displaced by trade. Government assistance to these workers can both help subsidize the cost of necessary human capital investment and help these workers move to new sectors, thus speeding the efficient reallocation of resources.

15. **Answer c.**   The costs of trade are not limited to affected markets, particularly since workers in other areas may experience increased uncertainty and risk as well as experiencing unpredictable swings in wages.

■ Problems

16a.   For the U.S., 1 unit of food costs 0.25 units of clothing. Conversely, 1 unit of clothing costs 4 units of food.

16b.   For China, 1 unit of food costs 0.5 units of clothing. Conversely, 1 unit of clothing costs 2 units of food.

16c.   The U.S. is the low-cost producer of food, China is the low-cost producer of clothing.

16d.   In the U.S., workers consume 2.4 units of food and 0.4 units of clothing per person, while in China, workers consume 0.2 units of food and 0.4 units of clothing per person.

16e.   The U.S. should specialize in food, China should specialize in clothing.

16f.   A unit of food would have to trade for at least 0.25 units of clothing (otherwise the U.S. would not cover its costs), but no more than 0.5 units of clothing (otherwise China could produce the food itself).

16g.   After specialization, the U.S. would have 400 units of food and no clothing. China would have 300 units of clothing and no food. Now suppose a trade of 150 units of food for 50 units of clothing were made. The U.S. would end up with 250 units of food and 50 units of clothing. China would end up with 150 units of food and 250 units of clothing. Per capita consumption levels would rise to 2.5 units of food and 0.5 units of clothing in the U.S., and 0.25 units of food and 0.4167 units of clothing in China. These figures represent an increase in living standards for both countries.

17. Barriers to trade are constructed to avoid the transitional job losses that trade imposes. For example, in this problem even though living standards improve, initially the U.S. would have lost clothing jobs to China. Eventually these would have been made up by new jobs in the food-producing sector, but this transition of resources is not always smooth or painless for many workers. To avoid making these kinds of adjustments, countries often look to devices like tariffs and import quotas to preserve existing industries and jobs.

18. Technological change and international trade are similar in that they both cause transitional job losses. With technological change, jobs are lost in the sectors producing outdated products, or through substitutions of capital for labor. Eventually, this labor is reabsorbed into the other expanding sectors of the economy that the technological change and increased efficiency has made possible, but the transition process is not always smooth or painless for many workers.

19a. The costs of trading across borders are significantly higher for many service-related industries. For example, it would not generally be cost-effective for a doctor to deliver medical care from another country; the transaction costs involved would simply be too high. On the other hand, unless the good being produced is unusually difficult or costly to transport, the cost of trading across borders, while significant, is not generally sufficient to make relocation of production facilities undesirable.

19b. Substitution effects are large because clothing production is relatively unskilled labor, and thus the elasticity of substitution between U.S. and foreign workers is large. Domestic workers remaining are likely to have jobs that are substitutes, not complements, to foreign production, and demand for these goods is elastic and thus very responsive to price/cost changes. Thus small changes in either the foreign wage or the domestic wage are likely to cause large changes in domestic employment, with no significant positive scale effects to offset them.

20a. Trade represents a reallocation of resources, not a permanent loss of resources. Jobs will be lost in those areas where Mexico can produce goods more cheaply, but at the same time, opportunities will grow in those areas where the U.S. is the low-cost producer. Because of specialization and trade, living standards (real wage rates) in both countries should rise.

20b. Import quotas do seem to preserve employment in those areas where they apply. However, if the import quotas result in more monopoly power for domestic firms, the price increases that result may reduce the number of jobs that are really preserved. Also, the reduction in competition may lead the domestic firms to grow sluggish and inefficient, leading to even more job losses in the future.